2026/Nov/17

BUILDING NETWORK MANAGEMENT TOOLS WITH TCL/TK

Dave Zeltserman

Gerard Puoplo

**Prentice Hall Series in
Computer Networking and Distributed Systems**
Radia Perlman, editor

BUILDING NETWORK MANAGEMENT TOOLS WITH TCL/TK

Dave Zeltserman

Gerard Puoplo

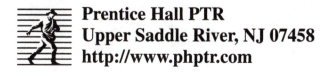

Prentice Hall PTR
Upper Saddle River, NJ 07458
http://www.phptr.com

Library of Congress Cataloging-in-Publication Data

Zeltserman, Dave.

Building network management tools with Tcl/Tk / Dave Zeltserman. Gerard Puoplo.

p. cm. — (Prentice Hall series in computer networking and distributed systems)

Includes index.

ISBN 0-13-080727-3 (alk. paper)

1. Tcl (Computer programming language) 2. Tk toolkit. 3. Computer networks—Management. I. Puoplo, Gerard. II. title. III. Series.

QA76.73.T44Z45 1998

005.13'3--dc21

98-14599

CIP

Editorial/Production Supervision: *Kathleen M. Caren*

Acquisitions Editor: *Mary Franz*

Cover Design Director: *Jerry Votta*

Cover Art: *Tom Post*

Art Director: *Gail Cocker-Boguz*

Manufacturing Manager: *Alexis R. Heydt*

Marketing Manager: *Miles Williams*

Editorial Assistant: *Noreen Regina*

 © 1998 Prentice Hall PTR

A Simon & Schuster Company

Upper Saddle River, New Jersey 07458

Prentice Hall books are widely used by corporations and government agencies for training, marketing, and resale.

The publisher offers discounts on this book when ordered in bulk quantities.

For more information, contact: Corporate Sales Department, Phone: 800-382-3419; FAX: 201-236-7141; E-mail: corpsales@prenhall.com

Or write: Corp. Sales Dept., Prentice Hall PTR, 1 Lake Street, Upper Saddle River, NJ 07458

Printed in the United States of America

10 9 8 7 6 5 4 3 2 1

ISBN 0-13-080727-3

Prentice-Hall International (UK) Limited, *London*

Prentice-Hall of Australia Pty. Limited, *Sydney*

Prentice-Hall Canada Inc., *Toronto*

Prentice-Hall Hispanoamericana, S.A., *Mexico*

Prentice-Hall of India Private Limited, *New Delhi*

Prentice-Hall of Japan, Inc., *Tokyo*

Simon & Schuster Asia Pte. Ltd., *Singapore*

Editora Prentice-Hall do Brasil, Ltda., *Rio de Janeiro*

Contents

Preface

I first became mildly interested in Tcl in 1993 when I was working with Digital Equipment Corporation. I was talking with Glenn Trewitt, a brilliant engineer with Digital's Western Research Laboratory, about an IP path tracing/diagnostic tool I was working on, and Glenn mentioned how he had just built an SNMP interface onto Tcl. At the time, the only thing I knew about Tcl was that it was an interpretive scripting language. I had spent the last three years programming in C and the previous eight years programming in assembly language, and the last thing I wanted to do was move to a scripting language, so I listened politely as Glenn described the interface he had built. Still, I had a great deal of respect for Glenn, great enough that I bought John Ousterhout's book *Tcl and the Tk Toolkit* book when it came out, but I wasn't yet motivated enough to take Tcl seriously.

At the end of 1993, I left Digtial to join LightStream Corporation. LightStream was building an ATM/Ethernet switch and I was given the opportunity to build a large bulk of the network management software. The test engineers were using Tcl/Tk to build their test platform. I was impressed with how quickly they were able to build their user interfaces using Tcl/Tk, but in my own mind, that just meant Tcl/Tk was good for building test tools. I still wasn't taking it seriously for network management.

By the end of 1994, we were purchased by Cisco. As a newly appointed Cisco employee, I visited the headquarters in San Jose and had a code walk-through of the CiscoView application—written completely in Tcl/Tk. For the first time, I began to see the power of building network management applications with Tcl.

A few months later, I left Cisco to join 3Com. One of the engineers in my group had discovered Scotty and wanted to develop on it (Scotty, among other things, provides an SNMP extension for Tcl). I was building a network monitoring/diagnostic tool for 3Com's LANplex switches and needed a tool to simulate the vast number of complex FDDI and system traps that the LANplex can generate, so I had this engineer build a trap simulation tool using Scotty. The tool was built quickly and was extremely powerful in how it simulated device traps. I was now more serious about Tcl.

The application I was building collected quite a bit of information from each interface on a switch and then ran the information through a series of expressions to determine how the switch was operating. The application supported up to several hundred switches at a time, and each switch could have 24–80 interfaces for which information would have to be gathered. Assuming about ten expressions per interface and a collection interval as short as 30 seconds, the application had a lot of expressions to evaluate every minute.

As an experiment, we replaced the C++ code that was performing expression evaluation with Tcl code. Performance quickly became a problem. It was just too many expressions for Tcl to keep up with. In my mind, this proved that Tcl was geared only toward a subset of tools and network management applications, and was not applicable for the large-scale network monitoring application I was working on. Besides, I was now developing in C++ and did not want to move to a scripting language.

For the next year and a half I ignored Tcl. Then I noticed Jerry Puoplo, who at the time was an engineering manager for Transcend at 3Com, building useful network management tools using Tcl with the TickleMan extensions. Mind you, this was a manager building tools at a much faster pace than any of the engineers in his group. And they were useful tools—like collecting network inventory information and performing a network discovery. It finally hit me. While Tcl may not be appropriate for large-scale applications that are computationally-intensive, it is perfectly suited for a large number of network management tools—especially the type typically built by network managers and network consultants.

My goal for this book is to help network managers and network consultants get to the point that it took me four years to get to—that very powerful and useful network management tools can be written quickly and easily with Tcl/Tk.

Dave Zeltserman

In the preface to their book, *How to Manage Your Network Using SNMP—The Network Management Practicum*, Marshall Rose and Keith McCloghrie categorized their book as a *preparedness* book. The topic of this book has much in common with Marshall and Keith's book: that this too is a preparedness book. It's a book to prepare you to create and maintain custom-built network management utilities.

Anyone who has worked in network operations knows that some of the best network management tools are custom-built tools developed by network managers or network management consultants. I have seen many NOCs (Network Operations Centers) and it's easy to see which ones have their heads above water and which are drowning. The ones swimming along merrily have a defined strategy for how to manage their network via management tools. Over time, they have developed a number of useful custom tools that they have integrated with their vendor-based tools.

Unfortunately, many network managers do not have a strategy for developing and evolving their own network management tools. Some may feel they don't have the skill set or largeness of scope to even think of this as they continue to fight fires without adequate tools. Others may be blindly using PERL scripts with the HP OpenView SNMP APIs without knowing of any other alternative.

You may also have the problem where your typical day at work is putting out fires and hence you never have time during your workday to be proactive. This for years delayed my progress implementing custom tools. However, all that changed when I was able to develop custom tools at home on my PC and later run the same tools at work on my UNIX management system.

Building custom management tools will empower network managers, network consultants and network support engineers. They have a wealth of useful utilities inside of them that would make them more productive if they knew how to use Tcl with SNMP extensions.

Recently, I was visiting a NOC in the midst of a major network problem. I watched the pain on the faces of the vendor's network support engineers as they tried to obtain data on device operations using a MIB browser. If those network engineers knew Tcl with SNMP, I bet one of the first things they would do is spend a few days building simple Tcl-based diagnostic tools.

This book is for them and others like them. The various sample applications it describes exist to prepare network managers, network consultants and network support engineers to build custom management utilities. Creating custom tools is both satisfying and effective in helping to manage a network.

Jerry Puoplo

NOTATION

Throughout this book we will use a Courier font for both source code listings and for commands typed at a console window. Furthermore, results for commands typed at a console will be preceded by a $\Rightarrow$. For example:

```
set x 100
```
$\Rightarrow$ 100

The Tcl command in this example, set x 100, appears in the Courier font. The result for this example, 100, appears on the following line. The $\Rightarrow$ symbol in the above example is not part of the return value.

In describing Tcl command syntax, the notation, ? *arg* ?, denotes an optional argument. The syntax, ? *arg ... arg*?, denotes one or more optional arguments.

BOOK ORGANIZATION

The chapters of this book are divided into three parts. The first part describes the motivation for using Tcl to build network management tools. Chapter 1 provides a brief introduction to Tcl and describes how it can be used to help manage a network. In Chapter 2 we expand on this theme and present the sample tools that we will be building later in the book and our motivation for originally building them (most of these tools were built before we ever conceived of this book).

In Part II, we start to lay a foundation for using Tcl to build network management tools. Chapters 3 and 4 provide both an introduction to Tcl and some basic Tcl procedures that will be used later with our sample tools. Chapter 5 examines two SNMP extension packages to Tcl, TickleMan, a commercial product available from SNMP Research, and Scotty, available both commercially and in some form as a freeware product. The freeware version of Scotty can be obtained over the Internet. In Chapter 6 we build a fairly robust SNMP polling loop and show how it can be used to periodically calculate several network statistics. In Chapter 7 we start to explore Tk, and use a step-by-step approach to build a sample user interface that can serve as a template for building network management application user interfaces. In Chapter 8 we build a simple table widget that will later be used by several of our sample tools. We also further explore Tk canvases, showing how to use them to draw an IP path. We end the chapter by exploring Itcl Mega-Widgets, and show how they can be used to build the same sample user interface that was built in Chapter 7. In Chapter 9 we explore sockets, building an example of a Web-accessible server.

In Part III, we provide four useful network management tools. In Chapter 10 we build a network response time monitoring tool; in Chapter 11 we build a network discovery tool; in Chapter 12 we design a status monitoring tool; in Chapter 13 we build an IP path tracing tool; and in Chapter 14 we build a series of scripts to help in RMONv2 configuration. Chapter 15 shows how to use Tcl plug-ins to access a server application, and also provides pointers to Tcl/Tk resources and a description of future Tcl/Tk work currently underway in the industry.

BOOK THANKS

We would like to thank our wives, Judy and Lucy, for their patience, support and help on this book.

Thanks to all of our reviewers, but especially David Levi for his TickleMan support, Juergen Schoenwaelder for getting us an early version of Tnm 3.0, his detailed review and his help with Scotty, and Brent Welch for his detailed review and for improving several of our code examples.

Thanks to the editors and staff at Prentice Hall. Mary Franz, Noreen Regina, Kathleen Caren and all the other editors and staff involved have done an amazing job getting this book published with the incredibly aggressive schedule that we had.

Finally, we would like to thank all of the end-users and customers we have worked with over the years for helping to educate us as to what's important in managing a network.

ABOUT NET MGMT SOLUTIONS

Net Mgmt Solutions provides network management tools, training, consulting services, and custom tool development. By using Tcl/Tk, we feel we can build tools that can be easily extended and modified by our customers, and can also be used as templates in building other tools.

To access the sample applications detailed in this book:

From the front page of our Web-site, www.net-mgmt-solutions.com, click on Customer Login, and use the Username "book-bnmtools", Password "MRB87125Z".

1 *Introduction*

This book is for anyone who is involved with managing TCP/IP networks. It is primarily intended for network managers and network consultants whose effectiveness depends on the tools at their disposal. This book will lay a foundation for quickly and easily building custom network management tools using the Tcl/Tk language. Several complete tools for managing computer networks will be provided.

Vendor-based network management tools typically have limitations. Often they lack specific reporting, monitoring and bulk configuration capabilities. Custom utilities are often needed to perform the following tasks:

- Reconfigure traps, community names, RMON thresholds or alarms on hundreds of different network devices. This task can take days to accomplish manually. Maintaining this information over the long term without bulk configuration tools can be an immense chore.

- Validate the consistency of device parameters across your network. Networks won't operate as intended when certain device parameters, such as the bridging mode on your LAN switches, are not all configured exactly alike. A utility that validates device configuration conformance allows you to detect and fix configuration problems quickly.

- Generate a timely, up-to-date device inventory of your multi-vendor network components. Provide notifications of additions to your network on a weekly basis.

- Monitor operations, such as spanning tree, across your LAN switches.

- Diagnose network faults. Examples include tools to look for broadcast storms or to diagnose an IP route.

By supplementing vendor-based management tools with your own custom developed utilities, you will manage your network more effectively. To be able to do this, all you need is a basic knowledge of SNMP and a quick and easy way to transfer this knowledge into actual tools. We advise our readers to first learn the basics of the SNMP protocol and MIBs. This knowledge is necessary to use most network management stations effectively. Second, we recommend you use a Tcl package like TickleMan or Scotty for developing custom SNMP-based management tools.

Learning the basics of SNMP is easy. There are a number of fine books on the subject identified in our reference section. There are also seminars given on this topic. Understanding MIB syntax and MIB content are key to compiling and using MIB data.

This book is a guide to developing custom network management utilities using Tcl with SNMP extensions. Sample applications contained in this book are based on the TickleMan product from SNMP Research International. Using Tcl with SNMP makes it easy to develop and maintain custom-built utilities on both UNIX and Windows. It also allows customers to integrate their own utilities with off-the-shelf tools in an effective manner.

We believe in learning by example. This book will show the basics of Tcl and Tk, and will provide a large number of coding examples along the way. Once a rich set of coding examples have been laid out, complete source code for several tools will be provided, along with descriptions of how to modify and extend these tools. This book, however, will not exhaustively describe the Tcl and Tk language. We believe there are several outstanding books on the market that already do that—including John Ousterhout's *Tcl and the Tk Toolkit* and Brent Welch's *Practical Programming in Tcl and Tk*.

The remainder of this chapter covers:

- System overview of Tcl
- Benefits of using Tcl
- Limitations of Tcl
- History of Tcl with SNMP
- Availability of Tcl with SNMP

SYSTEM OVERVIEW OF TCL

Tcl (pronounced "tickle") is a scripting language developed in the 1980s by John Ousterhout, while he was a professor at the University of California, Berkley. It is currently under the ownership of the Sunscript Group of Sun Microsystems Inc., managed by John Ousterhout. John and the rest of the Sunscript group have been actively evolving Tcl for years and have recently released version 8.0 of Tcl.

Tcl is extremely easy to use. A Tcl program is simply a bunch of commands. Since it is an interpreted language, every Tcl program is simply one or more files of textual commands that are executed by a Tcl interpreter program. On UNIX, the first line of a Tcl script identifies the Tcl interpreter to run; on Windows, unique file extensions are used to identify the Tcl interpreter to run.

The Sunscript group at Sun Microsystems provides two basic Tcl interpreter programs: **tclsh** and **wish**. Platform versions of **tclsh** and **wish** exist for just about every popular operating system in existence today, effectively making your Tcl programs platform-independent.

The **tclsh** interpreter launches a console window and executes the basic set of Tcl built-in commands. The **wish** interpreter launches a graphical window and executes both the basic set of Tcl commands plus the Tk (pronounced "tee-kay") extended commands for creating and controlling graphical widgets. Once running, Tcl script files can source additional Tcl script files.

Let's illustrate some Tcl and Tk commands right now !

- The following Tcl `puts` command writes the string "hello world" to standard output:

```
puts "hello world"
⇒ hello world
```

- The following Tk commands create a button widget with the text "hello world":

```
button .hello -text "hello world"
pack .hello
```

BENEFITS OF TCL

As we will keep repeating throughout this book (and hopefully proving): It is very easy to learn how to program in Tcl. To start, all you need is some knowledge of the Tcl command syntax. The easiest way to learn is through code examples. Since you can issue commands to the console directly, you can develop programs interactively with immediate feedback. This makes debugging simpler than with C or C++.

The interactive development nature of Tcl, combined with the fact that Tcl programs require far fewer lines of code than languages like C or C++, makes it fast and easy to develop in. It has been documented by numerous parties that developing in Tcl is typically one-tenth the work as developing in a procedural language like C or C++. Our own experience supports this impressive statistic.

You don't need to be a highly skilled programmer to create Tcl programs. Tcl is an excellent tools language that experts in many fields can take advantage of. The field we're focusing on in this book is network management. For example, if you're a network manager who needs a special reporting tool and you know what SNMP MIB information you need to collect, you can create your own tool quickly and easily with Tcl.

Tcl interpreters exist for most major operating systems. This makes Tcl scripts platform-independent. Tools built on Windows can be moved directly to UNIX workstations, and (of course) tools developed on UNIX can be moved directly to Windows.

There are numerous freely available Tcl tools. Tcl is used in many places by a growing community of people. There is a strong sense of code sharing among Tcl users. If you know where to look (and we'll guide you in later chapters), you can find a plethora of coding examples and Tcl-based tools scattered along the Internet. Similarly, there is a large population of Tcl-literate people to go to for help. System administrators have used Tcl for years for both system administration scripts and CGI-based Web server scripts. Network managers and vendor-based network management application developers have been developing SNMP-based network management applications in Tcl since 1991. What makes Tcl particularly useful for system and network management purposes is its basic and extended support for network communications, database integration and graphic display.

Tcl is Web-friendly. With native support for socket communications, it is easy to make Tcl applications Web-accessible. The folks at Sunscript have included a number of HTML parsing commands in Tcl 8.0, and have also distributed a free Tcl-based Web server that can be embedded within your Tcl applications. The Sunscript folks freely distribute the Tcl plug-ins for Netscape Navigator and Microsoft's Internet Explorer. They are also busy working to ensure that future releases of Tcl are synergistic with Java. As they explained at the Annual Tcl USENIX meeting held in July 1997 in Boston, MA, they are working to rewrite Tcl in Java and to allow the invocation of Java methods via Tcl commands.

LIMITATIONS OF TCL

Interpreted languages like Tcl are slower than languages like C or C++. The Tcl language has only a single datatype: strings. This can make handling large, complex data structures inefficient. The newly released version 8.0 of Tcl speeds things up significantly, and does a good job reducing the number of internal type conversions.

With today's systems being as fast as they are, Tcl 7.6 (the version most often used today) performance is usually acceptable for most custom tools. By developing in Tcl, you learn to quickly understand your logic bottlenecks better than systems programming languages. This results in developing more efficient applications.

When performance is an issue, C and C++ programmers can make selective use of Tcl within C/C++ code. Since most network managers are NOT C/C++ programmers, we advise you to keep your Tcl tools simple and not create overly large or complex applications. We advise this not only because of performance concerns, but also for tool maintenance reasons.

With Tcl, care must also be taken in dealing with SNMP counters, which in SNMPv1 are 32-bit non-negative integer types, and in SNMPv2 can be 64-bit counters. When performing evaluations on variables holding SNMP counters, it is very easy for Tcl to treat a large counter value as a negative number. Care must be taken to treat such counters as real values when performing arithmetic evaluations.

Basic Tcl is not object-oriented! To non-programmers this is a blessing, but for sophisticated programmers who intend to build very large applications, this is a limitation. There is a workaround, however. Object-oriented extensions to Tcl have been built. One well-known object-oriented extension is called [incr Tcl]. It was developed by Michael McLennan of Lucent Technologies. [incr Tcl] is to Tcl as C++ is to C. It provides an object-oriented programming paradigm to Tcl. [incr Tcl] is included with TickleMan and we have found that using its Mega-Widgets commands makes building user interfaces easier than using the standard set of Tk commands. Michael has a newly released book on building practical applications with Tcl that we also highly recommend.

HISTORY OF TCL USE WITH SNMP

In 1992, Poul-Henning Kamp made available on the Internet an SNMP extension package for Tcl that was based on the CMU (Carnegie Mellon University) SNMP source code and version 6.4 of Tcl.

In 1993, Glenn Trewitt and Poul-Henning Kamp drafted a Tcl-SNMP API called tclsnmp2, which included support for both SNMPv1 and SNMPv2 operations.

In 1994, Jürgen Schönwälder, working at the Technical University of Braunschweig, Germany, added to the previous work by releasing what is now known as Scotty. To this day, Juergen is still evolving Scotty.

In 1994, Marshall Rose and Keith McCloghrie released *How to Manage Your Network Using SNMP*. This book was basically a guide for network managers on how to access and use SNMP MIB data by using Tcl with SNMP extensions. Marshall and Keith's Tcl-SNMP interpreter was based on the ISODE SNMP stack. Unfortunately, non-programmers had difficulty getting this Tcl Interpreter up and running. Like Scotty, it took a fair amount of C programming expertise to compile and build.

Around this time, SNMP Research International developed and released TickleMan for UNIX. TickleMan is a pre-built Tcl interpreter that has turnkey installation. In 1997, SNMP Research released TickleMan/Lite for NT, which runs on both WIN NT and WIN95.

AVAILABILITY OF TCL WITH SNMP

In this book we will be looking at two SNMP extensions to Tcl: TickleMan and Scotty.

TickleMan is a commercial product available through SNMP Research. TickleMan is available in most flavors of UNIX and Windows 95/NT. The product provides tools for compiling MIBs, Tcl extensions for performing simple and complex SNMP operations and utility commands for making common operations easy. TickleMan also includes the itcl extensions. SNMP Research can be reached at: **www.snmp.com**.

Scotty is both available commercially and in some form as a freeware product, and is available on UNIX and Windows NT. Scotty is actually made up of several pieces, including a network map application and SNMP extensions, among other Tcl extensions. The SNMP extensions are part of a package called Tnm. It provides for automatic MIB compilation, and also provides Tcl extensions for performing both simple and complex SNMP operations. Tnm also allows for agent simulation and trap generation. The version we used in writing this book (Tnm 3.0 built on Tcl 8.0) was a pre-release of the commercial product. It was more turnkey than previous versions the authors have seen and includes a self-installing binary. No configuration was necessary to get Tnm working. The freely available sources for Scotty (not the commercial product) can be found by pointing your Web browser to:

```
http://wwwsnmp.cs.utwente.nl/~schoenw/scotty/
```

Chapter 5 will be examining both extensions in detail. To be consistent, we had to choose one of the extensions in which to build our sample tools, and we chose TickleMan. The SNMP component of our tools makes up less than ten percent of our code, and the amount of effort to port our TickleMan code to Scotty is relatively straightforward. As part of Chapter 5, we show an example of porting TickleMan code to Scotty.

2 *Overview*

In this chapter we will introduce the network management tools that we will build later in the book. We will further show how these tools can be used to help maintain a network and diagnose network faults.

DISCOVER

Understanding your network is critical to managing it. This includes knowing the "stuff you have" and knowing the "new stuff" as it is added to your network. It is also critical to make sure network devices are deployed and configured in a consistent manner.

Besides knowing what's in the network and what version of software is on each device, it's useful to know what IETF MIBs are supported by each device. Mainly, we look for things like RMON, RMONv2, OSPF, Bridge, ATM, Frame Relay and HOST MIB support. By understanding which devices support these MIBs, you can better set up management strategies like multi-vendor device monitoring.

We wrote Discover because initially we needed to know which host systems in a network supported the IETF Host MIB. This need was our initial reason for learning Tcl with SNMP extensions. In all, it took one weekend to pretty much learn enough Tcl to write a working version of Discover.

Discover creates a report listing every discovered device in a network, its sysObjectID, sysName, sysDescr, sysLocation, sysContact, sysDescr and list of supported IETF MIBs. Previously, we would have used a Network Management System (NMS) to discover a client's network. Then we would have written custom programs to pull the discovered information from the flat files or database of the NMS.

Although this type of solution is pretty straightforward, it has several shortcomings. First, it is restricted to a specific product implementation. Second, it isn't extendable in regards to the type of information that we may wish to obtain. It certainly couldn't provide the IETF MIB support knowledge we wanted.

Discover basically produces a device inventory report. So far, it has been easy to modify to change the information that is collected.

The input to the application `discover.itcl` is a file named `networks.txt`. It contains a list of Class B or C networks to discover. Each entry in this file has a list of community names to use when discovering each network. Below is a sample `network.txt` file. The first entry in this file requests a discover of the Class B network `158.101.*` using both 'public' and 'support' community names in the discover process. The second entry requests a discover of the Class C network `228.51.18` using only the community name 'public' in the discover process.

```
158 101 * public support
228 51 18 public
```

Upon completion, three files are created, namely:

- `discover.html`—HTML-formatted discover report
- `discover.txt`—text-delimited discover report
- `discover.1st`—text file listing discovered devices and their supported community names

The HTML-formatted report allows a distributed network operations staff to remotely look up information about any of the discovered nodes. The text-delimited format allows managers to import device information into Excel for budget and planning purposes. The device/community name file can be used to help set up monitoring tools and to properly group network devices by management domains. Network operations often will use different community strings to group devices into multiple NOC management domains. Thus, having a list of device/community associations helps us to identify NOC domains.

Figure 2.1 shows the output file `discover.txt` loaded into an Excel Spreadsheet. Note that this data was taken from a real network, so we have hidden or changed things like node addresses, names and other site-specific reference data. Also note that the same information would be presented in the file `discover.html`.

The code for `discover.itcl` is presented and explained in Chapter 11. You can also obtain this code and the code from all our sample applications from our Web site, www.net-mgmt-solutions.com.

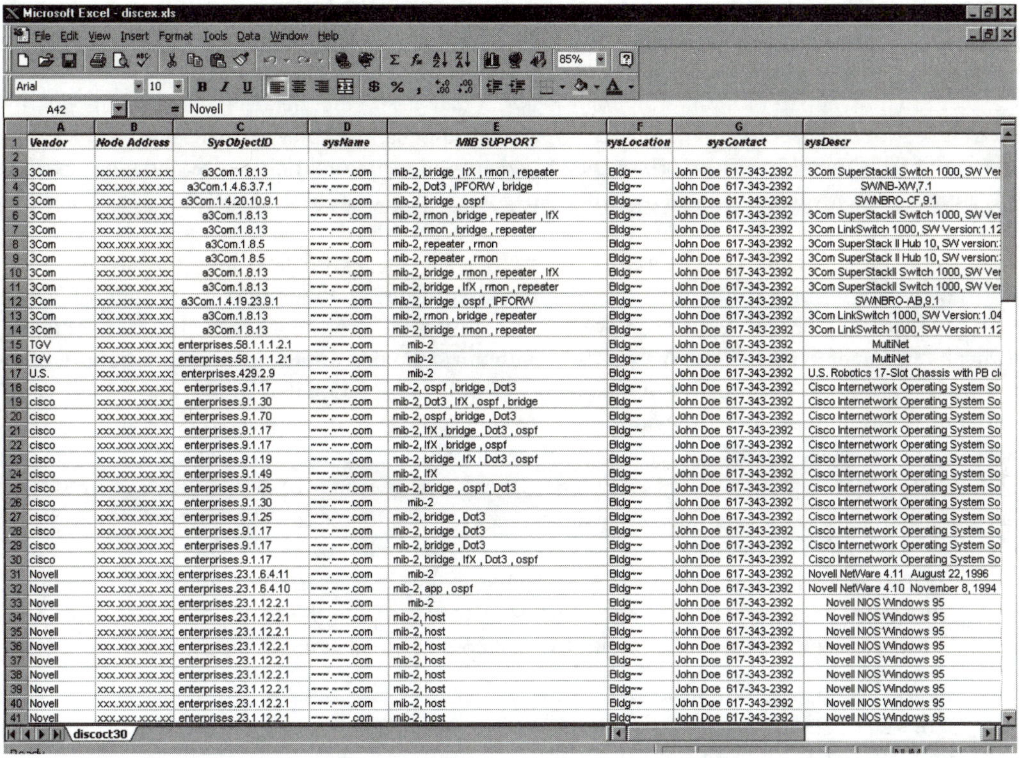

	A	B	C	D	E	F	G	
1	Vendor	Node Address	SysObjectID	sysName	MIB SUPPORT	sysLocation	sysContact	sysDescr
2								
3	3Com	xxx.xxx.xxx.xx	a3Com.1.8.13	~~~.~~~.com	mib-2, bridge , IfX , rmon , repeater	Bldg~~	John Doe 617-343-2392	3Com SuperStackII Switch 1000, SW Ver
4	3Com	xxx.xxx.xxx.xx	a3Com.1.4.6.3.7.1	~~~.~~~.com	mib-2, Dot3 , IPFORW , bridge	Bldg~~	John Doe 617-343-2392	SWNB-XW,7.1
5	3Com	xxx.xxx.xxx.xx	a3Com.1.4.20.10.9.1	~~~.~~~.com	mib-2, bridge , ospf	Bldg~~	John Doe 617-343-2392	SWNBRO-CF,9.1
6	3Com	xxx.xxx.xxx.xx	a3Com.1.8.13	~~~.~~~.com	mib-2, rmon , bridge , repeater , IfX	Bldg~~	John Doe 617-343-2392	3Com SuperStackII Switch 1000, SW Ver
7	3Com	xxx.xxx.xxx.xx	a3Com.1.8.13	~~~.~~~.com	mib-2, rmon , bridge , repeater	Bldg~~	John Doe 617-343-2392	3Com LinkSwitch 1000, SW Version:1.12
8	3Com	xxx.xxx.xxx.xx	a3Com.1.8.5	~~~.~~~.com	mib-2, repeater , rmon	Bldg~~	John Doe 617-343-2392	3Com SuperStack II Hub 10, SW version:
9	3Com	xxx.xxx.xxx.xx	a3Com.1.8.5	~~~.~~~.com	mib-2, repeater , rmon	Bldg~~	John Doe 617-343-2392	3Com SuperStack II Hub 10, SW version:
10	3Com	xxx.xxx.xxx.xx	a3Com.1.8.13	~~~.~~~.com	mib-2, bridge , rmon , repeater , IfX	Bldg~~	John Doe 617-343-2392	3Com SuperStackII Switch 1000, SW Ver
11	3Com	xxx.xxx.xxx.xx	a3Com.1.8.13	~~~.~~~.com	mib-2, bridge , IfX , rmon , repeater	Bldg~~	John Doe 617-343-2392	3Com SuperStackII Switch 1000, SW Ver
12	3Com	xxx.xxx.xxx.xx	a3Com.1.4.19.23.9.1	~~~.~~~.com	mib-2, bridge , ospf , IPFORW	Bldg~~	John Doe 617-343-2392	SWNBRO-AB,9.1
13	3Com	xxx.xxx.xxx.xx	a3Com.1.8.13	~~~.~~~.com	mib-2, rmon , bridge , repeater	Bldg~~	John Doe 617-343-2392	3Com LinkSwitch 1000, SW Version:1.04
14	3Com	xxx.xxx.xxx.xx	a3Com.1.8.13	~~~.~~~.com	mib-2, bridge , rmon , repeater	Bldg~~	John Doe 617-343-2392	3Com LinkSwitch 1000, SW Version:1.12
15	TGV	xxx.xxx.xxx.xx	enterprises.58.1.1.1.2.1	~~~.~~~.com	mib-2	Bldg~~	John Doe 617-343-2392	MultiNet
16	TGV	xxx.xxx.xxx.xx	enterprises.58.1.1.1.2.1	~~~.~~~.com	mib-2	Bldg~~	John Doe 617-343-2392	MultiNet
17	U.S.	xxx.xxx.xxx.xx	enterprises.429.2.9	~~~.~~~.com	mib-2	Bldg~~	John Doe 617-343-2392	U.S. Robotics 17-Slot Chassis with PB cl
18	cisco	xxx.xxx.xxx.xx	enterprises.9.1.17	~~~.~~~.com	mib-2, ospf , bridge , Dot3	Bldg~~	John Doe 617-343-2392	Cisco Internetwork Operating System So
19	cisco	xxx.xxx.xxx.xx	enterprises.9.1.30	~~~.~~~.com	mib-2, Dot3 , IfX , ospf , bridge	Bldg~~	John Doe 617-343-2392	Cisco Internetwork Operating System So
20	cisco	xxx.xxx.xxx.xx	enterprises.9.1.70	~~~.~~~.com	mib-2, ospf , bridge , Dot3	Bldg~~	John Doe 617-343-2392	Cisco Internetwork Operating System So
21	cisco	xxx.xxx.xxx.xx	enterprises.9.1.17	~~~.~~~.com	mib-2, IfX , bridge , Dot3 , ospf	Bldg~~	John Doe 617-343-2392	Cisco Internetwork Operating System So
22	cisco	xxx.xxx.xxx.xx	enterprises.9.1.17	~~~.~~~.com	mib-2, IfX , bridge , ospf	Bldg~~	John Doe 617-343-2392	Cisco Internetwork Operating System So
23	cisco	xxx.xxx.xxx.xx	enterprises.9.1.19	~~~.~~~.com	mib-2, bridge , IfX , Dot3 , ospf	Bldg~~	John Doe 617-343-2392	Cisco Internetwork Operating System So
24	cisco	xxx.xxx.xxx.xx	enterprises.9.1.49	~~~.~~~.com	mib-2, IfX	Bldg~~	John Doe 617-343-2392	Cisco Internetwork Operating System So
25	cisco	xxx.xxx.xxx.xx	enterprises.9.1.25	~~~.~~~.com	mib-2, bridge , ospf , Dot3	Bldg~~	John Doe 617-343-2392	Cisco Internetwork Operating System So
26	cisco	xxx.xxx.xxx.xx	enterprises.9.1.30	~~~.~~~.com	mib-2	Bldg~~	John Doe 617-343-2392	Cisco Internetwork Operating System So
27	cisco	xxx.xxx.xxx.xx	enterprises.9.1.25	~~~.~~~.com	mib-2, bridge , Dot3	Bldg~~	John Doe 617-343-2392	Cisco Internetwork Operating System So
28	cisco	xxx.xxx.xxx.xx	enterprises.9.1.17	~~~.~~~.com	mib-2, bridge , Dot3	Bldg~~	John Doe 617-343-2392	Cisco Internetwork Operating System So
29	cisco	xxx.xxx.xxx.xx	enterprises.9.1.17	~~~.~~~.com	mib-2, bridge , Dot3	Bldg~~	John Doe 617-343-2392	Cisco Internetwork Operating System So
30	cisco	xxx.xxx.xxx.xx	enterprises.9.1.17	~~~.~~~.com	mib-2, bridge , IfX , Dot3 , ospf	Bldg~~	John Doe 617-343-2392	Cisco Internetwork Operating System So
31	Novell	xxx.xxx.xxx.xx	enterprises.23.1.6.4.11	~~~.~~~.com	mib-2	Bldg~~	John Doe 617-343-2392	Novell NetWare 4.11 August 22, 1996
32	Novell	xxx.xxx.xxx.xx	enterprises.23.1.6.4.10	~~~.~~~.com	mib-2, app , ospf	Bldg~~	John Doe 617-343-2392	Novell NetWare 4.10 November 8, 1994
33	Novell	xxx.xxx.xxx.xx	enterprises.23.1.12.2.1	~~~.~~~.com	mib-2	Bldg~~	John Doe 617-343-2392	Novell NIOS Windows 95
34	Novell	xxx.xxx.xxx.xx	enterprises.23.1.12.2.1	~~~.~~~.com	mib-2, host	Bldg~~	John Doe 617-343-2392	Novell NIOS Windows 95
35	Novell	xxx.xxx.xxx.xx	enterprises.23.1.12.2.1	~~~.~~~.com	mib-2, host	Bldg~~	John Doe 617-343-2392	Novell NIOS Windows 95
36	Novell	xxx.xxx.xxx.xx	enterprises.23.1.12.2.1	~~~.~~~.com	mib-2, host	Bldg~~	John Doe 617-343-2392	Novell NIOS Windows 95
37	Novell	xxx.xxx.xxx.xx	enterprises.23.1.12.2.1	~~~.~~~.com	mib-2, host	Bldg~~	John Doe 617-343-2392	Novell NIOS Windows 95
38	Novell	xxx.xxx.xxx.xx	enterprises.23.1.12.2.1	~~~.~~~.com	mib-2, host	Bldg~~	John Doe 617-343-2392	Novell NIOS Windows 95
39	Novell	xxx.xxx.xxx.xx	enterprises.23.1.12.2.1	~~~.~~~.com	mib-2, host	Bldg~~	John Doe 617-343-2392	Novell NIOS Windows 95
40	Novell	xxx.xxx.xxx.xx	enterprises.23.1.12.2.1	~~~.~~~.com	mib-2, host	Bldg~~	John Doe 617-343-2392	Novell NIOS Windows 95
41	Novell	xxx.xxx.xxx.xx	enterprises.23.1.12.2.1	~~~.~~~.com	mib-2, host	Bldg~~	John Doe 617-343-2392	Novell NIOS Windows 95

Figure 2.1 Sample `discover.txt` file imported into Excel.

StatusMgr

An important part of managing your network is understanding how your network is working. This includes understanding which of your segments are over- or under-utilized, which of your devices have high packet throughputs or even how long your devices have been up and running. The more you observe the real-time network operational status of your network, the more you learn about it. By collecting real-time data, you can not only understand how your network is working, but you can also use this data to find network faults. For example, if you see high transmit broadcast rates on a large number of switch ports, but only see a high receive broadcast rate on a single port, you can identify and shut down a broadcast storm. If you consistently see high error rates on certain switch ports, you might be able to isolate the problem to bad cabling.

An important part of monitoring your network data is sharing this data with as many distributed network administrators as possible. By making this data Web-accessible, not only are you sharing this data with both network users and other administrators, but you're allowing yourself the ability to access the data from anywhere. If you get paged at three in the morning, instead of driving twenty miles to the NOC, you can dial in and access the data via a browser. Remote accessibility to management data is important to every aspect of successful network management.

We wrote the status monitoring application, StatusMgr, to do a quick health audit on a network. We basically needed an inexpensive, multi-platform, multi-vendor solution capable of monitoring a few hundred key nodes. We wanted minimum setup time; nothing more than simply identifying what nodes to monitor. We also wanted a Web-based solution that would allow us to access real-time status remotely over low-speed dial-up connections. And, we wanted to be able to easily visualize device status by defined groups. We needed this so we could isolate specific problems by both device and group. This would allow us to see if certain groups of devices were more or less healthier than others; for example, whether there were variations in network availability and performance according to differences in operational ownership and procedures.

To use StatusMgr, you need to create a file listing devices to monitor, their community names (normally only the read community name is required) and the group designation for each node. Below is a sample of a configuration file that could be loaded into StatusMgr:

```
<group> 3COM
158.101.122.1 public
158.101.122.2 public
158.101.122.3 public
<group> ACC
158.101.122.5 public
158.101.122.6 public
158.101.122.7 public
<group> Alantec
    .
    .
    .
```

That's it. No other tool setup is required. Sample screens are displayed in Figures 2.2 through 2.10. Note that sample screen displays shown throughout the book contain fictitious node address information.

Figure 2.2 shows the main StatusMgr GUI. In this screen, you can see from the tab display that we are looking at what we call the StatusMap. Green means the node and all its interfaces are healthy. Magenta means one or more interfaces that should be UP are DOWN. Orange means one or more threshold rules have been violated. Click on any node and a pop-up window is displayed that provides you reference data about the node and a list of any current problems.

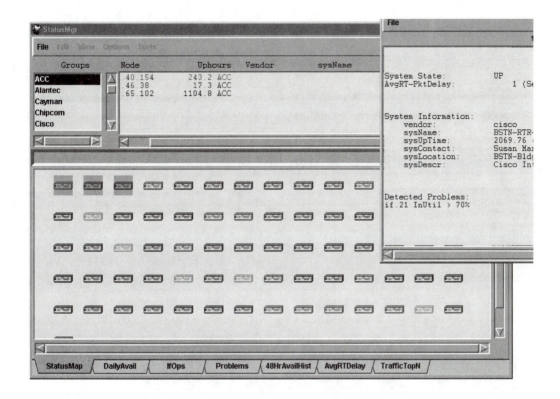

Figure 2.2   StatusMap with opened node pop-up window.

What we normally do is group nodes by either vendor, site or position in the network hierarchy. A network hierarchy group definition could easily consist of group names like "Level 1 Transit Routers", "Level 2 Transit Routers", "Backbone Edge Routers", "ATM Switches", "LAN Switches", "HUBS", "Servers" and "Clients". The Universal Group is a system-created group that includes all nodes.

Figure 2.3 shows the results of selecting StatusMgr's "DailyAvail" tab. For whatever group is selected, you see a report of devices. For each device, this report displays reset counts for that day, network availability for that day and the node's current system up-time. Select a different group, and that group's data is displayed. Very quickly we can see data for different groups.

Figure 2.4 shows the results of selecting the "IfOps" tab. For whatever group is selected, you'll see a list of interfaces and their current operational status. Select a different group, and that group's data is displayed.

Figure 2.5 shows the results of selecting the "Problems" tab. This report lists all down interfaces and all violated threshold rules for devices in the selected group. Threshold rules include:

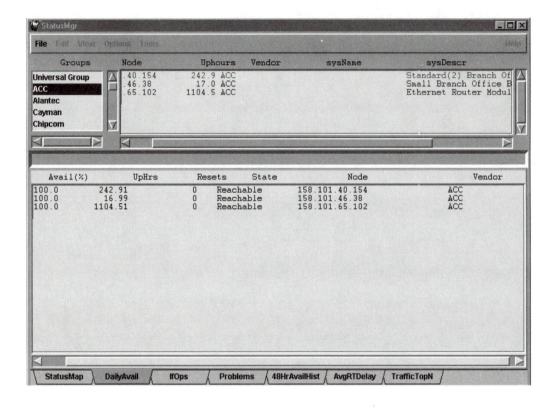

Figure 2.3 Daily network availability for nodes in a selected group.

- IP layer In Discards Rate > 1 pps
- IP layer Out Discards Rate > 1 pps
- IP layer Out No Routes Rate > 1 pps
- IP layer Routing Discards Rate > 1 pps
- Any change in ifLastTimeChange, indicating the interface experienced a reset
- Link layer In Utilization > 70%
- Link layer Out Utilization > 70 %
- Link layer In Discard Rates > 1 pps
- Link layer Out Discard Rate > 1 pps
- Link layer In Broadcast and Multicast Packet Rate > 500 pps
- Link layer Out Broadcast and Multicast Packet Rate > 500 pps
- Link layer In Error Rate > 1 pps
- Link layer Out Error Rate > 1 pps

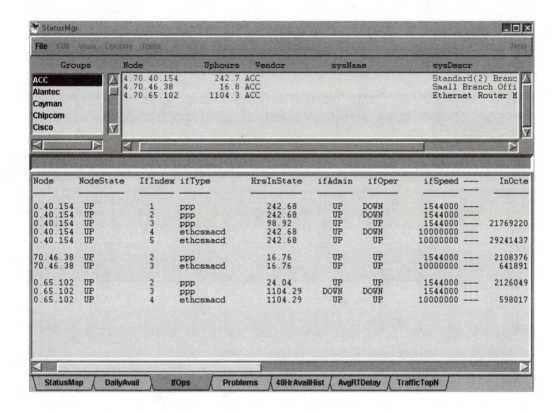

Figure 2.4   Interface operations for a selected group.

These threshold rules are defined in a procedure called `UpdateEvents`. Thus, it is easy to locate these rules in StatusMgr's code when you want to modify them.

Figure 2.6 shows the results of selecting the "48HrAvailHist" tab. This provides a summary of nodal availability for previously monitored hours for a selected group. In Figure 2.6, it shows that StatusMgr was recently started, so there are only two past monitored hours to report upon. It shows that for the selected group, Novell, operations are pretty stable. One server has been unreachable ever since we started monitoring with StatusMgr. All other servers have had full network availability over the past two hours. There have been no resets for any nodes in this selected group.

Figure 2.7 shows the results of selecting the "AvgRTDelay" tab. This provides a report that shows the average round-trip delay time for the last three successful polls to each node. This is normally used for assurance that the network is healthy and stable. Soft problems like OSPF experiencing frequent link state changes or convergence problems often are the most difficult to identify and troubleshoot.

In periods of chaos, high round-trip poll delays indicate that there is a major soft problem occurring in certain areas of your network. You may be surprised at the number of soft problems in networks that impact end-user performance. Soft problems are not detected by most management

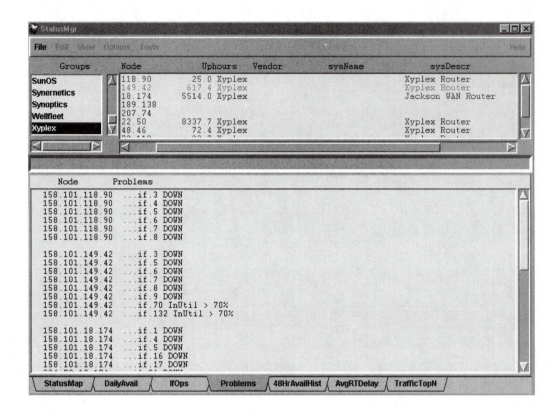

Figure 2.5   List of current problems for a selected group.

tools. Most management tool products with monitoring capabilities are primarily focused on detecting hard problems like interface failures and (on occasion) erroneous traffic counter thresholds.
Network packet delay and response time monitoring, even when not terribly accurate, are great in-
dicators of soft problems in the network. Fortunately, the monitoring of these soft problems is now
beginning to get widespread attention by off-the-shelf vendor products.

Figure 2.8 shows the results of selecting the "Traffic Top N" tab. This report shows the Top
N packet forwarders, the Top N packet receivers and the Top N packet senders. This report lets
you know how your network is working. For example, we have one router that we monitor that is a
critical router in its network. We know it always does over 13,000 pps of packet forwarding. We
would therefore be concerned if it was missing from the Top N traffic report for its group.

Remote users can get access to the real-time data of StatusMgr by directly connecting to the
application via a Web browser. All you need to do is point your Web browser to port number 2000
for whatever host system is running StatusMgr; or, on a centrally-located Web server, create an
HTML page with links to your StatusMgr host:2000.

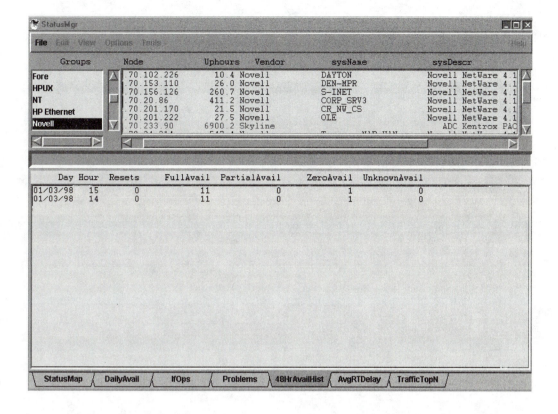

Figure 2.6 Availability summary for previous monitored hours.

StatusMgr's Web interface is simple but effective. It is described in detail in Chapter 9 where we discuss Tcl socket programming. When you remotely point your Web browser to a running instance of StatusMgr, your browser will display the StatusMgr Home Page illustrated in Figure 2.9. The Web interface provides basically the same information as the Tk GUI and is usually very fast to use as long as your membership in any one group isn't too large and you can avoid requesting reports on a large Universal Group as much as possible.

From the StatusMgr Home Page, you get to choose a group and a request. Valid requests include:

- Device Status
- Device Availability
- WAN Interface Status
- LAN Interface Status
- Historical Availability Summary

Figure 2.10 shows the results of requesting WAN Interface Status on the Universal Group from the StatusMgr's Home Page.

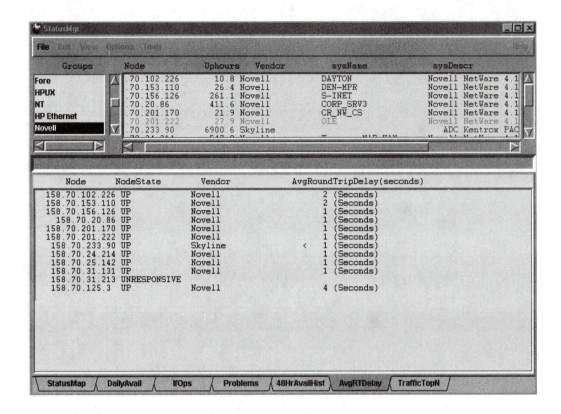

Figure 2.7 Average SNMP poll delay per node (over last three poll cycles).

RESPONSE TIME MONITORING TOOL

This tool, illustrated in Figure 2.11, provides network delay measurements from a host to a list of devices. By using this tool to measure network delay to a list of subnets, a network manager can gain insight as to how the network is performing at different strategic points. This tool can be used to help troubleshoot network performance problems. Specifically, the tool provides the following information for each address being tested:

- Current delay measurements
- Average delay measurements
- Peak delay measurements
- Percentage of tests that completed, which indicates the reachability of a device

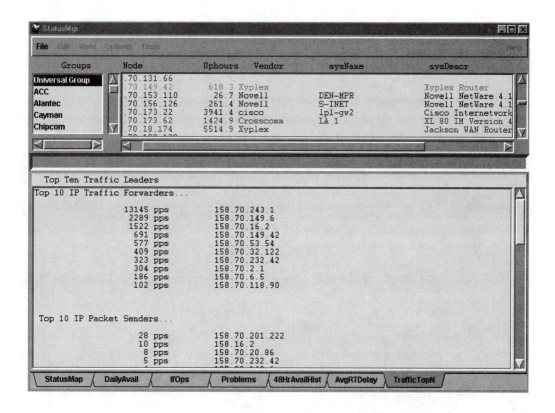

Figure 2.8   Top N traffic report for a selected group.

As mentioned already, stable response time and throughput values are good assurances that network operations are healthy and stable. Many network managers have custom ping programs that they find quite effective to monitor packet delays between end points. This is an extension of this basic concept.

The Response Time Monitoring Tool is especially useful for seeing who has TCP sessions opened to one or more of your host servers that are running this tool. Besides showing you who has an open TCP session to a server, it will also show you the average and peak round-trip packet delay for each of these sessions. The application is fully presented and discussed in Chapter 10.

The Response Time Monitoring Tool can also be used in other ways. For example, say you have five critical host servers under your domain. If these servers are on the same local segment as your management station, you can run invocations of this tool on your management station and get estimated measurements of packet delay from these servers to various other sites. (The network delay between a server and a remote client and a device on the same local segment of the server and the same remote client should be roughly the same.)

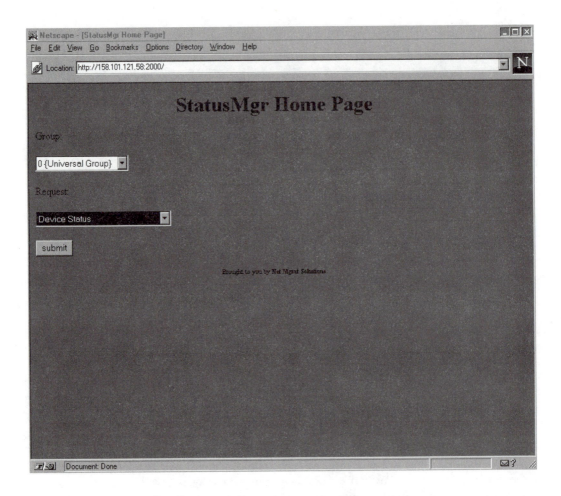

Figure 2.9 StatusMgr Web interface Home Page.

If these servers are on different segments, you could put the Response Time Monitoring Tool on each of these servers. You could then X-Display over to one of your host servers and start the Response Time Monitoring Tool. Sure enough, it will tell you who has TCP sessions opened to that server and what their average and peak round-trip packet delays are. Note that the application in this case is getting the TCP session address information from the host server's own MIB II TCP group.

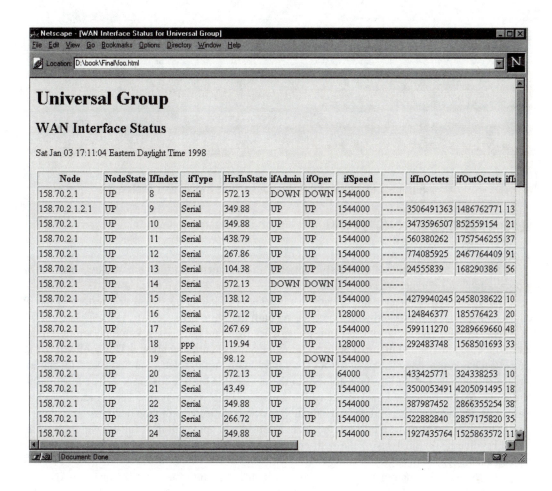

Figure 2.10   Example of WAN Interface Status report from StatusMgr's Web interface.

As currently written, the Response Time Monitoring Tool is more a utility than a full-blown application. If you use it as we just described, there are several ways to expand it. X-Display is usually only available on UNIX servers. Thus, what we just described wouldn't be applicable to many NT-based servers. If the Response Time Monitoring Tool is of interest to you, consider making it Web-accessible as we have done with StatusMgr. Consider expanding it by logging connect times, traffic volumes and response time data to some sort of report or database. It would be especially useful for planning purposes if it also combined other measures, such as host resource utilization, with user load and response times.

Device	Current Delay	Average Delay	Peak Delay	% Completed
www.cisco.com	217 msecs	367	888	100.0
www.3Com.com	230 msecs	369	858	100.0
www.baynetworks.com	220 msecs	505	1555	100.0
www.cabletron.com	183 msecs	192	237	100.0
www.ascend.com	247 msecs	255	300	100.0

Figure 2.11 GUI of the Response Time Monitoring Tool.

IP PATH TRACING TOOL

Another cardinal rule of successful network management is to have a strategy and set of tools available for diagnosing network problems.

For this book, we present the IP Path Tracing Tool in Chapter 13. The user interface of the IP Path Tracing Tool is illustrated with a mocked-up path in Figure 2.12.

Our IP Path Tracing Tool determines a network path and provides a path diagram that illustrates the components making up a path, and how busy these components are. This tool will list in a table each address along the path, the ifType for the outgoing interface, the line speed for the interface, the bit rate for the interface going into the device, the bit rate for the interface leading out of the device, the forwarded packet rate of the device and the vendor name. The bit rates and forwarded packet rates will be updated periodically as data is collected from the devices.

This is really more of a utility rather than a full-blown application. A full-blown application would involve health analysis of the path components as determined via add-on procedures that collect and analyze path data.

A problem with many network applications is that they are tested in a lab over a LAN connection. They are then deployed in a corporate network over a WAN with a higher incident of packet discards and round-trip delays. Sure enough, they run over connectionless UDP. Things work rather well most of the time, but occasionally users will have pretty bad connection performance. In such cases, you may want to do an echo test from point A to point B, or run a path trace/diagnostic tool.

Tracing an IP routing path between network devices can be especially useful for detecting client-server performance problems. By diagnosing the path, you can find problems such as congested interfaces, paths with large hop counts or low-speed WAN interfaces and nodes in the path with high Level 2/Level 3 packet discards or filtering rates.

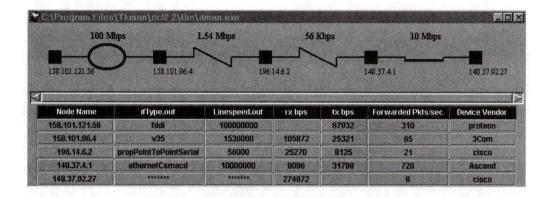

Figure 2.12 Path diagram of the IP Path Tracing Tool.

Node Name	ifType.out	Linespeed.out	rx bps	tx bps	Forwarded Pkts/sec	Device Vendor
158.101.121.56	fddi	100000000		87932	310	proteon
158.101.96.4	v35	1536000	105872	25321	65	3Com
196.14.6.2	propPointToPointSerial	56000	25270	8125	21	cisco
148.37.4.1	ethernetCsmacd	10000000	8096	31788	720	Ascend
148.37.92.27	*******	******	274872		8	cisco

RMONv2 CONFIGURATION MANAGER

RMON and RMONv2 are great additions to the network management solution space. Building inventory reports and configuring, collecting and analyzing RMON data are areas where custom tools can be very valuable.

Many hub and switch vendors today have network devices that support varying degrees of RMON and RMONv2. In addition, many of you have stand-alone RMON and RMONv2 probes. Unfortunately, RMON application products are sometimes limited in ways that cost you undue time and hardship.

First is the area of RMON configuration management. Few off-the-shelf tools support effective bulk configuration of RMON MIB control tables. Configuring tens or hundreds of probes individually is not how you should spend your time.

Second in the area of RMON deployment, few embedded network devices can afford to have all but a few RMON groups turned on at any one time. Thus, your investment in embedded RMON is not usable by many off-the-shelf reporting tools. Custom tools that selectively turn on RMON, grab data and turn off RMON can get around this problem and give you more utility out of embedded RMON and RMONv2 support.

In this book we provide several scripts to both configure RMONv2 tables and to inventory the configuration of your RMONv2 probes.

IN SUMMARY

The network management problem is sometimes overwhelming. Vendors have a tough challenge in building network management tools that work consistently for different devices built by different engineering groups, sometimes located in different countries. Customers also face a tough challenge when deploying network management tools from multiple vendors. In fact, the tasks are equally overwhelming on both sides.

We state this here because we don't want to minimize the difficulty of the network management problem. We do not want to sound like building custom tools is always simple. And, we don't want to sound like you don't need off-the-shelf management tools.

What we are stating is that off-the-shelf products often have limitations or high deployment costs. This forces you to implement customized solutions to get practical benefits out of combined vendor offerings. We have found a high value/low pain proposition that works for us—using Tcl with SNMP extensions to build specific utilities, applications and reporting mechanisms to individual client requirements. This can be an especially effective mechanism for network managers and consultants alike. We hope you will try it to supplement and extend your own use of off-the-shelf products with custom-built tools.

3 *Tcl Basics*

Tcl is a string-based command language. It has a simple syntax with none of the complexities of object-oriented languages such as C++. Still, it has similar constructs to other programming languages: variables, expression evaluation, arrays, control flow, procedures, file I/O and socket programming. It exceeds virtually any language we've encountered in its capabilities for:

- List processing
- String manipulation
- Building dynamic commands

This chapter takes you through the basics of the Tcl language syntax. Even though, as mentioned above, Tcl has similarities to other programming languages, it is well worth paying close attention to this chapter and the examples within it. The mindset for building Tcl programs is quite a bit different than that of building code with C or C++. While Tcl is a procedural language, with it you are basically doing a lot of list and string manipulation. One of the most powerful features of Tcl—being able to build dynamic commands—will be demonstrated over and over again throughout this text.

Tcl COMMAND SYNTAX

A Tcl program is made up of a collection of Tcl commands. When executing a Tcl program, each Tcl command will be interpreted in sequence until the program exits. The syntax for a Tcl command is simply:

```
command arg1 arg2 arg3 ...
```

where `command` is either a Tcl built-in command or a Tcl procedure. The number of arguments following the command depends purely on the command itself.

A pound character, #, is used for comments and must be at the beginning of a command. Since semicolons can be used to end a command, a trick for placing a comment at the end of a line is to put a semicolon in front of the pound character (the semicolon makes the pound character the start of the next command). For example:

```
set ipaddr 158.101.121.1  ;# Collect routing table.
```

VARIABLES

set

The set command is used to assign a value to a variable. A variable name can be any combination of characters and is case-sensitive. Variables are not typed, nor do they need to be declared before one can use them. Examples:

```
set x 87
⇒ 87

set x 87.65     ;# x can be used as a floating point.
⇒ 87.65

set x 87zz
⇒ 87zz

set x 158.101.121.1
⇒ 158.101.121.1
```

In the last example, x is set to a string that can be used to represent an IP address.

```
set x {sysUpTime sysDescr sysName }
⇒ sysUpTime sysDescr sysName
```

In the above example, x is set to a list of strings. Note that the braces used in the previous example are not part of the value, but instead group the value.

```
set x 100
⇒ 100

set x
⇒ 100
```

A set command with a single argument, as shown above, simply returns the value of the variable.

Tcl needs to be able to distinguish between a variable name and the value of a variable. This is done by putting a dollar sign, $, in front of a variable, which causes Tcl to perform variable substitution within the command. For example:

```
set a 100
⇒ 100

set b a      ;# Set b to the arbitrary string 'a'.
⇒ a

set b $a     ;# Set b to the value of variable a.
⇒ 100
```

incr

The incr command provides a simple way to change the value of a variable. incr takes two arguments: the name of a variable and an integer. The variable will be incremented by the integer amount, the integer being either positive or negative. If the integer is omitted from the command, the variable will be incremented by one.

```
set a 100
⇒ 100

incr a 20
⇒ 120

incr a -50
⇒ 70

incr a
⇒ 71
```

ARRAYS

An array in Tcl is a variable with any arbitrary string index. Indexes for an array can be created dynamically. Whole arrays or individual array elements can be deleted from memory with the unset command. As with variables, array elements are assigned values with the set command. Internally, arrays are accessed via a hash table and can be more efficient than processing large lists (more on that later!). Examples:

```
set val(ifInOctets) 100
⇒ 100

set val(1) {100 200 300}
⇒ 100 200 300

set val(1.x) "setting index 1.x to this string"
⇒ setting index 1.x to this string

unset val(1.x)  ;# Remove element from memory.
unset val       ;# Remove array from memory.
```

Multi-dimensional arrays can be simulated by using index strings with commas in them:

```
set val(ifInOctets,1) 100
⇒ 100
```

Note that a space within the index string will cause an error:

```
set val(ifInOctets, 1) 100
⇒ wrong # args: should be "set varName ?newValue?"
```

Also note that variable names and array names must be different:

```
set x 100
⇒ 100

set x(1) 200
⇒ can't set "x(1)": variable isn't array
```

Variable substitution is also accomplished with arrays by using a dollar sign, $, in front of the array name, and if a variable is being used as an index, in front of the array index. For example:

```
set i 100
⇒ 100

set arr($i) 28.6
⇒ 28.6

set val arr(i)   ;# This will set val to the string "arr(i)".
⇒ arr(i)

set val $arr(i)  ;# Wrong!
can't read "arr(i)": no such element in array

set val $arr($i)  ;# Correct!
⇒ 28.6
```

Tcl provides an `array` command to get various types of information about an array. This is best described (as with everything else we discuss in this book) with a set of examples:

```
set arr(ifInOctets) 1000
⇒ 1000

set arr(ifInErrors) 20
⇒ 20

set arr(ifSpeed) 56000
⇒ 56000
```

array exists

The `array exists` command will return 1 if a supplied argument is an array variable; otherwise, it will return 0.

```
array exists arr  ;# Returns 1 if arr is an array variable.
⇒ 1
```

array get

The `array get` command will return a list of alternating indices and values for an array.

```
array get arr
⇒ ifInErrors 20 ifInOctets 1000 ifSpeed 56000
```

Note that the list is returned in the order of its internal hash table.

```
array get arr *Octets
⇒ ifInOctets 1000
```

In the previous example, `*Octets` is used as a pattern to match against all the array indices being used. More will be said about pattern-matching later.

array set

The `array set` command is the inverse of the `array get` command. It will set array elements given an alternating list of indices and values.

```
array set arr {ifOutErrors 7 ifOutOctets 6000}
```

The example above, `array set` initializes `arr(ifOutErrors)` to 7 and `arr(ifOutOctets)` to 6000.

array names

The `array names` command returns a list of indices for an array.

```
array names arr
⇒ ifSpeed ifOutOctets ifInOctets ifInErrors ifSpeed

array names arr *Octets
⇒ ifOutOctets ifInOctets
```

In the examples above, `array names` returns a list of either all indices being used within the array or all the indices that match the optional pattern.

A common way to walk an array is to use the `array names` command with the `foreach` command that will be shown later in this chapter. The `foreach` command allows you to loop through the elements of a list.

```
set x [array names arr]
⇒ ifSpeed ifInOctets ifInErrors

foreach el $x {
  puts "$el $arr($el)"
}

⇒ ifSpeed 56000
ifInOctets 100
ifInErrors 20
```

array size

The `array size` command returns the number of elements in an array.

```
array size arr
⇒ 5
```

EXPRESSIONS

Tcl provides for both arithmetic and Boolean expressions with a syntax and precedence similar to ANSI C. If operands for an operator have different types, Tcl will convert one of the operands so that they both have the same type. If one operand is an integer and the other is a real, the integer will be converted to a real. The function double will convert an integer to a real explicitly. The functions int and round will convert a real value to an integer by either truncating or rounding.

Integers are represented internally with the C type int, which is usually stored internally as a 32-bit value. An integer with the most significant bit set will be treated as a negative number within an expression. Real numbers are represented internally with the C type double, which is stored internally as a 64-bit value. A common technique for monitoring network traffic is to periodically collect counter values from network devices and calculate bandwidth usage and error rates. If a variable is assigned an SNMP counter value (which are unsigned 32-bit values for SNMPv1), it could end up being treated as a negative number. If both counter values are large (both have the most significant bits set), calculating the difference between the two values will still yield the correct result.

```
set prevVal 4294965000    ;# Set to a very large number.
⇒ 4294965000

set lastVal 4294965500    ;# Set to a higher counter value.
⇒ 4294965500


expr $lastVal - $prevVal
⇒ 500
```

This is because the expression actually was (after converting the integers to negative numbers) -1796 – (-2296). When calculating the difference between two SNMP counters, you must check to see if a wraparound occurred (an SNMP counter, after reaching the maximum unsigned integer value for a 32-bit integer, will wrap to 0). This can cause problems if not dealt with properly.

```
set MAXINT 4294967295
⇒ 4294967295

set prevVal 4294965000
⇒ 4294965000
set lastVal 100
⇒ 100

if {$lastVal < $prevVal} {
   set delta [expr ($MAXINT - $prevVal) + $lastVal]
}
```

prevVal will be interpreted as a negative number and the conditional clause will fail. A simple way to get around this is to first convert both values to reals and then perform the comparsion:

```
append prevVal ".0"
```

```
append lastVal ".0"

if {$lastVal < $prevVal} {
   set delta [expr ($MAXINT - $prevVal) + $lastVal]
}
```

In the above examples, we introduced both the append command and if command. We also showed square brackets around the expr command. The append command simply appends text to the end of a variable. By appending a ".0" string to the end of an integer, we in effect convert the variable to a real. The if command will be discussed in more detail later. The square brackets introduce command substitution. In Tcl, the results of one command can be used as arguments for another command. In the command set delta [expr ($MAXINT - $prevVal) + $lastVal], the argument [expr ($MAXINT - $prevVal) + $lastVal] will be evaluated as a separate Tcl script, and the result of the script will be substituted in place of the bracketed argument.

Note that appending ".0" to the end of a variable will not work if the variable is already a real. If a variable, for example, had a value of 5.0, appending a ".0" to the end of the variable would create the string "5.0.0". A more expensive CPU-wise, but safer way to convert a variable prevVal to a real, would be:

```
scan $prevVal %f prevVal
```

which would convert either a real or an integer to a real. We will discuss this solution in more detail when we show the scan command later in this chapter.

Note that even though real numbers are internally stored as 64-bit values, an SNMP 64-bit counter cannot be stored as a real since the mantissa is shorter than 64 bits. To deal with SNMP 64-bit counters, you must split them up into two 32-bit reals, one representing the low 32 bits, the other the high 32 bits.

Table 3.1 provides a quick summary of Tcl arithmetic and logical operators by precedence.

Table 3.1

-, !, ~	unary minus, logical Not, bitwise complement
*, /, %	multiply, divide, remainder after division
+, -	add, subtract
<<, >>	left-shift, right-shift
<, >, <=, >=	less than, greater than, less than or equal, greater than or equal
==, !=	equal, not equal
&	bitwise AND
^	bitwise exclusive OR
|	bitwise OR
&&	logical AND
||	logical OR
x?y:z	if x is non-zero then y, else z

COMMAND SUBSTITUTION

Command substitution was introduced in the previous section. One point to keep in mind is that characters between brackets must constitute a valid Tcl script. The script, however, can be any number of Tcl commands separated by newlines or semicolons:

```
set rx_util [set linespeed 56000.0
set delta_inoctets 39872.0
set seconds 30.0
expr (($delta_inoctets * 8.0)/($linespeed*$seconds))*100.0]
⇒ 18.9867
```

BACKSLASH SUBSTITUTION

Tcl allows special characters, such as newlines or $, to be inserted into strings by prefacing the character with a backslash:

```
set x 100
⇒ 100

set y \$x
⇒ $x

expr $y+20
⇒ 120
```

Here, the script expr $y+20 gets converted after argument substitution to expr $x+20, which further gets converted to expr 100+20. The sequence backslash followed by a newline followed by a space will be converted to a single space character. This allows Tcl commands that span multiple lines to be written.

```
set percent_ip_rx_discards [expr (delta_ipInDiscards/ \
  (delta_ipInDelivers + delta_ipForwDatagrams \
  + delta_ipInDiscards))*100.0]
⇒ 2.56
```

QUOTING RULES

Double quotes are used to group words that contain spaces, newlines, curly brackets and semicolons. Variable substitutions, command substitutions and backslash substitutions all occur as usual within double quotes.

```
set rx_util 42.8
⇒  42.8

set result_str "Receive Utilization: {$rx_util}\n;;"
⇒  Receive Utilization: {42.8}
⇒  ;;

set x "Result = [expr 12*10]"
⇒  Result = 120
```

Braces provide a more radical form of quoting than double quotes. All special characters lose their meaning when within braces. No variable, command or backslash substitutions are performed when within braces. Spaces, tabs, newlines and semicolons are all treated as normal characters.

```
set x 100
⇒  100

set str {Value of x = $x}
⇒  Value of x = $x
```

However, if braces are within quotes, they are then treated as normal characters with substitution occurring.

```
set str "{Value of x = $x}"
⇒  {Value of x = 100}
```

Braces also allow for commands within the braces to be deferred until evaluation. This is an important concept for Tcl and will be described later.

PROCEDURES AND SCOPING

A procedure in Tcl is conceptually similar to a procedure in other languages. A procedure contains a name, a list of arguments and a body, and can return a value. Procedures are created with the `proc` command. We will now define a procedure, `TestWrapAround`, which will be passed two SNMP counter values and will return 1 if an SNMP counter wraparound has been detected, 0 otherwise.

```
proc TestWrapAround {firstVal secondVal} {

  append firstVal ".0"
  append secondVal ".0"

  if {$secondVal < $firstVal} {
    return 1
  }

  return 0
}


TestWrapAround 429465821 1057
⇒ 1

TestWrapAround 12000 82
⇒ 1

TestWrapAround 410873139 413912231
⇒ 0
```

The first argument to `proc` is the procedure name, the second argument is a list of variables for the procedure and the third argument is the body of the procedure. Once a procedure has been defined, it can be used as any Tcl command.

```
set result [TestWrapAround 429465821 1057]
⇒ 1
```

Procedures can access either local or global variables. Local and global variables can have the same name. These, of course, will be completely separate variables; modifying one will have no effect on the other. A procedure references global variables by using the Tcl `global` command within the procedure's body.

```
set MAXINT 4294967295.0
⇒ 4294967295.0
proc Delta {firstVal secondVal} {
global MAXINT

if {[TestWrapAround $firstVal $secondVal]} {
```

```
    append firstVal ".0"
    append secondVal ".0"

    set temp [expr $MAXINT - $firstVal]
    return [expr $temp + $secondVal]
}


    append firstVal ".0"
    append secondVal ".0"
    return [expr $secondVal - $firstVal]
}
```

In the above example, MAXINT is a global variable that has been defined outside the scope of the procedure, while temp is a local variable known only within the scope of the procedure. The function, given two SNMP counter values (assuming that the values are read from the same MIB variable at different points in time), will calculate the difference between the two values, checking for a possible wraparound condition. Note that MAXINT represents the largest SNMP counter value. Note also that if the time between reading the variable is long enough that the counter could have possibly wrapped around twice, then it would be impossible to calculate the difference between the two reads. The use in SNMPv2 of 64-bit counters makes this a virtual impossibility.

The function as defined is not the most efficient. The string ".0" is appended to the two counter values both within the TestWrapAround procedure and within Delta. Also, the procedure doesn't check whether the device has possibly rebooted between collecting the two samples, which would make Delta invalid (if a device reboots, the counter values are in an unknown state—the majority of network devices we have seen reinitialize counter values on reboots). Later in this chapter we will provide a more complete and efficient version of Delta.

As an aside, the Table 3.2 gives the fastest wraparound times for ifInOctets and ifOutOctets (assuming 32-bit counters) for different interface speeds.

Table 3.2

ifSpeed	Wraparound Time
10 Mbits	57.26 minutes
100 Mbits	5.73 minutes
155 Mbits	3.69 minutes
1 Gigabit	0.57 minutes

Several of the sample applications provided in this book will contain a procedure, Init-Globals, which will be responsible for initializing all global variables. This is purely our own convention, but seems like a reasonable way to structure our applications. The Tcl command up-level allows us to access variables at different stack levels. For example:

```
proc InitGlobals { } {
 uplevel #0 {
    set nodeInfo(sysDescr.0) ""
    set nodeInfo(sysName.0) ""
    set nodeInfo(sysObjectID.0) ""
    set nodeInfo(sysContact.0) ""
    set nodeInfo(sysUpTime.0) ""
  }
}
```

In the above example, we use a global array, `nodeInfo`, to store MIB II system information. `InitGlobals` initializes the elements of the array.

BUILDING AND MANIPULATING LISTS

One of the most powerful features of Tcl is its capability for building and manipulating lists. A list in Tcl is any ordered collection of strings. Lists can be nested within other lists. We will be using lists to represent more complex data structures. In time, we will also be using lists to dynamically build Tcl commands.

```
set system_mib {sysDescr sysObjectID sysUpTime \
    sysContact sysName sysLocation sysServices}
```

In the above example, variable `system_mib` is assigned a list containing the object-type descriptors of the MIB II system group. The backslash is used to continue the command line (as described previously, backslash-newline-space(s) is replaced by a space).

llength

The `llength` command returns the length of a list.

```
llength $system_mib    ;# Return length of list.
⇒  7

set x {{1 100} {2 140} {3 190}}
⇒  {1 100} {2 140} {3 190}

llength $x
⇒  3
```

In the above example, x consists of a list with three elements, all of which are lists themselves.

lindex

The `lindex` command allows you to access elements from a list. The format of the command is : `lindex list index`, where *index* is the ordered element in the list to be accessed (0 refers to the first element in the list).

```
lindex $system_mib 0
⇒ sysDescr

set i [lindex $x 1]
⇒ 2 140

lindex $i 1
⇒ 140
```

list

The `list` command will return a list with all the arguments specified in the command as elements.

```
list a b c d e
⇒ a b c d e
```

Let's assume that each element in list x represents a poll number and a value. Try adding another element to the end of the list representing poll 4, value 220, with the goal being forming the following list: `{{1 100} {2 140} {3 190} {4 220}}`.

```
set x [list $x 4 220]
⇒ {{1 100} {2 140} {3 190}} 4 220
```

This isn't quite the result we had in mind. Let's try again:

```
set x [list $x [list 4 220]]
⇒ {{1 100} {2 140} {3 190}} {4 220}
```

Still not what we're looking for. What we actually did was create a list with two elements: `{{1 100} {2 140} {3 190}}` and `{4 220}`.

lappend

The `lappend` command will append values to a list. The format for the command is: `lappend listName value ?value ...?`, where all the values specified in the command are appended to the list specified by *listName*.

```
lappend x {4 220}
⇒ {1 100} {2 140} {3 190} {4 220}
```

Finally, we get the result we were after!
Note that we could have gotten the same result with:

```
lappend x [list 4 220]
```

concat

The `concat` command will join multiple lists into a single list. Each element of each list will become an element of the resulting list. The format is: `concat` *?list ... list?*

```
concat $x [list 5 275]
⇒ {1 100} {2 140} {3 190} {4 220} 5 275
```

Again, we didn't get what we were looking for because the second list in the command, `[list 5 275]`, evaluates to a list with two elements, both of which are concatenated to the new list. However,

```
concat $x [list {5 275}]
⇒ {1 100} {2 140} {3 190} {4 220} {5 275}
```

returns the desired result since the list `{{5 275}}` consists of a single element, a nested list. Note that `concat` will create a new list, so the above example will not actually change x. To append the list `{{5 275}}` to the end of x, we would have to do the following:

```
set x [concat $x [list {5 275}]]
⇒ {1 100} {2 140} {3 190} {4 220} {5 275}
```

join

The `join` command takes a list and a string as arguments, concatenates the string between each element of the list and creates a new string.

```
set z {1 3 6 1 2 1 1 1}  ;# OID string for sysDescr
⇒ 1 3 6 1 2 1 1 1

set dotString [join $z .]
⇒ 1.3.6.1.2.1.1.1
```

split

The split command is the spiritual inverse of join, splitting up a string into list elements. The format is: split *string chars*, where *string* is the string to split up, and *chars* are the characters used to separate the elements in the string.

```
set ipaddr "158.101.121.36"
⇒ 158.101.121.36

split $ipaddr .
⇒ 158 101 121 36

lindex [split $ipaddr .] 0
⇒ 158

lindex [split $ipaddr .] 1
⇒ 101

lindex [split $ipaddr .] 2
⇒ 121

lindex [split $ipaddr .] 3
⇒ 36
```

linsert

The linsert command allows you to insert elements into a list. The format is: linsert *list* position *value ?value ...?* This command will actually build a new list, inserting all the values as list elements into *list* before the position specified (0 refers to the start of the list).

```
set collectOids {sysContact sysName sysLocation}
⇒ sysContact sysName sysLocation

linsert $collectOids 0 sysDescr sysObjectID
⇒ sysDescr sysObjectID sysUpTime sysContact sysName sysLocation
```

lrange

The lrange command returns a subset of an existing list. The format is: lrange *list* first last, where the subset is made up of the first through last elements of *list*. Note that if last equals "end", all the elements up to the end of the list are used.

```
set first 1
⇒ 1

set last 3
⇒ 3

lrange $collectOids $first $last
⇒ sysObjectID sysUpTime sysContact

lrange $collectOids [expr $first + 1] end
⇒ sysUpTime sysContact sysName sysLocation
```

lreplace

The `lreplace` command creates a new list by replacing elements within an existing list. The format is: `lreplace` *list* `first last` *?value* `value ...?`. Elements `first` through `last` will be replaced by the values specified.

```
lreplace {0 1 2 3 4 5 6 7 8 9} 1 3 {1 a} {2 b} {3 c}
⇒ 0 {1 a} {2 b} {3 c} 4 5 6 7 8 9

lreplace {0 1 2 3 4 5 6 7 8 9} 8 end zzzz
⇒ 0 1 2 3 4 5 6 7 zzzz
```

A slightly more practical example is:

```
set ipRouteDest {1 3 6 1 2 1 4 21 1 1}
⇒ 1 3 6 1 2 1 4 21 1 1

set instance {158 101 121 36}
⇒ 158 101 121 36

set oidStr [concat $ipRouteDest $instance]
⇒ 1 3 6 1 2 1 4 21 1 1 158 101 121 36
```

`oidstr` now equals a fully-instanced MIB variable. We can now use `lreplace` to replace the instance information:

```
set first [expr [llength $oidStr] - [[llength $instance]]
⇒ 10

lreplace $oidStr $first end 198 78 22 14
⇒ 1 3 6 1 2 1 4 21 1 1 198 78 22 14
```

lsearch

The lsearch command allows lists to be searched for specific patterns. The format is: lsearch ?-exact? ?-glob? ?-regexp? *list* pattern. Optional parameters: -exact, -glob, and -regexp specify which pattern-matching technique to use (the default is -glob). (More on Tcl pattern-matching techniques later.) The command returns −1 if the pattern is not found within the list; otherwise, the index number of the first element matching the pattern is returned.

Let's create a list of pairs, each pair representing an IP address and an SNMP community to use to access the device.

```
set commStrs {{158.101.121.1 public1} {158.101.121.2 public2} \
              {158.101.121.3 public3}}
 fi  {158.101.121.1 public1} {158.101.121.2 public2}
{158.101.121.3 public3}
```

Now let's create a procedure, GetCommString, which, given an IP address as a parameter, will either return the corresponding community string for that IP address or "public" if the IP address is not found within the the list commStrs.

```
proc GetCommString {ipAddr} {
  global commStrs
  set i [lsearch $commStrs "$ipAddr *"]
  if {$i == -1} {
    return public
  }
  set temp [lindex $commStrs $i]
  return [lindex $temp 1]
}
```

In the above procedure, if the IP address is found within commStrs, temp will be set to the nested sublist that contains the IP address and the community string. The community string is then returned as the second element within the list (remember, for lindex, 0 refers to the first element in the list).

```
GetCommString 158.101.121.2
⇒ public2

GetCommString 158.101.121.36
⇒ public
```

lsort

The `lsort` command returns a new sorted list. The format is: `lsort  ?-ascii?  ?-in-teger?  ?-real?  ?-command tcl-command?  ?-increasing?  ?-decreasing?  list`. The optional parameters allow you to control how the list is sorted. The default parameters are `-ascii` and `-increasing`. Examples:

```
set x {18 7 6 72 212 99}
⇒  18 7 6 72 212 99

lsort -integer -increasing $x
⇒  6 7 18 72 99 212

lsort -integer -decreasing $x
⇒  212 99 72 18 7 6

lsort $x
⇒  18 212 6 7 72 99
```

Note that in the last example, x is sorted by ascii values.

DELTA AND RATE EXAMPLES

A common technique used for performing status monitoring on network devices is to periodically poll devices for counter information (such as number of errors seen on an interface or number of bytes received on an interface). This collected data can then be stored in a circular buffer so that the values can be graphed or delta values or rates can be calculated from it. Now that we've built enough of a foundation in Tcl, let's build the following functions:

- Build a circular list for each instance of a variable, maintaining both value and timestamp information.
- From the circular list, calculate the delta value for a variable.
- From the circular list, calculate the rate value for a variable.

```
proc AddValueToList {var instance val timestamp} {
  global gValueList maxSampleSize

  lappend gValueList($var,$instance) [list $val $timestamp]

  set n [llength $gValueList($var,$instance)]
```

```
  if {$n <= $maxSampleSize} {
    return
  }

  set x [lrange $gValueList($var,$instance) 1 $n]
  set gValueList($var,$instance) $x
}
```

AddValueToList takes four parameters: a MIB variable name, an instance, a counter value and a timestamp value. The global gValueList is an array indexed by MIB variable name and instance. It is used for storing the {value timestamp} pairs. The global maxSample-Size defines the maximum size of a circular buffer. The function simply adds a new {value timestamp} list to the end of the list representing the circular buffer for that MIB variable, instance. If the size of the circular buffer becomes larger than the maximum size specified by maxSampleSize, the first element is chopped off by the lrange command.

```
proc GetDeltaSecs {tsPrev tsLast} {
   global MAXINT maxPollSeconds minPollSeconds
#
# GetDeltaSecs is passed two sysUpTime values
# and will either return -1 if a device reboot
# has been detected, or the delta difference in
# seconds between the two values.

#
# First convert TimeTicks values to float.
#
   append tsPrev ".0"
   append tsLast ".0"
#
# Check wraparound case.
#
   if {$tsLast < $tsPrev} {

        set temp [expr $MAXINT - $tsPrev]
        set deltaSecs [expr $temp + $tsLast]
#
# convert TimeTicks (1/100 seconds) to seconds.
#
        set deltaSecs [expr $deltaSecs/100.0]
        if {$deltaSecs > $maxPollSeconds} {
                return -1
        }
```

```
            return $deltaSecs
    }
    set deltaSecs [expr ($tsLast - $tsPrev)/100.0]
    if {$deltaSecs < $minPollSeconds} {
            return -1
    }
    return $deltaSecs

}
```

GetDeltaSecs is passed two sysUpTime values collected from the same device at different polls, and returns either –1 if a device reboot has been detected, or the difference in seconds between the two sysUpTime values. sysUpTime is reset when a device reboots. If a device hasn't rebooted, sysUpTime will wrap around every 497 days—not a very common occurrence!! However, some vendors build robust equipment and the case must be tested for. We determine that a device has rebooted if either of the following two conditions occur:

- The sysUpTime counter has wrapped around and the difference between the two TimeTick values is much larger than the polling period.
- The difference between the two TimeTick values is much smaller than the polling period. This condition will occur if a device reboots shortly before the first poll and also between the first and second poll.

Note that sysUpTime is actually reset when the network management portion of a device is reinitialized. Internal events, other than a reboot, can cause this to happen. The results, though, will be the same. Counters will be left in an unknown state.

GetDeltaSecs first converts both TimeTick values to reals, then checks whether the TimeTicks values have wrapped around. If they have, they have wrapped around either naturally or because a device reboot caused sysUpTime to be reset. If a wraparound occurred and the difference between the two values is much larger than the polling rate being used, a system reboot caused the wraparound and GetDeltaSecs returns –1. In the case where a wraparound didn't occur, GetDeltaSecs checks whether the difference between the two values is smaller than the polling rate being used—also indicating a reboot. maxPollSeconds can realistically be set to twice the polling interval. minPollSeconds can be set to some number of seconds less than the polling interval. Note that TimeTicks represent hundredths of seconds, which is why the values are divided by one hundred to convert to seconds.

```
proc Delta {var instance {ftype delta}} {
  global gValueList MAXINT

  if {![info exists gValueList($var,$instance)]} {
    return -1
  }
```

```tcl
set n [llength $gValueList($var,$instance)]

if {$n < 2} {
  return -1
}

set last [lindex $gValueList($var,$instance) [expr $n - 1]]
set prev [lindex $gValueList($var,$instance) [expr $n - 2]]

set tsLast [lindex $last 1]
set tsPrev [lindex $prev 1]

set deltaSecs [GetDeltaSecs $tsPrev $tsLast]
#
# If a device reboot occurred, causing sysUpTime to
# reset, GetDeltaSecs will return -1. In this case,
# previous counter values are invalid, so return -1.
#
if {$deltaSecs == -1} {return -1}

set lastVal [lindex $last 0]
set prevVal [lindex $prev 0]

append lastVal ".0"
append prevVal ".0"

#
# Check wraparound case.
#
if {$lastVal < $prevVal} {

  set delta [expr ($MAXINT - $prevVal) + $lastVal]
  if {$ftype == "delta"} {
      return $delta
  }
  #
  # Return rate.
  #
   return [expr $delta/$deltaSecs]
}

if {$ftype == "delta"} {
```

```
    return [expr $lastVal - $prevVal]
  }
#
# Return rate.
#
   return [expr ($lastVal - $prevVal)/$deltaSecs]
}
```

Delta takes a MIB variable name, an instance and a function type (either delta or rate), and returns either a delta value (difference) or a rate calculation (change in seconds) between the last two collected counter values for the MIB variable. If either a device reboot occurred between the last two polls or the circular buffer only contains a single value, -1 is returned. The timestamp values are pulled out of the list and used in a call to GetDeltaSecs to determine whether a device reboot occurred, and also for calculating a rate if requested.

Note that the Delta procedure uses the info command to check that an array variable exists before trying to access it. The info command will be discussed in Chapter 4. Delta also uses a default value for the parameter ftype. Default values for procedures will be discussed at the end of this chapter.

A Rate procedure can now be defined as:

```
proc Rate {var instance} {
   return [Delta $var $instance "rate"]
}
```

By overriding the default ftype parameter, the Delta procedure will calculate the rate of change per second for a specified counter value. Examples using these procedures:

```
set MAXINT 4294967295
set maxSampleSize 100
set maxPollSeconds 120   ;# Assuming a 60-second poll rate
set minPollSeconds 50

set gValueList(ifInOctets,1) ""

AddValueToList ifInOctets 1 4294965000 6000
AddValueToList ifInOctets 1 4294967228 12000

Delta ifInOctets 1
⇒ 2228.0

Rate ifInOctets 1
⇒ 37.1333
```

STRING MANIPULATION

Tcl provides a rich set of commands for both string manipulation and pattern-matching. This section will deal with the string manipulation functions. The next chapter will cover Tcl pattern-matching.

format

The `format` command is similar to the C procedure `printf`. It returns a string formatted by a `format` string with variable substitutions.

```
format "%x" 255
⇒ ff

format "%d" 0xff
⇒ 255

set linespeed 56000
⇒ 56000

set util 55.6
⇒ 55.6

format "Linespeed = %d, Utilization = %6.2f" $linespeed $util
⇒ Linespeed = 56000, Utilization = 55.60
```

Note that similar (but not exact) results can be obtained with simple variable substitution:

```
set str "Linespeed = $linespeed, Utilization = $util"
⇒ Linespeed = 56000, Utilization = 55.6
```

scan

The `scan` command is similar to the C procedure `scanf`.
The format is: `scan string format varName ?varName varName ...?`
`string` is parsed using the `format` string, placing the values that match the % sequences into the variables specified by the `varName` arguments. The function returns the number of variables matched.

```
set x "ifInOctets 5002"
⇒ ifInOctets 5002

scan $x "%s %d" mibName value
⇒ 2

puts $mibName
⇒ ifInOctets

puts $value
⇒ 5002
```

Getting back to an earlier example for converting either reals or integers to a real:

```
scan $value %f value
```

Note that the current value is used as the string to scan, %f is used as the format string to convert to a real and the variable value is used to get the result:

```
set value 4294965500
⇒ 4294965500

scan $value %f value ;# Convert integer to real.
⇒ 1

puts $value
⇒ 4294965500.0

scan $value %f value ;# Converting real doesn't cause problems.
⇒ 1

puts $value
⇒ 4294965500.0
```

string

The string command is used for comparing, searching, extracting and modifying strings. Examples:

```
set str "***abcde***"
⇒ ***abcde***
```

string length

The `string length` command will return the number of characters in a string.

```
string length $str
⇒ 11
```

string toupper

The `string toupper` command will convert a string to uppercase characters.

```
set str [string toupper $str]
⇒ ***ABCDE***
```

string tolower

The `string tolower` command will convert a string to lowercase characters.

```
set str [string tolower $str] ;# Convert to lowercase.
⇒ ***abcde***
```

string trimleft

The `string trimleft` command will remove specified characters from the front of a string.

```
string trimleft $str * ;# Remove leading *.
⇒ abcde***
```

string trimright

The `string trimright` command will remove specified characters from the end of a string.

```
string trimright $str * ;# Remove trailing *.
⇒ ***abcde
```

string trim

The `string` `trim` command will remove both leading and trailing characters from a string.

```
string trim $str * ;# Remove both leading and trailing *.
⇒ abcde
```

Note that the `toupper`, `tolower`, `trimleft`, `trimright` and `trim` string commands return new string values. They do not modify the string provided as an argument.

string compare

The `string` `compare` command returns either a –1, 0 or 1 if one string is lexicographically less than, equal to or greater than another string. The format is: `string` `compare` *string1 string2*

```
set str "aaa"
⇒ aaa

string compare "aaa" $str
⇒ 0

string compare "bbb" $str
⇒ 1

string compare $str "bbb"
⇒ -1
```

string first

The `string` `first` command searches for a substring within a string. If the substring is found, the index of the first matching character of the string is returned; otherwise, – 1 is returned. The format is: `string` `first` *substring string*

```
set sysDescrValue "3Com ethernet switch"
⇒ 3Com ethernet switch

string first "Cisco" $sysDescrValue
⇒ -1

string first "3Com" $sysDescrValue
⇒ 0
```

string last

The `string last` command is similar to the `string first` command, except that it will attempt to match the rightmost substring within the string. In other words, if a substring exists multiple times within a string, `string last` will match the rightmost occurrence of the substring.

```
string last zz zzaazz
⇒ 4

string last zz zzz
⇒ 1
```

string index

The `string index` command will return the character at the specified index within a given string. As usual, the first character in *string* has index 0. The format is: `string index` *string* n

```
string index "abcde" 0
⇒ a

string index "abcde" 4
⇒ e
```

string match

The `string match` command provides pattern-matching using Tcl's glob-style pattern-matching rules (more on Tcl pattern-matching in the next chapter). The command returns 1 if a pattern match occurs; otherwise, it returns 0. The format is: `string match pattern` *string*

```
string match *cisco* "returns 1 if cisco appears in string"
⇒ 1

string match cisco* "return 0 if cisco not a start of string"
⇒ 0
```

string range

The `string range` command returns a substring from a string.

The format is: `string range` *string* `first last`

where `first` and `last` specify the substring to return. Note that `last` may be the string "end", which refers to the last character in *string*.

```
set oidString 1.3.6.1.2.1.4.21.1.1.158.101.121.36
⇒  1.3.6.1.2.1.4.21.1.1.158.101.121.36

set i [string length $oidString]
⇒  35

set instance 158.101.121.36
⇒  158.101.121.36

set j [string length $instance]
⇒  14

string range $oidString 0 [expr $i - $j - 2]
⇒  1.3.6.1.2.1.4.21.1.1
```

The above, slightly cumbersome example, extracts the noninstanced portion of an Object-Identifer String. Note that we subtracted 2 instead of 1 within the expression to take care of the dot between the base OID and the instance.

```
string range $oidString [expr $i - $j] end
⇒  158.101.121.36
```

append

Finally, the `append` command, which we saw briefly before, appends a string to another string. In the example:

```
append integerVar ".0"
```

will append the string ".0" to whatever value `integerVar` has. If the value of `integerVar` is a string which can be parsed as an integer value, this will in effect convert `integerVar` to a real. For example:

```
set x 100
⇒  100
```

```
expr $x/8    ;# x is an integer, so result will be an integer.
⇒  12

append x ".0"
⇒  100.0

expr $x/8    ;# x is a real, so result will be a real.
⇒  12.5
```

CONTROL FLOW

Tcl has all the control flow constructs that you would recognize from other programming languages: `if-else`, `while loop`, `for loop`, and the `switch` statement. Tcl also provides `break` and `continue` commands to break and continue from loops. In keeping with its powerful list processing capabilities, Tcl provides a `foreach` command for cycling through a list.

if

The `if` command evaluates an expression, and if the expression evaluates to nonzero, it executes a script. For example:

```
if {![string length $x]} {
   set x $defaultStr
}
```

In the above example, the `if` command has two arguments: an expression and a Tcl script. The expression will evaluate to a nonzero value if x is empty. This would cause x to be set to `defaultStr`. Note that the open brace for the script must be on the same line as the expression. The following example:

```
if {![string length $x]}
{
   set x $defaultStr
}
```

would be interpreted as two commands: a poorly formed `if` command and a `set` command.

The format is: `if expr script ?elseif expr2 script2 elseif ...? ?else script?`

```
if {$i == 0} {
   ...
} elseif {$i == 2} {
   ...
} elseif {$i == 3} {
   ...
} else {
   ...
}
```

The above example simulates a switch statement with the final else acting as a default case.

while, for, foreach

Tcl provides three commands for looping: while, for and foreach. Both while and for are similar to their C counterparts; foreach allows looping through each element of a list. We will demonstrate all three commands by showing code examples to initialize the first 10 elements of an array:

```
set i 0
while {$i < 10} {
   set arr($i) 0
   incr i
}

for {set i 0} {$i < 10} {incr i 1} {
   set arr($i) 0
}

foreach el {0 1 2 3 4 5 6 7 8 9} {
   set arr($el) 0
}
```

In the for command example, similar to the corresponding C command, the first argument initializes the loop. If the expression provided as the second argument evaluates to nonzero, the body is executed as a Tcl script and then the third argument is executed. This is repeated until the second argument evaluates to zero.

switch

The switch command is again similar to the corresponding C statement. Based on a variable or expression matching one of a list of values execute a corresponding Tcl script. The switch command provides for a default case. The switch command will search through a list of pattern-body pairs for a match. If one is found, the Tcl-script representing the body will be evaluated. If the pattern associated with the last body is default, then this command body is executed if no other patterns match.

```
switch $error_code {
    timeout {incr timeout_count}
    tooBig -
    noSuchName -
    badValue {incr snmpError_count}
    default {incr miscError_count}
}
```

The dash following both tooBig and noSuchName causes the script{incr snmpError_count} to be executed if a match occurs. In the example above, if errorCode equals tooBig, noSuchName or badValue, snmpError_count will be incremented.

MORE ON TCL PROCEDURES

There are two additional procedure properties worth describing: defaults and variable number of arguments. Default values can be specified for the last arguments of a procedure. The special argument, args, is a list that contains all the remaining arguments.

The following function will calculate receive utilization given the change in the receive octet count for an interface, the time duration and the linespeed of the interface:

```
proc rx_util {delta_ifInOctets deltaSecs {linespeed 56000.0}}
{

    set x [expr ($delta_ifInOctets * 8.0)/$deltaSecs)]
    set x [expr $x/$linespeed * 100.0]
    return $x
}

rx_util 55000 60
⇒  13.0952
```

In the above example, the variable linespeed defaulted to 56000.0.

```
rx_util 55000 60 14400.0
⇒ 50.952
```

In the above example, a linespeed value of 14400.0 was used.

```
proc init {args} {
  global arr
  foreach el $args {
   set arr($el) 0
  }
}
```

The function init will initialize array elements for arr, given the indexes specified by args.

```
init ifInOctets ifInErrors ifOutOctets ifOutErrors
```

will create and initialize arr(ifInOctets), arr(ifInErrors), arr(ifOutOctets) and arr(ifOutErrors).

```
array get arr
⇒ ifOutErrors 0 ifInError 0 ifInOctets 0 ifOutOctets 0
```

IN SUMMARY

This chapter described the basics of Tcl, including list processing, string routines, expressions, arrays, procedures and control flow. We also started to set the foundation for building useful network management tools with Tcl.

4 *More Tcl*

This chapter describes additional Tcl commands and capabilities that are used in subsequent chapters, including descriptions on:

- `after`, `catch`, `clock`, `exec`, `error`, `eval`, `info`, `update` and `vwait`
- Predefined Tcl variables
- Tcl file I/O
- Event-driven programming with Tcl
- Pattern-matching techniques

MORE Tcl COMMANDS

after

The `after` command is used to delay execution of a program or to execute a script (i.e., a set of commands) sometime in the future. The `after` command has the following syntax:

```
after ms
after ms command
after cancel id
after cancel command
after idle command
after info ?id?
```

The following example will pause execution of a script for one second (or 1000 ms):

```
after 1000
⇒
```

When used in this context (without additional arguments), execution of the `after` command does not return until the specified time period has expired.

To execute a script, in this case a command to invoke a procedure named `SysPoll`, 30 seconds (30000 ms) in the future, simply specify:

```
after 30000 {SysPoll}
⇒ after#1
```

In this context, the execution of the `after` command returns immediately. In addition, the script specified with the `after` command, `SysPoll`, is executed after 30 seconds have passed.

In the preceding example code, the `after` command returned an ID, `after#1`, that can be used to cancel the pending execution of `SysPoll`. To do so, simply specify:

```
after cancel after#1
⇒
```

To find out if an `after` request corresponding to event ID `after#1` is still active, specify:

```
after info after#1
```

If the event does not exist, the following error is returned:

```
⇒ event "after#1" doesn't exist
```

If the event is found, the following is returned:

```
⇒ SysPoll
```

To invoke a procedure called `Discover` when the application is idle, specify:

```
after idle {Discover $nextsubnet}
⇒ after#2
```

You will use the `after` command a great deal as you write your programs, especially to invoke script execution after some specified time delay. Below is one more example using the `after` command. Here, during each iteration of a `for` loop, we issue the `after` command to invoke the procedure `Not` after a five-second delay:

```
proc Not {} {
   puts "She loves me not !"
}

for {set n 0} {$n <= 4} {incr n +1} {
   puts "She loves me !"
   after 5000 {Not}
}
```

Right away, we get back the following:

⇒ She loves me !
⇒ She loves me !
⇒ She loves me !
⇒ She loves me !
⇒ She loves me !

Then, after a five-second delay, we get:

⇒ She loves me not !
⇒ She loves me not !
⇒ She loves me not !
⇒ She loves me not !
⇒ She loves me not !

catch

The `catch` command is used to evaluate and trap errors on a specified script. The `catch` command has the following syntax:

```
catch script ?varName?
```

When `catch` executes a script, it catches any errors that may occur in the script. If a script executes without error, `catch` returns 0; otherwise, it returns 1. If an optional variable is specified with `catch`, it is assigned either whatever is returned by the script itself or an error message.

The following example code attempts to divide the integer 100 by zero. Normally this would result in abnormal termination of your application, but below we use the `catch` command to trap the error:

```
for {set n 5} {$n >= 0} {incr n -1} {
  set foo [catch {expr 100 / $n} result]
  puts "foo=$foo result=$result"
}
```

⇒ foo=0 result=20
⇒ foo=0 result=25
⇒ foo=0 result=33
⇒ foo=0 result=50
⇒ foo=0 result=100
⇒ foo=1 result=divide by zero

error

The error command raises an error condition that terminates a script, unless it is caught with the catch command. The command format is:

```
error message ?info? ?code?
```

If the ?info? command is provided, it is used to initialize the errorInfo global variable. The optional code argument provides a concise, machine-readable description of the error. It is stored into the global variable errorCode, and defaults to NONE.

An example using error:

```
proc procA {} {
  if [catch {procB} err] {
    puts "Error caught: $err"
  }
}

proc procB {} {
  procC
  puts "Here in procB!"
}

proc procC {} {
  error "Error raised in procC"
}

procA
Error caught: Error raised in procC
```

In this example, procA calls procB, which calls procC, which raises an error. The error will flow through procB before being caught by procA. Using the error and catch commands in your code is a good way to indicate procedure failure codes.

clock

The clock command performs one of several operations to obtain or manipulate strings or values that represent some notion of time. The clock command has the following syntax:

```
clock option ?arg arg ...?
```

where option is either clicks, seconds or format.

The `clicks` option of the `clock` command returns a high-resolution time value. This is useful for a relative measurement of elapsed time. The unit of the value here is system-dependent and is normally the highest resolution clock available on the system, such as a CPU cycle counter. In the example code below, the procedure `test1` sets the variable `t1` to the value of `[clock clicks]`, waits one second, sets the variable `t2` to the value of `[clock clicks]`, and then outputs the delta value of `t2` minus `t1`.

```
proc test1 { } {
    set t1 [clock clicks]
    after 1000
    set t2 [clock clicks]
    puts "Delta t2 - t1 = [expr $t2 - $t1] in clicks"
}
```

```
test1
⇒ Delta t1 - t1 = 1001 in clicks
```

Thus, on my system, there are roughly 1000 clicks per second.

The `seconds` option of the `clock` command returns the current date and time as a system-dependent integer value. The unit of the value here is seconds, allowing it to be used for relative time calculations. The value is usually defined as total elapsed time from an epoch. You shouldn't assume the value of the epoch. For example, on my system at this moment in time:

```
clock seconds
⇒ 878596599
```

The trivial example below uses `clock seconds` right before and right after a one-second pause. Then it outputs the delta value between these two timestamps.

```
proc test2 { } {
    set t1 [clock seconds]
    after 1000
    set t2 [clock seconds]
    puts "Delta t2 - t1 = [expr $t2 - $t1] in seconds"
}
```

```
test2
⇒ Delta t2 - t1 = 1 in seconds
```

The `format` option of the `clock` command converts the integer time value typically returned by `clock seconds` to human-readable form. If the `-format` argument is present, the next argument is a string that describes how the date and time are to be formatted. Field descriptors consist of a `%`, followed by a field descriptor character. For example:

```
clock format [clock seconds]
⇒ Mon Nov 03 17:42:57 Eastern Daylight Time 1997
```

There are numerous variations of using the `clock` command with the `-format` argument. In our `statusmgr.itk` sample program that is described later in this book, we use the following command to get current day (`%D`), hour (`%H`) and week (`%U`) values:

```
clock format [clock seconds] -format "%D %H %U"
⇒ 11/11/97 23 45
```

The following example will give you both the date and time:

```
clock format [clock seconds] -format "%B %d, %Y %I:%M %p"
⇒ November 11, 1997 11:17 PM
```

exec

The `exec` command is used to invoke platform-specific commands. It is used often to invoke system-available applications or subprocesses. The syntax of this command is:

```
exec ?switches? arg ?arg ...?
```

Switches in this command start with a - (dash). The arguments take the form of a standard shell pipeline, where each `arg` becomes one word of a command, and each distinct command becomes a subprocess.

In the example below, we use the `exec` command to invoke Window's command parser `command.com` to delete all files under the path `c:\$home\*.ofile`:

```
exec "command.com /c delete c:\\$home\\*.ofile"
```

Note that Tcl has its own `file` command that handles file system operations, such as deleting files. The previous example is platform-specific. You will soon see how Tcl's `file` command is a better way to delete local files.

The example below uses the `exec` command to invoke the application `notepad.exe` on the file `C:\$home\ops-diary.txt`:

```
exec notepad.exe c:\\$home\\ops-diary.tx
```

The following example uses the `exec` command to execute a local `ping` application from Tcl:

```
set addr 158.101.121.200
⇒

set ping_resp [exec ping $addr]
⇒
⇒
⇒ Pinging 158.101.121.200 with 32 bytes of data:
```

⇒
⇒
⇒ Reply from 158.101.121.200: bytes=32 time=2ms TTL=255
⇒
⇒ Reply from 158.101.121.200: bytes=32 time=2ms TTL=255
⇒
⇒ Reply from 158.101.121.200: bytes=32 time=1ms TTL=255
⇒
⇒ Reply from 158.101.121.200: bytes=32 time=2ms TTL=255

Be aware that the command syntax and capabilities of native ping applications will be different for different systems. Thus, the use of local ping applications prevents your applications from being system-independent.

Still, it's worth learning how to use your systems' native ping application. Native ping applications on most systems (including Windows 95 and NT) often have useful option switches for doing things like tracing paths and measuring hop-by-hop delays. You can write some useful diagnostic tools simply using Tcl with your system's native ping application. Also, be aware that both Scotty and TickleMan support ICMP echo requests. You can often use their ICMP echo request capabilities in place of your system's native ping application.

Be careful when you exec local applications like ping from within your Tcl scripts. In the preceding example, you would never get any response if your native application ran forever. Later in this chapter, we will show you how to invoke your local ping application using a file I/O pipeline.

eval

The eval command takes one or more arguments, which together comprise a Tcl script. The eval command returns the result of the evaluation or any error generated by it. The syntax of eval is as follows:

```
eval arg ?arg ...?
```

Later in the book we will use eval to execute SNMP poll requests. A quick peek into the future:

```
set sess [snmpsession sess1 -snmp]
set SysVBList [list sysUpTime.0 sysDescr.0]
for {set n 0} {$n <= $nn} {incr n +1} {
    set addr $nInfo($n,addr)
    set authinfo [list snmpv1 $nInfo($n,comm)]
    set cmd [list $sess get $addr $authinfo $SysVBList {} SysCallBk]
```

```
        eval $cmd
}
```

This example should not make much sense right now, but it demonstrates an important concept. The variable cmd varies with each iteration of the for loop. The eval command is used to execute the contents of cmd as a command. In effect, what we are doing is dynamically building a Tcl command.

info

The info command returns information about various internals from the Tcl interpreter. The syntax of the info command is:

```
    info option ?arg arg ...?
```

There are many options associated with the info command. Here we will describe two options that you will see later in our sample applications. First, we will describe how you can use the info command to get the hostname for the system on which you are running. Second, we will describe how you can use the info command to check whether a variable exists or not.

To get your system's hostname, use the info command with the hostname option as follows:

```
set hostname [info hostname]
⟹ nms-1
```

To check if a variable exists, use the info command with the exists option. The info command with the exists option will return 1 if the variable specified exists in the current context (either as a global or local variable); otherwise, it returns 0. Notice how in the following example code the info command is used to determine that nInfo(0,addr) exists, while nInfo(1,addr) does not.

```
# Procedure test3 outputs a node's address from
# its specified node index.

proc test3 { n } {
   global nInfo
   if { [info exists nInfo($n,addr)] == 1} {
     puts "Node $n has the address $nInfo($n,addr)"
   }
}

# Here we create nInfo(0,addr).
```

```
set nInfo(0,addr) 158.101.121.200
⇒  158.101.121.200

# Here we execute test3 on node index 0.
test3 0
⇒  Node 0 has the address 158.101.121.200

# Here we execute test3 on node index 1.
test3 1
⇒
```

update

The `update` command is used to bring an application up-to-date by entering the event loop repeatedly until all pending events (including idle callbacks) have been processed. The syntax of the `update` command is:

```
update ?idletasks?
```

Certain Tcl events, such as Tk screen updates, are implemented as idle callbacks, meaning they are not implemented immediately. If the `idletasks` keyword is specified as an argument to the `update` command, no new events or errors are processed; only idle callbacks are invoked. This causes operations that are normally deferred by Tcl, such as display updates and window layout calculations, to be performed immediately.

For example, say you have code to output a line to a scrolled list box or change the color of an icon on a network map. In these cases, if you don't want Tk to delay the screen update until the application is idle, you should issue an `update idletasks` or `update` at the point in your code right after you perform the screen update. If you invoke `update` without the `idletasks` argument, all pending events are processed before any new events are allowed onto the event queue.

Use the `update` command within procedures with long computations or processing requirements. This is especially important if you want to allow the application to respond to user interactions without long delays.

vwait

The `vwait` command will pause your script while it waits for a variable to be written. It normally returns as soon as the value of the specified variable is set. While the Tcl event handler waits, it continues to process events. The syntax of `vwait` is:

```
vwait ?varName?
```

Now, let's say you use vwait as follows:

```
set proceed false
after 1000 {set proceed true}
vwait proceed
```

If we simply used after 1000 instead of the above code, all application processing would stop during the one-second pause. By using vwait, as in the preceding example, we can cause a specified application to pause while allowing the application to continue processing other events.

BUILT-IN Tcl VARIABLES

The Tcl interpreter has several standard built-in variables. These built-in variables have global scope and are created and managed by the Tcl interpreter. Table 4.1 illustrates some commonly used built-in variables.

Table 4.1

argc	The number of command line arguments to the application.
argv	A list of the application's command line arguments.
argv0	this variable identifies the name of the script being executed.
auto_path	This variable identifies the search path that is used to look for Tcl package libraries (more on Tcl package libraries in Chapter 15).
env	This array contains variables that identify environment attributes. There are several variables in this array, including env(HOME), env(PATH), env(DISPLAY) and env(TEMP).
errorCode	This list contains information about the last error that occurred in your application. For example, if your application does a divide by zero, errorCode would be assigned the list value of {ARITH DIVZERO}
errorInfo	This variable holds the stack trace identifying the command that caused the last error.
tcl_platform	This array defines your platform attributes. The variables in this array are: tcl_platform(os), tcl_platform(osVersion), tcl_platform(machine) and tcl_platform(platform).

There are a number of cases where you will find Tcl's built-in variables useful, including:

1. Using `argc` and `argv` for integrating your applications with third-party network management platforms.
2. Using `errorCode` and `errorInfo` to help debug errors.
3. Using `tcl_platform(os)` to determine what operating system is in use.

Using `argc` and `argv` for Integrating with Third-Party Network Management Platforms

Command line arguments are often supported by network management tools to allow integration with third-party enterprise management tools like HP OpenView. When a user selects a node on the HP OpenView MAP and launches your application, your application need not prompt the user for such things as node address and community string. HP OpenView, via its registration files, can pass such information to your applications in the form of command line arguments. Where appropriate, use `argc` and `argv` to check and parse application command line arguments as follows:

```
if { $argc >= 2} {
    set node [lindex $argv 0]
    set comm [lindex $argv 1]
}
```

Using `errorCode` and `errorInfo` When Catching Errors

In Chapter 5, we will explain how to send out multiple SNMP requests simultaneously. With each request, a callback procedure can be specified to handle the response. This is called asynchronous polling. Asynchronous polling makes your applications significantly more efficient than synchronous polling, but you need a way to handle errors that occur within your callback procedures.

Errors in your callback procedures may not always terminate your application. Some may go unnoticed and corrupt your data by not completing normally. Other times, you may want to make certain they do not terminate your application and go unnoticed.

There are several ways you can define how different applications and procedures should behave when errors are encountered. Earlier, we demonstrated use of the `error` command for this. In some cases, you may want certain procedures to log a message to the console or to a log file, do some cleanup, and let the application continue without any error annunciation to the upper level. In other cases, you may want the application to notify the end-user immediately of an error and stop the application from proceeding further.

In the example below, we use the `catch` command alone to catch errors within a procedure called `ExampleCallBk`. Here we use the `errorCode` and `errorInfo` variables to identify the type of error and where it occurred. Upon encountering an error, the example here will write a message to the console but return no error to the upper level.

```
proc ExampleCallBk { } {
    set err [catch{
        ~~~~~~~~~~~
        ~~~~~~~~~~
        ~~~~~~~~~~
    }]

    if { $err != 0} {
        # OK we have an error, let's log what it is and
        # continue without annunciating the error to the
        # upper level.
        puts "Error in ExampleCallBk errorCode = \
                $errorCode, errorInfo=$errorInfo"
    }
}
```

Using `tcl_platform(os)` to Determine the Operating System in Use

As you write network management applications using packages like TickleMan or Scotty, there may be times when you need to know what operating system is running. For example, TickleMan's ICMP capability will not work on Windows 95. You may wish to make sure this feature is NOT used if the application is running on Windows 95 as follows:

```
if { $tcl_platform(os) == "Windows 95"} {
    set pinging OFF
}
```

FILE I/O WITH TCL

Tcl's file I/O support consists of:

- Using Tcl's `open` command to open a file for reading/writing. This returns a channel ID.
- Using Tcl's `close` command on the channel ID when done.
- Using Tcl's `puts`, `gets` and `read` commands to read and write to a channel ID.

Opening a File for Reading/Writing

The open command opens a file or command pipeline for reading/writing. Its syntax is:

```
open fileName
open fileName access
open fileName access permissions
```

The open command returns a channel ID, which is a string.

If present, the access argument indicates the way in which a file (or command pipeline) is to be accessed. There are two forms for the access argument, but we will only describe the form we most commonly use. In this form, the access argument may have any of the following values:

```
r           open for reading only
r+      open for reading and writing (file must exists)
w       open for writing only
w+          open for reading and writing (creates/over-
writes)
a       append
a+          open for reading/writing (creates/appends)
```

The permissions argument can be specified in cases where you know open may result in creating a new file. When specified, it assigns a UNIX-like file permission to the newly created file. Be aware, the default on some systems is to assign permission 0666 on newly created files. This makes the file readable and writeable to all.

Closing a File

The close command closes an open file. Its syntax is:

```
close channelId
```

READING/WRITING A FILE

The Tcl puts, gets, and read commands may all be used to read and write to files opened with suitable access. The syntax of the gets command is:

```
gets channelId ?varName?
```

The `gets` command reads the next line from `channelId`. If `varName` is omitted, the line is returned as the result of the command. If `varName` is specified, then it is set to the line and the number of characters in the line is returned. End-of-line character(s) are discarded.

In the following example, the file `events.log` is opened for reading. The `gets` command is used to read the file line-by-line and count the number of lines read:

```
set fileid [open events.log "r"]
⇒ file5

set numlines 0
⇒ 0

while {[gets $fileid line] >= 0} {
    incr numlines +1
}

close $fileid
⇒

puts "numlines = $numlines"
⇒ numlines = 3334
```

The `puts` command writes a string to a file. The syntax of the `puts` command is:

```
puts ?-nonewline? ?channelId? string
```

If `channelId` is not specified, it defaults to `stdout`. By default, `puts` writes a newline character after `string`, but this feature may be suppressed by specifying the `-nonewline` switch. Tcl will buffer data internally, so characters written with `puts` may not appear immediately in the output file or on the output device. Tcl will normally delay output until the buffer is full or the channel is closed. You can force output to appear immediately with the `flush` command, or you can use the command `fconfigure channelId -buffering line` to configure the channel to flush each line automatically on output.

In the code segment below, the `puts` command is used to write a timestamp to the file `temp.dat`.

```
set fileid [open temp.dat w]
⇒ file5

set timestamp [clock format [clock seconds] \
    -format "%B %d, %Y %I: %M %p"]
⇒ January 03, 1998 07: 26 PM
```

```
puts $fileid $timestamp
⇒

close $fileid
⇒
```

The read command allows you to read data from a file. It can either read a specified number of bytes or read to the end of a file. The format for the read command is:

```
read ?-nonewline? channelId
read channelId numBytes
```

The first form reads all of the data from channelId to the end of the file. If the −nonewline switch is specified, the last character of the file is discarded if it is a newline.

The second form uses an extra argument to specify the number of bytes to read. If fewer than that number of bytes are left in the file, the remaining bytes are returned.

In the following code segment, the read command is used to read the entire contents of the file foo.txt. The split command is then used to build a list, where each element of the list is a line from the file. Then a procedure called Process is called for each line.

```
set fileid [open foo.txt r]
⇒ file10

proc Process { line} {
    # Write line to console
    puts $line
}

foreach line [split [read $fileid] \n] {
    Process $line
}


close $fileid
⇒
```

Remember the earlier discussion on how to use the exec command to invoke your system's native ping application. The following example code is another way to exec ping using a pipeline channel:

```
set addr 158.101.121.200
⇒ 158.101.121.200

set pipe [open "| ping $addr"]
⇒ file5
```

```
while {[gets $pipe line] >= 0} {
    puts $line
}
⇒
⇒
⇒ Pinging 158.101.121.200 with 32 bytes of data:
⇒
⇒ Reply from 158.101.121.200: bytes=32 time=5ms TTL=255
⇒
⇒ Reply from 158.101.121.200: bytes=32 time=1ms TTL=255
⇒
⇒ Reply from 158.101.121.200: bytes=32 time=2ms TTL=255
⇒
⇒ Reply from 158.101.121.200: bytes=32 time=2ms TTL=255

close $pipe
```

Miscellaneous Tcl File I/O Commands and Features

Default File Descriptors

Standard output, `stdout`, standard input, `stdin`, and standard error, `stderr`, are default file descriptors. For example, the following two commands are equivalent; they both output the string `Hello` to standard output:

```
puts Hello
⇒ Hello

puts stdout Hello
⇒ Hello
```

eof

Tcl has an end-of-file command that has the following syntax:

```
eof channelId
```

This command returns 1 if an end of file condition occurs during the most recent input operation on `channelId` (such as `gets`); otherwise, it returns 0.

file

Suppose you want to check if a file exists before opening it. To do this and other operations on a file's name or attributes, there is the `file` command. Let's say you want to check if the file `c:/foo/problem.log` exists:

```
if { [file exists c:/foo/problem.log] == 1} {
  puts "c:/foo/problem.log exists"
}
```

If the file didn't exist, `[file exists c:/foo/problem.log]` would return 0. Note that even on Windows, within the command space of Tcl, filenames follow UNIX path definitions. In the preceding example , notice how even on a system running Windows 95 we used the path definition `c:/foo/problem.log` rather than `c:\foo\problem.log`.

flush

The `flush` command can be used with file and socket I/O. We will briefly introduce it here and expand upon its usage in more detail in the later chapter on socket programming.

The syntax of the `flush` command is:

```
flush channelId
```

The `flush` command flushes any output that has been buffered for `channelId`. The channel identifier returned by a previous `open` or `socket` command must have been opened for writing. If the channel is in blocking mode (which is explained later in the chapter on socket programming), the command does not return until all the buffered output has been flushed to the channel. If the channel is in nonblocking mode, the command may return before all buffered output has been flushed; the remainder will be flushed in the background as fast as the underlying file or device is able to absorb it.

The `flush` command can be used on `stdin` and `stdout`. The following code fragment makes sure that the prompt string written to `stdout` is flushed before attempting to read the user's input.

```
puts -nonewline stdout \
    {Enter List of Nodes or "quit" to exit: }
flush stdout
set line [gets stdin]
```

EXAMPLE: BUILDING HTML FILES

Many tools that network managers write are simple reporting utilities that collect information via SNMP and report on it. In Chapter 11 we will show you a sample application of ours named `discover.itcl`. The `discover.itcl` application finds and reports on the types of network devices that exist on specified networks. It outputs this information both as a delimited text file and as an HTML file. The advantage of the delimited text file is that it can be easily loaded into a spreadsheet like Excel or a database like DB Access. The advantage of the HTML file is that it makes the data readily available via a Web server to anyone needing access to it.

If you are going to create network management reports, you will probably want to output some of your reports in HTML format. A majority of the time, your HTML reports will be simple table reports. Here is an example showing how easy it is to do this while also reinforcing what we have discussed regarding Tcl file I/O:

```
# The following code fragments are from the sample application
# discover.itcl with minor simplification showing how to
# take nodal information from array nDisInfo and output the
# information in the form of a table to the html output file
# discover.html.

# Create and open output html file.
set html_fileid [open discover.html "w"]

# create html header and title with dated timestamp
set timestamp [clock format [clock seconds]]
puts $html_fileid \
    "<HTML> <HEAD> <TITLE>$timestamp</TITLE> </HEAD>"
puts $html_fileid {<BODY bgcolor="Beige">}
puts $html_fileid "<H1>$timestamp</H1>"

# Create an HTML table with border around cells.
puts $html_fileid "<TABLE BORDER>"

# Create column header for each column of the table.
set colnames [list Vendor NodeAddr ObjectId sysName \
        MIB-Support sysLocation sysContact sysDescr]
foreach el $colnames {
    puts $html_fileid "<TH>$el</TH>"
}
puts $html_fileid "<TR>"

# Output a row per node.
for { set n 0} {$n <= $nn} {incr n +1} {
    set columns [list vendorname %15s addr %15s \
        sysObjectID.0 %20s sysName.0 %20s mibsupport %10s \
```

```
     sysLocation.0 %20s sysContact.0 %20s sysDescr.0 %30s]
   foreach {el format} $columns {
     puts $html_fileid \
       [format "<TD>$format</TD>" $nDisInfo($n,$el)]
   }
   puts $html_fileid "<TR>"
   # Flush channel so if program abnormally
   # terminates we have at least partial data saved
   # to the output files.
   flush $html_fileid
}


# Close open HTML tags and close file.
puts $html_fileid "</TABLE> </BODY> </HTML>"
close $html_fileid
```

Figure 4.1 shows what the output looks like.

EVENT-DRIVEN PROGRAMMING WITH TCL

To make your applications as efficient as possible, you need to make your applications event-driven and non-blocking. This includes:

- Using callback routines when performing SNMP operations rather than waiting for completion of each request (we touched upon this already and will expand upon it more later).

- Using `vwait` where appropriate to pause a procedure from proceeding without stopping event handling from continuing for other procedures (as we discussed already).

- Binding events with Tk GUI operations (as we will see later in the chapters on Tk usage).

- Using the Tcl `update` command at appropriate places in your code to ensure timely GUI response (as we discussed already).

In addition, the Tcl `fileevent` command should be used where appropriate. We will introduce this command now and expand upon its usage more in the later chapter on socket programming.

The `fileevent` command executes a script when a channel becomes readable or writeable. The `channelId` argument to `fileevent` refers to an open channel, such as the return value from a previous `open` or `socket` command. The syntax of the `fileevent` command is:

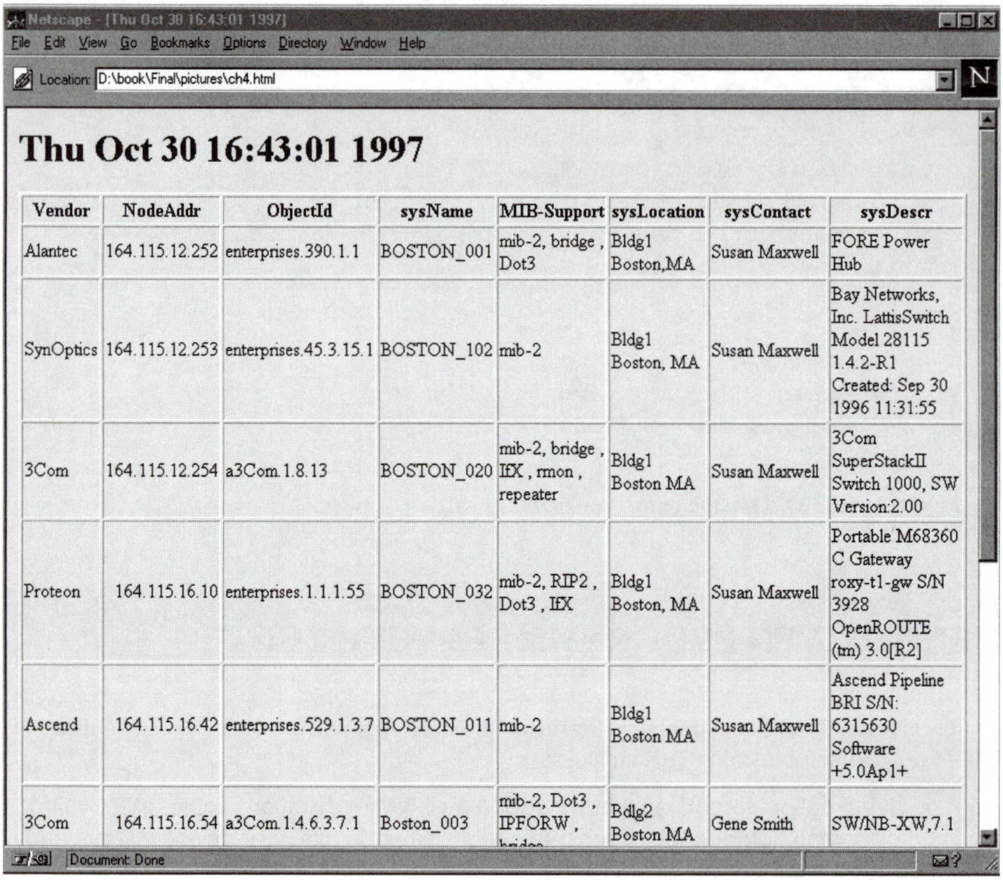

Vendor	NodeAddr	ObjectId	sysName	MIB-Support	sysLocation	sysContact	sysDescr
Alantec	164.115.12.252	enterprises.390.1.1	BOSTON_001	mib-2, bridge , Dot3	Bldg1 Boston,MA	Susan Maxwell	FORE Power Hub
SynOptics	164.115.12.253	enterprises.45.3.15.1	BOSTON_102	mib-2	Bldg1 Boston, MA	Susan Maxwell	Bay Networks, Inc. LattisSwitch Model 28115 1.4.2-R1 Created: Sep 30 1996 11:31:55
3Com	164.115.12.254	a3Com.1.8.13	BOSTON_020	mib-2, bridge , IfX , rmon , repeater	Bldg1 Boston MA	Susan Maxwell	3Com SuperStackII Switch 1000, SW Version:2.00
Proteon	164.115.16.10	enterprises.1.1.1.55	BOSTON_032	mib-2, RIP2 , Dot3 , IfX	Bldg1 Boston, MA	Susan Maxwell	Portable M68360 C Gateway roxy-t1-gw S/N 3928 OpenROUTE (tm) 3.0[R2]
Ascend	164.115.16.42	enterprises.529.1.3.7	BOSTON_011	mib-2	Bldg1 Boston MA	Susan Maxwell	Ascend Pipeline BRI S/N: 6315630 Software +5.0Ap1+
3Com	164.115.16.54	a3Com.1.4.6.3.7.1	Boston_003	mib-2, Dot3 , IPFORW ,	Bdlg2 Boston MA	Gene Smith	SW/NB-XW,7.1

Figure 4.1 HTML page created by the `Discover` application.

```
fileevent channelId readable ?script?
fileevent channelId writeable ?script?
```

If an application invokes `gets` or `read` on a blocking channel when there is no input data available, the process will block until data arrives. It will not be able to service other events and will appear to the user as if your application has frozen up. With `fileevent`, the application can be made to invoke a process that reads from the channel whenever data is present. (If you know the channel will return data in fixed-sized blocks, use `read` to process the data. If it is returned in line-oriented data, use `gets`.)

In our `statusmgr.itk` application, we use `fileevent` in a procedure called www as illustrated in the code below:

```
proc www {channel} {
  # When data is available on channel, www_receiver will be
  # called.

  fileevent $channel readable [list www_receiver $channel]
}
```

In the later chapter on socket programming, you will see how this is called after you open a server port within your application to allow remote users to access your application. For now, what is important to understand is that `fileevent`, as used in the above example, will not block other events from being processed as the application waits for data on the channel. The procedure www will call the procedure `www_receiver` whenever the channel has data to read.

PATTERN-MATCHING TECHNIQUES

Tcl supports two styles of pattern-matching: glob and regular expressions. Three Tcl commands are used strictly for pattern-matching, namely `glob`, `regexp` and `regsub`. The `glob` command supports glob-style pattern-matching. The `regexp` and `regsub` commands support regular expression-style pattern-matching.

In addition, glob and regular expression-style pattern-matching are used in other Tcl commands. For example, the Tcl `string match` command supports glob-style pattern-matching. The Tcl `switch` and `lsearch` commands support both glob and regular expression-style pattern-matching.

Glob-style Pattern-matching

Glob-style pattern-matching is very simple to use. It basically supports various types of wild-carding via special characters to search for a string match on character positioning.

Glob-style pattern-matching makes use of the following special characters:

?	Matches any single character.
*	Matches any sequence of zero or more characters.
[chars]	Matches any single character in chars. If chars contains a sequence of the form a-z, then any character between a and z (inclusive) will match.
\x	Matches the character x.
{a,b,...}	Matches any of the strings a, b, etc.

In the example below, the wildcard character * is used to compare the value of oid to see if it starts with the value 1.3.6.1.2.1. The string match command returns a value 1 if there is a match; otherwise, it returns a value of 0.

```
set oid 1.3.6.1.2.1.16
⇒ 1.3.6.1.2.1.16


string match 1.3.6.1.2.1.* $oid
⇒ 1
```

Here we are looking for a string that match the template of a telephone number:

```
set sysContact "Susan Maxwell (617) 343-6372"
⇒ Susan Maxwell (617) 343-6372


string match "*(???) ???-????*" $sysContact
⇒ 1
```

Glob-style pattern-matching uses brackets, as in [0-9], to mean any character between 0 and 9. If we specify [a-z], we mean match any lowercase letter. If you use brackets in a glob expression, you need to remember that brackets are special characters to the Tcl interpreter and hence must be preceded by \ or enclosed between braces:

```
set sysContact "Gene Smith (800) 555-5555"
⇒ Gene Smith (800) 555-5555


string match "*(\[8-9\]??) ???-????*" $sysContact
⇒ 1


string match {*([8-9]??) ???-????*} $sysContact
⇒ 1
```

The above code checks for a match on anything that follows the template of a phone number and looks like an 8xx or 9xx area code number.

Regular Expression-style Pattern-matching

A regular expression is zero or more pattern definitions separated by |. It attempts to match anything that matches one of the pattern definitions. Regular expressions can also use wildcard characters in pattern definitions. With regular expressions, you can match on whole or partial character patterns rather than on just character positions.

Regular expression pattern arguments may contain any of the following special characters:

.	Matches any single character.
*	Matches zero or more instances of the previous pattern.
+	Matches one or more instances of the previous pattern.
?	Matches zero or one instance of the previous pattern.
( )	Groups a pattern.
		The resulting regular expression matches either of the pattern definitions on either side of the	character.
[ ]	Matches any single character in a range. If ^ is used within the range, it means matches if NOT character.
^	Anchors the pattern to the beginning of the string.
$	Anchors the pattern to the end of the string.

Note that special characters in regular expressions have slightly different meanings than with glob-style pattern-matching. In regular expressions, the character * means matches zero or more instances of the previous pattern.

In the example below, we would get a match whenever the value of addr followed the template of an IP address:

```
switch -regexp $addr {
    [0-9]*.[0-9]*.[0-9]*.[0-9]* {puts "IP Address"}
    default              {puts "non-IP Address"}
}
```

Unfortunately, the string . . . would be a valid match for an IP address in the above code. We can fix this by changing the * character to the + character.

```
switch -regexp $addr {
    [0-9]+.[0-9]+.[0-9]+.[0-9]+ {puts "IP Address"}
    default              {puts "non-IP Address"}
}
```

The + character used in a regular expression means match on one or more instances of the previous pattern. The code now will not match on . . . as in the previous example, but it still has a problem since it will report that 1232.2.1.3 is an IP address.

As you can see, creating correct regular expressions can be tricky. Trying to use a regular expression with the switch command to check if a string is a valid IP address is proving to be difficult. Shortly we will solve this problem using the regexp command.

glob

The `glob` command returns a list of files whose names match the specified patterns. Naturally, it uses glob-style pattern-matching. It has the following syntax:

```
glob ?switches? pattern ?pattern ...?
```

If the initial arguments to `glob` start with -, they are treated as switches. The following switches are supported:

-nocomplain
  Allows an empty list to be returned without error. Without this switch, an error is returned if the result list would be empty.

--
  Marks the end of switches. The argument following this one will be treated as a pattern even if it starts with a dash.

If the first character in a pattern is ~, it refers to the home directory for the user whose name follows the ~. If the ~ is followed immediately by /, the value of the HOME environment variable is used.

Here are some examples using the `glob` command.

To find out if any `.txt` files exist in the directory `c:\Program Files\Tickleman\itcl2.2\bin`, simply specify:

```
glob "c:/Program Files/Tickleman/itcl2.2/bin/*.txt"
⇒ {c:/Program Files/Tickleman/itcl2.2/bin/foo.txt}
```

Below we see the result we get back if we `glob` for a filename that doesn't exist without using the -nocomplain switch. For example, to check whether a specified directory has any `*.cfg` files:

```
glob "c:/Program Files/Tickleman/itcl2.2/bin/*.cfg"
⇒ no files matched glob pattern
⇒ "c:/ProgramFiles/Tickleman/itcl2.2/bin/*.cfg"
```

Now, let's see the result we get back if we `glob` for a name that doesn't exist with the -nocomplain switch:

```
glob -nocomplain "c:/Program Files/Tickleman/itcl2.2/bin/*.cfg"
⇒
```

regexp

The `regexp` command matches a regular expression against a string. The syntax of the `regexp` command is as follows:

```
regexp ?switches? exp string ?matchVar? ?subMatchVar sub_MatchVar ...?
```

The `regexp` command determines whether the regular expression `exp` matches part or all of `string` and returns 1 if it does, 0 if it doesn't. It is also capable of extracting values from subexpression matches and saving these values into optionally specified variable arguments.

The `regexp` command supports the following switches:

`-nocase`
> Causes the pattern-matching to be case-insensitive.

`-indices`
> Changes what is stored in the `subMatchVars`. Instead of storing the matching characters from string, each variable will contain a list of two integer values, giving the indices in `string` the first and last positions in the matching range of characters.

`--`
> Marks the end of the switches. The argument following this one will be treated as exp, even if it starts with a dash.

During evaluation, `matchVar` is set to the string that matches all of `exp`. The first `subMatchVar` contains the characters in `string` that match the leftmost parenthesized subexpression within `exp`, the next `subMatchVar` contains the characters that match the next parenthesized subexpression to the right in `exp` and so on.

If there are more instances of `subMatchVar` specified than parenthesized subexpressions within `exp`, or if a particular subexpression in `exp` doesn't match the string, the corresponding `subMatchVar` will be set to `"-1 -1"` if `-indices` has been specified; otherwise, it will be set to an empty string.

In the procedure `GetVendorNum` below, we use `regexp` to get a vendor's enterprise number from a specified `sysObjectID`, such as `1.3.6.1.4.1.370.2.2`.

```
proc GetVendorNum { oid} {
    regexp {^(1.3.6.1.4.1.)([0-9]+)} $oid match sub1 sub2
    puts "oid=$oid match=$match sub1=$sub1 sub2=$sub2"
}
```

The `regexp` command in this procedure looks for the following:

- **That the first field of `$oid` starts with `1.3.6.1.4.1.`, as defined by the first subexpression `^(1.3.6.1.4.1.)`.**

- **That a second field of numbers exists after the first field, as defined by the second subexpression `([0-9]+)`**

For example:

```
% GetVendorNum 1.3.6.1.4.1.370
⇒ oid=1.3.6.1.4.1.370 match=1.3.6.1.4.1.370 sub1=1.3.6.1.4.1.
sub2=370
```

```
GetVendorNum 1.3.6.1.4.1.370.2.2
⇒ oid=1.3.6.1.4.1.370.2.2 match=1.3.6.1.4.1.370
sub1=1.3.6.1.4.1. sub2=370
```

Now to get back to the problem we tried to solve earlier, which is to check if a string is a valid IP address or mask, we use the procedure `CheckAddr` below, which uses a regular expression with four pattern or subexpression definitions:

```
proc CheckAddr { string } {
  set foo [regexp {(^[0-9]+).([0-9]+).([0-9]+).([0-9]+)} \
      $string match sub1 sub2 sub3 sub4]

  # If foo is not 1, then we did not match all patterns.

  if { $foo != 1} {
     puts "$string is NOT a valid IP address"
     return
  }

  # Now check if the values are less than or equal to 255.
  if { $sub1 <= 255 && $sub2 <= 255 && \
     $sub3 <= 255 && $sub4 <= 255} {
     puts "$string is a valid IP address or mask"
  } else {
     puts "$string is NOT a valid IP address or mask"
  }
}
```

Now to test it:
```
CheckAddr ...
⇒ ... is NOT a valid IP address
```

```
CheckAddr 256.21.23.1
⇒ 256.21.23.1 is NOT a valid IP address or mask
```

```
CheckAddr 158.101.121.200
⇒ 158.101.121.200 is a valid IP address or mask
```

Good! Now let's use the regexp command to check if the name Joe Smith is in the variable sysContact:

```
set sysContact "Joe Smith (555) 555-6473"
⇒ Joe Smith (555) 555-6473
```

We can either specify:

```
regexp {(Joe Smith)} $sysContact match name
⇒ 1
```

or:

```
regexp -indices {(Joe Smith)} $sysContact match name
⇒ 1
```

Using the `indices` switch above results in the following:

```
puts $match
⇒ 0 8
```

```
puts $name
⇒ 0 8
```

regsub

The `regsub` command performs substitutions based on regular expression pattern-matching. Its syntax is:

```
regsub ?switches? exp string subSpec varName
```

This command matches the regular expression `exp` against `string`, and it copies `string` to `varName`. If there is a match found while copying `string` to `varName`, the portion of `string` that matched `exp` is replaced with `subSpec`. The command returns the number of matching ranges that were found and replaced.

If the initial arguments to `regsub` start with `-`, they are treated as switches. The following switches are supported:

`-all`

All ranges in string that match `exp` are found and substitution is performed for each of these ranges. Without this switch, only the first matching range is found and substituted. If `-all` is specified, `&` and `\n` sequences are handled for each substitution using the information from the corresponding match.

`-nocase`

String-matching will be case-insensitive; however, substitutions specified by `subSpec` will use the original unconverted form of string.

`--`

Marks the end of switches. The argument following this one will be treated as `exp`, even if it starts with a dash.

The following procedure, FormatMac, converts the octet string value we get back from doing an SNMP poll for an interface's ifPhysicalAddress into a colon-delimited string that follows the typical format convention of an Ethernet MAC address. We test it below by setting the variable val to the octet string value 00 c0 d4 00 09 43. All it is doing is replacing a space with a colon.

```
proc FormatMac { val } {
    regsub -all " " $val : macaddress
  return $macaddress
 }

set val "00 c0 d4 00 09 43"
⇒ 00 c0 d4 00 09 43

set mac [FormatMac $val]
⇒ 00:c0:d4:00:09:43
```

5 *SNMP Tcl Extensions*

This chapter will cover both TickleMan and Scotty SNMP extensions.

TICKLEMAN

TickleMan provides Tcl command extensions for performing both simple and complex SNMP operations. Simple operations include SNMP Get, GetNext and Set commands. Complex operations include the retrieval of a MIB table. Both complex and simple operations can be done either synchronously or asynchronously. TickleMan also provides commands for processing SNMP traps, performing ICMP echo tests, accessing compiled MIB information and for converting ASN.1 objects. Finally, TickleMan supports SNMP v1, SNMP v2c and SNMP v2.

We will be focusing purely on SNMP v1. All of our examples and sample tools will be written for SNMP v1 agents. The reason for this is practical. Right now, most devices in operation are SNMP v1 devices. Second, the scope of SNMP v2 is so broad it merits its own book. Finally, the concepts we will be showing in this book are valid regardless of which version of SNMP is being used.

Okay, let's get to the fun stuff!!

TICKLEMAN—MANAGING SESSIONS

All SNMP operations are performed in the context of an SNMP session. An SNMP session is created with the following TickleMan command:

```
snmpsession ?name? ?option ... option?
```

The return value for the command is the name of the session, which in effect is a Tcl command that can be used to generate SNMP requests. Options, such as SNMP timeouts and retry counts, can be specified for a session. For example:

```
set sid [snmpsession session1 -snmp -timeout 300 -retries 2]
⇒ session1

puts $sid
⇒ session1
```

In the above example, the variable sid references the session created with the snmpsession command. The option -snmp specifies that the session is for SNMP communications. The option -timeout 300 specifies an SNMP timeout value of three seconds (the value is specified in 1/100 seconds). The option -retries 2 specifies an SNMP retry count of 2. Note that the session can be referenced either by the name given, session1, or indirectly by the variable sid.

Once a session has been created, it can be used for performing SNMP operations to any number of host devices. A possible reason for creating more than one session is if you need different session option values for different SNMP operations. For example, you may need different retry and timeout values for accessing different devices. Another reason is if you want to be able to cancel certain outstanding SNMP operations. More on this later.

The option values for a session can be both retrieved and modified via an SNMP session configure command:

```
$sid configure
⇒ {-timeout 300} {-retries 2} {-nonRepeaters 0}
{-maxRepetitions 10} {-retransA1 0} {-retransA2 1} {-retransB1
1} {-retransB2 1} {-retransC1 0} {-retransC2 1} {-tableRows
4294967295} {-tableMaxRows 4294967295} {-size 32}
```

All of the options for the session are returned. In the above example, you can see both the SNMP timeout and retry values that were set, plus the default values for other options. We will be describing the options relevant to SNMP v1 later in this chapter.

A specific option value can be obtained:

```
$sid configure -timeout
⇒ 300
```

Also, a specific option value can be modified:

```
$sid configure -timeout 500
$sid configure -timeout
⇒ 500
```

Finally, a session can be destroyed, which will both remove any outstanding SNMP operations for that session and free up any internal storage being used by the session. If you had set up different sessions for different groups of devices, you could cancel all outstanding SNMP requests to a specific group by destroying the session being used for that group.

```
$sid destroy
```

There is no return value given when destroying a session.

TICKLEMAN—BUILDING VARBIND LISTS

A variable binding list, or `varbind` list, defines either which MIB variables to retrieve or which MIB variables to set for different SNMP operations. A `varbind` list takes the form:

```
{ ?varbind ... varbind? }
```

For SNMP Get or GetNext operations, each `varbind` takes the form:

```
{ oid }
```

`oid` may either be a dotted form OID Number or an OID Name, with an optional instance appended to it. If it is an OID Name, it must be defined within the `snmpinfo.dat` file provided with TickleMan. More on `snmpinfo.dat` later. Examples of valid `oid` values:

```
1.3.6.1.2.1.1.1
sysDescr
sysDescr.0
```

Also, a variable can be used to reference an OID Name:

```
set sysDescr 1.3.6.1.2.1.1.1
⇒ 1.3.6.1.2.1.1.1
```

```
set oidStr $sysDescr.0
⇒ 1.3.6.1.2.1.1.1.0
```

For SNMP `set` operations, each `varbind` takes the form:

```
{ oid ?type? value }
```

`type` describes the ASN.1 type that the value is representing, and may have one of the following values, as shown in Table 5.1.

- INTEGER
- OctetString
- IpAddress
- ObjectID
- Counter
- Gauge
- TimeTicks

If only two fields are present in the `varbind`, the second is taken as the value, and the type is determined by searching the `snmpinfo.dat` file for the `oid`. Based on the type, the following formats for the value are:

Table 5.1

INTEGER	Integer
OctetString	text string or
	xx:xx:xx: ... :xx where xx is a two-digit hex value or
	xx xx xx ... xx where xx is a two-digit hex value or
	d.d.d. ... .d where d is a decimal value ranging from 0 – 255
IpAddress	IP address in dot notation
ObjectID	Same format previously defined for oid
Counter	Unsigned integer
Gauge	Unsigned integer
TimeTicks	Unsigned integer

The following is an example of a `varbindList` that could be used for a `set` operation:

```
set varbindList { {sysName.0 OctetString \
{6e 65 77 4e 61 6d 65}} {sysContact.0 \
OctetString {6e 65 77 43 6f 6e 74 61 63 74}} }
⇒ {sysName.0 OctetString {6e 65 77 4e 61 6d 65}}
{sysContact.0 OctetString {6e 65 77 43 6f 6e 74 61 63 74}}
```

Note that variable substitution will not occur within braces. If you had used a variable in the above example instead of actual text, you would not get the desired result. A preferred way to create `varbindList` would be:

```
set name [text2octet "newName"]
⇒ 6e 65 77 4e 61 6d 65
```

```
set contact [text2octet "newContact"]
⇒ 6e 65 77 43 6f 6e 74 61 63 74

set varbindList [list \
[list sysName.0 OctetString $name] \
[list sysContact.0 OctetString $contact]]
```

Here, we were able to use the `text2octet` routine offered by TickleMan to convert a text string to an `OctetString`, and since variable substitution can now be used, create an identical `varbindList`.

TICKLEMAN—PERFORMING SNMPv1 OPERATIONS

TickleMan supports Get, GetNext and Set operations. The command format for performing these operations are:

```
<session> <op> <addr> <authinfo> <vblist> options ?callback?
```

where

`<session>` is a session name returned by an `snmpsession` command.

`<op>` can be `get`, `next` or `set`.

`<addr>` is either an IP address in dot notation or a hostname.

`<authinfo>` specifies both the SNMP version and authentication information to be used for sending the request. The format is:

```
{ snmpv1 ?communityString? }
```

where `?communityString?` specifies the community string to be used for the request. If it is not provided, `public` will be used.

`<vblist>` specifies the list of variable bindings to be sent in the request.

`options` allows any of the session option values to be overridden for this operation.

If `?callback?` is set to `wait`, the command will block until the SNMP operation is completed, and the return value will be a list containing the request results. This in effect will cause SNMP operations to be performed synchronously.

If ?callback? is specified as any other string, the request results will be appended to this string, which will then be executed as a Tcl script command. This can be used to perform asynchronous SNMP operations. When the request is completed or destroyed, the command is also destroyed.

If ?callback? is omitted, the request will be performed and the results will be discarded. In this case, the return value will be an empty string. A possible reason for doing this might be to exercise an agent implementation where you don't care about the results being returned.

The following example demonstrates a blocking (synchronous) SNMP Get request:

```
set id [snmpsession session1 -snmp]
⇒ session1

set authinfo {snmpv1 public}
⇒ snmpv1 public

set vb {sysDescr.0 sysUpTime.0}
⇒ sysDescr.0 sysUpTime.0

set result [$id get $ipaddr $authinfo $vb {} wait]
⇒ session1 req508800 noError 0 {{sysDescr.0 OctetString "43
69 73 63 6f 20 49 6e 74 65 72 6e 65 74 77 6f 72 6b 20 4f 70 65
72 61 74 69 6e 67 20 53 79 73 74 65 6d 20 53 6f 66 74 77 61 72
65"} {sysUpTime.0 TimeTicks "56216405"}}
```

Let's examine both the SNMP Get request and the result. First, we hid the IP address in the variable $ipaddr, but the value is an IP address in standard dot notation. Second, the community string public is used. The option list provided is blank, meaning the options set for the session will be used. Finally, setting the callback to the string wait will cause the SNMP Get request to block.

The result returned is a list with five elements. The first element is the name of the session used for the request:

```
set sessionName [lindex $result 0]
⇒ session1
```

The next element is the unique request identifier associated with the request:

```
set requestID [lindex $result 1]
⇒ req508800
```

The next element is the SNMP error status returned for the request:

```
set errorStatus [lindex $result 2]
⇒ noError
```

The next element is the SNMP error index returned for the request:

```
set errorIndex [lindex $result 3]
⇒ 0
```

The final element is the `resultVblist`:

```
set resultVbList [lindex $result 4]
⇒ {sysDescr.0 OctetString "43 69 73 63 6f 20 49 6e 74 65 72
6e 65 74 77 6f 72 6b 20 4f 70 65 72 61 74 69 6e 67 20 53 79 73
74 65 6d 20 53 6f 66 74 77 61 72 65"} {sysUpTime.0 TimeTicks
"56216405"}
```

The `varbind` list returned contains two elements: the first contains the `varbind` result for `sysDescr.0` and the second contains the `varbind` result for `sysUpTime.0`.

```
set vb1 [lindex $resultVbList 0]
⇒ sysDescr.0 OctetString "43 69 73 63 6f 20 49 6e 74 65 72 6e
65 74 77 6f 72 6b 20 4f 70 65 72 61 74 69 6e 67 20 53 79 73 74 4
65 6d 20 53 6f 66 74 77 61 72 65"
```

The resulting list contains three elements of the form:

```
{ oid type value }
```

which should seem familiar from the section on building `varbind` lists. Now:

```
set oid [lindex $vb1 0]
⇒ sysDescr.0
```

The `oid` value matches the original `oid` value requested.

```
set type [lindex $vb1 1]
⇒ OctetString
```

The type, `OctetString`, indicates the value returned is an octet string.

```
set value [lindex $vb1 2]
⇒ 43 69 73 63 6f 20 49 6e 74 65 72 6e 65 74 77 6f 72 6b 20 4f
70 65 72 61 74 69 6e 67 20 53 79 73 74 65 6d 20 53 6f 66 74 77
61 72 65
```

The octet string returned is in hex format. Fortunately, TickleMan provides convenient commands for converting data to more readable or usable formats. The `octet2text` command will convert an octet string in hex format to a display string.

```
octet2text $value
⇒ Cisco Internetwork Operating System Software
```

Now let's look at the second `varbind` returned:

```
set vb2 [lindex $resultVbList 1]
⇒ sysUpTime.0 TimeTicks "56216405"
```

Again, the first element in the list is the `oid` value, the second element specifies the type of the value returned and the third element is the value returned.

```
set value [lindex $vb2 2]
⇒ 56216405
```

`TimeTicks`, as mentioned previously, is in one-hundredths of a second. To make the returned `sysUpTime` value meaningful, let's write a conversion procedure:

```
proc ConvertTimeTicks {ticks} {

  set seconds [expr $ticks/100]

  set days [expr $seconds/86400]
  set seconds [expr $seconds - ($days*86400)]

  set hours [expr $seconds/3600]
  set seconds [expr $seconds - ($hours*3600)]

  set minutes [expr $seconds/60]
  set seconds [expr $seconds - ($minutes*60)]

return "$days days, $hours hours, $minutes minutes, \
$seconds seconds"
}
```

`ConvertTimeTicks` is fairly straightforward. It takes a `TimeTicks` value, converts it to seconds and then figures out how many days, hours, minutes and seconds can fit into that value. Finally, it returns a string, using variable substitution, to include the number of days, hours, minutes and seconds calculated.

```
set resultStr [ConvertTimeTicks $value]
⇒ 6 days, 12 hours, 9 minutes, 24 seconds
```

Let's now write a procedure which will return `sysDescr` and `sysUpTime` **MIB** values for a device in displayable format:

```
proc GetSystemInfo {sid addr cstr} {

  set vb {sysDescr sysUpTime}
  set authinfo [list snmpv1 $cstr]
```

```
   set result [$sid next $addr $authinfo $vb {} wait]
#
#  Check error status, if error return list with error code.
#
   set errorStatus [lindex $result 2]

   if {$errorStatus != "noError"} {
       return [list $errorStatus]
   }
#
#  Get sysDescr value and convert to displayable string.
#
   set resultVB [lindex $result 4]

   set vb1 [lindex $resultVB 0]
   set temp [lindex $vb1 2]
   set descrVal [octet2text $temp]
#
#  Get sysUpTime value and convert to displayable string.
#
   set vb2 [lindex $resultVB 1]
   set temp [lindex $vb2 2]
   set timeVal [ConvertTimeTicks $temp]

   return [list $descrVal $timeVal]
}

set id [snmpsession session1 -snmp]
⇒ session1

set x [GetSystemInfo $id $ipaddr public]
⇒ {Cisco Internetwork Operating System Software } {9 days, 12
hours, 43 minutes, 50 seconds}

set x [GetSystemInfo $id $ipaddr badCommString]
⇒ timeout
```

In GetSystemInfo, we provide as arguments an SNMP session ID, an IP address and an SNMP community string. An SNMP GetNext operation is used to retrieve sysDescr and sysUpTime MIB variable information (which is why the MIB variables in the varbind list contain no instance information). Once the operation completes, the error status is checked. If it is something other than "noError", it is an indication that the SNMP GetNext operation failed and the procedure returns a list with a single element containing the error status. Otherwise, the values for sysDescr and sysUpTime are pulled out of the returned varbind list and converted to displayable strings.

Throughout the example, the lindex command is used to pull elements out of the returned list. This results in somewhat cryptic code. We can make the code more readable by abstracting the details of the returned list.

The following procedures will provide an abstraction between the SNMP result and the list returned:

```
proc GetSessionName {result} {
   return [lindex $result 0]
}

proc GetReqID {result} {
   return [lindex $result 1]
}

proc GetErrorStatus {result} {
   return [lindex $result 2]
}

proc GetErrorIndex {result} {
   return [lindex $result 3]
}

proc GetVarBindList {result} {
   return [lindex $result 4]
}

proc GetVarBind {vblist pos} {
   return [lindex $vblist [expr $pos - 1]]
}

proc GetOID {vb} {
   return [lindex $vb 0]
}

proc GetType {vb} {
   return [lindex $vb 1]
}

proc GetValue {vb} {
```

```
    return [lindex $vb 2]
}

proc GetInstance {oid m} {
  set n [expr [string length $m] + 1]
  return [string range $oid $n end]
}
```

Note that the procedure GetVarBind expects pos to start at 1. The procedure GetInstance will return the instance portion of an oid given the original OID string used in the request.

Now given these routines, we will rewrite GetSystemInfo:

```
proc GetSystemInfo {sid addr cstr} {

  set vb {sysDescr sysUpTime}
  set authinfo [list snmpv1 $cstr]

  set result [$sid next $addr $authinfo $vb {} wait]

#
#  Check error status, if error return empty list.
#
  set errorStatus [GetErrorStatus $result]

  if {$errorStatus != "noError"} {
      return [list $errorStatus]
  }
#
#  Get sysDescr value and convert to displayable string.
#
  set resultVB [GetVarBindList $result]

  set vb1 [GetVarBind $resultVB 1]
  set val [GetValue $vb1]
  set descrVal [octet2text $val]
#
#  Get sysUpTime value and convert to displayable string.
#
  set vb2 [GetVarBind $resultVB 2]
  set val [GetValue $vb2]
  set timeVal [ConvertTimeTicks $val]
```

```
    return [list $descrVal $timeVal]
}
```

Procedures are more CPU-intensive than in-line code. In our example, this translates to roughly fifteen percent more processing (approximately 4,200 microseconds in elapsed time for the more readable version of GetSystemInfo compared to 3,600 microseconds of elapsed time for the original version). Unless performance becomes an issue (and for the small diagnostic and configuration tools that we are advocating it shouldn't be), we feel for code readability that these abstraction routines should be used.

At this point, we will tie in several of the procedures from Chapter 3 to build a procedure, CalcEthUtil, which will calculate Ethernet utilization for a given interface:

```
source book-ch3.itcl

proc GetEthUtilVars {sid addr inst cstr} {

    global linespeed

    set vb [list ifSpeed.$inst ifInOctets.$inst \
            ifOutOctets.$inst sysUpTime.0]

    set authinfo [list snmpv1 $cstr]

    set result [$sid get $addr $authinfo $vb {} wait]
    set errorStatus [GetErrorStatus $result]

    if {$errorStatus != "noError"} {
            return $errorStatus
    }
#
#   Get ifSpeed, ifInOctets, ifOutOctets.
#
    set resultVB [GetVarBindList $result]

    set timevb [GetVarBind $resultVB 4]
    set ticks [GetValue $timevb]

    set vb1 [GetVarBind $resultVB 1]
    set linespeed [GetValue $vb1]

    set vb2 [GetVarBind $resultVB 2]
    set val [GetValue $vb2]
```

```
   AddValueToList ifInOctets $inst $val $ticks

   set vb3 [GetVarBind $resultVB 3]
   set val [GetValue $vb3]
   AddValueToList ifOutOctets $inst $val $ticks

   return $errorStatus
}


proc CalcEthUtil {sid addr inst cstr} {

# Procedure will return -1 if utilization cannot
# be calculated. Otherwise, utilization value will be
# returned.

   global linespeed minPollSeconds maxPollSeconds

   set minPollSeconds 8
   set maxPollSeconds 20

   set status [GetEthUtilVars $sid $addr $inst $cstr]
   if {$status != "noError"} {
        return -1
   }

   after 10000

   set status [GetEthUtilVars $sid $addr $inst $cstr]
   if {$status != "noError"} {
        return -1
   }
#
# At this point, two samples have been collected
# 10 seconds apart.
#
   set dInOctets [Delta ifInOctets $inst]
   if {$dInOctets == -1} {
        return -1
   }
```

```
    set dOutOctets [Delta ifOutOctets $inst]
    if {$dOutOctets == -1} {
         return -1
    }

   set rxUtil [expr (($dInOctets * 8.0) / (10.0 *\
   $linespeed))*100.0]

   set txUtil [expr (($dOutOctets * 8.0) / (10.0 *\
   $linespeed))*100.0]

    return [expr $rxUtil + $txUtil]

   }



   CalcEthUtil $sid $ipaddr 1 public
   ⇒ 4.64096
```

The first thing we do is source a file that contains the procedures from Chapter 3 so we can access AddValueToList and Delta. GetEthUtilVars will collect ifSpeed, ifInOctets and ifOutOctets for a specified interface, and then add the results to a circular buffer using AddValueToList. GetEthUtilVars will also collect sysUpTime, which is passed along to AddValueToList as well. CalcEthUtil calls GetEthUtilVars, waits ten seconds and then calls GetEthUtilVars again. Now with two collections, CalcEthUtil can calculate the delta difference for ifInOctets and ifOutOctets. Finally, Ethernet utilization is calculated as the sum of the receive and transmit utilizations. The expressions for the receive and transmit utilizations are similar: the number of bytes transmitted or received during some time period times eight bits/per byte divided by both the linespeed and the time duration in seconds. Finally, the result is multiplied by 100 to convert a decimal to a percent.

This procedure ignores the intergap delay between frames on an Ethernet segment. To be precise, we would have to calculate the total number of packets both received and transmitted during the measured time interval and factor in the unutilized bandwidth due to this intergap delay. However, this factor is so small that it is not worth bothering with. Also, the expression used is for standard half-duplex Ethernet. Full-duplex Ethernet is beginning to show up in vendor switch products. In this case, receive and transmit utilization would be calculated as above and would be the values of interest to the user.

TICKLEMAN—NONBLOCKING SNMP OPERATIONS

So far, we have only demonstrated blocking (synchronous) SNMP operations. TickleMan also supports nonblocking (asynchronous) SNMP operations. As we stated in the previous section,

if the ?callback? parameter in an SNMP command equals the string wait the SNMP operation will be performed in a blocking manner. However, if the ?callback? parameter is any
other string, the SNMP operation will be performed nonblocking, with the ?callback? parameter executed as a script after the SNMP operation completes. For example:

```
proc SimpleNonBlockingTest {sid addr cstr} {

    set vb {sysUpTime}
    set authinfo [list snmpv1 $cstr]

    set reqid [$sid next $addr $authinfo $vb {} {puts }]
    puts "SNMP GetNext sent!"
}

SimpleNonBlockingTest $sid $ipaddr public
⇒ SNMP GetNext sent!
⇒ session1 req50c5c0 noError 0 {{sysUpTime.0 TimeTicks
"39712199"}}
```

In the above eaample, the SNMP GetNext operation is performed in the background while the
rest of the Tcl script executes. Once the SNMP operation completes, an event will be generated.
Processing the event will cause the result string to be appended to the script and the script to be executed. Since the script is simply puts, the result string is appended to it, causing the script
{puts $result-string} to be executed.

Using nonblocking SNMP operations is extremely powerful. Multiple outstanding SNMP
operations can be issued while the rest of a Tcl script executes normally. Callback routines can be
written to catch and process the results. A more useful demonstration of nonblocking SNMP operations is a script which will simultaneously collect sysUpTime values from a list of devices and
store the results in an array:

```
proc CollectSysUpTime {sid addrList} {

    global gArray reqCount colDone

    set reqCount 0
    set vb {sysUpTime.0}
    foreach el $addrList {
#
#  Format of list elements { ipAddress communityString }:
#
            set addr [lindex $el 0]
            set cstr [lindex $el 1]

            set authinfo [list snmpv1 $cstr]
```

```
        set cb [list CollectSysUpTimeCB $addr]
        set reqid [$sid get $addr $authinfo $vb {} $cb]
        incr reqCount
    }
    vwait colDone
    foreach index [array names gArray] {
        puts $gArray($index)
    }
}

proc CollectSysUpTimeCB {node result} {

    global gArray reqCount colDone

    set gArray($node,sysUpTime) $result
    incr reqCount -1
    if {$reqCount == 0} {
        set colDone 1
    }

}

set sid [snmpsession s1 -snmp]
⇒ s1

set addrList [list [list $addr1 $cstr1] [list $addr2 $cstr2]]

CollectSysUpTime $sid $addrList
⇒ s1 req559320 noError 0 {{sysUpTime.0 TimeTicks "47499725"}}
⇒ s1 req559bd0 noError 0 {{sysUpTime.0 TimeTicks
"103106743"}}
```

CollectSysUpTime is passed an SNMP session and a list of IP addresses and community strings. For each IP address community string pair, an SNMP Get operation is performed and a global request count is incremented. When the operation completes (successfully, with an error, or times out) a script:

```
        CollectSysUpTimeCB $addr $result-string
```

is executed. CollectSysUpTimeCB stores the result string in a global array and decrements the global request count. When the count is decremented to zero (indicating that all requests have been processed), a global flag, colDone, is set, waking up the CollectSysUpTime procedure. At this point, the contents of the array are dumped.

Note that in this example, we assigned one parameter, the IP address of the device being polled, when we defined the callback script. TickleMan automatically added the second parameter, the result string, just before the callback was made. The ability to pass additional information to our callback routines is critical, and is something we will be doing over and over again throughout this book.

Lastly, a nonblocking SNMP command will return the SNMP request identifier associated with the operation.:

```
set reqid [$sid get $addr $authinfo $vblist {} {puts}]
puts $reqid
⇒ req510140
```

The operation can be stopped before it completes by:

```
$reqid destroy
```

TICKLEMAN—SNMP SET OPERATIONS

The syntax for performing SNMP Set operations is identical to that of performing Get or GetNext operations. For example:

```
#
# GetRandom will generate a random number between
# 1 and 65536.
#
proc GetRandom { } {
  set a [random_byte] ;# random_byte generates a random.
  set b [random_byte] ;# Value between 0 and 255.
  return [expr ($a + 1)*($b + 1)]
}

set ciscoPingEntryStatus 1.3.6.1.4.1.9.9.16.1.1.1.16
⇒ 1.3.6.1.4.1.9.9.16.1.1.1.16

set inst [GetRandom]
⇒ 9607

set vblist [list [list $ciscoPingEntryStatus.$inst INTEGER 5]]
⇒ {1.3.6.1.4.1.9.9.16.1.1.1.16.9607 INTEGER 5}
```

```
set result [$sid set $ipaddr [list snmpv1 $cstr] $vb {} wait]
⇒ s1 req513d90 noError 0 {{enterprises.9.9.16.1.1.1.16.9607
INTEGER "5"}}
```

The GetRandom procedure returns a random number, which we use as an instance for creating a Cisco Ping entry row. We specified the OID string for ciscoPingEntryStatus since it was not found within snmpinfo.dat. Also, the varbind list had to be created in the format {{varbind}}. The command:

```
set vblist [list $ciscoPingEntryStatus.$inst INTEGER 5]
```

would have caused the SNMP Set operation to fail since each element in the varbind list was expected to be a list containing minimally an OID string and a value. We had to specify the value type since ciscoPingEntryStatus was not defined within snmpinfo.dat. Finally, the result string returned was identical in format to the result strings returned from Get or GetNext operations.

As a little background to our simple Set operation example, Cisco supports a private MIB called the Cisco Ping MIB. This MIB allows you to direct a Cisco device to send ICMP echo requests to a remote device and measure the delay in receiving ICMP echo replies. This is very powerful. Instead of measuring response time delays from your workstation to remote devices, you can direct Cisco devices throughout your network to measure response time delays to devices within other subnets. This could help you generate a mapping of response time delays between all the subnets of your network. BayNetwork devices, NetScout probes and other vendor equipment support similar private MIBs.

We will now build a Tcl program to direct a device supporting the Cisco Ping MIB to ping a remote device and to measure the response time delay. The program is going to be written using nonblocking SNMP operations, and hence is going to be a series of callback routines chained together. The program is made up of 11 procedures, roughly 200 lines of Tcl code. Outside of the main driver routine, CiscoPing, all other routine names will have the prefix CP_ to make it clear that they are part of the CiscoPing application. Note that if we used blocking SNMP operations, the code could have been written as one large procedure.

The routines making up this program are:

- CiscoPing acts as the main driver. It is passed an SNMP session ID, an address of a Cisco device to configure, an address of a remote address for the Cisco device to ping and a read-write community string. This routine will call CP_StartCiscoPing.

- CP_StartCiscoPing will attempt to find a valid Cisco Ping serial number to use. It generates a nonblocking SNMP Get command, using callback routine CP_SerialNumCB.

- CP_SerialNumCB will call CP_StartCiscoPing if the serial number being tried is invalid. Otherwise, it will attempt to configure a Cisco Ping row by issuing a nonblocking SNMP Set command, using callback routine CP_InitialSetCB.

- `CP_InitialSetCB` will attempt to configure the rest of the Cisco Ping row by issuing a nonblocking SNMP Set command, using callback routine `CP_Test-SetCB`.
- `CP_TestSetCB` will make the row "active", starting the ping test. A nonblocking SNMP Set command is issued, using callback routine `CP_TestNextCB`.
- `CP_TestNextCB` will be set up to call `CP_TryAgain` in 10 seconds.
- `CP_TryAgain` issues a nonblocking SNMP Get command to determine if the ping test has completed, using callback routine `CP_WaitForCompletionCB`.
- `CP_WaitForCompletionCB` will call `CP_CollectResults` if the test has completed; otherwise, `CP_TryAgain` will be called in five seconds.
- `CP_CollectResults` issues a nonblocking SNMP Get command to retrieve the results of the test, using callback routine `CP_CollectResultsCB`.
- `CP_CollectResultsCB` processes the results of the test and signals to `CiscoPing` that the test has completed.
- `CP_TestFailed` is a convenience routine for handling an unexpected SNMP error.

```
set ciscoPingProtocol          1.3.6.1.4.1.9.9.16.1.1.1.2
set ciscoPingAddress           1.3.6.1.4.1.9.9.16.1.1.1.3
set ciscoPingPacketCount       1.3.6.1.4.1.9.9.16.1.1.1.4
set ciscoPingPacketSize        1.3.6.1.4.1.9.9.16.1.1.1.5
set ciscoPingPacketTimeout     1.3.6.1.4.1.9.9.16.1.1.1.6
set ciscoPingDelay             1.3.6.1.4.1.9.9.16.1.1.1.7
set ciscoPingSentPackets       1.3.6.1.4.1.9.9.16.1.1.1.9
set ciscoPingReceivedPackets   1.3.6.1.4.1.9.9.16.1.1.1.10
set ciscoPingMinRtt            1.3.6.1.4.1.9.9.16.1.1.1.11
set ciscoPingAvgRtt            1.3.6.1.4.1.9.9.16.1.1.1.12
set ciscoPingMaxRtt            1.3.6.1.4.1.9.9.16.1.1.1.13
set ciscoPingCompleted         1.3.6.1.4.1.9.9.16.1.1.1.14
set ciscoPingEntryOwner        1.3.6.1.4.1.9.9.16.1.1.1.15
set ciscoPingEntryStatus       1.3.6.1.4.1.9.9.16.1.1.1.16


proc CiscoPing {sid addr remoteAddr cstr} {
   global gDoneFlag gResult

   set gDoneFlag 0
   CP_StartCiscoPing $sid $addr $remoteAddr $cstr

   vwait gDoneFlag
```

```
        puts $gResult
    }
```

CiscoPing is the main routine. It takes as arguments an SNMP session, an address of a device supporting the Cisco Ping MIB, an IP address of a remote device to test and a community string. CiscoPing starts things rolling by calling CP_StartCiscoPing, and then waits for gDoneFlag to be set. gDoneFlag will be set by one of the underlying procedures when the Cisco Ping test completes (either successfully or unsuccessfully). If the test completes unsuccessfully, gResult will be set to a list containing the name of the procedure where the test failed, the SNMP error status which caused the failure and the corresponding SNMP error index. If the test completes successfully, gResult will be set to a list containing the number of ping packets received, the number of packets sent, the minimum delay time measured, the average delay time measured and the maximum delay time measured.

```
    proc CP_StartCiscoPing {sid addr remoteAddr cstr} {
        global gInst ciscoPingEntryStatus
    #
    #    First, find a valid serial number. This is done
    #    by picking one at random and making sure it is
    #    not being used.
    #
       set authinfo [list snmpv1 $cstr]
       set gInst [GetRandom]
       set vb [list $ciscoPingEntryStatus.$gInst]
       set cb [list CP_SerialNumCB $sid $addr $remoteAddr $cstr]

       $sid get $addr $authinfo $vb {} $cb
    }
```

CP_StartCiscoPing will pick a random number to try to use as a serial number. It will then issue an SNMP Get operation, trying to retrieve the ciscoPingEntryStatus MIB variable associated with the selected serial number. If the operation completes with no error, the serial number is already being used and another one will have to be tried. Note that the SNMP operation, as all operations in this program, is nonblocking. When the operation completes, CP_Serial-NumCB will be called. Also note that the term "serial number" is simply a Cisco Ping MIB convention that refers to a unique instance number.

```
    proc CP_SerialNumCB {sid addr remoteAddr cstr result} {
    #
    #    If error status == noError, serial number already
    #    being used, choose another.
    #
    #    If error status == noSuchName, we found an unused
```

```
#     serial number and can proceed with the test.
#
#     Any other error causes test to fail.
#
  global gInst gDoneFlag gResult
  global ciscoPingEntryStatus ciscoPingEntryOwner
  global ciscoPingProtocol ciscoPingAddress

  set errorStatus [GetErrorStatus $result]
  if {$errorStatus == "noError"} {
      CP_StartCiscoPing $sid $addr $remoteAddr $cstr
      return
  }

  if {$errorStatus != "noSuchName"} {
      CP_TestFailed "CP_SerialNumCB" $result
      return
  }

  set authinfo [list snmpv1 $cstr]

  set dest [host2addr $remoteAddr]

  set vb1 [list $ciscoPingEntryStatus.$gInst INTEGER 5]
  set vb2 [list $ciscoPingProtocol.$gInst INTEGER 1]
  set vb3 [list $ciscoPingAddress.$gInst OctetString $dest]

  set vblist [list $vb1 $vb2 $vb3]
  set cb [list CP_InitialSetCB $sid $addr $cstr]

  $sid set $addr $authinfo $vblist {} $cb
}
```

If `CP_SerialNumCB` sees an error status of "noError", it calls `CP_StartCiscoPing` to try another random serial number. If the error status is anything other than "noSuchName", the test fails; otherwise, a Set operation is performed, setting `ciscoPingEntryStatus` to the value corresponding to "createAndWait", `ciscoPingProtocol` to the value corresponding to "IP", and `ciscoPingAddress` to an octet string representing the destination address to test.

```
proc CP_InitialSetCB {sid addr cstr result} {
   global gDoneFlag gResult
   global gInst ciscoPingPacketCount ciscoPingPacketSize
   global ciscoPingDelay
```

```
    set errorStatus [GetErrorStatus $result]
    if {$errorStatus != "noError"} {
        CP_TestFailed "CP_InitialSetCB" $result
        return
    }
    set authinfo [list snmpv1 $cstr]

    set vb1 [list $ciscoPingPacketCount.$gInst INTEGER 10]
    set vb2 [list $ciscoPingPacketSize.$gInst INTEGER 128]
    set vb3 [list $ciscoPingDelay.$gInst INTEGER 1000]

    set vblist [list $vb1 $vb2 $vb3]

    set cb [list CP_TestSetCB $sid $addr $cstr]

    $sid set $addr $authinfo $vblist {} $cb

}
```

CP_InitialSetCB is called when the Set operation triggered by CP_SerialNumCB completes. If the Set succeeded, another Set operation is issued, configuring the Cisco Ping test to send ten packets, using a packet size of 128 bytes and a sending delay of 1000 milliseconds (1 second) between each packet.

```
proc CP_TestSetCB {sid addr cstr result} {
    global gDoneFlag gResult
    global gInst ciscoPingEntryStatus
#
#   Test has been set up - make it active!!
#
    set errorStatus [GetErrorStatus $result]
    if {$errorStatus != "noError"} {
        CP_TestFailed "CP_TestSetCB" $result
        return
    }
    set authinfo [list snmpv1 $cstr]

    set vb1 [list $ciscoPingEntryStatus.$gInst INTEGER 1]

    set vblist [list $vb1]
    set cb [list CP_TestNextCB $sid $addr $cstr]
```

```
      $sid set $addr $authinfo $vblist {} $cb


}
```

CP_TestSetCB is called when the Set operation triggered by CP_InitialSetCB completes. If the Set succeeded, CP_TestSetCB sets ciscoPingEntryStatus to the value corresponding to "active".

```
proc CP_TestNextCB {sid addr cstr result} {
  global gDoneFlag gResult
#
#   Test has been made active!!
#   Check if it has completed.
#
  set errorStatus [GetErrorStatus $result]
  if {$errorStatus != "noError"} {
      CP_TestFailed "CP_TestNextCB" $result
      return
  }
  set cb [list CP_TryAgain $sid $addr $cstr]
  after 10000 $cb
}
```

CP_TestNextCB is next in our chain of callback procedures. At this point, if everything has worked properly, the Cisco Ping is in an active state and we simply want to periodically poll the device to see when the device completes. Since the test comprises 10 pings, each ping being sent one second apart, it makes no sense to test for completion until at least 10 seconds have elapsed. This is done by calling CP_TryAgain after 10000 milliseconds (ten seconds).

```
proc CP_TryAgain {sid addr cstr} {
  global gInst ciscoPingCompleted

  set authinfo [list snmpv1 $cstr]
  set vb [list $ciscoPingCompleted.$gInst]

  set cb [list CP_WaitForCompletionCB $sid $addr $cstr]

  $sid get $addr $authinfo $vb {} $cb
}


proc CP_WaitForCompletionCB {sid addr cstr result} {
  global gDoneFlag gResult
#
```

```
#    Periodically query until test completed.
#
  set errorStatus [GetErrorStatus $result]
  if {$errorStatus != "noError"} {
      CP_TestFailed "CP_WaitForCompletionCB" $result
      return
  }

  set resultVB [GetVarBindList $result]

  set vb1 [GetVarBind $resultVB 1]
  set val [GetValue $vb1]

  if {$val != 1} {
      set cb [list CP_TryAgain $sid $addr $cstr]
      after 5000 $cb
      return
  }

#
#  Test completed! Collect results!
#
  CP_CollectResults $sid $addr $cstr
}
```

CP_WaitForCompletionCB will check the value of ciscoPingCompleted to determine if the test has completed internally within the device. If the test hasn't completed, CP_TryAgain will be called after five seconds to poll again for test completion. If the test has completed, CP_CollectResults will be called.

```
  proc CP_CollectResults {sid addr cstr} {

    global gInst
    global ciscoPingReceivedPackets ciscoPingSentPackets
    global ciscoPingMinRtt ciscoPingAvgRtt ciscoPingMaxRtt

    set authinfo [list snmpv1 $cstr]
    set vblist [list  $ciscoPingReceivedPackets.$gInst \
                      $ciscoPingSentPackets.$gInst \
                      $ciscoPingMinRtt.$gInst \
                      $ciscoPingAvgRtt.$gInst \
                      $ciscoPingMaxRtt.$gInst ]
```

```
    set cb [list CP_CollectResultsCB]

    $sid get $addr $authinfo $vblist {} $cb
}
```

CP_CollectResults issues an SNMP Get command to collect the results of the test. The information collected includes:

- Number of responses received
- Number of packets sent
- Minimum delay time measured
- Average delay time measured
- Maximum delay time measured

```
proc CP_CollectResultsCB {result} {
    global gResult gDoneFlag

    set errorStatus [GetErrorStatus $result]
    if {$errorStatus != "noError"} {
        CP_TestFailed "CP_CollectResultsCB" $result
        return
    }

#
#  Parse varbind list to build test result string.
#
    set descriptions {"Packets Received" "Packets Sent" \
        "Min. Delay" "Average Delay" \
        "Max. Delay"}

    set resultVB [GetVarBindList $result]

    foreach el $resultVB descr $descriptions {
        set val [GetValue $el]
        lappend resultStr [list $descr $val]
    }

    set gResult $resultStr
    set gDoneFlag 1
}
```

CP_CollectResultsCB processes the results, building a list of {description value} pairs. Finally, gResult is set to the list and gDoneFlag is set to notify the CiscoPing procedure that the test completed. Note that Cisco's implementation of this MIB is that if no ICMP echo responses are received, entries for ciscoPingMinRtt, ciscoPing-AvgRtt and ciscoPingMaxRtt are not created. This will cause our SNMP Get operation to return an error of noSuchName.

```
proc CP_TestFailed {name result} {
  global gResult gDoneFlag

  set es [GetErrorStatus $result]
  set ei [GetErrorIndex $result]
  set gResult [list $name $es $ei]
  set gDoneFlag 1
}
```

Wrapping up this example, CP_TestFailed is simply a convenience routine to call if an SNMP operation fails unexpectedly. CP_TestFailed takes as arguments the name of the procedure which detected the failed operation and the corresponding result string. gResult is set to a list containing the procedure name, the error status and the error index. gDoneFlag is then set to notify the CiscoPing procedure that the test completed (unsuccessfully).

```
CiscoPing $sid $ipAddr $remoteAddr $cstr
⇒ {{Packets Received} 10} {{Packets Sent} 10} {{Min. Delay}
104} {{Average Delay} 150} {{Max. Delay} 312}
```

TICKLEMAN—TABLE OPERATIONS

TickleMan offers a powerful table retrieval command. The format for the command is:

```
<session> table <addr> <authinfo> <vblist> \
  <initialInstance> options ?callback?
```

The command should look similar to the SNMP Get, GetNext and Set commands previously discussed. The main differences are:

- <vblist> specifies the columns to be retrieved. The columns can be selected from more than one MIB table; however, if the indices of the tables do not match, the results will not be useful.
- <initialInstance> specifies the starting point within the table. The table command uses the GetNext operation for retrieval, so the next row after

> <initialInstance> will be the first row retrieved. The value must be a dotted form OID. For example, if we wanted to read ipRouteDest entries after address 158.0.0.0, the value of <initialInstance> would have to be set to 158.0.0.0

- For the command to be meaningful, ?callback? must specify a script. If ?callback? is set to the string "wait", the command will be ignored.
- The use of options, as before, allows you to override session options. Two option values are unique to the table command:

  -tableRows controls how many rows are returned at a time.

  -tableMaxRows controls the total number of rows the operation can return.

  Note that the default settings for -tableRows and tableMaxRows are both 4,294,967,295. It is strongly suggested that these values be overridden to something more practical. Also, the command specified by ?callback? is invoked for each set of rows retrieved.

An example of the table command:

```
set op {-tableRows 5 -tableMaxRows 5}
⇒ -tableRows 5 -tableMaxRows 5

set vb {ifType ifAdminStatus ifOperStatus}
⇒ ifType ifAdminStatus ifOperStatus


$sid table $addr {snmpv1 public} $vb {0} $op {puts}
⇒ req510600
⇒ s1 req510600 endOfTable 0 {{ifType.1 INTEGER "6"}
{ifAdminStatus.1 INTEGER "1"} {ifOperStatus.1 INTEGER "1"}
{ifType.2 INTEGER "6"} {ifAdminStatus.2 INTEGER "1"}
{ifOperStatus.2 INTEGER "1"} {ifType.3 INTEGER "39"}
{ifAdminStatus.3 INTEGER "1"} {ifOperStatus.3 INTEGER "1"}
{ifType.4 INTEGER "6"} {ifAdminStatus.4 INTEGER "2"}
{ifOperStatus.4 INTEGER "2"} {ifType.5 INTEGER "6"}
{ifAdminStatus.5 INTEGER "2"} {ifOperStatus.5 INTEGER "2"}}
```

The request identifier associated with the command is returned immediately. Later, when table retrieval completes, the script {puts result-str} is executed. The format of the result string is identical to the string returned by a Get or GetNext operation. For this example, the error status is set to endOfTable. endOfTable indicates that either all the rows from the tables have been retrieved or the number of rows retrieved equals tableMaxRows. In the example we gave, both tableRows and tableMaxRows were set to 5. This caused only five rows to be returned, all at one time.

The following example will retrieve all the rows from a table, one row at a time, and store each row in a global array:

```
proc TableExample {sid addr cstr} {
   global gRowCount gDoneFlag gArray

   set gRowCount 0

   set authinfo [list snmpv1 $cstr]
   set vb {ifType ifAdminStatus ifOperStatus}
   set op {-tableRows 1}
   set cb [list TableExampleCB]

   $sid table $addr $authinfo $vb {0} $op $cb

   vwait gDoneFlag
   puts "Number of rows: $gRowCount"
}

proc TableExampleCB {result} {

   global gRowCount gDoneFlag

   incr gRowCount
   set vblist [GetVarBindList $result]

   AddVarBind $vblist
   set errorStatus [GetErrorStatus $result]
   if {$errorStatus == "endOfTable"} {
       set gDoneFlag 1
   }

}

proc AddVarBind {vblist} {
   global gArray gRowCount
   set gArray($gRowCount) $vblist
}


TableExample $sid $addr public
⇒ Number of rows: 26
```

```
puts $gArray(1)
⇒ {ifType.1 INTEGER "6"} {ifAdminStatus.1 INTEGER "1"}
  {ifOperStatus.1 INTEGER "1"}
```

TICKLEMAN—TRAP HANDLING

With TickleMan, you can perform SNMP trap processing by creating a trap filter and a callback script. The format for creating an SNMP trap filter is:

```
<session> v1trap <options> <callback>
```

where

`<session>` is the name of an SNMP session created with the `-trap` option.

`<options>` can be any of the following:

```
-from <addr>

-genType <integer>

-specType <integer>

-enterprise <OID>
```

which allow you to filter on the IP address of the device generating the trap, the generic trap type, the specific trap code or the type of object generating the trap.

`<callback>` is a string that will be invoked as a script when a trap is received that matches this filter. The following will be appended to this string before it is invoked:

```
<session>
<filter>
<attributes>
<varBindList>
```

An example of this:

```
set tid [snmpsession traps -trap 0.0.0.0:162]
⇒ traps

set cb [list TrapCallback 158.101.121.36]
⇒ TrapCallback 158.101.121.36
```

```
set filterId [$tid v1trap -from 158.101.121.36 $cb]
⇒ filt511f50

proc TrapCallback {addr result} {
  puts "Trap sent from $addr"
  puts $result
}
```

The filter will cause the script {TrapCallback 158.101.121.36 $result-str} to be executed whenever a trap is received from address 158.101.121.36. On receiving a trap, the following output produced by TrapCallback would be something along the lines of:

```
⇒ Trap sent from 158.101.121.36
⇒ traps filt511f50 4 0 enterprises.1575 public 151183 {{}}
```

where the first element in the result string is the session name, followed by the filter name, the generic trap type, the specific trap code, the enterprise number of the device generating the trap, the community string from the trap, the sysUpTime value of the device when the trap was generated and the varbind list associated with the trap. In our example, the generic trap type is 4, indicating an authentication failure. Also, the varbind list is empty.

The following convenience routines can be used to parse a trap result string:

```
proc GetTrapSession {result} {
  return [lindex $result 0]
}

proc GetTrapFilterName {result} {
  return [lindex $result 1]
}

proc GetTrapGenericNum {result} {
  return [lindex $result 2]
}

proc GetTrapSpecificNum {result} {
  return [lindex $result 3]
}

proc GetTrapEnterprise {result} {
  return [lindex $result 4]
}

proc GetTrapCommString {result} {
  return [lindex $result 5]
}
```

```
proc GetTrapSysUpTime {result} {
  return [lindex $result 6]
}

proc GetTrapVarBindList {result} {
  return [lindex $result 7]
}
```

TICKLEMAN—PERFORMING ICMP ECHO REQUESTS

TickleMan allows you to perform ping testing. This is useful in both determining device reachability and measuring network delay. The command format for performing ICMP echo tests is:

```
<session> ping <dest> <size> [?option ...?] wait
```

where,

`<session>` is the name of an SNMP session created with the `-icmp` option.

`<dest>` is an IP address of a remote system to send ICMP echo requests to.

`<size>` is an integer specifying how many bytes of data to place in the ICMP echo request.

`?option?` can override a session option value. The only option value that makes sense for an ICMP test is `-timeout`.

According to the TickleMan documentation, the ICMP echo test should be able to be performed in either blocking or nonblocking mode. During our testing of TickleMan version 14.2, we were only able to use blocking mode. We fully expect this to be fixed by the time this book goes to print. However, our code examples will be for blocking mode only.

```
set sid [snmp s2 -icmp]
⇒ s2

set result [$sid ping www.cisco.com 128 {} wait]
⇒ s2 req554b00 noError
```

First we create a session initialized for ICMP communications. Next we send an ICMP echo request with a data size of 128 bytes to address `www.cisco.com`. The request completes and gives us a result string with the following elements: session name, request identifier and error status. The only two error statuses possible are `noError` and `timeout`. Status `noError` indicates the test was successful; `timeout` indicates the test failed.

The previous example verified that address www.cisco.com was reachable from our workstation. If we wanted to measure the network delay time, we would have used the time command as follows:

```
set cmd [list $sid ping www.cisco.com 128 { } wait]
⇒ s2 ping www.cisco.com 128 { } wait

set x [time {set y [eval $cmd]}]
⇒ 471000 microseconds per iteration
```

which indicates that the test took 471 milliseconds to complete. The time command has the following format: time {*script*}, and it returns a string indicating in microseconds how long it took to execute the given script. In our example, to verify that the test completed successfully and did not time out, we need to examine the variable y:

```
puts $y
⇒ s2 req553a80 noError
```

We could also use the following code to search for the string timeout within y:

```
set n [string first timeout $y]
⇒ -1
```

which will return either –1 if the string timeout is not found within variable y, or a positive number indicating the index of where timeout is found within y.

TICKLEMAN—MIB TREE OPERATIONS

As we showed earlier, OID names can be used instead of OID numbers in an SNMP operation. This is because TickleMan uses a compiled MIB, C:\srconf\mgr\snmpinfo.dat, to obtain the necessary information from an OID name to build an SNMP request. The version of snmpinfo.dat shipped with TickleMan contains standard MIB II. The TickleMan product also contains utilities for compiling MIBs and merging compiled MIBs into snmpinfo.dat.

TickleMan provides several commands for both obtaining information about compiled MIBs and loading in compiled MIBs. The mib_attr will return attributes about a MIB variable. The format for the command is:

```
mib_attr ?-name? ?-oid? ?-type? ?-access? ?-enumers? ?-index?
         ?-size? ?-range? ?-exact? ?acceptLeafParent? <string>
```

Examples of using the `mib_attr` command:

```
mib_attr ifInErrors
⇒ ifInErrors 1.3.6.1.2.1.2.2.1.14 Counter read-only {}
{ifIndex 0} {} {}

mib_attr -oid ifType
⇒ 1.3.6.1.2.1.2.2.1.3

mib_attr -name 1.3.6.1.2.1.2.2.1.3.1
⇒ ifType
```

In the above example, we provided as a string an OID number with an instance appended to it.

```
mib_attr -type -access ifType
⇒ INTEGER read-only

mib_attr -index ifType
⇒ {ifIndex 0}
```

The 0 in the list indicates that the length of the last index is not implied; a 1 would indicate that the length of the last index is implied.

```
mib_attr -size sysDescr
⇒ {{0 255}}

mib_attr -enumers ifType
⇒ {{1 other} {2 regular1822} {3 hdh1822} {4 ddn-x25} {5
rfc877-x25} {6 ethernet-csmacd} {7 iso88023-csmacd} {8
iso88024-tokenBus} {9 iso88025-tokenRing} {10 iso88026-man}
{11 starLan} {12 proteon-10Mbit} {13 proteon-80Mbit} {14 hy-
perchannel} {15 fddi} {16 lapb} {17 sdlc} {18 ds1} {19 e1} {20
basicISDN} {21 primaryISDN} {22 propPointToPointSerial} {23
ppp} {24 softwareLoopback} {25 eon} {26 ethernet-3Mbit} {27
nsip} {28 slip} {29 ultra} {30 ds3} {31 sip} {32 frame-relay}}
```

The above example shows the enumerated values for MIB variable `ifType` mapped to their corresponding string descriptions. We will now write a simple routine which, given a MIB variable and an enumerated value, will return the corresponding string value. If no mapping is found, the enumerated value is simply returned. This procedure will allow you to translate the results from an SNMP Get operation into a more meaningful string.

```
proc MapEnumToString {mibvar enumval} {
```

```
set result [mib_attr -enumers $mibvar]
if {[llength $result] == 0} {return $enumval}
set x [lindex $result 0]
foreach el $x {
       if {[lindex $el 0] == $enumval} {
             return [lindex $el 1]
       }
}
return $enumval
}


MapEnumToString ifType 6
⇒ ethernet-csmacd

MapEnumToString ifType 15
⇒ fddi
```

If the specified MIB variable has not been loaded, `mib_attr` will return information about the first parent object loaded. If the `-acceptLeafParent` option is specified, only a parent object which is also a leaf node (i.e, not an entry or table object) will be used. If the `-exact` option is specified, only the specified object will be used.

TICKLEMAN—CONVENIENCE COMMANDS

TickleMan provides a set of miscellaneous conversion commands.
The **char_to_int** command converts a character to its ascii decimal value.

```
char_to_int A
⇒ 65
```

The **random_byte** command returns a random value from 0 to 255.

```
random_byte
⇒ 247
```

```
random_byte
⇒ 89
```

The **oid2dot** command converts an OID Name to an OID Number in dotted format.

```
oid2dot sysName
⇒ 1.3.6.1.2.1.1.5
```

The **dot2oid** command converts a dotted form OID Number to an OID Name.

```
dot2oid 1.3.6.1.2.1.1.5.0
⇒ sysName.0
```

The **xor_key** commands takes a two-octet string in "xx:xx:xx: ... :xx" form, both of the same length, and performs an exclusive or operation on each byte.

```
xor_keys "f0:0f" "f0:f0"
⇒ 00 ff
```

The **octet2text** command converts an octet string to a text string.

```
octet2text {54 69 63 6b 6c 65 4d 61 6e}
⇒ TickleMan
```

The **text2octet** command coverts a text string to an octet string.

```
text2octet "TickleMan"
⇒ 54 69 63 6b 6c 65 4d 61 6e
```

The **octet2inst** command converts an octet string to a dotted OID instance.

```
octet2inst {c0 1f 07 82}
⇒ 192.31.7.130
```

The **host2addr** command converts a hostname or a dotted IP address to an octet string.

```
host2addr www.cisco.com
⇒ c0 1f 07 82
```

```
host2addr 192.31.7.130
⇒ c0 1f 07 82
```

SCOTTY

The Tnm (Tcl extensions for network management applications) package within Scotty is rather broad in scope. For this book, we will be focussing on four of the commands within Tnm:

- `snmp`, which provides for SNMP extensions.
- `mib`, which allows SNMP MIB definitions to be loaded and queried.
- `icmp`, which allows you to send ICMP messages.
- `dns`, which among other things, allows you to translate a domain name to an IP address.

In writing this book, we used an early version of the commercially available version of Tnm 3.0. Hopefully, there will only be at most a few minor changes between what we describe in this chapter and what is eventually released. For those of you familiar with earlier versions of Tnm, you will notice that SNMP sessions are now created differently and that the `mib` command has been extended.

Tnm 3.0 is based on Tcl 8.0 and will not work with earlier versions of Tcl. To use the Tnm commands, you must first load the Tnm package and then import its namespace by using the following commands:

```
package require Tnm 3.0
namespace import Tnm::*
```

As a final note, the snapshot we were given did not support receiving traps. We have been told that this will be fixed by the time Tnm 3.0 is released to the public.

SCOTTY—MANAGING SESSIONS

Just as with TickleMan, all SNMP operations within Scotty are performed within the context of a session. For Tnm 3.0, the `snmp` command to create a session has changed slightly. To create a session that can generate an SNMP request, you use the `snmp generator` command:

```
snmp generator
⇒ snmp0
```

A generator session can be configured with the following options:

-address, IP address to send SNMP requests to. The value may be in either dotted notation or a hostname that can be resolved to an IP address (default:127.0.0.1).

-port, UDP port number to send SNMP requests to (default 161).

-version, SNMP version to use (default SNMPv1).

-community, read community string (default public).

-writecommunity, write community string (default private).

-timeout, SNMP timeout value in seconds (default 5 seconds).

-retries, SNMP retry count (default 3).

-window, the number of asynchronous requests that can be outstanding. This option is used to keep a script from accidentally flooding an agent with SNMP requests (default 10).

-delay, the amount of delay in milliseconds to introduce between consecutive SNMP requests (default 0).

-tags, a list of arbitrary tag values that can be assigned to a session. The snmp find command can be used to find all sessions with associated tags.

The following example will create an SNMP session that can generate SNMP requests to IP address 158.101.121.58, using read community string xpublic and write community string xprivate:

```
set s [snmp generator -address 158.101.121.58 \
                -community xpublic \
                -writecommunity xprivate]
⇒ snmp1
```

The above command returns the name of the newly created session. Once a session is created, its configuration can be both obtained and changed. The command:

```
$s configure
⇒ -address 158.101.121.58 -port 161 -version SNMPv1 -commu-
nity xpublic -writecommunity xprivate -timeout 5 -retries 3 -
window 10 -delay 0 -tags {}
```

returns the configuration for the session. The command:

```
$s cget -address
⇒ 158.101.121.58
```

can be used to return a single option value for a session. To change the configuration of a session, you can use the configure command with pairs of option names and values. For example:

```
$s configure -delay 10 -window 30
⇒ -address 158.101.121.58 -port 161 -version SNMPv1 -commu-
nity xpublic -writecommunity xprivate -timeout 5 -retries 3 -
window 30 -delay 10 -tags {}
```

Changing a session's configuration will cause the command to block until all pending SNMP requests for that session have completed. Once all pending SNMP requests have completed, the session's configuration will be modified. Because of this, it is recommended that you create a session for every IP address/community string value pair (a chassis device using a proxy mechanism could require different community strings to access different MIB objects) that you use. You can manage your SNMP sessions with the following routines:

```
proc getSession {addr rcomm wrcomm} {

    set s [snmp find -tags "$addr,$rcomm,$wrcomm"]
    if {[string length $s] > 0} {return [lindex $s 0]}
```

```
    return [snmp generator -address $addr \
            -community $rcomm \
            -writecommunity $wrcomm \
            -tags "$addr,$rcomm,$wrcomm"]
}

proc destroySession {addr rcomm wrcomm} {
    set slist [snmp find -tags "$addr,$rcomm,$wrcomm"]
    foreach el $slist {
        $el destroy
    }
}
```

In the routine destroy session, the command:

```
$el destroy
```

destroys the session. All data associated with the session is removed and any pending asynchronous SNMP requests are canceled.

The following command will either create a new session if one doesn't exist for IP address `158.101.121.58`, with read community string `xpublic` and read-write community string `xprivate` or return the previously created session.

```
set s [getSession 158.101.121.58 xpublic xprivate]
⇒ snmp1
```

We will wrap up this section by showing that you can create aliases for common configuration options, and you can use these aliases in configuring a session. Typically, aliases are used to bundle options for a specific device or a set of devices. The format for the `snmp alias` command is:

```
snmp alias aliasName "-optionName value ?-optionName value?"
```

For example:

```
snmp alias hub-cstr "-community hubpublic \
   -writecommunity hubprivate"
snmp alias slow "-window 2 -delay 5"
```

will create aliases with the names `hub-cstr` and `slow`. We can then use these aliases in configuring a session:

```
$s configure -alias hub-cstr -alias slow
```

SCOTTY—BUILDING VARBIND LISTS

Building a varbind list in Scotty is virtually identical to building one in TickleMan. In Scotty, as with TickleMan, you can use either an OID Name (if you have loaded the corresponding MIB) or an OID Number with an optional instance appended to it. With Scotty, MIB II is automatically loaded. The following is an example varbind list that can be used for the SNMP Get operation:

```
set vblist [list ifInOctets.1 ifInErrors.1 ifInDiscards.1]
```

For an SNMP Set operation, if you're using MIB variables from a loaded MIB file, each varbind within a varbind list must be a list containing minimally an OID and a value. If you are using MIB variables from a MIB that has not been loaded, each varbind must be a list consisiting of an OID, a type and a value. Again, if you are using MIB variables from a loaded MIB file, you may use either the enumerated string (if the MIB variable has one defined) for a value or the actual integer value. The following are valid varbind lists that can be used in an SNMP Set operation:

```
#
# Create a varbind using MIB variables that have been loaded.
#
set vblist [list [list ifAdminStatus.1 up] \
                 [list ifAdminStatus.2 down]]


#
# Create a varbind using OID Numbers.
#

set protoclDirHostConfig     1.3.6.1.2.1.16.11.2.1.7
set protocolDirMatrixConfig  1.3.6.1.2.1.16.11.2.1.8

set vblist [list \
[list $protocolDirHostConfig.$prot.$param INTEGER 2] \
[list $protocolDirMatrixConfig.$prot.$param INTEGER 2]]
```

In the above example, `$prot.$param` defines the instance for these two RMONv2 MIB variables.

Finally, if you are specifying the type within a varbind, Scotty expects the type to be one of the following:

```
OCTET STRING, OBJECT IDENTIFIER, IpAddress, TimeTicks, INTE-
GER, Integer32, Counter, Counter32, Gauge, Gauge32, Unsigned32 or
Counter64.
```

SCOTTY—PERFORMING SNMPv1 OPERATIONS

Scotty has identical capabilities to TickleMan in being able to perform either blocking or nonblocking SNMP Get, GetNext and Set operations. In this section, we will briefly show how to perform blocking SNMP operations; in the following section we will demonstrate how to perform nonblocking or asynchronous operations.

The format for an SNMP Get, GetNext or Set command is:

```
sessionId command varbindlist
```

where `command` is either `get`, `getnext` or `set`. If the operation completes successfully, the varbind list of the resulting string is returned. For example:

```
set result [$s get [list ifInOctets.1 ifInErrors.1]]
⇒ {1.3.6.1.2.1.2.2.1.10.1 Counter32 200156886}
{1.3.6.1.2.1.2.2.1.14.1 Counter32 72}

llength $result
⇒ 2
```

However, if an SNMP error occurred, an error would be thrown, with an error string being made up of a list composed of the SNMP error, error index and varbind list. For example:

```
set result [$s get [list ifInOctets.1 ifInErrors.4]]
⇒ noSuchName 1 {1.3.6.1.2.1.2.2.1.10.1 NULL {}}
{1.3.6.1.2.1.2.2.1.14.4 NULL {}}
```

In the above example, the error index is 1. Tnm uses Tcl index values for varbind lists that start from 0 instead of SNMP index values that start from 1. So, an error index of 1 refers to the second varbind in the list. TickleMan uses error index values starting at 1, so in the above example, it would return an error index of 2.

If an SNMP timeout occurs, an error is thrown with an error string `noResponse`. Because of this behavior, SNMP commands should be performed within a `catch` command. For example:

```
catch {set result [$s get $vblist]} err
```

would return 0 if the SNMP Get operation completed successfully; otherwise, it would return 1 and set `err` to the thrown error string.

If you are using a loaded MIB, and you are using MIB variables with enumerated string values, the enumerated value will be substituted for the corresponding integer value within the returned varbind. For example:

```
$s get ifOperStatus.1
⇒ {1.3.6.1.2.1.2.2.1.8.1 INTEGER up}
```

If you want to convert "up" to its actual integer value, you have to do it explicitly. We will show how to do this later when we discuss the `mib` command.

In the past, Tnm would return a TimeTicks value as a string, representing the value as a number of days, hours, minutes and seconds. This would be inconvenient if you needed the value represented as an integer so, for example, it could be used to generate an RMONv2 time filter. Tnm 3.0 fixes this by returning TimeTicks as a number.

Tnm automatically applies display-hints defined in SNMPv2 MIBs. In the example below, the `OctetString` returned for `sysDescr` is converted to text. Formatting `DisplayStrings` is just one example of this general feature. It also works for `PhysAddress`, `MacAddress` or `DateAndTime`.

```
$s get sysDescr.0
⇒ {1.3.6.1.2.1.1.1.0 {OCTET STRING} {NetScout Model 6010
V4.0.0}}
```

We will wrap up this section by demonstrating an SNMP Set operation.

```
set vblist [list [list ifAdminStatus.3 2]]
⇒ {ifAdminStatus.3 2}

catch {set result [$s set $vblist]} err
⇒ 0

puts $result
⇒ {1.3.6.1.2.1.2.2.1.7.3 INTEGER down}
```

In the above example, we first built a varbind list composed of a single varbind with an OID Name and value. We were able to ignore the type since the MIB variable is part of a loaded MIB. The `catch` command returned a zero, indicating that the SNMP Set operation completed successfully. The returned varbind list has a single varbind, with the enumerated string value down substituted for the integer 2.

SCOTTY—NONBLOCKING SNMP OPERATIONS

Scotty, like TickleMan, allows you to perform nonblocking or asynchronous SNMP operations. By appending an optional script to the end of an SNMP Get, GetNext or Set command, the command will send the corresponding SNMP command immediately and return. The result of the command is the request ID for the asynchronous request. When the SNMP command completes, the script will be called. Special % escape sequences can be used in the callback script to access details contained in the SNMP response. These escape sequences are substituted before the callback script is evaluated. The following % escape sequences are defined:

   `%%`   replace with a single percent character.

%V   replace with the resulting varbind list.

%R   replace with the resulting request ID.

%S   replace with the session name.

%E   replace with the error status. Possible values:

noError, tooBig, noSuchName, badValue, readOnly, gen-
Err, noAccess, wrongType, wrongLength, wrongEncoding,
wrongValue, noCreation, inconsistentValue, resource-
Unavailable, commitFailed, undoFailed, authorizationError,
notWriteable, inconsistentName and noResponse.

%I   replace with the error index, starting at position 0.

%A   replace with the IP address of the device sending the SNMP packet.

%P   replace with the port number of the device sending the SNMP packet.

%T   replace with the SNMP PDU type. Possible values:

get-request, get-next-request, response, snmpV1-trap,
set-request, get-bulk-request, inform-request, snmpV2-trap
and report.

The following callback script will generate a list identical to the result string that an asynchronous TickleMan SNMP command produces:

```
set cb "cbroutine {%S %R %E %I {%V} %A \
        {[list snmpv1 $comm]}}"
```

For example:

```
proc cbroutine {result} {
    puts "SessionName = [GetSessionName $result]"
    puts "RequestID = [GetReqID $result]"
    puts "ErrorStatus = [GetErrorStatus $result]"
    puts "ErrorIndex = [GetErrorIndex $result]"
    puts "VarBindList = [GetVarBindList $result]"
}

catch {set result [$s getnext sysDescr  $cb]} err
⇒ 0
```

will produce a 0 as the result of the catch command. When the SNMP GetNext operation completes, cbroutine will be called, generating the following output:

```
SessionName = snmp1
RequestID = 6102
ErrorStatus = noError
ErrorIndex = -1
```

```
VarBindList = {1.3.6.1.2.1.1.1.0 {OCTET STRING} {NetScout
Model 6010 V4.0.0}}
```

You can block until all ayncbronous requests for a session have been processed by using the `session# wait` command. For example:

```
proc demoWait {addr comm} {

    set s [snmp generator -address $addr -community $comm]
    $s get {ifIndex.1 ifInErrors.1 ifInOctets.1} {puts "%V"}
    $s get {ifIndex.2 ifInErrors.2 ifInOctets.2} {puts "%V"}
    $s get {ifIndex.3 ifInErrors.3 ifInOctets.3} {puts "%V"}

    $s wait
    puts "completed!"
}

demoWait $addr $comm
⇒ {1.3.6.1.2.1.2.2.1.1.1 INTEGER 1} {1.3.6.1.2.1.2.2.1.14.1
Counter32 72} {1.3.6.1.2.1.2.2.1.10.1 Counter32 206809184}
⇒ {1.3.6.1.2.1.2.2.1.1.2 INTEGER 2} {1.3.6.1.2.1.2.2.1.14.2
Counter32 0} {1.3.6.1.2.1.2.2.1.10.2 Counter32 0}
⇒ {1.3.6.1.2.1.2.2.1.1.3 INTEGER 3} {1.3.6.1.2.1.2.2.1.14.3
Counter32 0} {1.3.6.1.2.1.2.2.1.10.3 Counter32 0}
⇒ completed!
```

To wrap up this section, we will now provide the complete `CiscoPing` application, which we built earlier under TickleMan. It now has been converted to run under Scotty.

```
set ciscoPingProtocol        1.3.6.1.4.1.9.9.16.1.1.1.2
set ciscoPingAddress         1.3.6.1.4.1.9.9.16.1.1.1.3
set ciscoPingPacketCount     1.3.6.1.4.1.9.9.16.1.1.1.4
set ciscoPingPacketSize      1.3.6.1.4.1.9.9.16.1.1.1.5
set ciscoPingPacketTimeout   1.3.6.1.4.1.9.9.16.1.1.1.6
set ciscoPingDelay           1.3.6.1.4.1.9.9.16.1.1.1.7
set ciscoPingSentPackets     1.3.6.1.4.1.9.9.16.1.1.1.9
set ciscoPingReceivedPackets 1.3.6.1.4.1.9.9.16.1.1.1.10
set ciscoPingMinRtt          1.3.6.1.4.1.9.9.16.1.1.1.11
set ciscoPingAvgRtt          1.3.6.1.4.1.9.9.16.1.1.1.12
set ciscoPingMaxRtt          1.3.6.1.4.1.9.9.16.1.1.1.13
set ciscoPingCompleted       1.3.6.1.4.1.9.9.16.1.1.1.14
set ciscoPingEntryOwner      1.3.6.1.4.1.9.9.16.1.1.1.15
set ciscoPingEntryStatus     1.3.6.1.4.1.9.9.16.1.1.1.16
```

```
set gRSFormat {%S %R %E %I {%V}}

proc convertAddressToOctetString {addr} {
    set n [split $addr .]
    set x [format "%02x:%02x:%02x:%02x" \
            [lindex $n 0] [lindex $n 1] \
            [lindex $n 2] [lindex $n 3]]
    return $x
}
```

In our TickleMan example, we used the TickleMan routine host2addr to convert an IP address to an octet string. Here we provide the routine convertAddressToOctetString to perform conversion. To convert the address, we first split it into a list of four numbers and then use the format command to convert each number into a hex value. Note that the reason we used the format string "%02x:%02x:%02x:%02x" is that each element of the octet string had to be a two-digit hex value for Scotty to work properly.

```
proc GetRandom {} {
    return [expr int(rand() * 65536 + 1)]
}
```

The GetRandom routine, which we showed earlier, made use of a TickleMan convenience routine, random_byte, to generate a random number. Here we use the Tcl 8.0 rand() function to generate a random number between 0 and 1.

```
proc CiscoPing {addr remoteAddr cstr} {
    global gDoneFlag gResult

    set s [getSession $addr $cstr $cstr]

    set gDoneFlag 0
    CP_StartCiscoPing $s $addr $remoteAddr

    vwait gDoneFlag

    puts $gResult
}
```

In the CiscoPing routine we used the getSession routine, which we built earlier in this Scotty section. Subsequent routines making up the CiscoPing application required only minor changes to port them from TickleMan to Scotty. By using the format string {%S %R %E %I {%V}}, we were able to provide the callback routines with the same result string format that was used in the original TickleMan code. In the TickleMan version, we passed the community string value into the procedures needing to generate SNMP commands. We no longer have to do this since the community string is configured into the SNMP session that we built. The only other difference between this code and the original TickleMan example is the format of the snmp command.

```
proc CP_StartCiscoPing {s addr remoteAddr} {
    global gInst ciscoPingEntryStatus gRSFormat
#
#    First, find a valid serial number. This is done
#    by picking one at random and making sure it is not being
#    used.
#
    set gInst [GetRandom]
    set vb [list $ciscoPingEntryStatus.$gInst]
    set cb [list CP_SerialNumberCB $s $addr $remoteAddr \
        $gRSFormat]

    set result [$s get $vb $cb]
}

proc CP_SerialNumberCB {s addr remoteAddr result} {
#
#    If error status == noError, serial number already being
#    used, choose another.
#
#    If error status == noSuchName, we found an unused serial
#        number and can proceed with the test.
#
#    Any other error, cause test to fail.
#
    global gInst gDoneFlag gResult gRSFormat
    global ciscoPingEntryStatus ciscoPingEntryOwner
    global ciscoPingProtocol ciscoPingAddress

    set errorStatus [GetErrorStatus $result]
    if {$errorStatus == "noError"} {
        CP_StartCiscoPing $s $addr $remoteAddr
        return
    }

    if {$errorStatus != "noSuchName"} {
        CP_TestFailed "CP_SerialNumberCB" $result
        return
```

```
    }

    set os [convertAddressToOctetString $remoteAddr]

    set vb1 [list $ciscoPingEntryStatus.$gInst INTEGER 5]
    set vb2 [list $ciscoPingProtocol.$gInst INTEGER 1]
    set vb3 [list $ciscoPingAddress.$gInst \
        {OCTET STRING} $os]

    set vblist [list $vb1 $vb2 $vb3]

    set cb [list CP_InitialSetCB $s $addr \
        $gRSFormat]

    set result [$s set $vblist $cb]
}


proc CP_InitialSetCB {s addr result} {
    global gDoneFlag gResult gRSFormat
    global gInst ciscoPingPacketCount ciscoPingPacketSize
    global ciscoPingDelay

    set errorStatus [GetErrorStatus $result]
    if {$errorStatus != "noError"} {
        CP_TestFailed "CP_InitialSetCB" $result
        return
    }

    set vb1 [list $ciscoPingPacketCount.$gInst INTEGER 10]
    set vb2 [list $ciscoPingPacketSize.$gInst INTEGER 128]
    set vb3 [list $ciscoPingDelay.$gInst INTEGER 1000]

    set vblist [list $vb1 $vb2 $vb3]

    set cb [list CP_TestSetCB $s $addr \
        $gRSFormat]

    set result [$s set $vblist $cb]

}
```

```
proc CP_TestSetCB {s addr result} {
  global gDoneFlag gResult gRSFormat
  global gInst ciscoPingEntryStatus
#
#   Test has been set up - make it active!!
#
  set errorStatus [GetErrorStatus $result]
  if {$errorStatus != "noError"} {
      CP_TestFailed "CP_TestSetCB" $result
      return
  }

  set vb1 [list $ciscoPingEntryStatus.$gInst INTEGER 1]

  set vblist [list $vb1]
  set cb [list CP_TestNextCB $s $addr $gRSFormat]

  set result [$s set $vblist $cb]

}

proc CP_TestNextCB {s addr result} {
  global gDoneFlag gResult
#
#   Test has been made active!!
#   Check if it has completed.
#
  set errorStatus [GetErrorStatus $result]
  if {$errorStatus != "noError"} {
      CP_TestFailed "CP_TestNextCB" $result
      return
  }

  set cb [list CP_TryAgain $s $addr]
  after 10000 $cb

}


proc CP_TryAgain {s addr} {
  global gInst ciscoPingCompleted gRSFormat
```

```
    set vb [list $ciscoPingCompleted.$gInst]

    set cb [list CP_WaitForCompletionCB $s $addr $gRSFormat]

    set result [$s get $vb $cb]
}

proc CP_WaitForCompletionCB {s addr result} {
  global gDoneFlag gResult
#
#   Periodically query until test completed.
#
  set errorStatus [GetErrorStatus $result]
  if {$errorStatus != "noError"} {
        CP_TestFailed "CP_WaitForCompletionCB" $result
        return
  }

  set vblist [GetVarBindList $result]
  set vb [GetVarBind $vblist 1]
  set val [GetValue $vb]

  if {$val != 1} {
        puts "Polling For Test Complete!"
        set cb [list CP_TryAgain $s $addr]
        after 5000 $cb
        return
  }

#
#  Test completed! Collect results!
#
  CP_CollectResults $s $addr
}


proc CP_CollectResults {s addr} {

  global gInst gRSFormat
  global ciscoPingReceivedPackets ciscoPingSentPackets
```

```
    global ciscoPingMinRtt ciscoPingAvgRtt ciscoPingMaxRtt

    set vblist [list  $ciscoPingReceivedPackets.$gInst \
                      $ciscoPingSentPackets.$gInst \
                      $ciscoPingMinRtt.$gInst \
                      $ciscoPingAvgRtt.$gInst \
                      $ciscoPingMaxRtt.$gInst ]

    set cb [list CP_CollectResultsCB $gRSFormat]

    set result [$s get $vblist $cb]
}

proc CP_CollectResultsCB {result} {
    global gResult gDoneFlag

    set errorStatus [GetErrorStatus $result]
    if {$errorStatus != "noError"} {
        CP_TestFailed "CP_CollectResultsCB" $result
        return
    }

#
#  Parse varbind list to build test result string.
#
    set descriptions {"Packets Received" "Packets Sent" \
            "Min. Delay"  "Average Delay" "Max. Delay"}

    set resultVB [GetVarBindList $result]

    foreach el $resultVB descr $descriptions {
        set val [GetValue $el]
        lappend resultStr [list $descr $val]
    }

    set gResult $resultStr
    set gDoneFlag 1
}

proc CP_TestFailed {name result} {
    global gResult gDoneFlag
```

```
    set es [GetErrorStatus $result]
    set ei [GetErrorIndex $result]
    set gResult [list $name $es $ei]
    set gDoneFlag 1
}
```

SCOTTY—SNMP WALK COMMAND

Scotty provides two commands to collect subtrees from a MIB table. The first command, walk, is in practice similar to TickleMan's `table` operation with several exceptions. First, the command will block until the collection is complete, while TickleMan's `table` operation is performed asynchronously. Second, you cannot specify a starting instance. For example, with Tickle-Man, you could collect a subset of the IP route table information after a certain address. With Scotty, you must collect the complete subtree.

The format for the `walk` command is:

```
sessionId walk varName varbindlist script
```

For example:

```
set s [snmp generator -address $addr -community $comm]
$s walk x {ifInOctets ifOutOctets} {puts $x}
⇒ {1.3.6.1.2.1.2.2.1.10.1 Counter32 206887523}
{1.3.6.1.2.1.2.2.1.16.1 Counter32 0}
{1.3.6.1.2.1.2.2.1.10.2 Counter32 0} {1.3.6.1.2.1.2.2.1.16.2
Counter32 0}
{1.3.6.1.2.1.2.2.1.10.3 Counter32 0} {1.3.6.1.2.1.2.2.1.16.3
Counter32 0}
```

In the above example, after each collection, variable x is assigned the response varbind list before executing the script `puts $x`.

The second command, tentatively named `zzz`, allows you to perform an asynchronous walk:

```
$s zzz {ifInOctets ifInErrors} {puts "%E %V"}
⇒ noError {1.3.6.1.2.1.2.2.1.10.1 Counter32 234973315}
{1.3.6.1.2.1.2.2.1.14.1 Counter32 72}
⇒ noError {1.3.6.1.2.1.2.2.1.10.2 Counter32 0}
{1.3.6.1.2.1.2.2.1.14.2 Counter32 0}
⇒ noError {1.3.6.1.2.1.2.2.1.10.3 Counter32 0}
{1.3.6.1.2.1.2.2.1.14.3 Counter32 0}
```

Rewriting `TableExample` from the TickleMan section to use the `zzz` command:

```
proc TableExample {addr cstr} {
      global gArray
      set vb [list ifType ifAdminStatus ifOperStatus]
      set s [snmp generator -address \
                  $addr -community $cstr]
      $s zzz $vb {
          if {"%E" == "noError"} {
              set gArray([expr [array size gArray] + 1]) "%V"
          }
      }
      $s wait
      $s destroy
      puts "Number of rows: [array size gArray]"
      parray gArray
}
```

```
TableExample $addr public
⇒ Number of rows: 3
gArray(1) = {1.3.6.1.2.1.2.2.1.3.1 INTEGER ethernetCsmacd}
{1.3.6.1.2.1.2.2.1.7.1 INTEGER up} {1.3.6.1.2.1.2.2.1.8.1 IN-
TEGER up}
gArray(2) = {1.3.6.1.2.1.2.2.1.3.2 INTEGER slip}
{1.3.6.1.2.1.2.2.1.7.2 INTEGER up} {1.3.6.1.2.1.2.2.1.8.2 IN-
TEGER up}
gArray(3) = {1.3.6.1.2.1.2.2.1.3.3 INTEGER ethernetCsmacd}
{1.3.6.1.2.1.2.2.1.7.3 INTEGER up} {1.3.6.1.2.1.2.2.1.8.3 IN-
TEGER up}
```

We have been told that a status code will be added to indicate when the end of a walk has been reached. This will allow the `zzz` command to be used similarly to TickleMan's `table` command.

SCOTTY—GENERATING TRAPS

Scotty provides a mechanism for generating traps. If you are building a network management tool to process device traps, having the capability to simulate traps is invaluable. Equally invaluable is being able to send application-specific traps to a platform such as HP OpenView. With this capability you could distribute status monitoring tools throughout your network and sync event information, such as a high error rate detected on a device interface, to a single point.

To generate an SNMP trap, you first must create an SNMP session with the `snmp notifier` command. You can then use the SNMP `trap` command to generate a trap message. The format for the SNMP `trap` command is:

```
sessionId trap snmpTrapOid varbindlist
```

For example:

```
set s2 [snmp notifier -address $addr]
$s2 trap coldStart [list [list sysDescr.0 "bogus"]]
```

will send a cold start trap to the address specified by the variable `addr`. The trap will have the varbind list `{{sysDescr.0 "bogus"}}`. Note that the value of `sysUpTime.0` is automatically added to the trap message.

An enterprise-specific trap can be sent by appending the generic trap type and specific trap code to the enterpise OID Number. Given the enterprise number for Cisco is 9, the following example will generate a Cisco enterprise-specific trap, with the specific trap number `100` (the authors have no idea if this is a defined Cisco trap):

```
$s2 trap enterprises.9.6.100 [list [list ifOperStatus.1 1]]
```

The default configuration for a session created by `snmp notifier` can be obtained by using the `configure` command:

```
set trapsession [snmp notifier]
$trapsession configure
⇒ -address 127.0.0.1 -port 162 -version SNMPv1 -community
public -timeout 5 -retries 3 -window 10 -delay 0 -tags {}
```

The –timeout and –retries options, however, do not apply to SNMPv1 traps.

SCOTTY—NAME-TO-IP ADDRESS TRANSLATION

Scotty provides a `dns` command that allows you to translate a domain name into an IP address, and vice versa. With the `dns` command, you can specify as options which DNS servers to use (`-server`, the default, is a list of DNS servers configured on the local machine), the timeout value to use (`-timeout`, default 2 seconds) and a retry count (`-retries`, default 2). The `dns` command always asks a DNS server to resolve names or addresses, thus you cannot resolve names that are not known by the DNS.

To translate a hostname into an IP address:

```
dns address ?-option value ... option value? name
```

For example:

```
dns address www.cisco.com
⇒ 192.31.7.130
```

```
dns address 192.31.7.130
⇒ 192.31.7.130
```

To translate an IP address into a domain name:

```
dns name ?-option value ... option value? name
```

For example:

```
dns name 192.31.7.130
⇒ cio-sys.cisco.com
```

SCOTTY—PERFORMING ICMP ECHO REQUESTS

Scotty allows you to send ICMP echo requests, which you can use to perform network reachability tests, network delay measurements and traceroutes. We will be focusing on two `icmp` commands: one that returns network delay and another in which you can set the time-to-live (ttl) field, to obtain either the destination address or the address of the device that discarded the packet (this will be used for performing a traceroute). The format for these two commands is:

```
icmp ?-option value ... -option value? echo hosts
```

or

```
icmp ?-option value ... -option value? trace num hosts
```

Possible options are:

-timeout, the time in seconds the `icmp` command will wait for a response (default 5 seconds).

-retries, how many times a request is retransmitted during the timeout interval (default 2).

-delay, the minimum delay in milliseconds between sending two ICMP packets (default 0).

-size, the size of the ICMP packet in bytes (default 64).

-window, the maximum number of active asynchronous requests that can be outstanding (default 10). A value of 0 turns the windowing mechanism off.

Examples of using icmp to measure both reachability and network delay:

```
set hosts [list www.cisco.com www.3Com.com www.baynetworks.com]
set result [icmp echo $hosts]
⇒ www.cisco.com 221 www.3Com.com 251 www.baynetworks.com 321


foreach {host rtt} $result {puts "$host $rtt"}
⇒ www.cisco.com 221
www.3Com.com 251
www.baynetworks.com 321
```

In the following example, you can see that the round-trip time increases as we increase the packet size from 64 bytes (the default) to 128 bytes:

```
icmp -size 128 echo $hosts
www.cisco.com 251 www.3Com.com 291 www.baynetworks.com 411
```

We will now use the icmp trace command to trace a route to a destination address:

```
proc traceroute {addr} {

  set route ""

  set addr [dns address $addr]
  set i 1
  while {1} {

        if [catch {icmp trace $i $addr} result] {
            return $route
        }

        set dest [lindex $result 0]
        if {$dest == [lrange $route end end]} {
            return $route
        }
        lappend route $dest
        if {$dest == $addr} {
            return $route
```

```
        }

        incr i
    }
}
```

The first thing we do is use the `dns address` command to make sure the address we are using is in dotted notation. We then simply go through a loop, starting with a ttl value of 1, and perform a trace, incrementing the ttl value after each iteration. When the destination address equals the address we are trying to trace a route to, we return. Note that if a timeout occurs, we will catch it and return the partial route that we calculated. Also, to protect against an endless loop on a multi-homed device, we check to see if the current returned address equals the previously returned address, and return if it does.

```
traceroute www.cisco.com
⇒ 206.115.150.129 207.76.44.2 137.39.82.22 137.39.22.121
4.0.2.73 4.0.2.249 4.0.2.246 4.0.3.166 4.0.2.198 131.119.0.201
131.119.26.10 192.31.7.39 192.31.7.130
```

SCOTTY—MIB COMMAND

The `mib` command has been extended significantly for Tnm 3.0. In this section we will focus on what we consider the most useful of these extended commands.

mib load

The `mib load` command allows you to load SNMP MIB files and access SNMP MIB definitions. Scotty comes packaged with a large number of RFC MIB files in the `$tnm(library)/mibs` directory. The `mib load` command will automatically try to locate the file in the `$tnm(library)/site` and the `$tnm(library)/mibs` directory if the file does not exist in the current directory.

By loading a MIB, you can use OID Names and enumerated values within your code, instead of having to define the corresponding OID Numbers and integer values. Also, when performing a SET operation, you can build a varbind consisting of the OID and value, as opposed to building a varbind with the OID, type and value. If we use the `mib load` command to load the RMONv2 MIB definition (rfc2021), we can then refer to the RMON2 MIB variables by their OID Names:

```
mib load rfc2021.mib
set s [snmp generator -address $addr]
$s getnext {protocolDirLocalIndex protocolDirDescr \
        protocolDirStatus}
⇒ {1.3.6.1.2.1.16.11.2.1.3.8.1.0.0.1.0.0.0.240.2.0.0 INTEGER
917511} {1.3.6.1.2.1.16.11.2.1.4.8.1.0.0.1.0.0.0.240.2.0.0
{OCTET STRING} NETB}
{1.3.6.1.2.1.16.11.2.1.10.8.1.0.0.1.0.0.0.240.2.0.0 INTEGER
active}
```

Notice in this example that the enumerated string value "active" for `protocolDirStatus` was substituted for the returned integer value (1).

We could have performed the same operation without loading the `rfc2021` MIB by providing the OID Numbers directly:

```
set protocolDirLocalIndex 1.3.6.1.2.1.16.11.2.1.3
set protocolDirDescr      1.3.6.1.2.1.16.11.2.1.4
set protocolDirStatus     1.3.6.1.2.1.16.11.2.1.10
$s getnext [list $protocolDirLocalIndex \
      $protocolDirDescr $protocolDirStatus]
⇒ {1.3.6.1.2.1.16.11.2.1.3.8.1.0.0.1.0.0.0.240.2.0.0 INTEGER
917511} {1.3.6.1.2.1.16.11.2.1.4.8.1.0.0.1.0.0.0.240.2.0.0
{OCTET STRING} 4E:45:54:42:00}
{1.3.6.1.2.1.16.11.2.1.10.8.1.0.0.1.0.0.0.240.2.0.0 INTEGER 1}
```

You can control the MIB files that get loaded automatically through two global Tcl variables: `$tnm(mib:core)` and `$tnm(mibs)`. `$tnm(mib:core)` contains the names of the MIB files that make up the SNMPv1 and SNMPv2 core definitions; `$tnm(mibs)` contains a list of MIB file names that are useful for your site. You can customize this set of MIB files in the `$tnm(library)/site/init.tcl` script.

`mib` `enums` returns the enumerations associated with a type. The RMONv2 `protocolDirStatus` is defined as type `RowStatus`. Using the `mib` `enums` command, we can obtain the enumerations possible for `protocolDirStatus`.

```
mib enums RowStatus
⇒ active 1 notInService 2 notReady 3 createAndGo 4
createAndWait 5 destroy 6
```

`mib` `format` maps an integer value into an enumerated string for either a type or an OID.

```
mib format RowStatus 1
⇒ active
```

```
mib format protocolDirStatus 2
⇒ notInService
```

mib scan provides the inverse function to the mib format command; it will map an enumerated string back to an integer value.

```
mib scan RowStatus active
⇒ 1
```

```
mib scan protocolDirStatus createAndWait
⇒ 5
```

mib oid returns the OID Number for a given OID.

```
mib oid sysDescr
⇒ 1.3.6.1.2.1.1.1
```

mib name returns the fully-qualified name associated with an OID.

```
mib name 1.3.6.1.2.1.1.1
⇒ SNMPv2-MIB!sysDescr
```

mib instance returns the instance portion of an OID.

```
mib instance sysDescr.0
⇒ 0
```

```
mib instance 1.3.6.1.2.1.1.1.0
⇒ 0
```

mib subtree will compare two OIDS and will return 1 if the second OID is within the subtree defined by the first OID; otherwise, it will return 0.

```
mib subtree sysDescr sysDescr.0
⇒ 1
```

```
mib subtree sysDescr 1.3.6.1.2.1.1.2.0
⇒ 0
```

mib length returns the length of an OID.

```
mib length sysDescr
⇒ 8
```

```
mib length sysDescr.0
⇒ 9
```

`mib file` returns the file name in which an OID or type was defined.

```
mib file RowStatus
⇒ C:/PROGRA~1/Scotty/lib/tnm3.0.0/mibs/rfc1903.tc
```

```
mib file protocolDirStatus
⇒ C:/PROGRA~1/Scotty/lib/tnm3.0.0/mibs/rfc2021.mib
```

`mib description` returns the textual description for either an OID or type.

```
mib description sysDescr
⇒ A textual description of the entity. This value should
include the full name and version identification of the
system's hardware type, software operating-system, and
networking software.
```

IN SUMMARY

This chapter showed how to use both the TickleMan and Scotty extensions for performing SNMP operations, performing table retrievals, measuring network delay and retrieving loaded MIB tree information. We showed with TickleMan how to receive and process traps; we showed with Scotty how to generate traps. We also showed for both extensions how to use blocking (synchronous) and nonblocking (asynchronous) modes for performing SNMP operations, and we showed how to make result strings returned by an asynchronous operation identical, regardless of which extension you are using. Further, we provided procedures for converting TimeTicks to a readable string, measuring Ethernet utilization on an interface and collecting sysUpTime values for a list of devices. We provided a series of routines with the TickleMan extensions which used the Cisco Ping MIB to measure network delay times. We later provided an identical series of routines which were modified slightly to use Scotty's extensions.

6 *Building A Polling Loop*

There are any number of reasons for periodically collecting information from a group of devices. You might want to collect utilization and traffic rates for a set of interfaces across your network. Or you might want to log protocol distribution information that is available from a group of RMONv2 probes, or look for certain error conditions, or keep track of interface availability. Just about any status monitoring or diagnostic tool requires some periodic data collection.

This chapter builds a polling loop that can be used for this type of periodic data collection. First, we will build a procedure, GetPollingInfo, which will return the community string, SNMP retry count and SNMP timeout values to be used for accessing a device. Next, we will design the data structures for maintaining the information necessary for polling a device. Finally, we will build a procedure, PollingLoop, which we will use to obtain utilization, broadcast rate and error rate statistics for a group of interfaces.

MAINTAINING SNMP ACCESS INFORMATION

Certain information is necessary to access/configure a device with SNMP. This includes the device's read and read-write community strings, SNMP timeout value and SNMP retry count. We want to be able to obtain this information in a consistent way for any of the devices we might poll. Also, we want to make it easy to maintain this information. In a network with thousands of devices, it could be an impossible task to maintain this information for each device. A better and more manageable solution might be to use the same information for all devices within the same subnet; or, maybe for most of the devices within a subnet, but allow this information to be overridden for select devices. Of course, the simplest solution is to have default values that all devices use.

The solution we will build will allow you to look up this information either for a specific device address, a subnet or, if no match is found, use default values. A file, CommStringVars.itcl, will maintain this information. A procedure, `GetPollingInfo`, will be passed an IP address. It will first check to see if device-specific information exists. If not, it will check for subnet-specific information. If this also fails, it will return a set of default values.

The file, `CommStringVars.itcl`, will maintain the SNMP polling information by defining an array to represent information for specific addresses, a list for representing subnet information and a list for the default values. The file would look something like this (with, of course, made-up addresses and community strings):

```
array set gCommStrAddr {
   158.101.121.1 {public1 private1 300 4}
   158.101.121.2 {public2 public2 500 2}
}
set gCommStrSubnetList [list \
    {158.101.121.0 255.255.255.0 pubX privX 300 2} \
    {158.101.122.0 255.255.255.0 pubZ privZ 300 2} \
    ]
set gCommStrDefault {public private 500 2}
```

where the format of the array values of gCommStrAddr are: read community string, read-write community string, SNMP timeout value (in one-hundredths of a second) and SNMP retry count. The format of the list elements of gCommStrSubnetList is similar, except the first component represents a subnet address and the second represents a subnet mask address—a match being determined if an IP address ANDed with the subnet mask equals the subnet address. gCommStrDefault provides the default community strings, timeout and retry count values.

By maintaining the configuration information as Tcl scripts (as opposed to a specially formated text file that needs to be parsed), we can parse the file by performing the command :

```
source CommStringVars.itcl
```

The configuration information is instantly read in and can be used by accessing the globals gCommStrAddr, gCommStrSubnetList and gCommStrDefault.

The code for `GetPollingInfo` is as follows:

```
source CommStringVars.itcl

proc GetPollingInfo {addr} {
#
#   Return list {readCommStr writeCommStr timeout retries}.
#
    global gCommStrDefault gCommStrAddr gCommStrSubnetList
#
#   If device name given - convert to IP address in dotted
#   form.
#
    set addr [ConvertNameToIpAddr $addr]
```

```
    if {[llength $addr] == 0} {
          return $gCommStrDefault
    }

#
# First, try to find an exact match within gCommStrAddr.
#
    if {[info exists gCommStrAddr($addr)]} {
          return $gCommStrAddr($addr)
    }

#
# Next, try to find a subnet match.
#
    set a [split $addr .]
    foreach el $gCommStrSubnetList {
          set subnet [lindex $el 0]
          set mask [lindex $el 1]

          #
          # Compare address && mask with subnet.
          #

          set m [split $mask .]
          set result [list [MaskField $a $m 0] \
                            [MaskField $a $m 1] \
                            [MaskField $a $m 2] \
                            [MaskField $a $m 3]]

          set result [join $result .]
          if {$result == $subnet} {
                return [lrange $el 2 5]
          }
    }
#
#     Neither an exact match nor subnet match were found,
#     return the defaults.
#
    return $gCommStrDefault
}
```

The first thing `GetPollingInfo` does is reference the structures defined within the `Comm-StringVars.itcl` file as globals. The command, `set addr [ConvertNameToIpAddr $addr]`, will convert a hostname to an IP address in dotted form. If addr is originally an IP address in dotted form, ConvertNameToIpAddr will have no effect on it.

The code used to search through gCommStrSubnetList for a subnet match uses the split command to convert both the address and mask values from dotted form to lists containing four elements. A new list is then formed by performing a bitwise AND on the corresponding address and mask elements. For example, if the address was *a1.a2.a3.a4* and the mask value was *m1.m2.m3.m4*, a list with the values { (*a1* & *m1*) (*a2* & *m2*) (*a3* & *m3*) (*a4* & *m4*) } would be created. This list is then converted to an IP address in dotted form by the join command.

```
proc MaskField {addr mask index} {
   set x [lindex $addr $index]
   set y [lindex $mask $index]

   return [expr $x & $y]
}

proc ConvertNameToIpAddr {addr} {
   set temp [host2addr $addr]
   if {[llength $temp] == 0} {
        return {}
   }
   return [octet2inst $temp]
}
```

Again, ConvertNameToIpAddr will have no effect on an IP address already in IP dotted form notation, but will convert a device name (if it can be translated by the DNS server) to an IP address. For example:

```
ConvertNameToIpAddr www.cisco.com
⇒ 192.31.7.130

ConvertNameToIpAddr 192.31.7.130
⇒ 192.31.7.130
```

At this point, we require CommStringVars.itcl to be manually edited. Ideally, we would like a simple application for adding, changing and deleting information from this file. To build this application we would need a user interface, a procedure for modifying the lists in memory and a procedure for creating a new CommStringVars.itcl from the modified lists. We will now supply two pieces of this application, UpdatePollingInfo and WritePolling-Info.

```
proc UpdatePollingInfo {newlist} {

   global gCommStrDefault gCommStrAddr gCommStrSubnetList
#
```

```
#   If deleting a record from gCommStrAddr, newlist has format:
#
#   address
#
  if {[llength $newlist] == 1} {
        set addr [lindex $newlist 0]
        if {[info exists gCommStrAddr($addr)]} {
              unset gCommStrAddr($addr)
        }
        return
  }
#
#   If deleting a record from gCommStrSubnetList, newlist has
£   format:
#
#   address mask
#
  if {[llength $newlist] == 2} {
        set addr [lindex $newlist 0]
        set mask [lindex $newlist 1]
        set i [lsearch $gCommStrSubnetList "$addr $mask *"]
        if {$i == -1} {return}
        set gCommStrSubnetList \
              [lreplace $gCommStrSubnetList $i $i]
        return;
  }


#
#   If replacing default values, newlist has format:
#
#   readCommStr writeCommStr timeout retries
#
  if {[llength $newlist] == 4} {
        set gCommStrDefault $newlist
        return
  }
#
#   If adding/replacing an address, newlist has format:
#
#   address readCommStr writeCommStr timeout retries
#
  if {[llength $newlist] == 5} {
```

```
            set addr [lindex $newlist 0]
            set gCommStrAddr($addr) [lrange $newlist 1 4]
    }
    #
    #  If adding/replacing a subnet address, newlist has format:
    #
    #  address mask readCommStr writeCommStr timeout retries
    #
    if {[llength $newlist] != 6} {
        return
    }

    set addr [lindex $newlist 0]
    set mask [lindex $newlist 1]
    set i [lsearch $gCommStrSubnetList "$addr $mask *"]
    if {$i != -1} {
        set gCommStrSubnetList \
                [lreplace $gCommStrSubnetList $i $i $newlist]
        return
    }

    lappend gCommStrSubnetList $newlist
}
```

UpdatePollingInfo determines from the length of the list passed to it which list or array defined within CommStringVars.itcl to modify. It also determines from the length whether to delete a specific address or subnet entry, or to either update or add a new entry. If the list contains a single item, the item identifies the address of the entry to delete from gComm-StrAddr. If the list contains two items, the items identify the subnet address and mask of the entry to delete from gCommStrSubnetList. If it contains four items, the list is used for setting gCommStrDefault. If it contains five items, it is used to add or replace an entry within gCommStrAddr. Finally, if it contains six items, it is used to add or replace an entry within gCommStrSubnetList.

```
    proc WritePollingInfo {} {
        global gCommStrDefault gCommStrAddr gCommStrSubnetList

        set fid [open "CommStringVars2.itcl" w]
    #
    #  First, write address array, each array element on a line.
    #
        puts $fid "array set gCommStrAddr {"
        foreach el [array names gCommStrAddr] {
```

```
             puts $fid \t[list $el $gCommStrAddr($el)]
      }
      puts $fid "}"

      puts $fid
#
#  Next, write subnet list, each element on a line.
#
      puts $fid "set gCommStrSubnetList \[list \\"
      foreach el $gCommStrSubnetList {
            set str [list $el]
            puts $fid "    $str \\"
      }
      puts $fid "    ]"
      puts $fid
#
# Finish up by writing default string assignment.
#
      set str [list $gCommStrDefault]
      puts $fid "set gCommStrDefault $str"
      flush $fid
      close $fid
}
```

WritePollingInfo creates a new CommStringVars.itcl file using the current values of gCommStrDefault, gCommStrAddr and gCommStrSubnetList.

DESIGNING A POLLING LOOP

We will now design a polling loop which will periodically poll a list of devices for MIB information. The MIB information to poll for will be referenced by the global variable gMibs, and will have the format: { MIB-Group1 ... ? MIB-Groupi ... MIB-Groupn?}, where each MIB-Group represents a list of MIB variables grouped together by common instances. For example, if we were going to poll for a subset of ipRoute MIB variables and a subset of ifTable MIB variables, gMibs would be defined as follows:

```
set gMibs \
    [list \
       [list ipInReceives ipOutRequests] \
       [list ifInOctets ifOutOctets ifInDiscards ifInErrors] \
    ]
```

For each device, we need to specify a list of instances to be collected for each MIB-Group. For example, if we wanted to collect the ipRoute MIB variables for DeviceA and the ifTable MIB variables for interfaces 1 through 4, we would specify the following list:

```
set pollListA { {0} {1 2 3 4} }
```

If we wanted to collect only the ifTable MIB variables for DeviceB for interfaces 2, 5, 7, we would specify:

```
set pollListB { {} {2 5 7}}
```

It is sometimes necessary to use a different community string per MIB variable instance. This usually happens when you try to access different boards within a chassis-type device. While there is a proposed standard chassis MIB, most vendors have come up with their own proprietary solutions. Some simply assign different IP addresses to different boards. Others append a string which ties the board number to the device's community string. Still others require proprietary MIB tables to be accessed to decipher the correct community string to use. Because of all this, we need a way to override the device's community string for any instance.

An instance can be defined as either an instance identifier or a sublist containing the instance identifier and the community string to use. If, for DeviceB we needed to override the community string used for interface 5, we would define `pollListB` as follows:

```
set pollListB { {} {2 {5 overrideCS} 7}}
```

The polling loop will be made up of several procedures. It is started by calling `PollingLoop` and passing it a list containing the devices and instances to poll for and a callback script to execute when MIB information is retrieved.

```
proc PollingLoop {pollList cb} {
#
#   pollList defines which devices and instances to poll.
#   Format of list is: {{addr igrp1 ? ... igrpn?} ?... {...}?},
#   where igrpi is a sublist defining a group of instances to
#   use against mib group i.
#
#   cb defines a callback routine to call when SNMP data is
#   collected. sysUpTime value, node name, a unique node
#   identifier, instance and the varbind list from the snmp
#   request will be appended to cb, and then the script will
#   be executed.
#

    global gNodeInfo gNodeIpAddr gActivePolls gSid gPollingState
    global gNodeID
```

```
set gNodeID 0

set gSid [snmpsession -snmp]
foreach el $pollList {
        set addr [lindex $el 0]
        set ipaddr [ConvertNameToIpAddr $addr]
        set nid [GetNodeId $ipaddr]
        if {$nid == -1} {
            incr gNodeID
            set nid $gNodeID
        }

        set pinfo [GetPollingInfo $ipaddr]

        set gNodeIpAddr($nid) $ipaddr

        set gNodeInfo($nid,name) $addr
        set gNodeInfo($nid,cb) $cb
        set gNodeInfo($nid,pinfo) $pinfo
        set gNodeInfo($nid,inst) [lrange $el 1 end]
        set gNodeInfo($nid,time) 0
        set gNodeInfo($nid,pflag) idle
        set gNodeInfo($nid,removecmds) ""
        set gNodeInfo($nid,cmdcount) 0

        PL_BuildCommands $nid $ipaddr $pinfo
    }
  set gPollingState "on"
  set gActivePolls 0
  PL_Timer
}
```

gNodeInfo is used to maintain the following information about each device being polled:

- Device name
- User-specified callback script
- SNMP access information retrieved by GetPollingInfo.
- Instances by group to collect
- A time count

  Every second the time count will be decremented. When it reaches 0 and the poll flag for the device equals "idle", polling will start for the device. When polling is finished, the time count will be reinitialized to the poll rate.

- A polling flag that indicates the state of polling for the device

  While waiting for the next poll cycle, the flag will equal "idle". While in the process of sending polls, the flag will be set to "waiting". After all the polls have been sent, but not all responses have yet been received, the flag will be set to "polling". If an SNMP timeout error is received, the flag will be set to "timeout". It will be reset back to "idle" when all the outstanding SNMP requests have been received.

- A list indicating the instances to stop polling for

  If an SNMP `noSuchName` error is received, the instance associated with the error will be added to this list.

- A list of SNMP commands to use for polling the device

- A count of the number of commands being used

- Counts of the number of SNMP messages sent and received during the current polling cycle

  These counts are used both for determining when polling is complete and for throttling the number of outstanding SNMP requests that can be sent to a device.

`gNodeIpAddr` is used for accessing the IP addresses being polled. `gSid` references an SNMP session used for the polling. `gActivePolls` keeps track of the number of outstanding polls that have been issued for all devices. To control the total number of outstanding polls that we can put out on the network, we throttle the polling based on high and low threshold settings. If the number of outstanding polls exceeds the high threshold value, referenced by `gHiThreshold`, polling will be suspended until the number of outstanding polls falls below `gLowThreshold`. `gPollingState` will indicate whether polling is "on" or "suspended."

`PollingLoop` will perform the necessary initialization, cause all the SNMP commands to be pre-built and then enter a one-second timer routine. Note that `GetNodeId` will associate a unique integer value to each device being polled. `gNodeInfo` and `gNodeIPAddr` will be indexed using this node identifier. Using an integer as an array index is more manageable than using an IP address or device name.

The polling will be performed using SNMP Get commands instead of table retrieval commands. By using SNMP Get, we can selectively choose which interfaces to collect as opposed to collecting whole columns. Also, the `table` command performs a series of SNMP GetNext commands until the columns are collected. By using SNMP Get, we can send out multiple commands at one time, speeding up the collection period. Equally important, using SNMP Get, we can retrieve the `sysUpTime` value with each poll (which we cannot do using the `table` command), allowing us to accurately calculate rate changes among counter values.

```
proc PL_BuildCommands {n addr pinfo} {
```

```
    global gNodeInfo
#
# Build SNMP commands for each interface for a node and
# save as a list in gNodeInfo(node_id,cmdlist).
#
    set cstr [lindex $pinfo 0]
    set tmout [lindex $pinfo 2]
    set retries [lindex $pinfo 3]

    set cmdlist ""
    set instlist $gNodeInfo($n,inst)
    set grpid 0
    foreach group $instlist {
          foreach el $group {
#
#    An instance within the instance list can be either a
#    value or a list element containing an instance value and
#    a community string. This allows us to override a node's
#    community string for a particular instance.
#
                if {[llength $el] == 1} {
                      set i $el
                      set cs $cstr
                } else {
                      set i   [lindex $el 0]
                      set cs [lindex $el 1]
                }

                set cmd [PL_BuildGetCommand $n $grpid $i $addr \
                        $cs $tmout $retries]
                lappend cmdlist $cmd
                incr gNodeInfo($n,cmdcount)
          }
          incr grpid
    }
    set gNodeInfo($n,cmdlist) $cmdlist
}
```

PL_BuildCommands will cycle through each instance of each MIB-Group, building the SNMP Get command to access the corresponding MIB information. By pre-building SNMP Get commands before polling starts, we are trading off memory for performance. This trade-off is well worth making. The amount of space to store an SNMP Get command is obviously dependent on the number of MIB variables being collected, but is still going to be relatively small—somewhere along the lines of a couple of hundred characters. The amount of processing we save by not re-building each SNMP command for each polling cycle is significant.

```
proc PL_BuildGetCommand {n gid inst addr cstr tmout retries} {

    global gNodeInfo gNodeIpAddr gMibs gSid
#
#   Build varbind list for instance inst.
#
    set mibs [lindex $gMibs $gid]
    set vb "sysUpTime.0"
    foreach el $mibs {
        lappend vb "$el.$inst"
    }

    set authinfo [list snmpv1 $cstr]
    set options [list "-timeout" $tmout "-retries" $retries]
    set cb [list PL_GetCallback $n $gid $inst]

    return [list $gSid get $addr $authinfo $vb $options $cb]
}
```

PL_BuildGetCommand builds the SNMP Get command. The MIB-Group identified by gid is used for building the varbind list. sysUpTime is added to the front of the varbind list, so that the system TimeTicks value is returned with each SNMP poll.

```
proc PL_RemoveCommands {n} {
#
#   Remove commands corresponding to instances in
#   list gNodeInfo($n,removecmds).
#
    global gNodeInfo
    foreach el $gNodeInfo($n,removecmds) {
        set gid [lindex $el 0]
        set i [lindex $el 1]
        set group [lindex $gNodeInfo($n,inst) $gid]
#
#   Find instance i in instance group. Note that instances can
#   be in a group list as either single elements or as sublists
#   represented by {instance commString}.
        set k [lsearch $group $i]
        if {$k == -1} {
            set k [lsearch $group "$i *"]
```

```
        }
        if {$k != -1} {
                PL_RemoveFromCommandList $n $gid $k
                set group \
                        [lreplace $group $k $k]
                set gNodeInfo($n,inst) \
                        [lreplace $gNodeInfo($n,inst)\
                                $gid $gid $group]
        }
    }
    set gNodeInfo($n,removecmds) ""
}

proc PL_RemoveFromCommandList {n gid i} {
#
#    Remove command corresponding to the ith instance
#    in instance group gid.
#
    global gNodeInfo
    set j 0
    set k 0
    while {$j < $gid} {
            set k [expr $k +\
        [llength [lindex $gNodeInfo($n,inst) $j]]]
            incr j
    }
    set k [expr $k + $i]
    set gNodeInfo($n,cmdlist) \
            [lreplace $gNodeInfo($n,cmdlist) $k $k]
    incr gNodeInfo($n,cmdcount) -1
}
```

As mentioned earlier, we want to remove any SNMP Get commands that cause an SNMP noSuchName error. If a noSuchName error is detected, a sublist identifying the MIB-Group and the specific instance is added to a device's removecmds list. PL_RemoveCommands will be called before the next poll cycle to clean up the instance information maintained for a device. PL_RemoveFromCommandList removes the corresponding SNMP Get command from a device's command list. While the position within the local MIB-Group is given, the position within the overall command list must be calculated by first summing the number of commands from the previous MIB groups.

```
    proc PL_Timer { } {
```

```
    PL_CheckPolling
    after 1000 PL_Timer
}

proc PL_CheckPolling {} {
    global gNodeInfo gNodeIpAddr gActivePolls

    set flag 0
    set nlist [array names gNodeIpAddr]
    foreach n $nlist {

        if {$gNodeInfo($n,time) > 0} {
            incr gNodeInfo($n,time) -1
        }
        if {($gNodeInfo($n,time) == 0) && \
            ($gNodeInfo($n,pflag) == "idle")} {
            if {[llength $gNodeInfo($n,removecmds)] > 0} {
                PL_RemoveCommands $n
            }
            set gNodeInfo($n,pflag) waiting
            set gNodeInfo($n,next) 0
            set gNodeInfo($n,psent) 0
            set gNodeInfo($n,precv) 0
            set flag 1
        }
    }
#
# Note that if active polls, PL_DoPolls will be called after
# callback routine is entered.
#
    if {($gActivePolls == 0) && ($flag == 1)} {
        PL_DoPolls
    }
}
```

PL_Timer implements a one-second timer. PL_CheckPolling is called by the timer, and is responsible for decrementing each device's time count and transitioning a device from "idle" to "waiting". If a device is transitioned to "waiting", the procedure PL_DoPolls will be called if there are no active polls. If there are active polls, PL_DoPolls will be called after the next SNMP response is received.

```
proc PL_DoPolls {} {
    global gNodeInfo gNodeIpAddr gPollRate gPollingState
```

```
        global gActivePolls gHiThreshold gLowThreshold
gDeviceThreshold

if {$gPollingState == "suspend"} {

        if {$gActivePolls >= $gLowThreshold} {
             return
        }

        set gPollingState "on"
}

set nlist [array names gNodeIpAddr]
foreach n $nlist {

        if {$gNodeInfo($n,pflag) != "waiting"} continue
        if {[expr $gNodeInfo($n,psent) -\
$gNodeInfo($n,precv)] > \
$gDeviceThreshold} continue

#
#   Found node waiting to send polls.
#
        set i $gNodeInfo($n,next)
        set flag true
        while {$flag == "true"} {

                PL_SendPoll $n $i
                incr i
                set gNodeInfo($n,next) $i

                incr gNodeInfo($n,psent)
                if {$i >= $gNodeInfo($n,cmdcount)} {
                     set gNodeInfo($n,pflag) "polling"
                     set flag "false"
                }
                incr gActivePolls
                if {$gActivePolls >= $gHiThreshold} {
                     set gPollingState "suspend"
                     update
                     return
                }
```

```
        if {[expr $gNodeInfo($n,psent) - \
            $gNodeInfo($n,precv)] > \
            $gDeviceThreshold} break
        }
    }
    update
}
```

PL_DoPolls will simply return if the polling state is suspended and the number of active polls hasn't yet fallen below the low watermark. Otherwise, PL_DoPolls will search for devices in the "waiting" state and will attempt to send out polls for those devices. PL_DoPolls is responsible for transitioning a device's polling state from "waiting" to "polling", indicating that all the polls for that polling cycle have been sent. PL_DoPolls is also responsible for transitioning the overall polling state to "suspend" if the number of outstanding requests exceeds the high watermark. Note that the update command is executed at the completion of PL_DoPolls to guarantee the constant flushing of pending events.

```
proc PL_SendPoll {n i} {
    global gNodeInfo
#
#   Send out poll command for ith element in command list.
#   Format of elements in cmdlist: {intf cmd}
#
    set cmd [lindex $gNodeInfo($n,cmdlist) $i]
    eval $cmd
}

proc PL_GetCallback {n gid i result} {
    global gNodeInfo gActivePolls gPollRate

    incr gActivePolls -1
    incr gNodeInfo($n,precv) 1

    if {$gNodeInfo($n,pflag) == "timeout"} {
        if {$gNodeInfo($n,psent) == $gNodeInfo($n,precv)} {
            set gNodeInfo($n,pflag) "idle"
            set gNodeInfo($n,time) $gPollRate
        }
        PL_DoPolls
        return
    }

#
```

```
#  If error status of "timeout" received, disable any more
#  collection from device for this poll cycle (assume device
#  is too busy to be polled now!).
#  If error status "noSuchName" sent, remove associated
#  command from poll list.
#  Otherwise, execute script
#       [usercallback timeticks name node_id intf
#          varbindList].
#
  set errorStatus [GetErrorStatus $result]
  if {$errorStatus == "timeout"} {
       PL_HandleTimeOut $n
       PL_DoPolls
       return
  }

  if {$errorStatus == "noSuchName"} {
       lappend gNodeInfo($n,removecmds) [list $gid $i]
       PL_CheckDone $n
       PL_DoPolls
       return
  }

  if {$errorStatus != "noError"} {
       puts $result
       PL_CheckDone $n
       PL_DoPolls
       return
  }

  set vblist [GetVarBindList $result]
  set vb [GetVarBind $vblist 1]
  set timeticks [GetValue $vb]

  set vblist [lrange $vblist 1 end]

  eval [list $gNodeInfo($n,cb) $timeticks \
          $gNodeInfo($n,name) $n $i $vblist]

  PL_CheckDone $n
  PL_DoPolls
}
```

PL_GetCallback gets executed as a callback script whenever any SNMP Get command completes. The node identifier, MIB-Group identifier, instance and result string are passed as arguments. If an SNMP error status of "timeout" is returned, the polling state for the device is transitioned to "timeout", which in effect stops any more polling for the device for the current polling cycle. The reason for this is if the device is too busy to respond to an SNMP request, or the network is too congested to get an SNMP request to the device, we don't want to compound the problem by sending more requests. It's better to give the system a chance to stabilize and wait for the next poll cycle. If a noSuchName error is returned, we remove the corresponding instance from being polled.

If a noError status is returned, the sysUpTime value is pulled out of the varbind list. The user-specified callback script is then appended with the sysUpTime value, the node name, the node identifier, the instance and the returned varbind list. The script is then executed.

```
proc PL_CheckDone {n} {
   global gNodeInfo gPollRate

   if {($gNodeInfo($n,psent) == $gNodeInfo($n,precv)) && \
          ($gNodeInfo($n,pflag) == "polling")} {
      set gNodeInfo($n,pflag) "idle"
      set gNodeInfo($n,time) $gPollRate
      return 1
   }
   return 0
}


proc PL_HandleTimeOut {n} {
   global gNodeInfo

   if {[PL_CheckDone $n] == 1} return
   set gNodeInfo($n,pflag) "timeout"
}

proc GetNodeId {ipaddr} {
#
#   Return Node id associated with IP address.
#   Return -1 if IP address not assigned a Node id yet.
#
   global gNodeID gNodeIpAddr

   set x [array get gNodeIpAddr]
   set i [lsearch $x $ipaddr]
   if {$i != -1} {
```

```
            return [lindex $x [expr $i - 1] ]
      }
      return -1
   }
```

USING THE POLLING LOOP

We will now build a callback routine, myCallback, which will save collected MIB values using the procedure AddValueToList, which we built in Chapter 3. Afterwards, we will write routines to calculate utilization, broadcast rates and error statistics for a device and an interface.

```
proc myCallback {timeticks name nid inst vblist} {
   set i [string length $inst]
   foreach vb $vblist {
         set val [GetValue $vb]
         set oid [GetOID $vb]
         set j [string length $oid]
         set mibVar [string range $oid 0 [expr $j - $i - 2]]
         AddValueToList $mibVar "$nid,$inst" $val $timeticks
#
#  If ifOperStatus not "up", flush all collected values
#  for interface. Don't bother logging any more data.
#
         if {$mibVar == "ifOperStatus"} {
               if {$val != 1} {
                     FlushAllValues "$nid,$inst"
                     AddValueToList $mibVar "$nid,$inst" \
                           $val $timeticks
                     return
               }
         }
      }
   }
}
```

In myCallback, we introduce a procedure, FlushAllValues, which, given an instance, removes all related samples from the circular buffers maintained by AddValueToList. If the ifOperStatus is down (or testing), any previously collected values for that interface are no longer valid since the counter values have all been reset. In this case, we flush all collected values for the interface, re-add the ifOperStatus value (since it was just flushed out) and exit, since there is no point to adding any other collected values for the interface. The code for `FlushAll-Values` is simply:

```
proc FlushAllValues {inst} {
   global gValueList

   set x [array names gValueList *,$inst]
   foreach el $x {
        set gValueList($el)  ""
   }
}
```

Note that `AddValueToList` was orginally defined to take as arguments an OID name, an instance, a value and a TimeTicks. Here, instead of passing it an instance, we're passing it a string composed of the node identifier and the instance, separated by a comma. This will end up building array indexes like "`ifInOctets,3,2`", which will work fine.

Now that we're saving the values using `AddValueToList`, we can use the previously defined `Delta` and `Rate` procedures to build routines to calculate the desired statistics.

```
proc GetEthUtil {addr inst} {

   set ipaddr [ConvertNameToIpAddr $addr]
   set nid [GetNodeId $ipaddr]
   if {$nid == -1} {
        error "Not collecting for $addr"
   }

   CheckReady $nid
   CheckOperStatus $nid $inst
#
#   util = txUtil + rxUtil, where
#        txUtil = (rate(ifOutOctets)*8/linespeed)*100
#         rxUtil = (rate(ifInOctets)*8/linespeed)*100
#
   set linespeed [GetLastValue ifSpeed "$nid,$inst"]
   if {$linespeed == -1} {
        error "Unable to collect ifSpeed"
   }

   set rOutOctets [Rate ifOutOctets "$nid,$inst"]
   if {$rOutOctets == -1} {
        error "Unable to calculate r(ifOutOctets)"
   }
   set txUtil [expr ($rOutOctets*8.0/$linespeed)*100.0]
```

```
    set rInOctets [Rate ifInOctets "$nid,$inst"]
    if {$rInOctets == -1} {
         error "Unable to calculate r(ifInOctets)"
    }
    set rxUtil [expr ($rInOctets*8.0/$linespeed)*100.0]

    return [expr $txUtil + $rxUtil]
}
```

GetEthUtil uses three new utility routines: CheckReady, CheckOperStatus and GetLastValue. CheckReady takes advantage of the information stored within gNodeInfo to wait until a node's polling status is set to "idle" before continuing. This is so we don't start calculating utilization while we're in the middle of processing a poll. CheckOperStatus is a simple convenience routine that verifies whether or not ifOperStatus for the specified interface is "up". If it isn't, or if the ifOperStatus is unknown (hasn't been collected yet), it will raise an error which will cause GetEthUtil to terminate since it isn't being caught. Calculating utilization or any of the other statistics we will be showing is meaningless if the operational status for the interface is not up. GetLastValue extends the Delta and Rate procedures to return the last collected value for a MIB variable for a specific interface. The three routines are defined as follows:

```
proc CheckReady {nid} {
  global gNodeInfo
#
#  If in the process of polling, wait until complete.
#
  set flag 1
  while {$flag == 1} {
       if {$gNodeInfo($nid,pflag) == "idle"} {
          return
       }
       vwait $gNodeInfo($nid,pflag)
  }
}


proc CheckOperStatus {nid inst} {
  set operStatus [GetLastValue ifOperStatus "$nid,$inst"]
  if {$operStatus == -1} {
       error "Unable to collect data"
  }
  if {$operStatus != 1} {
       error "Operational status down for interface."
```

```
        }
    }

    proc GetLastValue {var instance} {
        global gValueList

        if {![info exists gValueList($var,$instance)]} {
         return -1
        }

        set n [llength $gValueList($var,$instance)]
        if {$n == 0} {
         return -1
        }
        set x [lindex $gValueList($var,$instance) end]
        return [lindex $x 0]
    }
```

The procedures GetTxBCastRate, GetRxBCastRate, GetPercentTxErrors and GetPercentRxErrors calculate transmit broadcast rates in packets per second, receive broadcast rates in packets per second, percentage of transmit packets discarded due to errors or resource limitations and percentage of receive packets discarded due to errors or resource limitations respectively. The code for these procedures is given in the following pages. Note that the code collects ifInNUcastPkts and ifOutNUcastPkts, which have been deprecated. If you are running this code against agents that support the IF-MIB from RFC 2233, you should replace these variables with ifInBroadcastPkts and ifOutBroadcastPkts, respectively. Also note that all these routines, as well as GetEthUtil, will raise an error if they are unable to calculate the expected statistic. By doing this, a surrounding application can handle the error as it wants.

```
    proc GetTxBCastRate {addr inst} {
        set ipaddr [ConvertNameToIpAddr $addr]
        set nid [GetNodeId $ipaddr]
        if {$nid == -1} {
            error "Not collecting for $addr"
        }

        CheckReady $nid
        CheckOperStatus $nid $inst
    #
    #
    # txBroadcastRate = rate(ifOutNUcastPkts)
    #
```

```
    set rOutNUcastPkts [Rate ifOutNUcastPkts "$nid,$inst"]
    if {$rOutNUcastPkts == -1} {
         error "Unable to calculate r(ifOutNUcastPkts)"
    }
    return $rOutNUcastPkts
}

proc GetRxBCastRate {addr inst} {
   set ipaddr [ConvertNameToIpAddr $addr]
   set nid [GetNodeId $ipaddr]
   if {$nid == -1} {
         error "Not collecting for $addr"
   }

   CheckReady $nid
   CheckOperStatus $nid $inst
#
# rxBroadcastRate = rate(ifInNUcastPkts)
#
   set rInNUcastPkts [Rate ifInNUcastPkts "$nid,$inst"]
   if {$rInNUcastPkts == -1} {
         error "Unable to calculate r(ifInNUcastPkts)"
   }
   return $rInNUcastPkts
}

proc GetPercentRxErrors {addr inst} {
   set ipaddr [ConvertNameToIpAddr $addr]
   set nid [GetNodeId $ipaddr]
   if {$nid == -1} {
         error "Not collecting for $addr"
   }

   CheckReady $nid
   CheckOperStatus $nid $inst
#
# errorPkts = d(ifInErrors)+d(ifInDiscards)+d(ifUnknownProtos)
# percentErrs = errorPkts/(d(ifInUcastPkts)+d(ifInNUcastPkts)+
#       errorPkts)*100
#
   set dInErrors [Delta ifInErrors "$nid,$inst"]
   if {$dInErrors == -1} {
```

```
            error "Unable to calculate r(ifInErrors)"
    }

    set dInDiscards [Delta ifInDiscards "$nid,$inst"]
    if {$dInDiscards == -1} {
            error "Unable to calculate r(ifInDiscards)"
    }

    set dInUnknownProtos [Delta ifInUnknownProtos "$nid,$inst"]
    if {$dInUnknownProtos == -1} {
            error "Unable to calculate r(ifInUnknownProtos)"
    }

    set dInUcastPkts [Delta ifInUcastPkts "$nid,$inst"]
    if {$dInUcastPkts == -1} {
            error "Unable to calculate r(ifInUcastPkts)"
    }

    set dInNUcastPkts [Delta ifInNUcastPkts "$nid,$inst"]
    if {$dInNUcastPkts == -1} {
            error "Unable to calculate r(ifInNUcastPkts)"
    }

    set errorPkts [expr $dInErrors + $dInDiscards + \
                    $dInUnknownProtos]

    set totalPkts [expr $errorPkts + $dInUcastPkts + \
              $dInNUcastPkts]

    set percentErrs [expr ($errorPkts/$totalPkts)*100.0]
    return $percentErrs
}

proc GetPercentTxErrors {addr inst} {
  set ipaddr [ConvertNameToIpAddr $addr]
  set nid [GetNodeId $ipaddr]
  if {$nid == -1} {
          error "Not collecting for $addr"
  }

  CheckReady $nid
  CheckOperStatus $nid $inst
```

```
#
# errorPkts = d(ifOutErrors)+d(ifOutDiscards)
# percentErrs = errorPkts/(d(ifOutUcastPkts)+
# d(ifOutNUcastPkts)+
#        errorPkts)*100
#
  set dOutErrors [Delta ifOutErrors "$nid,$inst"]
  if {$dOutErrors == -1} {
       error "Unable to calculate r(ifOutErrors)"
  }

  set dOutDiscards [Delta ifOutDiscards "$nid,$inst"]
  if {$dOutDiscards == -1} {
       error "Unable to calculate r(ifOutDiscards)"
  }

  set dOutUcastPkts [Delta ifOutUcastPkts "$nid,$inst"]
  if {$dOutUcastPkts == -1} {
       error "Unable to calculate r(ifOutUcastPkts)"
  }

  set dOutNUcastPkts [Delta ifOutNUcastPkts "$nid,$inst"]
  if {$dOutNUcastPkts == -1} {
       error "Unable to calculate r(ifOutNUcastPkts)"
  }

  set errorPkts [expr $dOutErrors + $dOutDiscards]

  set totalPkts [expr $errorPkts + $dOutUcastPkts + \
       $dOutNUcastPkts]

  set percentErrs [expr ($errorPkts/$totalPkts)*100.0]
  return $percentErrs
}
```

Now, let's define the necessary globals to start using the polling loop and these statistic routines:

```
set gPollRate 60
set maxPollSeconds [expr $gPollRate * 10]
set minPollSeconds [expr $gPollRate - 5]
```

```
set gHiThreshold 15
set gLowThreshold 10
set gDeviceThreshold 5
set gMibs { \
        {ifOperStatus ifSpeed ifInOctets ifOutOctets \
        ifOutNUcastPkts ifOutUcastPkts ifInNUcastPkts \
        ifInUcastPkts ifInDiscards ifInErrors \
          ifInUnknownProtos ifOutErrors ifOutDiscards} \
        }
```

Let's also define the address and interface list to poll for:

```
set pList [list [list $ipaddr1 {1 2 3 4 5 6 7}] \
                [list $ipaddr2 {1 2 3 4}] \
                [list $ipaddr3 {1 2 3 4}]]
```

where again, we've hidden the IP addresses in variables `ipaddr1`, `ipaddr2`, and `ipaddr3`. `pList` defines that for `ipaddr1`, we will collect data for interfaces 1—7, for `ipaddr2`, we will collect for interfaces 1—4, and for `ipaddr3`, we will collect for interfaces 1—4. Now to start the collection, we simply issue the command:

```
PollingLoop $pList myCallback
```

Later, we can issue the following commands to get information about a device's interface:

```
GetPercentRxErrors $ipaddr1 1
⇒ 5.40407

GetEthUtil $ipaddr1 1
⇒ 16.6069

GetEthUtil $ipaddr1 4
⇒ Operational status down for interface.

GetRxBCastRate $ipaddr1 1
⇒ 23.0132

GetTxBCastRate $ipaddr1 1
⇒ 0.198675

GetTxBCastRate $ipaddr1 7
⇒ 0.347395
```

As an aside, let's show how to build a list of Ethernet interfaces for a device using the table command. We will write a procedure, CollectEthInterfaces, which will issue a table command to collect the ifType column. The callback routine will add interface numbers to a list if the ifType is equal to "6" (corresponding to Ethernet). These routines could be easily modified to collect only Ethernet interfaces with ifOperStatus equal to "up".

```
proc CollectEthInterfaces {sid addr} {
    global gList gDone

    set gList ""
    set gDone 0

    set vb {ifType}
    set addr [ConvertNameToIpAddr $addr]
    set pinfo [GetPollingInfo $addr]
    set cstr [lindex $pinfo 0]
    set authinfo [list snmpv1 $cstr]
    set cb [list CollectCallback]
    set options {-tableRows 1}

    $sid table $addr $authinfo $vb {0} $options $cb

    vwait gDone
    puts $gList
}

proc CollectCallback {result} {
    global gList gDone

    set n [expr [string length "ifType"] + 1]
    set errorStatus [GetErrorStatus $result]
    set vblist [GetVarBindList $result]
    set vb [GetVarBind $vblist 1]
    set val [GetValue $vb]
    set oid [GetOID $vb]
    if {$val == 6} {
        set x [string range $oid $n end]
        lappend gList $x
    }
    if {$errorStatus == "endOfTable"} {
        set gDone 1
    }
}
```

IN SUMMARY

This chapter provided routines for retrieving SNMP access information maintained within a Tcl script. We also showed how to update and rewrite this information. Further, we designed, step-by-step, a nonblocking polling loop capable of polling different MIB group information for a set of devices. Within the polling loop we throttled the number of outstanding SNMP packets that can be sent to control the number of requests we put on the network at any one time. We also throttled the number of outstanding packets that can be sent to a single device to keep the device from being overworked. We built the polling loop using SNMP Get commands instead of the `table` command for several reasons, including being able to control which instances we collected information for and being able to collect `sysUpTime` with each poll. Also, some network devices are more efficient in handling SNMP Get commands than in handling SNMP GetNext commands, which the `table` command breaks down to. In our examples of using the polling loop, we built several routines for showing useful statistics about an interface. We also tied in several procedures built in Chapters 3–5. Scattered throughout the chapter we showed useful tidbits, such as checking for `ifOperStatus` to verify whether or not `ifTable` counter values have any significance.

7 *Tk Basics*

This chapter describes Tk and its commands for building Graphical User Interfaces (GUIs). Besides being easy to learn, Tk is one of the most effective methods available today for developing multi-platform graphical applications that run on both UNIX and Windows. After showing the basic Tk components, we will build a network management GUI framework. Both the concepts and components used in building this GUI can be used for building a large number of network management applications.

TK FUNDAMENTALS

Tk's Console and Display Windows

The Tk Toolkit is an extension for Tcl which allows you to implement GUIs. To use Tk commands, you must invoke a Tcl interpreter, such as **wish**, that supports the Tk extension.

When you start a Tcl/Tk interpreter program like **wish** on a Windows system, it will create two windows: a Console Window and a Display Window, as illustrated in Figure 7.1.

The Console Window is used mainly for developing or debugging your applications. If you invoke a Tcl script file that launches a specified interpreter, the Console Window does not get created. The Display Window is the main application window that displays your GUI. It is what is called a top-level widget or window.

Basic Steps in Using Tk

Typical steps in using Tk to build your GUI include:

- Assigning attributes like a title to your top-level application window
- Creating instances of various classes of Tk widgets
- Positioning and displaying your Tk widgets using one of Tk's Geometry Managers
- Invoking method commands on your Tk widgets
- Associating application events with your Tk widgets

Figure 7.1   Tk's Console and Display Windows.

Widgets

A widget is a visible GUI component, like a listbox, scrollbar or button. It is also a software object with a well-documented programming interface and its own set of configuration options and methods.

Widgets are more than just display items. Most have built-in behaviors that are associated with mouse events. Most also support the `-command` option that allows you to specify a Tcl command (or script) to invoke when the widget is selected. And finally, you can use the Tcl `bind` command or bind method to associate how a widget or group of widgets should behave for specified mouse or keyboard events.

Like all command extensions to Tcl, there are two categories of Tk widgets. The first category is the built-in Tk widgets that are distributed with Tcl by Sunscript. The second category is the extended Tk widgets that are typically made available from the general Tcl user community via Tcl extension packages.

This chapter discusses only built-in Tk widgets. Later in Chapter 8, we will discuss Itcl Mega-Widgets, which are part of the [incr Tcl] extension package.

In this chapter, we will be discussing the Tk commands for building the following Tk widgets: `button`, `canvas`, `frame`, `entry`, `label`, `listbox`, `menu`, `menubutton`, `message`, `radiobutton`, `scrollbar` and `text`.

COMMAND SYNTAX FOR CREATING AND MANIPULATING WIDGETS

Being an extension of Tcl, you create and interact with Tk widgets through commands. Tk widgets commands have one syntax for creating new instances of a widget and another syntax for applying methods to an existing widget instance.

The syntax for creating a new instance of a widget is:

```
<widget class name> <widget instance name > ?option?...
```

For example:

```
button .hello -text "Hello, world"
```

The syntax for invoking a supported method on an existing instance of a widget is:

```
<widget instance name> <method> ?args?...
```

For example:

```
.hello configure -background red
```

Each class of widget has its own set of supported options. Widget options have a - (dash) in front of the option's name. Options such as -background, -foreground, -width and -height are supported by most widgets.

The "Hello, world" Example

Widget instances follow a strict hierarchical naming convention that is similar to absolute pathnames used by file systems. This allows you to do things like create widgets inside of specific widgets and top-level windows. You must use a period as the first character in widget instance names.

Earlier, we showed some example code that created a Tk button widget which displayed the text "Hello, world". The command that created this widget was:

```
button .hello -text "Hello, world"
⇒ .hello
```

When you create a widget, its name defines its hierarchical place in regard to its top-level window. Note the terms "slave", "master", "parent", and "child" are used a lot in the Tk man pages to differentiate the hierarchical relationship of widgets. In our "Hello, world" example, .hello is a child widget of the default top-level window, . (period).

The winfo command is useful for obtaining information on widgets, including hierarchical information. For example, to see the children widgets of the top-level window, . , we simply specify:

```
winfo children .
⇒ .hello
```

Be aware that in our "Hello, world" example, nothing changes in our application window until the following command is processed:

```
pack .hello
⇒
```

The above command, pack .hello, is using what is called the Packer Geometry Manager. pack executes low-level routines to display our widget in the appropriate top-level window.

At the time we created the button .hello, we could have given it attribute values different than its default values. Any time after creation, we can also configure the widget with different attribute values. For example, to make the background color of the .hello button red, we can create it as follows:

```
button .hello -text "Hello, world" -background red
⇒ .hello
```

or at any time later (as long as the .hello button exists), we can simply enter:

```
.hello configure -background red
⇒
```

Now, to make the application exit whenever we click on the .hello button with Mouse Button-1, we can create it as follows:

```
button .hello -text "Hello, world" -background red \
    -command { exit }
⇒ .hello
```

or at any time later (as long as the .hello button exists), we can simply enter:

```
.hello configure  -command {exit}
⇒
```

If at any time we want to unpack the .hello button, we simply enter:

```
pack forget .hello
⇒
```

The .hello button still exists, but it is no longer positioned or visible in the Tk Display Window. To make sure it still exists, we simply enter:

```
winfo exists .hello
⇒ 1
```

We can pack the .hello button again if we want to position it in the Tk Display Window. Or, we can destroy the .hello widget by simply entering:

```
destroy .hello
⇒ 1
```

Geometry Managers

A Geometry Manager is low-level software. Its job is to control the size and location of widgets on the screen. Widgets are displayed on the screen after the Geometry Manager computes their size and location. The three existing Tcl/Tk Geometry Managers are: the Packer, the Grid and the Place Geometry Managers. Each does basically the same thing, so it's really a user preference regarding which one to use. The Packer Geometry Manager is invoked using the `pack` command; the Grid Geometry Manager is invoked using the `grid` command; and the Place Geometry Manager is invoked using the `place` command.

The Packer is Tcl's original Geometry Manager and it is the one most often used in practice. The Packer simply packs around the edges of a cavity, as we will soon explain. The Grid uses a grid layout to place widgets and is very useful when you have complex layouts of many widgets. The Place Geometry Manager uses actual screen coordinates to place widgets and is the least used of the three Geometry Managers because of the complexity of using screen coordinates. In this book, we only use and discuss the Packer.

pack

The `pack` command is used to communicate with the Packer to display and arrange widgets. It arranges widgets by packing them in order around the edges of the parent. The `pack` command has the following forms:

```
pack slave ?slave ...? ?options?
pack configure slave ?slave ...? ?options?
pack forget slave ?slave ...?
pack info slave
pack propagate master ?boolean?
pack slaves master
```

Let's create three buttons and pack them side by side horizontally, as illustrated in Figure 7.2. To do this, we will use the `pack` command with the `-side` option as an argument. The `-side` option specifies the positioning order used to pack the widget.

```
button .b1 -text "Node Status"
⇒ .b1

button .b2 -text "Link Status"
⇒ .b2

button .b3 -text "Recent Traps"
⇒ .b3

pack .b1 .b2 .b3 -side left
⇒
```

Figure 7.2 Packing three buttons horizontally.

When you execute the above code, you will see that the main window automatically adjusts itself to the appropriate size. We could have prevented this resizing from automatically happening by issuing the method command, `pack propagate . false`, before packing our buttons. If we did this, we risk not seeing all the buttons unless we manually enlarge the main window ... so let's not do this.

Now, let's experiment with the `pack` command to rearrange the three button widgets we created already, namely `.b1`, `.b2` and `.b3`. First, let's arrange them one on top of the other and centered horizontally, as illustrated in Figure 7.3 (a). We do so by specifying:

```
pack .b1 .b2 .b3 -side top
```

Let's arrange them so they are left-aligned, as illustrated in Figure 7.3 (b), by specifying:

```
pack configure .b1 .b2 .b3 -anchor w
```

Let's fill out the buttons horizontally so that their widths are equal, as illustrated in Figure 7.3 (c), by specifying:

```
pack configure .b1 .b2 .b3 -fill x
```

Now, let's destroy these widgets:

```
destroy .b1 .b2 .b3
```

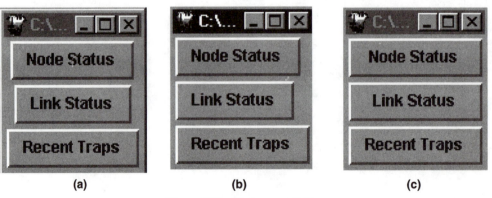

Figure 7.3 Packer example.

The Packer's Algorithm

When you create a widget, it normally becomes a slave widget to its parent or master widget. The Packer maintains an ordered list of slave widgets (called the packing list) for each master.

The Packer arranges the slaves for a master by scanning the packing list in order. At the time it processes each slave, a rectangular area called the cavity within the master is still unallocated. Thus, the area reserved for the first slave is the entire area of the master.

For each slave, the Packer carries out the following steps:

1. The Packer allocates a rectangular parcel for the slave along the side of the cavity given by the slave's -side option. The parcel may be enlarged further by the -expand option.

2. The Packer chooses the dimensions of the slave based on its needs or requested width and height. The dimensions of the slave may be enlarged to fill the entire parcel horizontally or vertically by the -fill option.

3. If the slave is smaller than the available cavity, it is packed accordingly within the cavity and the area of its parcel is subtracted from the cavity.

4. The top-level window resizes itself to fit the needs of the entire hierarchy of master-slave widgets.

Table 7.1 describes the various option arguments that can be used with the pack command.

Table 7.1 Options Available with the pack Command

-after other	This insert slaves just after other in the packing order.
-anchor anchor	anchor must be a valid anchor position, such as: center n s e w nw ne sw se It specifies where to position each slave in its parcel. Defaults to center.
-before other	This inserts the specified slaves just before other in the packing order.
-expand boolean	A Boolean value of 1 expands the specified slaves to consume extra space in their master parcel. If not specified, defaults to 0.
-fill style	This option is used to stretch the slave to fill its parcel. Valid values for style include:
	none Don't fill. This is the default.
	x Stretch horizontally to fill the entire width of the parcel.

Table 7.1 (continued)

`-fill style`	`y`	Stretch vertically to fill the entire height of the parcel.
	`both`	Stretch both horizontally and vertically.
`-in other`		Insert the slaves at the end of the packing order for the master window given by `other`.
`-ipadx amount`		Specifies how much horizontal internal padding to leave on each side of the slaves. `amount` must be a valid screen dis tance, such as 2 or .5c. It defaults to 0. (The default unit is screen pixels; a specification of .5c means .5 centimeters; a specification of 1i means 1 inch.)
`-ipady amount`		Specifies how much vertical internal padding to leave on each side of the slaves. `amount` defaults to 0.
`-padx amount`		Specifies how much horizontal external padding to leave on each side of the slaves. `amount` defaults to 0.
`-pady amount`		Specifies how much vertical external padding to leave on each side of the slaves. `amount` defaults to 0.
`-side side`		Specifies which side of the cavity to pack against. Must be `left`, `right`, `top` or `bottom`. Defaults to `top`.

bind

The `bind` command allows you to invoke a Tcl script whenever specific mouse or keyboard events occur for a specified widget or group of widgets. This binding can be specified either with the `bind` command or by using the bind method with specific widgets. The syntax of the `bind` command is as follows:

```
bind widget/tag eventsequence script
```

Let's illustrate the `bind` command with our "Hello, world" example. The following code sets up a binding so that whenever Mouse Button-3 is pressed with the cursor over our `.hello` button, we output the screen coordinates of the position of the mouse to the console.

```
bind .hello <Button-3> {puts "Current coordinates are: %x
%y"}
```

Now, when the user clicks Mouse Button-3 over any area of the `.hello` button, the screen coordinates of the exact mouse position are output to the console as follows:

```
⇒ Current coordinates are: 38 9
```

When used with widgets, the interpreter substitutes %x with the x coordinates of the current mouse position and %y with the y coordinates of the current mouse position. Later we will show you how we use %x and %y in conjunction with the bind command to track the position of items on a canvas as we allow users to move items to new positions.

BASIC TK WIDGETS

button

The button widget displays a button with a specified text string, bitmap or image inside of it. With the -relief option, it can be made to appear raised, sunken or flat. With the -command option, it can be made to invoke a Tcl command whenever a user presses Mouse Button-1 with the cursor over the button. The button command has the following syntax:

```
button pathName ?options?
```

You have seen Tk's button widget in action already with our simple "Hello, world" example. There, the button widget displayed the text "Hello, world" and invoked the simple command exit when pressed with Mouse Button-1.

canvas

The canvas command creates a canvas window that can be used to display and manipulate graphical items such as bitmaps, images, circles, lines, etc. Items in the canvas can be assigned tags and Tcl scripts can be bound to them. The syntax of the command to create the canvas widget is:

```
canvas pathName ?options?
```

In the following code, we create a canvas, .c, and in this canvas we create two oval objects representing nodes. We will make the color of the nodes green and connect the ovals with a line. The results are illustrated in Figure 7.4.

```
canvas .c -width 250 -height 250 -background beige \
  -relief raised
⇒ .c

pack .c -side top -fill both
⇒
```

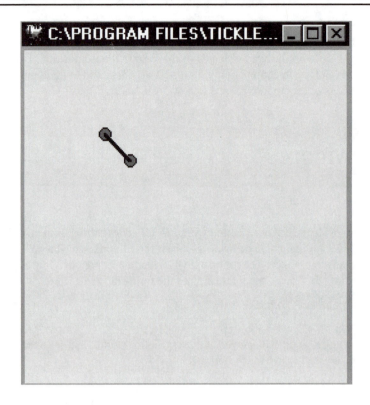

Figure 7.4   Canvas widget example.

```
set id1 [.c create oval 60 60 70 70 -tag node -fill green]
⇒ 1

set id2 [.c create oval 80 80 90 90 -tag node -fill green]
⇒ 2

set id3 [.c create line 65 65 85 85 -tag line -width 2]
⇒ 3
```

When we create items in the canvas, they are automatically assigned unique identifying numbers that are called ids. Our first oval was assigned id 1, our second id 2, and our line was assigned id 3. The id of an item never changes and id numbers are never re-used within the lifetime of a `canvas` widget. If we want to delete an item, we can do so using its id. For example, to delete our line we can simply specify:

```
.c delete 3
```

Each item may also have any number of tags associated with it. A tag is just a string of characters, and it may take any form except that of an integer. In our example above, we assigned the two ovals the tag `node` and the line the tag `line`.

When specifying items in `canvas` widget commands, if the specifier is an integer, it is assumed to refer to the single item with that id. If the specifier is not an integer, it is assumed to refer to all of the items in the canvas that have a tag matching the specifier. For example, to delete all nodes from our canvas, we can do so simply by specifying: `.c delete node`.

The tag `current` is managed automatically by Tk; it applies to the topmost item whose drawn area has the mouse cursor over it. If the mouse is not in the `canvas` widget or is not over an item, then no item has the `current` tag. Let's say we want the user to select which item to delete using Mouse Button-1. We can have the user make his/her selection and then in our code delete the item selected by specifying: `.c delete current`.

When you create items in a canvas, you must specify the coordinates for each item. Coordinates are specified as: `x1 y1 x2 y2`, where `x` is the horizontal distance from the left edge of the canvas and `y` is the vertical distance from the top edge of the canvas. When we used `60 60 70 70` for drawing our first oval, we specifyied the left top corner of our oval and the right bottom corner of our oval. Notice how when we drew our line, we actually specified the midpoints of our two ovals.

All coordinates related to canvases are stored as floating-point numbers. Coordinates and distances are specified in screen units, which are floating-point numbers optionally followed by one of several letters. If no letter is supplied, then the distance is in pixels; if the letter is m, the distance is in millimeters; if it is c, the distance is in centimeters; i means inches; and p means printer's points (1/72 inch).

Normally the origin of the canvas coordinate system is at the upper left corner of the window containing the canvas. It is possible to adjust the origin of the canvas coordinate system relative to the origin of the window using the `xview` and `yview` widget commands; this is typically used for scrolling.

entry

The `entry` widget is used to create a one-line text widget that can be both editable and scrollable by the user. The syntax of the command to create an `entry` widget is:

```
entry pathName ?options?
```

In the example below, we create a procedure, `GetRefData`, that uses multiple `entry` widgets to display and modify reference data, such as `sysName`, `sysLocation` and `sysContact`, for a specified node. Then we define some sample data for a node and invoke this procedure on that node. The results are illustrated in Figure 7.5.

```
proc GetRefData { n } {

    global nInfo
```

Figure 7.5 entry widget example.

```
set w [toplevel .$n]
wm minsize $w 250 250
wm title $w  $nInfo($n,addr)
wm iconname $w $nInfo($n,addr)
frame $w.frame
entry $w.frame.addr -textvariable nInfo($n,addr)  \
     -width 30 -state disabled
entry $w.frame.name -textvariable nInfo($n,sysName.0) \
     -width 30
entry $w.frame.location \
     -textvariable nInfo($n,sysLocation.0)  -width 30
entry $w.frame.contact \
     -textvariable nInfo($n,sysContact.0)  -width 30
entry $w.frame.rcomm -textvariable nInfo($n,rcomm)  \
     -width 30 -state disabled
```

```
        entry $w.frame.wcomm  -textvariable nInfo($n,wcomm) \
                -width 30 -show * -state disabled
        pack $w.frame.addr $w.frame.name $w.frame.location \
                $w.frame.contact $w.frame.rcomm $w.frame.wcomm
        pack $w.frame  -side left -fill both -expand true
        button $w.frame.close -text "Close" -command "destroy $w"
        pack $w.frame.close -anchor se

}

set nInfo(0,addr)                158.102.122.2
set nInfo(0,sysName.0)           Rtr-001
set nInfo(0,sysLocation.0)       " "
set nInfo(0,sysContact.0)        "Susan Maxwell"
set nInfo(0,rcomm)               public
set nInfo(0,wcomm)               private

GetRefData 0
```

This example first creates a top-level window for displaying or changing node reference data. Note that we didn't have to create a top-level window just to use the `entry` widget. We created a top-level window because we wanted the effect of a pop-up window here.

After creating the top-level window, we created a frame within the top-level window and then an `entry` widget for each attribute that we wanted to display. By using the `-state disabled` option, we inhibited the user from changing either the address or community name information in the above window. By using the `-show *` option, we ensured that * would be displayed for each character in the write community name. If the user edits any other field, he/she is modifying the array `nInfo` directly for the specified node.

frame

The `frame` widget acts as a spacer or container in window layouts. You may specify a background color for a frame and an optional 3-D border to make the frame appear raised or sunken. The syntax of the `frame` command is:

```
frame pathName ?options?
```

Frames are normally invisible to the user unless you assign them a background color that makes them distinguishable. Frames help tremendously in controlling the layout of your GUI. You have already seen us use the `frame` widget in the `entry` widget code example. You will also see us use the `frame` widget in several more subsequent examples.

label

The label widget can display a text string, bitmap or image. If text is displayed, it must all be in a single font, but it can occupy multiple lines. The syntax of the command to create a label widget is:

```
label pathName ?options?
```

The code below is a modification of the procedure GetRefData that was used in the previous example. This new code example allocates a label to each entry. The results of the code are illustrated in Figure 7.6.

```
proc DisplayRefData { n } {

    global nInfo

    set w [toplevel .$n]
    wm minsize $w 250 250
    wm title $w  $nInfo($n,addr)
    wm iconname $w $nInfo($n,addr)
    frame $w.f1
    label $w.f1.label1 -text "Address:" -width 30
    entry $w.f1.addr -textvariable nInfo($n,addr)  \
            -width 30 -state disabled
    pack $w.f1.label1 $w.f1.addr -side left
    pack $w.f1 -anchor w -fill x -expand true
    frame $w.f2
```

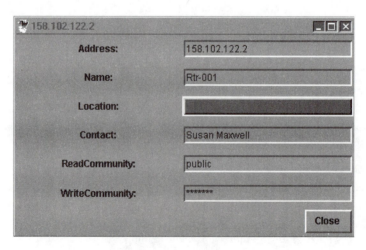

Figure 7.6 label widget example.

```
        label $w.f2.label2 -text "Name:" -width 30
        entry $w.f2.name -textvariable nInfo($n,sysName.0)    \
              -width 30
        pack $w.f2.label2 $w.f2.name -side left
        pack $w.f2 -anchor w -fill x -expand true
        frame $w.f3
        label $w.f3.label3 -text "Location:" -width 30
        entry $w.f3.location \
              -textvariable nInfo($n,sysLocation.0)\
              -width 30
        pack $w.f3.label3 $w.f3.location -side left
        pack $w.f3 -anchor w -fill x -expand true
        frame $w.f4
        label $w.f4.label4 -text "Contact:" -width 30
        entry $w.f4.contact -textvariable nInfo($n,sysContact.0) \
              -width 30
        pack $w.f4.label4 $w.f4.contact -side left
        pack $w.f4 -anchor w -fill x -expand true
        frame $w.f5
        label $w.f5.label5 -text "ReadCommunity:" -width 30
        entry $w.f5.rcomm -textvariable nInfo($n,rcomm)    \
              -width 30 -state disabled
        pack $w.f5.label5 $w.f5.rcomm -side left
        pack $w.f5 -anchor w -fill x -expand true
        frame $w.f6
        label $w.f6.label6 -text "WriteCommunity:" -width 30
        entry $w.f6.wcomm  -textvariable nInfo($n,wcomm)   \
              -width 30 -show * -state disabled
        pack $w.f6.label6 $w.f6.wcomm -side left
        pack $w.f6 -anchor w -fill x -expand true
        button $w.close -text "Close" -command "destroy $w"
        pack $w.close -anchor se

}
set nInfo(0,addr)                158.102.122.2
set nInfo(0,sysName.0)            Rtr-001
set nInfo(0,sysLocation.0)       " "
set nInfo(0,sysContact.0)        "Susan Maxwell"
set nInfo(0,rcomm)               public
set nInfo(0,wcomm)               private
set n 0
DisplayRefData $n
```

listbox

The listbox widget displays a list of strings, one per line. The intent is for the user to select an item in the list. When first created, a new listbox has no elements. Elements are added and deleted using method commands such as insert and delete. The command to create a listbox has the following syntax:

```
listbox pathName ?options?
```

Below we create a listbox that displays the names of some groups of network devices. By using the -selectmode single option, only a single group name at a time can be selected by the user. The results of the code below are illustrated in Figure 7.7.

```
listbox .groups -selectmode single
⇒ .groups

pack .groups
foreach group {"Universal Group" Cisco 3COM} {
    .groups insert end $group
}
```

Figure 7.7   listbox widget example.

To see which item in a listbox is selected, we first get the index of the selected item, and then we get the value of a specified index as illustrated below:

```
.groups curselection
⇒ 2


.groups get 2
⇒ 3COM
```

Below, we create a binding that outputs the group name to the console whenever a group name is selected by the user:

```
bind .groups <ButtonRelease-1> {
    set item [.groups get [.groups curselection]]
    puts "$item is selected"
}
```

message

The message widget displays a given text string and breaks it into a multi-line message. The line breaks are chosen at word boundaries wherever possible. The command to create a message widget has the following syntax:

```
message pathName ?options?
```

The message widget is very simple. The code below displays a long text string as a multi-line message. The results are illustrated in Figure 7.8.

```
set msg "This software is furnished under a license. It may be\
used and copied only in accordance with the terms of its\
license. This software and any copies thereof may not be\
provided or otherwise made available to any other person."\
⇒ This software is furnished under a license. It may be\
⇒ used and copied only in accordance with the terms of its\
⇒ license. This software and any copies thereof may not be\
⇒ provided or otherwise made available to any other person.

message .license -text $msg -width 300
⇒ .license

pack .license
```

This software is furnished under a license. It may be used and copied only in accordance with the terms of its license. This software and any copies thereof may not be provided or otherwise made available to any other person.

Figure 7.8 message widget example.

radiobutton

The radiobutton widget is normally used when you want the user to select one option from a set of two or more options. Radio buttons have a selector box that makes it apparent to the user which radio button is currently selected. The command to create a radio button has the following syntax:

```
radiobutton pathName ?options?
```

In the example code below, we use the radiobutton widget to allow the user to set a variable view. The results are illustrated in Figure 7.9.

```
frame .view
⇒ .view

radiobutton .view.statusmap -text "StatusMap" \
    -variable view -value StatusMap -anchor w
⇒ .view.statusmap

radiobutton .view.deviceview -text "DeviceView" \
    -variable view -value DeviceView -anchor w
⇒ .view.deviceview

pack .view.statusmap .view.deviceview -fill x -expand yes
pack .view
```

Notice how in Figure 7.9 neither button is selected. We can assign a selection by specifying the following:

```
.view.statusmap invoke
```

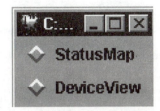

Figure 7.9   radiobutton widget example.

This results in the variable view being set to the value StatusMap. If the user selects De-viceView, the value of view gets set to the value DeviceView.

scrollbar

Scrollbars are used when you have a limited viewing area that is insufficient for what needs to be displayed. The command to create a scrollbar widget is as follows:

```
scrollbar pathName ?options?
```

Scrollbars are assigned to work with other widgets. For example, below we expand upon our previous listbox example by creating a scrollable listbox for displaying group names. The results are illustrated in Figure 7.10.

```
frame .f -height 75 -width 400
⇒ .f

pack .f -side top -fill x
listbox .f.groups -selectmode single \
  -xscrollcommand ".f.sx set" \
  -yscrollcommand ".f.sy set"
⇒ .f.groups

scrollbar .f.sx -orient horizontal -command ".f.groups xview"
⇒ .f.sx

scrollbar .f.sy -orient vertical \
     -command ".f.groups yview"
⇒ .f.sy

pack .f.sx -side bottom -fill x
```

```
pack .f.sy -side right -fill y
pack .f.groups -side left -fill both -expand true
foreach group {"Universal Group" Cisco 3COM} {
        .f.groups insert end $group
}
```

In the code above, we create two scrollbar widgets, namely .f.sx and .f.sy, and associate them with the listbox widget .f.groups. Each scrollbar contains a slider whose size and position represents the area of the listbox that is visible to the user. As we move a scrollbar, the visible portion of the associated widget changes. As it changes, the scrollbar sliders reflect the visible portion of the associated widget.

In Figure 7.10, the entire listbox is visible and both sliders represent this. If we were to resize our listbox so that it was too small in height to display all listbox entries, the size and position of the .f.sy slider would change accordingly.

When a user moves the horizontal scrollbar, .f.sx, the command .f.groups xview is invoked with each movement of the slider. When a user moves the vertical scrollbar, .f.sy, the command .f.groups yview is invoked with each movement of the slider. This changes the visible area of the listbox .f.groups.

The associated widget, .f.groups, in turn defines –xscrollcommand ".f.sx set" and –yscrollcommand "f.sy set". As its visible area changes with scrolling, it correspondingly changes the size and position of the associated scrollbar slider.

text

The text widget displays one or more lines of editable text. The command to create a text widget has the following syntax:

```
text pathName ?options?
```

text widgets support three different kinds of annotations on text: tags, marks and embedded windows. Tags allow different portions of the text to be displayed with different fonts and colors. In addition, Tcl commands can be associated with tags so that scripts are invoked when particular actions such as keystrokes and mouse button presses occur in particular ranges of the text.

The second form of annotation consists of marks, which are floating markers in the text. Marks are used to keep track of various positions in the text as it is edited.

The third form of annotation allows arbitrary windows to be embedded in a text widget.

The procedure below, NodeList, creates a scrollable text widget that we will use to display a line of nodal information (e.g., address, uptime, vendor, system name and system description) for each node in the global array nInfo:

```
proc NodeList { } {

        global nInfo nn
```

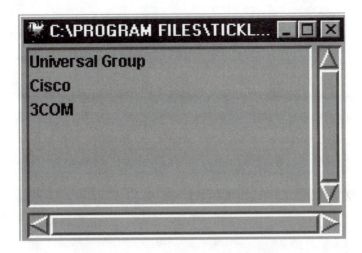

Figure 7.10 scrollbar widget example.

```
# This procedure displays node information in a
# scrollable textbox. The nodal information is
# contained in the array nInfo and nn is the
# last index value in nInfo.

# If it doesn't exist, create the scrolled text box,
# else make sure it's empty and editable.
  if { [winfo exists .nodes.text] != 1} {
     frame .nodes
     pack .nodes -side top -expand yes
     text .nodes.text -wrap none -height 10 -width 300 \
             -yscrollcommand ".nodes.sy set" \
             -xscrollcommand ".nodes.sx set"
     scrollbar .nodes.sx -orient horizontal \
             -command ".nodes.text xview"
     scrollbar .nodes.sy -orient vertical \
             -command ".nodes.text yview"
     pack .nodes.sx -side bottom -fill x
     pack .nodes.sy -side right -fill y
     pack .nodes.text -side left -fill both -expand true
  } else {
     .nodes.text configure -state normal
     .nodes.text delete 0.0 end
  }
```

```
    # Insert a line of info per node into .nodes.text.
     for {set n 0} {$n <= $nn} {incr n +1} {
       if { $nInfo($n,state) == 1} {
          set line [format "%-15s %9.1f %-15s %-20s %-40s\n" \
             $nInfo($n,addr) $nInfo($n,uphrs) \
             $nInfo($n,vendor) $nInfo($n,sysName) \
             $nInfo($n,sysDescr)]
       } else {
          set line [format "%-15s %9s %-15s %-20s %-40s\n" \
             $nInfo($n,addr) " " $nInfo($n,vendor) \
             $nInfo($n,sysName) $nInfo($n,sysDescr)]
       }
       set tag $nInfo($n,addr)
       .nodes.text  insert end $line $tag
    }

    # Change the state of .nodes.text so its no longer
    # editable.
     .nodes.text configure -state disabled
}
```

To test the procedure, we put it together with the procedure gInit. This procedure simply creates sample data in the array nInfo, as you can see below:

```
proc gInit { } {

    global nInfo nn

    set sampledata [list \
          {1 1.3.6.1.4.1.9.1.12 158.121.122.1 Rtr-001 Cisco \
          123.3 "Susan Maxwell (617) 232-2373" \
          "Bldg-001 Boston MA" \
          "Cisco Internetworking Operating System" -1} \
          {0 1.3.6.1.4.1.9.1.9 158.121.122.2 Rtr-002 Cisco \
          1243.3 "Susan Maxwell (617) 232-2373" \
          "Bldg-001 Boston MA" \
          "Cisco Internetworking Operating System" -1} \
          {1 1.3.6.1.4.1.114.1.3.3.1.7 158.121.122.3 \
          Sw-001 3Com 1.6 "Susan Maxwell (617) 232-2373" \
          "Bldg-001 Boston MA" "Lanplex Rev 4.3" -1} \
          {1 1.3.6.1.4.1.114.1.3.3.1.7 158.121.122.4 \
```

```
         Sw-002 3Com 2.4 "Susan Maxwell (617) 232-2373" \
         "Bldg-001 Boston MA" "Lanplex Rev 4.3" -1}]

    set n 0
    foreach el $sampledata {
        set nInfo($n,state)        [lindex $el 0]
        set nInfo($n,sysOID)       [lindex $el 1]
        set nInfo($n,addr)         [lindex $el 2]
        set nInfo($n,sysName)      [lindex $el 3]
        set nInfo($n,vendor)       [lindex $el 4]
        set nInfo($n,uphrs)        [lindex $el 5]
        set nInfo($n,sysContact)   [lindex $el 6]
        set nInfo($n,sysLocation)  [lindex $el 7]
        set nInfo($n,sysDescr)     [lindex $el 8]
        set nInfo($n,id)           [lindex $el 9]
        incr n +1
    }
    set nn [expr $n -1]
}
```

Now, we will invoke `gInit` and `NodeList`; the results are illustrated in Figure 7.11.

```
    gInit
    NodeList
```

In `NodeList`, the `-state` option is used to make the `text` widget either editable (normal) or not (disabled). The `text` widget's `insert` method command is used to insert items onto the `text` widget. The `text` widget's `delete` method is used to delete items from the `text` widget. Note that items in the `text` widget are indexed by `line.word`, so the command `.nodes.text delete 0.0 end` deletes the entire contents of our `text` widget.

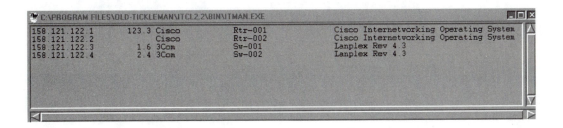

Figure 7.11 text widget example.

The -nowrap option prevents long text strings from wraparound, which is one reason why we implement the above with a horizontal scrollbar.

Notice that when we inserted lines into the text widget, we assigned each line a tag that was the address for the node associated with the given line. We can use this tag later to reference a given line of text. For example, if we wanted to change the color of the line with the address 158.121.122.1 to red, we would simply specify the following:

```
.nodes.text tag configure 158.101.122.1 -foreground red
```

EXAMPLE: BUILDING A MAIN APPLICATION WINDOW

We will now show the code for CreateMainWindow, which builds the main application window shown in Figure 7.12. This main window is suitable for many different types of network management applications. It has a menu bar, a scrolled listbox to show node groups, a scrolled text box to show node information, a label to display status messages and a canvas to display a status map.

We will use the lower frame .bottom, to display different contextual views. We will toggle between conceptual views by packing and unpacking each of them. The default view is StatusMap. The user will be able to toggle back and forth between the StatusMap view or some other application-specific view.

CreateMainWindow

CreateMainWindow uses two convenience routines: ScrolledListbox and ScrolledTextbox. These routines build a scrolled listbox and a scrolled textbox, respectively. CreateMainWindow creates the main window shown in Figure 7.12.

```
proc ScrolledListbox { parent args } {
    # Creates a scrolled list box.
    frame $parent
    eval {listbox $parent.listbox -bg beige \
        -yscrollcommand [list $parent.sy set] \
        -xscrollcommand [list $parent.sx set]} $args
    scrollbar $parent.sx -orient horizontal \
        -command [list $parent.listbox xview]
    scrollbar $parent.sy -orient vertical \
        -command [list $parent.listbox yview]
    pack $parent.sx -side bottom -fill x
```

TITLE
MENUBAR
LISTBOX
WITH
SCROLLBARS
TEXT WITH
SCROLLBARS
LABEL
WIDGET

CANVAS
WITH
SCROLLBARS

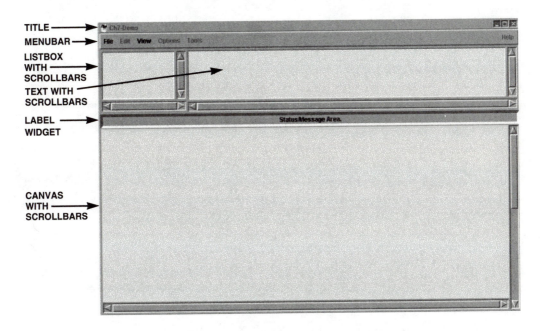

Figure 7.12   Main application window created by CreateMainWindow.

```
        pack $parent.sy -side right -fill y
        pack $parent.listbox -side left -fill both -expand true
}

proc ScrolledTextbox { parent args } {
        # Creates a scrolled text box.
        frame $parent
        eval {text $parent.text -bg beige -wrap none \
            -yscrollcommand [list $parent.sy set] \
            -xscrollcommand [list $parent.sx set]} $args
        scrollbar $parent.sx -orient horizontal \
            -command [list $parent.text xview]
        scrollbar $parent.sy -orient vertical \
            -command [list $parent.text yview]
        pack $parent.sx -side bottom -fill x
        pack $parent.sy -side right -fill y
        pack $parent.text -side left -fill both -expand true
}
```

```
proc CreateMainWindow { } {

    global view curr_view

    #   Step 1: Define main window attributes.

    wm minsize . 800 550
    wm   title .  Ch7-Demo
    wm iconname . Ch7-Demo

    # Step 2: Define broad frame layout of main window.

    frame .menubar -height 18 -relief raised \
        -borderwidth 2  -bg grey
    pack .menubar -side top -fill x
    frame .top -height 75  -borderwidth 2
    pack .top -side top -fill x
    frame .status -height 18 -borderwidth 3 \
        -relief sunken -bg grey
    pack .status -side top -fill x
    frame .bottom
    pack .bottom -side top -fill both -expand true

    # Step 3a: Define menubar main menu selections
    #          within the frame .menubar.

    # Create menubutton .menubar.file with submenu
    # .menubar.file.menu.
    menubutton .menubar.file -text "File" \
        -menu .menubar.file.menu
    menu .menubar.file.menu
    pack .menubar.file -side left

    # Create menubutton .menubar.edit with submenu
    # .menubar.edit.menu.
    menubutton .menubar.edit -text "Edit" \
        -menu .menubar.edit.menu -state disabled
    menu .menubar.edit.menu
    pack .menubar.edit -side left

    # Create menubutton .menubar.view with submenu
```

```
# .menubar.view.menu.
menubutton .menubar.view -text "View" \
  -menu .menubar.view.menu
menu .menubar.view.menu
pack .menubar.view  -side left


# Create menubutton .menubar.options with submenu
# .menubar.options.menu.
menubutton .menubar.options -text "Options" \
    -menu .menubar.options.menu -state disabled
menu .menubar.options.menu
pack .menubar.options  -side left


# Create menubutton .menubar.tools with submenu
# .menubar.tools.menu.
menubutton .menubar.tools  -text "Tools" \
    -menu .menubar.tools.menu -state disabled
menu .menubar.tools.menu
pack .menubar.tools  -side left


# Create menubutton .menubar.help with submenu
# .menubar.help.menu.
menubutton .menubar.help -text "Help" \
    -menu .menubar.help.menu -state disabled
menu .menubar.help.menu
pack .menubar.help -side right


# Step 3b: Define submenu selections.
# Add selections to the submenu .menubar.file.menu.

.menubar.file.menu add command -label "Open Device File" \
      -command  {# OpenNodeFile}
.menubar.file.menu add command  -label "Exit" \
      -command {exit}


# Create view menubutton with associated submenu choices.
.menubar.view.menu add radiobutton -label "StatusMap" \
    -variable view -value .bottom.statusmap \
    -command { pack forget $curr_view
                pack .bottom.statusmap  -side top  \
                  -fill both -expand yes
```

```
                    set curr_view .bottom.statusmap
}
set view .bottom.statusmap
set curr_view .bottom.statusmap

# Step 4a: Create scrolled listbox for group
# display and selection.

ScrolledListbox .top.groups -height 5 -selectmode single
pack .top.groups -side left

# Step 4b: Create scrolled textbox for node display and
# selection.

ScrolledTextbox .top.nodes -height 7
pack .top.nodes  -side left  -fill x -expand yes

# Step 5:  Create a label within frame .status to
# display status messages.

label .status.label  -text "Status/Message Area." \
      -bg grey    -relief sunken -height 1
pack .status.label -fill x -anchor ne -expand yes

# Step 6: Create a canvas to display StatusMap.

canvas .bottom.statusmap -confine false \
    -bg beige  -relief raised \
    -xscrollcommand ".bottom.statusmap.sx set" \
    -yscrollcommand ".bottom.statusmap.sy set"
scrollbar .bottom.statusmap.sx \
    -command ".bottom.statusmap xview" -orient horizontal
scrollbar .bottom.statusmap.sy \
    -command ".bottom.statusmap yview"
.bottom.statusmap configure -scrollregion "0 0 800  800"
pack  .bottom.statusmap.sy -side right  -fill y
pack  .bottom.statusmap.sx  -side bottom -fill x
pack  .bottom.statusmap  -side top  -fill both -expand yes

}
```

The code in `CreateMainWindow` is organized into the following six steps:

STEP 1: ASSIGN MINSIZE, TITLE AND ICONNAME TO MAIN WINDOW

Step 1 uses the wm command to assign a minimum size, title and icon name to our application window. The wm command interacts with the Window Manager to control attributes associated with a top-level window. The syntax of the wm command is as follows:

```
wm option window ?args
```

Various options are associated with the wm command, but they all expect window to be the path name for a top-level window.

STEP 2: ORGANIZE OUR MAIN WINDOW INTO FRAMES

Step 2 organizes the layout of our main window into four frames. The uppermost frame in our application window is .menubar. Underneath it is a frame called .top; underneath that is a frame called .status; and underneath that is a frame called .bottom. We assigned a height to each frame except .bottom, so that we can get a general idea of screen layout.

STEP 3: ADD MENUBAR AND MENU SELECTIONS TO OUR MAIN WINDOW

Step 3 first adds menu buttons to .menubar. Next, it adds menu selections to the File and View menu buttons. The File menu button has two selections: "Open Device File" and "Exit." Open Device File" calls the procedure OpenNodeFile, but we commented this out for now. "Exit" simply exits the application. The View menu button has one RadioSelection, and it sets the variable view to StatusMap. This is used to get back to the StatusMap view whenever the application is in a different contextual view.

STEP 4: ADD SCROLLED LISTBOX AND SCROLLED TEXT TO OUR MAIN WINDOW

Step 4 adds a scrolled listbox for group display and selection, plus a scrolled text area for node display using the convenience routines ScrolledListbox and ScrolledTextbox. These two convenience routines will be replaced by Itcl Mega-Widgets in Chapter 8.

STEP 5: ADD STATUS MESSAGE LINE

Step 5 creates the label widget .status.label, which we will use to display status messages to the user.

STEP 6: CREATE A CANVAS FOR STATUSMAP AND DEVICEVIEW

Step 6 creates a scrolled canvas area, `.bottom.statusmap`. Our applications can create additional views in the `.bottom` frame and toggle between views by unpacking one before packing the other. The canvas, `.bottom.statusmap`, will be used later to display device status via color coded bitmaps.

Test Driver

We will now build a test driver for `CreateMainWindow`. The results of running this driver are displayed in Figures 7.13 and 7.14. Figure 7.13 shows the StatusMap view; red indicates that the node is DOWN, green that the node is UP and HEALTHY. Double-clicking on any node will change the view to the node's DeviceView, as illustrated in Figure 7.14.

The code for our test driver is as follows:

```
source ch7-demo.itk ;# Contains CreateMainWindow.
source ginit.itk     ;# Contains gInit.

proc DisplayNodeList { } {

        global nn gi nInfo groups
```

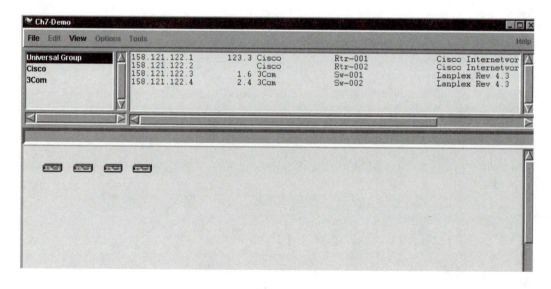

Figure 7.13   StatusMap view.

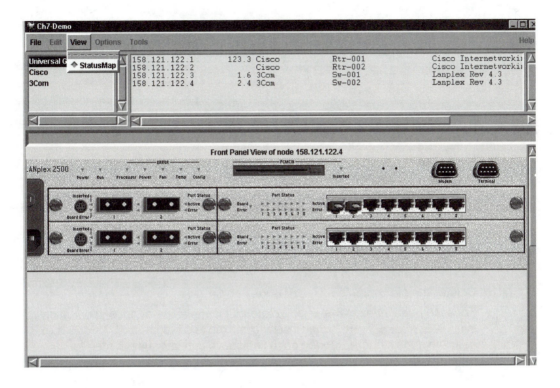

Figure 7.14 DeviceView view.

```
# Displays a specified group of nodes in the
# scrolled textbox at the upper right of the window.
set gi [.top.groups.listbox curselection]
if { [info exists groups($gi,nodelist)] != 1} { return }
if { [llength $groups($gi,nodelist)] <= 0} {return}

.top.nodes.text configure -state normal
.top.nodes.text delete 0.0 end

foreach n $groups($gi,nodelist) {
  if { $nInfo($n,state) == 1} {
    set line [format "%-15s %9.1f %-15s %-20s %-40s\n" \
        $nInfo($n,addr) $nInfo($n,uphrs) \
        $nInfo($n,vendor) $nInfo($n,sysName) \
        $nInfo($n,sysDescr)]
    } else {
```

```
            set line [format "%-15s %9s %-15s %-20s %-40s\n" \
                $nInfo($n,addr) " " $nInfo($n,vendor) \
                $nInfo($n,sysName) $nInfo($n,sysDescr)]
        }
        set tag $nInfo($n,addr)
        .top.nodes.text  insert end $line $tag
    }
    .top.nodes.text configure -state disabled
}
```

The procedure `DisplayNodeList` does the following:

- Gets the index of the selected item in `.top.groups.listbox`.
- From this index, obtains the list of node indexes that are members of the selected group.
- Changes the state of `.top.nodes.text` to normal from disabled. This allows it to modify the contents of `.top.nodes.text`.
- Deletes the old contents of `.top.nodes.text`.
- For each node index in the selected group, inserts a line of node information into `.top.nodes.text`. When inserting into the text widget `.top.nodes.text`, uses the node's address to tag each line so we can later use the tag to reference the line.
- Changes the state of `.top.nodes.text` to disabled so its contents cannot be modified by the user.

```
proc AddDevice { nindex  } {

    global x y xpos ypos nInfo nn gi width

    # This proc adds a node to the .bottom.statusmap canvas
    # and is called the first time we learn of a new node.

    # Set initial screen coordinates for the new node.
    set view [expr $width -100]
    if {$xpos < $view} { incr xpos 50
    } else { set xpos 50; incr ypos 50}
    set id [ .bottom.statusmap create bitmap \
        $xpos  $ypos  -bitmap @node.xbm -foreground black]
    .bottom.statusmap bind current <Enter> {
        set tag [.bottom.statusmap find withtag current]
        for {set n 0} {$n <=$nn} {incr n +1} {
            if {$nInfo($n,id) == $tag} {
```

```
            .status.label config -text $nInfo($n,addr)
            break
        }
    }
}


# Bind it so the statusbar clears whenever the
# mouse moves off the node.
.bottom.statusmap bind current <Leave> {
    .status.label config -text ""
}


# Bind it so that screen coordinates are made known
# whenever the mouse is over the node.
.bottom.statusmap bind  current  <Button-1> {
    global x y
    set x %x
    set y %y
}


# Bind it so the node moves with mouse drags.
.bottom.statusmap bind  current  <B1-Motion> {
    global x y; set newx %x;  set newy %y
    set distx [expr $newx - $x]
    set disty [expr $newy - $y]
    .bottom.statusmap move current $distx $disty
    # Store values for next time.
        set x $newx
        set y $newy
 }


# Bind it so that the user can double-click on the node
# and change from StatusMap view to device front panel.
.bottom.statusmap bind $id <Double-Button-1> {
    .bottom.statusmap itemconfigure all -background {}
    set tag [.bottom.statusmap find with tag current]
    for {set n 0} {$n <=$nn} {incr n +1} {
        if {$nInfo($n,id) == $tag} {
            DisplayFrontPanel $n
            break
        }
    }
```

```
    }

    return $id

}
```

The procedure `AddDevice` does the following:

- Gets the screen coordinates of the last node added to `.bottom.statusmap` and calculates a new set of screen coordinates for the new node to be added.
- Takes the bitmap from the file `node.xbm` and uses it to add the new node icon to the StatusMap canvas.
- Creates a bind association so whenever the user moves the mouse over the node, `.status.label` displays the address of the node.
- Creates a bind association so whenever the user moves the mouse off the node, `.status.label` is cleared.
- Creates a bind association so whenever the user clicks Mouse Button-1 over the node, the global variables `x` and `y` are set to the current coordinates of the mouse.
- Creates a bind association so the user can move the node with Mouse Button-1.
- Creates a bind association so the user launches the procedure `DisplayFrontPanel` by double-clicking the node with Mouse Button-1.

```
proc DisplayFrontPanel {nindex} {

    global  nInfo view width height curr_view

    # This routine displays a frontpanel bitmap of a 3Com
    # Lanplex 2500. It also makes hot spots on the bitmap.

    # Create .bottom.deviceview canvas if it does not exist.
    if { [winfo exists .bottom.deviceview] != 1} {
        canvas .bottom.deviceview -confine false -bg beige \
                -relief raised \
                -xscrollcommand ".bottom.deviceview.sx set" \
                -yscrollcommand ".bottom.deviceview.sy set"
        scrollbar .bottom.deviceview.sx \
            -command ".bottom.deviceview xview" \
            -orient horizontal
        scrollbar .bottom.deviceview.sy \
            -command ".bottom.deviceview yview"
```

```
    .bottom.deviceview configure \
        -scrollregion "0 0 800  800"
    pack  .bottom.deviceview.sy -side right  -fill y
    pack  .bottom.deviceview.sx  -side bottom -fill x
}

pack forget $curr_view
pack .bottom.deviceview -anchor nw -fill both \
    -expand yes -side left
.bottom.deviceview delete all
set view .bottom.deviceview
set curr_view .bottom.deviceview

# Check if the node is a 3Com Lanplex 2500.
if { [string compare 1.3.6.1.4.1.114.1.3.3.1.7 \
    $nInfo($nindex,sysOID)] == 0} {
    # Device is a supported 3Com Lanplex
    image create photo chassis -file "3comchas.gif"
    image create photo greenport -file "greenport.gif"
    set image chassis
    set heading \
        "Front Panel View of node $nInfo($nindex,addr)"
    if { [winfo exists .bottom.deviceview.label] != 1} {
        label .bottom.deviceview.label -text $heading \
            -width 60 -bg beige -fg black
        pack .bottom.deviceview.label  -side top -fill x
    } else {
        .bottom.deviceview.label configure -text $heading
    }

    .bottom.deviceview create image 400 100  \
        -image $image -tag chassis
    .bottom.deviceview create image 520 100 \
        -image greenport -tag port1
    .bottom.deviceview bind port1 <Button-1> {
        .status.label config -text "Port 1 selected"
    }
    .bottom.deviceview create image 550 100 \
        -image greenport -tag port2
    .bottom.deviceview bind port2 <Button-1> {
        .status.label conf -text "Port 2 selected"
    }
```

```
      .bottom.deviceview bind  chassis <Button-1> {
            .status.label conf -text "Chassis Selected"
      }
  }


}
```

The procedure `DisplayFrontPanel` does the following:

- Creates the canvas `.bottom.deviceview` if it doesn't already exist.
- Unpacks the value of the variable `curr_view`, packs `.bottom.deviceview` and sets `curr_view` to `.bottom.deviceview`.
- Checks if the specified node's System Object ID is that of a 3Com Lanplex 2500; if not, the precedure returns, else it displays the image of a Lanplex 2500 from the file `3comchas.gif` into `.bottom.deviceview` and gives this image the tag `chassis`.
- Creates images of port 1 and port 2, set them green, and tags each of these images respectively as `port1` and `port2`.
- Binds it so that `.status.label` displays a message whenever `chassis`, `port1` or `port2` is selected by the user.

```
proc UpdateStatus { n } {

    global nn nInfo

    # Make the color of the nodes and node info lines such
    # that they reflect the operational state of the node.
    if { $nInfo($n,state) == 1} {
        .top.nodes.text tag configure $nInfo($n,addr) \
            -foreground darkgreen
        .bottom.statusmap itemconfigure $nInfo($n,id) \
            -foreground darkgreen
    } elseif  { $nInfo($n,state) == 0} {
        .top.nodes.text tag configure $nInfo($n,addr) \
            -foreground red
        .bottom.statusmap itemconfigure $nInfo($n,id) \
            -foreground red
    }


}
```

The procedure `UpdateStatus` does the following:

- Checks the state of the node. If the state is 1 (UP), changes the color on the corresponding node in .bottom.statusmap and the corresponding line in .top.nodes.text to GREEN; if the state is 0 (DOWN), changes the color of both to RED.

Now, let's put everything together:

```
proc MainApp {} {
  uplevel #0 {

    # Initialize.

    set xpos 0
    set ypos 0
    set x 0
    set y 0
    set width  800
    set height 550

    CreateMainWindow

    # Add three groups to the group listbox.

    .top.groups.listbox insert end "Universal Group"
    .top.groups.listbox insert end "Cisco"
    .top.groups.listbox insert end "3Com"

    # Populate nInfo with some sample data using the
    # procedure gInit from the earlier text widget example.

    gInit

    # Create a list of nodes for each group.

    set groups(0,nodelist) [list 0 1 2 3]
    set groups(1,nodelist) [list 0 1]
    set groups(2,nodelist) [list 2 3]

    # Select index 0 "Universal Group".

    .top.groups.listbox selection set 0
    DisplayNodeList
```

```
# Add nodes to the StatusMap.

for {set n 0} {$n <= $nn} {incr n +1} {
    set nInfo($n,id) [AddDevice $n]
}

# Set up things so when the user selects an entry in
# .top.groups.list,
# its corresponding nodes are displayed in
# .top.nodes.text.

bind .top.groups.listbox <ButtonRelease-1> {
    DisplayNodeList
}

# Update status color for each node.

for { set n 0} {$n <= $nn} {incr n +1} {
    UpdateStatus $n
}

vwait forever

    }

}
```

Note that our example application window displays group names in the listbox
`.top.groups.listbox` and node information in the text widget `.top.nodes.text`. The
test driver binds Mouse Button-1 so that as users make group selections, the application displays
the nodes that are in that group. Each node has a node icon in the StatusMap that is color-coded to
its operational status. The node's operational status is also reflected by the color of the text line in
the node listbox. Double-clicking on a node icon will launch `DisplayFrontPanel`. This will
bring up a front-panel view of the node if the node's sysObjectID is that of a 3Com Lanplex 2500.
The front-panel bitmap has hot spots on its chassis and ports. The statusbar displays a message
whenever you touch a hot spot.

The following is a walk-through of the logic of `MainApp`:

- Initialize the variables that represent the initial width and height of our
  StatusMap canvas area, plus the x and y coordinates of where to place the
  first node.
- Invoke `CreateMainWindow`.

- Add three groups to `.top.groups.listbox`: "Universal Group", "Cisco", "3Com".
- Invoke `gInit`, which creates four nodes: two Cisco routers and two 3Com LANplexes.
- Assign the two Cisco routers to the Cisco group and the two 3Com LANplexes to the 3Com group. (Note that "Universal Group" contains all nodes.)
- Select "Universal Group" in `.top.groups.listbox` and invoke `DisplayNodeList` to display the appropriate nodes in `.top.nodes.text`.
- Bind `.top.groups.listbox` to call `DisplayNodeList` whenever the user releases Mouse Button-1 from a group selection.
- For each node, call `UpdateStatus`, which changes the color of the node in `.bottom.statusmap` and the color of the line in `.top.nodes.text` to green if the node is UP, and red if the state of the node is DOWN.
- End the main control path with `vwait forever` to keep the application from exiting.

IN SUMMARY

This chapter described how to create and use Tk widgets with the Packer Geometry Manager. We showed how to use the following widgets: `frame`, `button`, `canvas`, `listbox`, `text`, `entry`, `scrollbar` and `message`. We demonstrated building a top-level window using the `toplevel` command. We also showed several uses of the `winfo` command.

After laying the groundwork with Tk basic widgets, we provided the sample GUI code for `CreateMainWindow` and its test driver. `CreateMainWindow` can be used as a template for building a wide variety of network management GUIs.

In Chapter 8, we will show you more example code using Tk widgets. We will also introduce Itcl Mega-Widgets, and we will rewrite `CreateMainWindow` to use them. You will see how creating this GUI with Mega-Widgets is simpler than using Tk. In Chapter 15 you will see how you can use the Tk plug-in to extend the power of Tk via the Web.

8 *More Tk*

In this chapter, we will delve deeper into Tk. We will first build a simple table widget using Tk components. This simple table widget will allow data to be presented in an easy-to-view, tabular format, and will be used by several of our sample applications. Next, we will take another look at Tk canvases, showing a real-world example of using canvases to represent an IP path. Finally, we will explore the Itcl Mega-Widgets, and we will rebuild the GUI shown in Chapter 7 by replacing Tk code with Mega-Widgets.

A SIMPLE TABLE WIDGET

The justification for the simple table widget is straightforward: Data in tabular format is easier to view and digest than the same data presented in a listbox. What we want to do with the simple table widget is produce a frame that can be packed into a more complex GUI. When we build the IP path tracing tool in Chapter 13, we will be building a user interface with one main frame and several subframes packed within it, including the simple table widget and a scrolled canvas.

We will write a procedure which will build a table with a specified number of rows and columns. We will then write a related procedure which will allow you to populate each cell of the table. Figure 8.1 shows the same information from Figure 7.11 now represented as a table.

IP Address	Up Hours	Vendor	SysName	SysDescr
158.121.122.1	123.3	Cisco	Rtr-001	Cisco Internetworking Operating System
158.121.122.2	1243.3	Cisco	Rtr-002	Cisco Internetworking Operating System
158.121.122.3	1.6	3Com	Sw-001	Lanplex Rev 4.3
158.121.122.4	2.4	3Com	Sw-002	Lanplex Rev 4.3

Figure 8.1 Simple table widget example.

BUILDING A SIMPLE TABLE WIDGET

We will build a procedure, `MakeTable`, which will be passed a unique string to identify the table, the number of rows in the table and a variable number of strings to be used for the column headings. `MakeTable` will create a frame to hold the table, frames to represent each row in the table and labels to represent each cell. Each row frame will be packed into the table frame, and labels will be packed into the corresponding row frames. The code for `MakeTable` is as follows:

```
proc MakeTable {name rows args} {
  global gTableInternals
#
#  Create table of label widgets, then pack them.
#
#  Note that the name of each entry is:
#        .name_Table_frame.ri.cj, where name is the
#        name of the table and i and j are the row
#        and column numbers.
#

#  Create main frame.

        set f .${name}_Table_frame
  frame $f

  set columns [llength $args]
#
# Format for gTableInternals: # rows, #columns, start, end
#
  set gTableInternals($name) [list $rows $columns 1 $rows]

#
#  Create row frames to stick the label widgets in.
#
  for {set i 0} {$i <= $rows} {incr i 1} {
      frame $f.r$i
  }

  Table_CreateCells $f $rows $columns $args
  Table_PackFrames $f $rows
  return $f
}
```

Note that a global array, gTableInternals, is used to maintain certain information about each table, specifically the number of rows in the table, number of columns, the first row being displayed and the last row being displayed. At the moment, all rows are displayed, but this will change when we later add a vertical scrollbar. Also, the table frame is left unpacked and is returned by the procedure. Finally, frame row 0 is created to hold the column headings.

```
proc Table_CreateCells {f rows columns headers} {

   for {set i 0} {$i <= $rows} {incr i 1} {
        for {set j 0} {$j < $columns} {incr j 1} {
                set w $f.r$i.c$j
                set header [lindex $headers $j]
                set n [string length $header]
                label $w -width $n -justify center \
        -relief groove
                $w configure -text ""
                if {$i == 0} {
                    $w configure -text $header \
                        -fg white -bg blue -relief raised
                }
                pack $w -side left
        }
    }
}
```

Table_CreateCells is passed the table frame, the number of rows in the table, the number of columns and a list containing the header strings. This procedure creates a label to represent each cell. The cells within row 0 represent headers for the columns, and a corresponding text string is placed within each of these cells. Note that the width of each cell is determined by the length of the corresponding column header string.

```
proc Table_PackFrames {f rows} {
   global gTableInternals
#
#   Pack each frame on top of the other.
#
   for {set i 0} {$i <= $rows} {incr i 1} {
        pack $f.r$i -side top
   }
}
```

Table_PackFrames simply packs each row frame underneath each other within the table frame.

```
proc SetTableValue {name row column val} {
#
#    rows, columns start at [1, 1]
#
   set column [expr $column - 1]

   set w .${name}_Table_frame.r$row.c$column
   $w configure -text $val
}
```

SetTableValue is passed a string identifying a table, a row number, a column number and a value. The value is written into the cell identified by the row and column.

To demonstrate MakeTable, we will build a table with ten rows and three columns. A routine, MT_Driver, will populate each cell with row and column numbers. Figure 8.2 shows the results.

```
proc MT_Driver {name rows cols} {
   for {set i 1} {$i <= $rows} {incr i} {
        for {set j 1} {$j <= $cols} {incr j} {
             SetTableValue $name $i $j "$i,$j"
        }
   }
}

set f [MakeTable x 10 " First " " Second " " Third "]
pack $f
MT_Driver x 10 3
```

ADDING A SCROLLBAR TO THE SIMPLE TABLE WIDGET

So far, our simple table widget will display each row in the table. Obviously this will cause problems if we have more rows than can be displayed on a screen. We need a vertical scrollbar! As discussed in Chapter 7, scrollbars work very nicely with entry, listbox, text and canvas widgets. For the remainder of this section, we will show how a vertical scrollbar can be manually added to MakeTable to extend it to support scrolling. In fact, what we will be doing is making a scrollbar work with a complex, composite Tk widget.

As an aside: If our goal was to build the simple table widget within a toplevel window, we could have implemented scrolling easily by using an Itcl scrolledframe Mega-Widget, or even by building a scrolled canvas. However, our goal was to build a frame that could be packed within other frames, and we needed to be able to control both the number of rows and columns that were displayed. For example, using an Itcl scrolledframe, we can specify the width and height of a frame, and if it is placed within a toplevel window, the user can stretch it to the desired

First	Second	Third
1,1	1,2	1,3
2,1	2,2	2,3
3,1	3,2	3,3
4,1	4,2	4,3
5,1	5,2	5,3
6,1	6,2	6,3
7,1	7,2	7,3
8,1	8,2	8,3
9,1	9,2	9,3
10,1	10,2	10,3

Figure 8.2 MakeTable **example.**

size. However, figuring out what width and height to use so you can automatically control how many rows and columns are visible is not an easy task!

Getting back to the subject at hand, to implement vertical scrolling within our simple table widget we need to modify MakeTable and add two new procedures, Table_BuildVScroll-Bar and Scroll_call:

```
proc MakeTable {name rows displayRows args} {
  global gTableInternals
#
#  Create table of entry widgets, then pack them.
#
#  Note that the name of each entry is:
#        .{$name}_row{$i}col{$j}, where name is the
#        name of the table and i and j are the row
#        and column numbers.
#

#  create main frame

    set f .${name}_Table_frame
```

```
    frame $f

    set columns [llength $args]

    set n $displayRows
    if {$rows < $displayRows} {
        set n $rows
    }
#
# format for gTableInternals: # rows, #columns, start, end
#
    set gTableInternals($name) [list $rows $columns 1 $n]

    Table_BuildVScrollBar $name $rows $displayRows
#
#  Create frames to stick the entry widgets in.
#
    for {set i 0} {$i <= $rows} {incr i 1} {
        frame $f.r$i
    }

    Table_CreateCells $f $rows $columns $args
    Table_PackFrames $f [lindex $gTableInternals($name) 3]
    return $f
}
```

MakeTable needed to be modified slightly to pass it the number of rows to display and to call Table_BuildVScrollBar:

```
proc Table_BuildVScrollBar {name rows displayRows} {
    global gTableInternals

    if {$rows <= $displayRows} {
        return
    }

    set sc ${name}_Table_frame.xscroll

    append rows ".0"
    append displayRows ".0"
    set x [expr $displayRows/$rows]

    scrollbar .${name}_Table_frame.xscroll -orient vertical \
```

```
            -command [list Scroll_call .$sc $name $x xview]
        .$sc set 0.0 $x
        pack .${name}_Table_frame.xscroll -side right -fill y

    }
```

`Table_BuildVScrollBar` will build a vertical scrollbar if the number of rows in the table is greater than the number of rows to display. If either of the scrollbar arrows are clicked or the slider moved, the command:

```
    Scroll_call .$sc $name $x xview
```

will be executed. `$sc` references the `scrollbar` widget created by the routine, `$name` is a unique string identifying the table and `$x` is a ratio of the number of rows to display to the total number of rows. `xview` will generate the string `xview scroll -1 units` if the scrollbar's up arrow is clicked, `xview scroll 1 units` if the down arrow is clicked and `xview moveto pos` if the slider is moved (*pos* being a real number between 0 and 1, indicating the relative position of the slider within the scrollbar).

```
    proc Scroll_call {sc name offset args} {
        global gTableInternals

        set rows [lindex $gTableInternals($name) 0]
        set cols [lindex $gTableInternals($name) 1]
        set start [lindex $gTableInternals($name) 2]
        set end [lindex $gTableInternals($name) 3]

        set new_start $start
        set new_end $end
        set n "$rows.0"
    #
    #   If length of args = 4, scroll button was pushed.
    #
        if {[llength $args] == 4} {
            set i [lindex $args 2]
            if {([expr $start + $i] >= 1) && \
                ([expr $end + $i] <= $rows)} {
                    incr new_start $i
                    incr new_end $i
            }
            set pos [expr ($new_start - 1)/$n]
        }
    #
    #   If length of args = 3, scroll bar was dragged.
```

```
        #
    if {[llength $args] == 3} {
         set pos [lindex $args 2]
         if {$pos < 0.0} {
              set pos 0.0
         }
         if {[expr $pos + $offset] > 1.0} {
              set pos [expr 1 - $offset]
         }

         set new_start [expr $pos * $n + 1]
         set new_start [expr int($new_start)]

         set new_end [expr ($pos + $offset) * $n]
         set new_end [expr int($new_end)]
    }

    $sc set $pos [expr $pos + $offset]
    if {$start == $new_start} return

    set f .${name}_Table_frame
    if {$new_start < $start} {
         for {set i 0; set j $new_start} {$j < $start} \
              {incr i; incr j} {

              set x1 [expr $end - $i]
              set x2 [expr $start - $i - 1]
              set x3 [expr $x2 + 1]

              pack forget $f.r$x1
              pack $f.r$x2 -before $f.r$x3
         }
    }

    if {$start < $new_start} {
         for {set i 0; set j $start} {$j < $new_start} \
              {incr i; incr j} {

              set x1 [expr $start + $i]
              set x2 [expr $end + $i + 1]
              set x3 [expr $end + $i]
```

```
            pack forget $f.r$x1
            pack $f.r$x2 -after $f.r$x3
        }
    }

    set gTableInternals($name) \
    [list $rows $cols $new_start $new_end]
}
```

`Scroll_call` uses the unique name string passed to it to get information about the table generating the scroll event. Specifically, it needs the number of rows in the table, the first row currently being displayed and the last row currently being displayed. Based on the string produced by `xview`, it calculates which rows should be displayed. If these values haven't changed from the last saved settings, the routine simply returns.

If different rows need to be displayed, the outdated rows will be unpacked while the new rows that are currently unpacked are packed. The order of the rows will be maintained by properly using the `-before` and `-after` switches.

The following example builds a table with 100 rows, but displays only 10 (see Figure 8.3).

```
set f [MakeTable x 100 10 " First " " Second " " Third "]
pack $f
MT_Driver x 100 3
```

Lastly, we will provide a procedure, `DestroyTable`, which will destroy all the Tk widgets associated with a table, and free any associated memory from `gTableInternals`. Note that the row frames and cells are created as children of the table frame, so in destroying the table frame, we automatically destroy all the children.

```
proc DestroyTable {name} {
    global gTableInternals
    if {![info exists gTableInternals($name)]} {
        return
    }

    destroy .${name}_Table_frame
    unset gTableInternals($name)
}
```

In building the simple table, we used label widgets to represent cells. We did this for simplicity. With some minor tweaking, entry widgets could've been used, which would have allowed us to associate mouse button bindings to the cells, allowed the cells to be edited, and allowed large strings to be placed in a cell and scrolled. Even canvases could've been used to represent cells, which would have allowed us to build tables of bitmaps.

In our example, we showed how to implement a vertical scrollbar. Implementing a horizontal scrollbar would've been more difficult, but possible. To scroll the display horizontally, a combina-

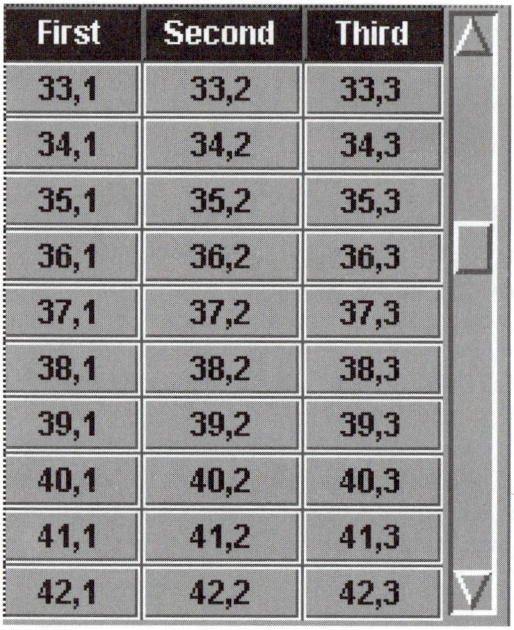

Figure 8.3   Example of a table with a vertical scrollbar.

tion of packing and unpacking cells, along with adjusting the width of the last displayed column, would have to be done.

A SECOND LOOK AT CANVASES

In the previous chapter, we briefly mentioned Tk canvases. In this section we are going to take a closer look at them, and show an example of using a canvas to represent an IP path. In our example, we will build a scrolled canvas, draw an IP path (which another procedure first calculates), allow individual nodes or connections to indicate status by changing their colors, trap mouse clicks on a specific node, and finally, allow an additional label window to pop up if a mouse sits on a node for three seconds.

This basic IP path drawing will be broken into the following procedures:

- `IpPath` acts as the main driver code for this example. It also sets up all the mouse event bindings for the canvas.
- `BuildCanvas` builds a scrolled canvas.
- `DrawIpPath` controls drawing an IP path into a canvas.
- `DrawNode` draws a node into the canvas.

- DrawEthConn draws an Ethernet connection between two nodes.
- DrawRingConn draws a ring connection between two nodes to represent either a Token Ring or FDDI connection.
- DrawSerialConn draws a serial connection between two nodes. This is used to represent any number of WAN connections.
- ConvertSpeedToStr converts an ifSpeed value to a displayable string.

```
proc IpPath {} {
  global gNodeSize gConnSize gxOffset gyOffset gMouseMoved
  global path gAfterId

  set path [list \
             [list start-node eth 10000000] \
             [list 158.101.121.106 serial 256000] \
             [list 198.2.1.1 ring 1540000] \
             [list 136.54.7.5 ring 100000000] \
             [list 207.14.171.4 eth 100000000] \
             [list dest none 0] \
             ]

  set gNodeSize 20
  set gConnSize 150
  set gxOffset  30
  set gyOffset  40
  set gAfterId  ""
  set gMouseMoved 0

  set t [toplevel .t]
  set f [BuildCanvas $t.f [llength $path]]
  pack $f

  DrawIpPath $f.c $path
  $f.c bind node <Button-1> {NodeSelected %x %y %W}
  $f.c bind node <Enter> {NodeEntered %x %y %W}
  $f.c bind node <Leave> {NodeLeft %x %y %W}
  bind $f.c <Motion> {MouseMoved}
}
```

IpPath initializes globals used in the example. It builds a toplevel window, places a scrolled canvas within it, draws the IP path represented by path and sets up mouse bindings for each drawn device within the canvas and for the canvas itself. Each drawn node is given the tag 'node', so the commands:

```
$f.c bind node <Button-1> {NodeSelected %x %y %W}
$f.c bind node <Enter> {NodeEntered %x %y %W}
$f.c bind node <Leave> {NodeLeft %x %y %W}
```

will set up bindings for whenever a mouse button is clicked within a node, a mouse enters a node or a mouse leaves a node. The command:

```
bind $f.c <Motion> {MouseMoved}
```

will set up a binding for whenever the mouse is moved within the canvas.

Each element within a path represents a device name or IP address, a connection type to the next device along the path and the linespeed of the connection.

```
proc BuildCanvas {p n} {
#
#   Build a canvas to represent n objects within
#   an ip path.
#
    global gNodeSize gConnSize gxOffset gyOffset
    set f [frame $p]

    set size [expr (($n-1) * ($gConnSize + $gNodeSize)) \
                + ($gxOffset * 2) + $gNodeSize]
    if {$size < 800} {
        set size 800
    }

    canvas $f.c \
            -xscrollcommand [list $f.xscroll set] \
            -width 800 -height 100 \
            -scrollregion [list 0 0 $size 100]

    scrollbar $f.xscroll -orient horizontal \
            -command [list $f.c xview]

    pack $f.xscroll -side bottom -fill x
    pack $f.c -side top -fill both -expand true
    return $f
}
```

BuildCanvas calculates the needed size of the scrolling window based on the number of devices within the IP path. It builds a frame, canvas and scrollbar, placing the canvas and scrollbar within the frame.

```
proc DrawIpPath {c path} {

    set i 0
    foreach el $path {

            set nodeName [lindex $el 0]
            set connType [lindex $el 1]
            set ifSpeed  [lindex $el 2]

            DrawNode $c $i $nodeName
            switch $connType {
               eth {DrawEthConn $c $i $ifSpeed}
               ring {DrawRingConn $c $i $ifSpeed}
               serial {DrawSerialConn $c $i $ifSpeed}
            }
            incr i
    }
}
```

DrawIpPath simply cycles through each element of the path, drawing both the node and connection to the next node. The last node in the path will have connection type none, which causes the switch statement to do nothing.

```
proc DrawNode {c i name} {
   global gNodeSize gConnSize gxOffset gyOffset

   set x0 [expr ($i * ($gConnSize + $gNodeSize)) + $gxOffset]
   set x1 [expr $x0 + $gNodeSize]
   set y0 $gyOffset
   set y1 [expr $y0 + $gNodeSize]

   $c create rect $x0 $y0 $x1 $y1 -fill black \
           -tag [list node$i node]

   $c create text $x0 [expr $y1 + 20] -text $name \
           -anchor sw -justify center -font {times 12 Normal}
}
```

DrawNode is passed the canvas, the position of a node within the path and a name of a node. It draws a rectangle within the canvas, assigning tags, node and nodei. The tag node is used for the mouse event bindings set up within IpPath. The tag nodei will be unique for each node, allowing individual nodes to have their statuses changed and to be able to distinguish in which node a mouse button was clicked. DrawNode also draws a text object under the rectangle, identifying the name of the device.

The following three procedures, DrawEthConn, DrawRingConn, and DrawSerial-Conn, draw different types of connections between two devices. DrawEthConn was used to draw the connection between the first and second nodes in Figure 8.4, DrawSerialConn was used to draw the connection between the second and third nodes and DrawRingConn drew the connection between the third and fourth nodes.

```
proc DrawEthConn {c i speed} {
    global gNodeSize gConnSize gxOffset gyOffset
#
# Draw five lines to represent an ethernet connection.
#
    set n [expr $gConnSize/2]

    set xa0 [expr ($i * ($gConnSize + $gNodeSize)) \
                + $gxOffset + $gNodeSize]
    set ya0 [expr $gyOffset + ($gNodeSize/2)]
    set xa1 [expr $xa0 + $n - 30]
    set ya1 $ya0

    $c create line $xa0 $ya0 $xa1 $ya1 \
            -width 2 -tag conn$i

    set xb0 $xa1
    set yb0 [expr $ya0 + 5]
    set xb1 [expr $xb0 + 60]
    set yb1 $yb0

    $c create line $xb0 $yb0 $xb1 $yb1 \
            -width 4 -tag conn$i

    $c create line $xb0 $ya0 $xb0 $yb0 \
            -width 2 -tag conn$i

    set xc0 [expr $xb1 + 2]
    set yc0 $ya0
    set xc1 [expr (($i+1) * ($gConnSize + $gNodeSize)) \
```

```
                           + $gxOffset]
      set yc1 $yc0

      $c create line $xc0 $yc0 $xc1 $yc1 \
           -width 2 -tag conn$i

      $c create line $xc0 $ya0 $xc0 $yb0 \
           -width 2 -tag conn$i

      $c create text [expr $xa0 + $n] \
           [expr $ya0 - 25] -text [ConvertSpeedToStr $speed] \
           -anchor s -justify center -font {times 14 Bold} \
           -tag conn$i
}
```

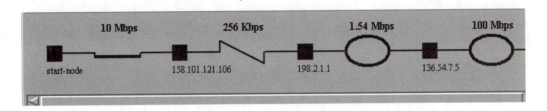

Figure 8.4 Drawing an IP path in a canvas.

DrawEthConn draws an Ethernet connection by drawing five lines, each assigned the tag conni. The linespeed of the connection is drawn above the middle of the connection.

```
proc DrawRingConn {c i speed} {
   global gNodeSize gConnSize gxOffset gyOffset
#
#  Draw a line, an oval and another line to represent
#  a token ring or FDDI connection.
#
   set n [expr $gConnSize/2]

   set xa0 [expr ($i * ($gConnSize + $gNodeSize)) \
                + $gxOffset + $gNodeSize]
   set ya0 [expr $gyOffset + ($gNodeSize/2)]
   set xa1 [expr $xa0 + $n - 30]
   set ya1 $ya0

   $c create line $xa0 $ya0 $xa1 $ya1 \
```

```
                 -width 2 -tag conn$i

    set xb0 $xa1
    set yb0 [expr $gyOffset - 10]
    set xb1 [expr $xb0 + 60]
    set yb1 [expr $gyOffset + $gNodeSize + 10]

    $c create oval $xb0 $yb0 $xb1 $yb1 \
            -width 4 -tag connRing$i

    set xc0 $xb1
    set yc0 $ya0
    set xc1 [expr (($i+1) * ($gConnSize + $gNodeSize)) \
                + $gxOffset]
    set yc1 $ya0

    $c create line $xc0 $yc0 $xc1 $yc1 \
            -width 2 -tag conn$i

    $c create text [expr $xa0 + $n] \
            [expr $ya0 - 25] -text [ConvertSpeedToStr $speed] \
            -anchor s -justify center -font {times 14 Bold} \
            -tag conn$i
    }
```

DrawRingConn draws a Token Ring or FDDI connection by drawing two lines and an oval. Again, the tag conni is assigned to each drawing making up the connection.

```
proc DrawSerialConn {c i speed} {
    global gNodeSize gConnSize gxOffset gyOffset
    #
    #  Draw a series of lines to represent a serial connection.
    #
    set n [expr $gConnSize/2]

    set xa0 [expr ($i * ($gConnSize + $gNodeSize)) \
                + $gxOffset + $gNodeSize]
    set ya0 [expr $gyOffset + ($gNodeSize/2)]
    set xa1 [expr $xa0 + $n - 30]
    set ya1 $ya0

    $c create line $xa0 $ya0 $xa1 $ya1 \
            -width 2 -tag conn$i
```

```
#
#  Draw a line going up.
#

   set xb0 $xa1
   set yb0 $ya0
   set xb1 $xa1
   set yb1 [expr $yb0 - 15]

   $c create line $xb0 $yb0 $xb1 $yb1 \
         -width 2 -tag conn$i
#
#  Draw a diagonal line.
#
   set xc0 $xb0
   set yc0 $yb1
   set xc1 [expr $xb0 + 60]
   set yc1 [expr $yb0 + 15]

   $c create line $xc0 $yc0 $xc1 $yc1 \
         -width 2 -tag conn$i
#
#  Draw a line going up.
#
   set xd0 $xc1
   set yd0 $yc1
   set xd1 $xc1
   set yd1 $ya0

   $c create line $xd0 $yd0 $xd1 $yd1 \
         -width 2 -tag conn$i
#
#  Draw a line to next node.
#
   set xe0 $xd0
   set ye0 $ya0
   set xe1 [expr (($i+1) * ($gConnSize + $gNodeSize)) \
               + $gxOffset]
   set ye1 $ya0

   $c create line $xe0 $ye0 $xe1 $ye1 \
```

```
        -width 2 -tag conn$i

$c create text [expr $xa0 + $n] \
        [expr $ya0 - 25] -text [ConvertSpeedToStr $speed] \
        -anchor s -justify center -font {times 14 Bold} \
        -tag conn$i
}
```

DrawSerialConn draws a serial connection as a series of five lines. And once again, the tag conni is assigned to each part of the connection.

```
proc ConvertSpeedToStr {speed} {

    if {$speed < 1000000} {
        set n [expr $speed/1000.0]
        set s [format "%7.2f" $n]
        set s [string trimright $s "0"]
        set s [string trimright $s "."]
        return "$s Kbps"
    }

    if {$speed < 1000000000} {
        set n [expr $speed/1000000.0]
        set s [format "%7.2f" $n]
        set s [string trimright $s "0"]
        set s [string trimright $s "."]
        return "$s Mbps"
    }

    set n [expr $speed/1000000000.0]
    set s [format "%7.2f" $n]
    set s [string trimright $s "0"]
    set s [string trimright $s "."]
    return "$s Gbps"
}
```

ConvertSpeedToStr simply converts a linespeed to an appropriate displayable string. For example, a linespeed of 10000000 will be converted to 10 Mbps, a linespeed of 56000 will be converted to 56 Kbps.

The following procedures handle both mouse events and setting node and connection statuses:

- GetNodeTag, given the x,y coordinates of a mouse click, returns the tag associated with the closest node.

- NodeSelected is a callback routine for a mouse button pressed event.

- SetNodeStatus sets the color of a specific node.
- SetConnStatus sets the color of a specific connection.
- NodeEntered is a callback routine for a mouse enter event.
- NodeLeft is a callback routine for a mouse leave event.
- MouseMoved is a callback routine for a mouse move event.
- ProcessNodeStuff pops up a label window if a mouse sits on a node for three seconds.

```
proc GetNodeTag {x y c} {
    set x [$c canvasx $x]
    set y [$c canvasy $y]
    set t [$c find closest $x $y]
    set tags [$c gettags $t]

    foreach el $tags {
        set rc [scan $el "node%d" n]
        if {$rc == 1} {
            return $el
        }
    }
    return none
}
```

In GetNodeTag, the commands:

```
set x [$c canvasx $x]
set y [$c canvasy $y]
```

map the x and y screen coordinates to the canvas coordinates. The command:

```
set t [$c find closest $x $y]
```

sets t to the ID of the drawn object closest to the x and y coordinates given. Finally, the command:

```
set tags [$c gettags $t]
```

returns a list of tags assigned to the given ID. Since each node was assigned the tags node and nodei, we need to cycle through the list and find the nodei tags which uniquely identify the node.

```
proc NodeEntered {x y c} {
    global gAfterId gMouseMoved

    if {$gMouseMoved == 1} return
```

```
if {[winfo exists $c.labelInfo] == 1} {
    $c delete info
    destroy $c.labelInfo
}

if {[string length $gAfterId] > 0} {
    after cancel $gAfterId
    set gAfterId ""
}

set tag [GetNodeTag $x $y $c]
set gAfterId [after 3000 ProcessNodeStuff $tag $c $x $y]
}
```

NodeEntered gets called by the binding set up for a mouse enter event, passing it the x and y coodinates along with the associated window. This routine will get called when a mouse enters any of the areas associated with the tag node. The command:

```
set gAfterId [after 3000 ProcessNodeStuff $c $x $y]
```

will cause ProcessNodeStuff to be called after three seconds. The ID associated with the after command is assigned to gAfterId so that the registered command can be cancelled if a mouse leave event is detected within three seconds.

```
proc NodeLeft {x y c} {
    global gAfterId gMouseMoved

    if {$gMouseMoved == 1} return

    if {[winfo exists $c.labelInfo] == 1} {
        $c delete info
        destroy $c.labelInfo
    }

    set tag [GetNodeTag $x $y $c]
    if {[string length $gAfterId] > 0} {
        after cancel $gAfterId
        set gAfterId ""
    }
}
```

NodeLeft will get called when a mouse leaves any of the areas associated with the tag node. If an after command is pending due to NodeEntered, it will be cancelled.

```
proc MouseMoved {} {
```

```
    global gMouseMoved

    set gMouseMoved 0
}
```

MouseMoved will be called if a mouse move event occurs anywhere within the canvas. This simply clears a global variable that was set by ProcessNodeStuff. More about this a little later.

```
proc ProcessNodeStuff {tag c x y} {
  global path gMouseMoved

  set x [$c canvasx $x]
  set y [$c canvasy $y]

  if {[winfo exists $c.labelInfo] == 1} {
      $c delete info
      destroy $c.labelInfo
  }

  if {[$c itemcget $tag -fill] == "black"} {
      set status "Normal"
  } else {
      set status "Critical"
  }

  set gMouseMoved 1
  set info [label $c.labelInfo \
      -bg white -fg blue  \
      -relief raised -text $status]
  $c create window $x $y -anchor w -window $info \
      -tag info
}
```

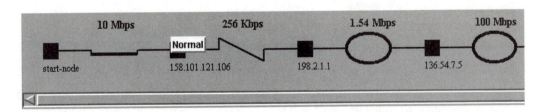

Figure 8.5 Pop-up label added to the canvas.

ProcessNodeStuff simply pops up a window in the canvas identifying the status of the node on which the mouse has been sitting (see Figure 8.5). The variable gMouseMoved is used to keep track of whether the mouse has moved since the label window was created. This is necessary because if the label is placed on top of where the mouse is currently sitting, a mouse leave event will be generated. Tracking when the mouse actually moves, we can distinguish between genuine mouse leave events (which will cause this pop-up window to be deleted) and the phantom type just mentioned.

```
proc NodeSelected {x y c} {

    set tag [GetNodeTag $x $y $c]

    if {$tag == "none"} return

    #
    #  If current status black, set to red;
    #  else set back to black.
    #

    if {[$c itemcget $tag -fill] == "black"} {
       set status red
    } else {
         set status black
    }

    $c itemconfigure $tag -fill $status
}
```

NodeSelected is called when a mouse button press event occurs within a node. It simply toggles the color of a node from black to red.

```
proc SetNodeStatus {c n color} {
    $c itemconfigure node$n -fill $color
}

proc SetConnStatus {c n color} {
    $c itemconfigure conn$n -fill $color
    $c itemconfigure connRing$n -outline $color
}
```

Wrapping up our canvas example, SetNodeStatus and SetConnStatus simply use the unique tag value associated with each node and connection to set the node and connection colors, respectively.

ITCL MEGA-WIDGETS

In this section, we will discuss the Itcl extension package, introduce the set of Mega-Widgets that come with it and show examples of a few Mega-Widgets. Then we will rewrite the procedure `CreateMainWindow` from Chapter 7 using Itcl Mega-Widgets.

SNMP Research's TickleMan product ships with Version 2.2 of Itcl. Its **itmansh** and **itman** interpreters support both SNMP and Itcl extension commands. If you are a Scotty user and want to use Itcl, you can freely obtain Itcl from http://www.tcltk.com/itcl.

First and foremost, the Itcl extension package can greatly simplify application coding while maintaining compatibility with Tcl/Tk. Second, it is very useful for creating new widgets. Third, it comes with [incr Widgets]—a set of pre-built Mega-Widgets.

ITCL INTRODUCTION

Michael McLennan of Lucent Technologies introduced [incr Tcl], pronounced "inker tickle," in1993 and has been leading its evolution ever since. This very popular extension package provides extra language support for building Tcl/Tk applications via an object-oriented paradigm.

Included with the Itcl extension package are:

- [incr Tcl], which provides object-oriented language extensions to Tcl.
- [incr Tk], which allows you to build high-level Mega-Widgets without C programming.
- [incr Widgets], which is a set of useful Mega-Widgets built from [incr Tk].

To get full advantage of the Itcl extension package, you need to learn to build [incr Tcl] classes. This is beyond the scope of this book and is best left to after you have gained a basic proficiency with Tcl/Tk. Once you are ready for this, we recommend the book *Tcl/Tk Tools* by Mark Harrison. It has descriptions of several useful Tcl extension packages with two chapters written by Michael McLennan on [incr Tcl] and [incr Tk], plus a chapter by Mark Ulfer on [incr Widgets].

If your Tcl installation is like TickleMan and supports Itcl, don't delay learning how to use [incr Widgets], the set of Mega-Widgets that come packaged with Itcl. You create and use Mega-Widgets just like regular widgets. The fact that they are built using [incr Tk] is transparent to you.

[Incr Widgets] Mega-Widgets

The [incr Widget] set of Mega-Widgets is created and managed just like Tk widgets, but they are actually made up of a number of sub-widgets.

Remember in Chapter 7, in our procedure `CreateMainWindow`, we needed a scrolled list-box. There we defined a convenience routine call `ScrolledListbox` to create one. Our

ScrolledListbox procedure had the undesired complexity of making us manually create and manage the several individual widget components that made up our scrolled listbox.

Well, life gets simpler when we use the Itcl extension package. It provides a scrolledlistbox widget that does exactly what we need plus more. Using Itcl's scrolledlistbox, we only need to create and manage one widget, not several. In addition, our high-level Mega-Widget will support normal Tk methods commands like configure and cget, while also supporting most of the normal methods and options of its Tk sub-widgets.

Table 8.1 Itcl Mega-Widget Commands

Table 8.1 lists the various Mega-Widgets commands that are available with Version 2.2 of Itcl.

buttonbox	Manager widget for adding pushbuttons.
canvasprintbox	Print box for printing the contents of a canvas widget to a printer or a file.
canvasprintdialog	Print dialog for printing the contents of a canvas widget to a printer or a file.
combobox	Enhanced entry field widget with an optional associated label and a scrollable list of choices. When an item is selected in the list area of a Combobox, its value is then displayed in the entry field text area.
dialog	Dialog box providing standard buttons and a childsite for use in derived classes. The buttons include ok, apply, cancel and help.
dialogshell	Dialog shell which is a top level widget composed of a button box, separator and childsite area. Also has methods to control button construction.
entryfield	Enhanced text entry widget with an optional associated label. Additional options support validation and length control on the entry field.
feedback	Feedback widget to display feedback on the current status of an ongoing operation to the user. Display is given as a percentage and as a thermometer-type bar. Options exist for adding a label and controlling its position.
fileselectionbox	File selection box composed of directory and file scrolled lists, as well as filter and selection entry fields.

	Table 8.1 *(continued)*
`fileselectiondialog`	File selection dialog that is derived from the `Dialog` class and is composed of a `fileselectionbox` with attributes set to manipulate the dialog buttons.
`hyperhelp`	HTML hypertext help viewer. This is a shell window with a pulldown menu showing a list of topics. The topics are displayed by importing an HTML-formatted file named helpdir/topic.html.
`labeledwidget`	Labeled widget which contains a label and childsite.
`menubar`	Widget that simplifies the task of creating menu hierarchies. It encapsulates a frame widget, as well as menubuttons, menus and menu entries.
`messagedialog`	Message dialog composite widget that is composed of an image and associated message text with commands to manipulate the dialog buttons.
`notebook`	Notebook widget that contains a set of pages. Each page is a childsite frame. When a new page is selected, the previously selected page's childsite frame is automatically unpacked from the notebook and the newly selected page's childsite is packed. Pages may be added or deleted using widget commands.
`optionmenu`	Option menu widget, which is a frame containing a label and a button. Press the button and a pop-up menu of choices appears.
`panedwindow`	Widget that can support multiple childsites from which you display multiple panes.
`promptdialog`	Prompt dialog widget that is derived from the dialog class and is composed of an `entryfield` with commands to manipulate the dialog button.
`pushbutton`	Pushbutton with an optional default ring.
`radiobox`	Radio button box widget capable of adding, inserting, deleting, selecting and configuring radiobuttons, as well as obtaining the currently selected button.
`scrolledcanvas`	Scrolled canvas.

Table 8.1 (continued)

`scrolledframe`	Scrolled frame.
`scrolledhtml`	Scrolled text widget with the additional capability to display HTML-formatted documents.
`scrolledlistbox`	Scrolled listbox
`scrolledtext`	Scrolled text widget with additional options to manage scrollbars. Options also exist for adding a label to the scrolled text area and controlling its position. Import/export of methods are provided for file I/O.
`selectionbox`	Scrolled list of items and a selection entry field. The user may choose any of the items displayed in the scrolled list of alternatives and the selection field will be filled with the choice. The user is also free to enter a new value in the selection entry field. Both the list and entry areas have labels. A childsite is also provided in which the user may create other widgets to be used in conjunction with the selection box.
`selectiondialog`	Selection box to allow the user to select from a list of choices. Provides a childsite so it can be extended.
`shell`	Toplevel window shell that serves as a based class for many other Mega-Widgets, such as the `dialogshell`.
`spindate`	Set of spinners for use in date value entry. The set includes a month, day and year spinner widget.
`spinint`	Widget that displays a label, an entry field and up/down arrow buttons that allow "spinning" of integer values within a specified range with wrap support.
`spinner`	Widget that is composed of an `entryfield`, plus up and down arrow buttons. This basic class is used by `spinint`, `spintime` and `spindate`.
`spintime`	Set of spinners for use in time value entry. The set includes an hour, minute and second spinner widget.
`tabnotebook`	Like the `notebook` widget, but this command creates a `tabnotebook` with the look of a series of folders with tabs.
`tabset`	Widget usually used to add tab buttons to some other widget.
`toolbar`	Widget often used with bitmaps to create an icon toolbar.

[Incr Widgets] Inheritance Hierarchy

All of the [incr Widgets] Mega-Widgets are derived from the `itk::widget` and `itk::toplevel` base classes of [incr Tk]. In turn, several [incr Widgets] Mega-Widgets are themselves derived from other Mega-Widgets. For example, the `scrolledlistbox`, `optionmenu`, `entryfield`, `scrolledtext`, `scrolledcanvas`, `scrolledframe` and `feedback` Mega-Widgets are all derived from the `labeledwidget` Mega-Widget. Likewise, the `messagedialog`, `promptdialog`, `selectiondialog`, `fileselectiondialog` and `canvasprintdialog` are all derived from the `dialog` Mega-Widget.

Childsites

Most Mega-Widgets support something called a childsite or childsite frame. A childsite frame is a standard Tk frame widget that is an optional child widget of your Mega-Widget. You can acquire the path of this frame widget with the childsite command. Using this command, you can extend a Mega-Widget by sticking other widgets or Mega-Widgets within the childsite frame.

Example—buttonbox

The `buttonbox` Mega-Widget creates and manages a box of pushbuttons, which are themselves Mega-Widgets. The command to create a buttonbox has the following syntax:

```
buttonbox pathName ?options?
```

In the example below, we create a buttonbox `.bb` and add to it three pushbuttons. The results of this are illustrated in Figure 8.6.

```
buttonbox .bb
⇒ .bb

.bb add b1 -text "Node Status" -command {puts "Node Status"}
.bb add b2 -text "Link Status" -command {puts "Link Status"}
.bb add b3 -text "Recent Traps" -command {puts "Recent Traps"}
pack .bb -expand yes -fill both
```

If we wanted to change the background of our buttonbox `.bb` to beige, we would simply specify the following:

```
.bb configure -background beige
```

Each of the buttons have an index number corresponding to their left or topmost position. For example, The "Node Status" button has an assigned index of zero. We can hide this button by issuing the following command:

```
.bb hide 0
```

Now, the "Node Status" button still exists; we didn't delete it. Note that we can reference any button either by its tag or index. Above, we hide the "Node Status" button using its index. We could just as easily hide it using its tag as follows:

```
.bb hide b1
```

To destroy our buttonbox, we simply specify:

```
destroy .bb
```

Example—canvasprintdialog

The `canvasprintdialog` Mega-Widget displays a top-level print dialog for printing the contents of a canvas widget to a printer or a file in postscript format. It is possible to specify page orientation, the number of pages to print the image on and if the output should be stretched to fit the page. The command to create a `canvasprintdialog` has the following syntax:

```
canvasprintdialog pathName ?options?
```

For example, say we have multiple canvases in our application and we want to give the user the capability of printing the contents of the various canvases to a file or printer. We can use either the `canvasprintbox` or `canvasprintdialog` Mega-Widget for this. Here we use `canvasprintdialog` as follows:

First, we create the `canvasprintdialog` widget:

```
canvasprintdialog .cpd
```

Second, when we want to print a canvas, in this case `$v2tab1.deviceview`, we use the `setcanvas` method on `.cpd` to define which canvas to print:

```
.cpd setcanvas $v2tab1.deviceview
⇒ after#59
```

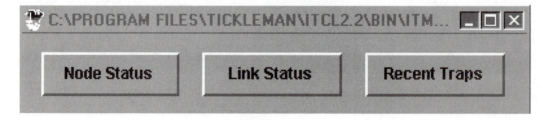

Figure 8.6 `buttonbox` Mega-Widget.

Next, we use the `activate` method on `.cpd`:

```
.cpd activate
```

As soon as we activate `.cpd`, the user will see the `canvasprintdialog` screen, as illustrated in Figure 8.7.

Example—hyperhelp

The `hyperhelp` Mega-Widget displays a top-level shell window that is used for selecting and displaying the contents of HTML-formatted help files. It provides a pulldown menu showing a list of topics and a scrolled area for displaying the contents of whatever HTML file is selected. The topics correspond to individual HTML help files. As you select a topic, its associated HTML file is displayed in the scrolled area. A `showtopic` command is used to initialize or change topics. The syntax of the command to create a `hyperhelp` Mega-Widget is:

```
hyperhelp pathName ?options
```

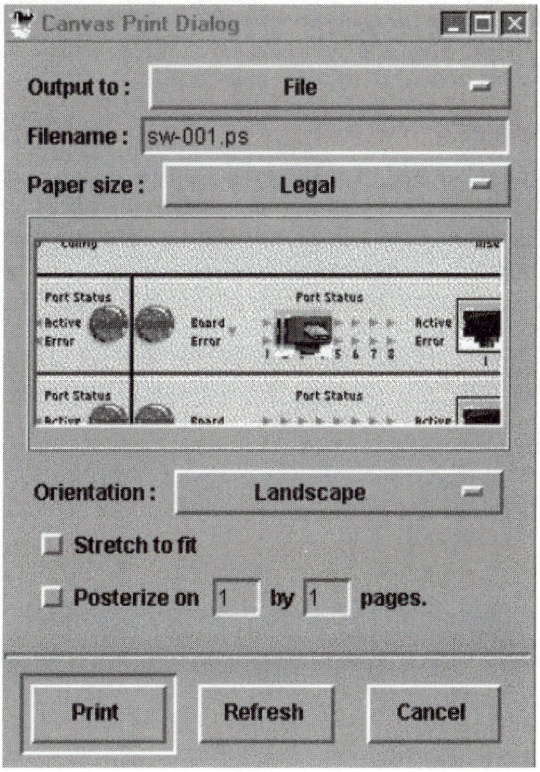

Figure 8.7 `canvasprintdialog` Mega-Widget.

Later in this chapter, you will see the following code in an updated version of the procedure `CreateMainWindow`. The code below launches the `hyperhelp` widget via menu selection. It defines four topics, each referencing the files `intro.html`, `ch1.html`, `ch2.html` and `ch3.html`, which are located in the relative directory `./help`. It initializes the viewer so that `intro.html` is displayed as soon as the viewer is launched. Figure 8.8 shows the results of this.

```
.menubar add command .help.manual -label "On-Line Help" \
    -command {
        set help [hyperhelp .#auto -topics {intro ch1 ch2 ch3 } \
            -helpdir ./help]
        $help showtopic intro
        $help activate
}
```

Example—menubar

The `menubar` command displays a menubar and simplifies the task of creating menu entries. The syntax of the command to create a menubar is:

```
menubar pathName ?options?
```

In the example code below, we create a menubar called `.menubar`. Then we add menubuttons to `.menubar` and finally, we add submenu entries to each menubutton. The resulting menubar is displayed in Figure 8.9. This same menubar is used later in our rewritten `CreateMainWindow`. To simplify reading the code below, we left each command statement empty. Later in CreateMainWindow, we will include code to execute in each `-command` option.

```
menubar .menubar -height 18  -borderwidth 2  -background grey
pack .menubar -side top -fill x

.menubar configure -menubuttons {
        menubutton file    -text "File"
        menubutton edit    -text "Edit"     -state disabled
        menubutton view    -text "View"
        menubutton options -text "Options" -state disabled
        menubutton tools   -text "Tools"    -state disabled
        menubutton help    -text "Help"
}

.menubar add command .file.open -label "Open Device File" \
        -command {}
.menubar add command .file.edit -label "Exit"  -command {}
```

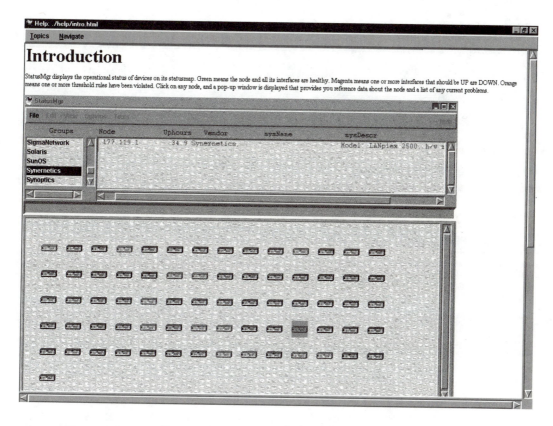

Figure 8.8 `hyperhelp` Mega-Widget—navigating and displaying HTML help files.

```
.menubar add radiobutton .view.curr_view \
        -variable view -label "Status View"  -value .view1 \
        -command {}
.menubar add command .help.manual -label "On-Line Help" \
        -command {}
.menubar add command .help.about -label "About Ch8-Demo" \
        -command {}
```

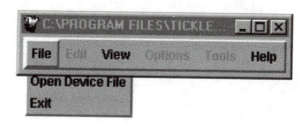

Figure 8.9 `menubar` Mega-Widget.

messagedialog

The `messagedialog` widget displays a top-level dialog shell that shows image and text data. It has a number of predefined buttons, such as OK, Apply, Cancel and Help. The syntax of the command to create a messagedialog is:

```
menubar pathName ?options?
```

Later in this section, our updated version of `CreateMainWindow` will contain the following code that creates the messagedialog window that is illustrated in Figure 8.10:

```
menubar add command .help.about -label "About Ch8-Demo"
-command {
        if { [winfo exists .md ] != 1} {
            image create photo logo -file "nms.gif"
            messagedialog .md -title "About Ch8-Demo" \
    -image logo \
                -imagepos w -text "Ch8-Demo \n Version 1.0"
        .md hide Apply
        .md hide Cancel
        .md hide Help
        .md activate
    }
```

Note that in the above code, we hid the Apply, Cancel and Help buttons. The remaining OK button has a default command assignment to deactivate our Mega-Widget when pressed.

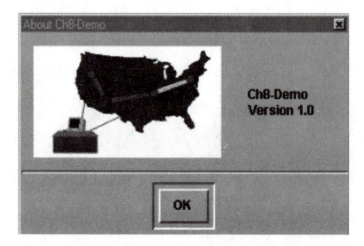

Figure 8.10 `messagedialog` Mega-Widget.

scrolledcanvas

The `scrolledcanvas` Mega-Widget displays a labeled scrolled canvas. The syntax of the command to create a scrolled canvas is:

```
scrolledcanvas pathName ?options?
```

In the example below (see Figure 8.11), we take our canvas example from Chapter 7, but this time we make one change. Instead of using the `canvas` command, we use the `scrolledcanvas` command:

```
scrolledcanvas .c -width 250 -height 250 -background beige \
        -relief raised
⇒ .c

pack .c -side top -fill both
set id1 [.c create oval 60 60 70 70 -tag node -fill green]
⇒ 1

set id2 [.c create oval 80 80 90 90 -tag node -fill green]
⇒ 2

set id3 [.c create line 65 65 85 85 -tag line -width 2]
⇒ 3
```

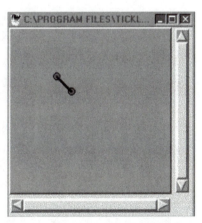

Figure 8.11 `scrolledcanvas` Mega-Widget.

Notice that the `-background` option used above made the scrollbar components of the Mega-Widget beige, but not the canvas component. To change the background color of the canvas component, we need to use the `-textbackground` option as follows:

```
.c configure -textbackground skyblue
```

Now the scrollbars will be beige and the canvas skyblue.

scrolledlistbox

The `scrolledlistbox` Mega-Widget displays a labelled scrolled listbox. The syntax of the command to create a `scrolledlistbox` Mega-Widget is:

```
scrolledlistbox pathName ?options?
```

In the example below, we take our listbox example from Chapter 7, but this time we make two changes. Instead of using the `listbox` command, we use the `scrolledlistbox` command. In addition, we use the `-labeltext` option to label the listbox. The results are shown in Figure 8.12.

```
scrolledlistbox .groups -selectmode single \
    -vscrollmode static -hscrollmode static \
    -labeltext "Groups"
⇒ .groups

pack .groups
foreach group {"Universal Group" Cisco 3COM} {
    .groups insert end $group
}
```

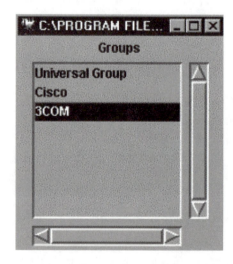

Figure 8.12 `scrolledlistbox` Mega-Widget.

The following code displays the selected item in the scrolledlistbox.

```
.groups curselection
⇒ 2

.groups get 2
⇒ 3COM
```

Now, let's create a binding that outputs to the console whenever a group name is selected. Here, things are somewhat different from what they were in Chapter 7. Instead of using the `bind` command, we will use the `-selectioncommand` option that is supported by the `scrolledlistbox` Mega-Widget.

```
.groups configure -selectioncommand {
    set item [.groups get [.groups curselection]]
    puts "$item is selected"
}
```

scrolledtext

The `scrolledtext` Mega-Widget displays a labeled scrolled text area. The syntax of the command to create a `scrolledtext` Mega-Widget is:

```
scrolledtext pathName ?options?
```

Below is the procedure `NodeList` from Chapter 7, now rewritten using the `scrolledtext` widget. The results are shown in Figure 8.13. Here we added a label to our newly created `scrolledtext` widget. Other than that, there are no other real changes except we now have only a single widget to create and manage. As you can see, the text widget methods and options we used in Chapter 7 are all supported by the `scrolledtext` Mega-Widget.

```
proc NodeList { } {

    global nInfo nn

    # This procedure displays node information in a
    # scrollable textbox. The nodal information is
    # contained in the array nInfo and nn is the
    # last index value in nInfo.

    # If it doesn't exist, create the scrolled text box;
    # else make sure it's empty and editable.
      if { [winfo exists .nodes] != 1} {
         set labelfont \
```

```
            {-*-Courier-Medium-R-Normal--*-120-*-*-*-*-*-*}
            set header [format "%4s %12s %8s %13s %11s %8s" \
            "Node" "             Uphours"  " Vendor" \
            "       sysName" " " "sysDescr"]
            scrolledtext .nodes -labeltext $header \
            -labelpos nw \
            -height 1.5i -width 800 \
            -labelfont $labelfont \
            -wrap none
            pack .nodes -side left -fill x -expand yes
        } else {
          .nodes configure -state normal
          .nodes delete 0.0 end
        }

    # Insert a line of info per node into .nodes.text.
     for {set n 0} {$n <= $nn} {incr n +1} {
      if { $nInfo($n,state) == 1} {
          set line [format "%-15s %9.1f %-15s %-20s %-40s\n" \
             $nInfo($n,addr) $nInfo($n,uphrs) \
             $nInfo($n,vendor) $nInfo($n,sysName) \
             $nInfo($n,sysDescr)]
        } else {
          set line [format "%-15s %9s %-15s %-20s %-40s\n" \
             $nInfo($n,addr) " " $nInfo($n,vendor) \
             $nInfo($n,sysName) $nInfo($n,sysDescr)]
        }
        set tag $nInfo($n,addr)
        .nodes insert end $line $tag
    }

  # Change the state of .nodes so it's no longer editable.

  .nodes configure -state disabled
}
```

To change the color of the line using its associated tag, use the same command as in Chapter 7, namely:

```
.nodes tag configure 158.121.122.1 -foreground red
```

Figure 8.13 scrolledtext Mega-Widget.

Mega-Widget Example—selectiondialog

The selectiondialog Mega-Widget displays a top-level dialog shell with a listbox, buttons and editable entry. The syntax of the command to create a selectiondialog Mega-Widget is:

```
selectiondialog pathName ?options?
```

Figure 8.14 illustrates a selectiondialog Mega-Widget that allows users to select a group name from a list of groups. We create our selectiondialog Mega-Widget as follows:

```
selectiondialog .grps -title "Select Group" -itemslabel Groups
⇒ .grps

foreach group {"Universal Group" Cisco 3Com} {
    .grps insert items end $group
}

.grps activate
```

tabnotebook

The tabnotebook Mega-Widget is used to display one page at a time from a set of tabbed pages. A 3-D tab displays a user-defined page label and serves as a page selector. The tabs are displayed as a group, along the left, top, right or bottom edge. When first created, a tabnotebook has no pages. The default behavior is for the tabnotebook to automatically handle the unpacking and packing of pages as they are selected. This behavior is defined by the -auto option, which has a default value of true. The syntax of the command to create a tabnotebook Mega-Widget is:

```
tabnotebook pathName? options?
```

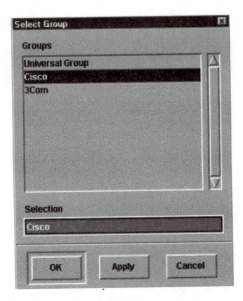

Figure 8.14 `selectiondialog` Mega-Widget.

Many of the method commands for a `tabnotebook` take an index argument to indicate the page of the notebook on which to operate. A page index can be specified as:

- `<number>`, specifies the page numerically, where 0 corresponds to the first page, 1 to the second and so on.
- `select`, specifies the currently selected page's index. If no page is selected, returns −1.
- `end`, specifies the last page in the notebook's index. If the notebook is empty, returns -1.

In other cases, a page argument may be a pattern, which is then pattern-matched against the label of each page in the notebook, in order from the first to the last page, until a matching entry is found.

Below is example code that creates a `tabnotebook` called `.view1`. The notebook has several tabbed pages, which are illustrated in Figure 8.15.

```
tabnotebook .view1 -background skyblue
⇒ .view1

pack .view1 -anchor nw -fill both -expand yes -side left
# Add pages to the tabnotebook.
.view1 add -label "StatusMap" -command {}
```

```
⇒ .view1.canvas.notebook.cs.page1.cs

.view1 add -label "DailyAvail" -command {}
⇒ .view1.canvas.notebook.cs.page2.cs

.view1 add -label "IfOps" -command {}
⇒ .view1.canvas.notebook.cs.page3.cs

.view1 add -label "Problems" -command {}
⇒ .view1.canvas.notebook.cs.page4.cs

.view1 add -label "48HrAvailHist" -command {}
⇒ .view1.canvas.notebook.cs.page5.cs

.view1 add -label "AvgRTDelay" -command {}
⇒ .view1.canvas.notebook.cs.page6.cs

.view1 add -label "TrafficTopN" -command {}
⇒ .view1.canvas.notebook.cs.page7.cs
```

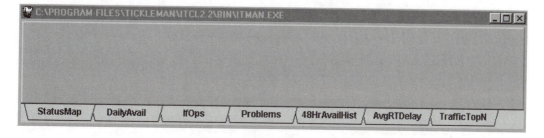

Figure 8.15 tabnotebook Mega-Widget.

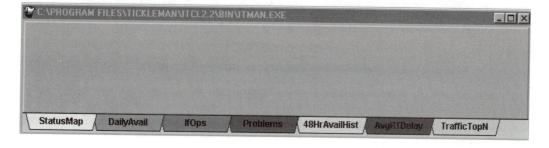

Figure 8.16 tabnotebook with different colored tabs.

Each tab is indexed, starting from zero. To make each tab a different color, we simply specify the following (see Figure 8.16):

```
% .view1 pageconfigure 0 -background beige
% .view1 pageconfigure 1 -background orange
% .view1 pageconfigure 2 -background green
% .view1 pageconfigure 3 -background magenta
% .view1 pageconfigure 4 -background yellow
% .view1 pageconfigure 5 -background purple
```

To insert into each page, we must first create a childsite frame for each page as shown below. Later, we can insert into each childsite frame as desired.

```
set v1tab1 [.view1 childsite 0]
set v1tab2 [.view1 childsite 1]
set v1tab3 [.view1 childsite 2]
set v1tab4 [.view1 childsite 3]
set v1tab5 [.view1 childsite 4]
set v1tab6 [.view1 childsite 5]
set v1tab7 [.view1 childsite 6]
```

EXAMPLE: MAIN APPLICATION WINDOW USING MEGA-WIDGETS

As promised, we will now rewrite a new and improved `CreateMainWindow` (from Chapter 7) using Itcl Mega-Widgets.

This main window will allow us to develop over time different management views of a network without providing numerous top-level windows to the user. Some of the example views we had in mind when we designed this GUI include:

- An overall network status view (shown here as our StatusView view)
- A view of Level 3 routing operations
- A view of Level 2 LAN switching operations
- A view of operations for a single device (shown here as our DeviceView view)

In each view, we wanted multiple subviews and the ability to move between views and subviews easily. With Tcl/Tk, making different views visible is as easy as packing and unpacking a master widget. Handling different subviews simply involves making each subview a separate page in a tabnotebook.

Figure 8.17 shows our example main application window in the context of its StatusView view. It also points out the various Mega-Widgets in use. Within this StatusView view, we illustrate to the user via a tabnotebook various subviews that exist within this context. Figure 8.18 shows our example main application window in the context of a DeviceView view, as defined by the sample driver program, which is also shown here.

The code that builds this main window is shown here as our newly rewritten `CreateMain-Window`. Also shown here is a sample driver program which is similar to the one used in Chapter 7 to populate the main application window with data.

The `CreateMainWindow` and sample driver code we show here are not very different from those shown in Chapter 7. Mainly, we created Mega-Widgets like `menubar`, `scrolledlistbox` and `scrolledtext` in place of their Tk counterparts. In addition, we made use of `tabnotebook`, `hyperhelp` and `messagedialog` widgets to give us the added functionality of subviews and on-line help.

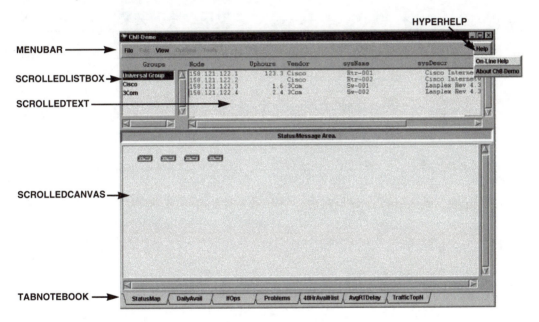

Figure 8.17 Main application window with Mega-Widgets showing StatusView.

Rewritten CreateMainWindow Using Itcl Mega-Widgets

Below is an updated version of `CreateMainWindow`. It looks basically the same as the main application window in Chapter 7, but it uses Itcl Mega-Widgets in several places to simplify the code. This procedure is used in our status monitoring application, `StatusMgr`. Thus, you will

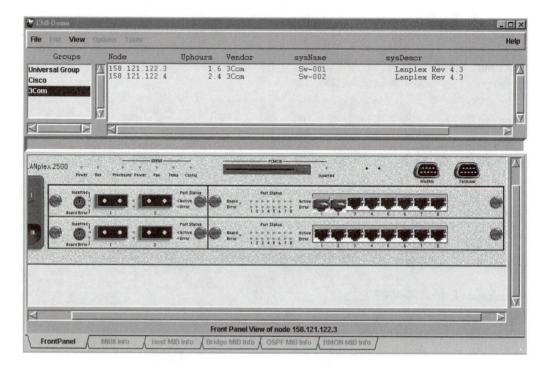

Figure 8.18 Main application window with Mega-Widgets showing StatusView.

see in the code below various lines that have been commented out. These are mainly calls to procedures that are used by `StatusMgr`, but were not applicable to this chapter.

```
proc CreateMainWindow { } {

    global view curr_view
    global v1tab1 v1tab2 v1tab3 v1tab4 v1tab5 v1tab6 v1tab7

    #  Step 1: Define main window attributes.
    wm minsize . 800 550
    wm title .  Ch8-Demo
    wm iconname . Ch8-Demo


    # Step 2: Define broad frame layout of main window.
    menubar .menubar -height 18  -borderwidth 2 \
        -background grey
```

```
pack .menubar -side top -fill x
frame .top -height 75  -borderwidth 2
pack .top -side top -fill x
frame .status -height 18 -borderwidth 3 \
    -relief sunken -bg grey
pack .status -side top -fill x
tabnotebook .view1
pack .view1 -anchor nw -fill both -expand yes -side left
# Add pages to the tabnotebook group view.
.view1 add -label "StatusMap" \
    -command {# DisplayMap}
.view1 add -label "DailyAvail" \
    -command {# DisplayAvail}
.view1 add -label "IfOps" \
    -command {# DisplayIfOps}
.view1 add -label "Problems" \
    -command {# DisplayProblems}
.view1 add -label "48HrAvailHist" \
    -command {# DisplayHistory}
.view1 add -label "AvgRTDelay" \
    -command {# DisplayDelay}
.view1 add -label "TrafficTopN" \
    -command {# DisplayTrafficLdrs}
# Get the childsite frames of these tab pages.
set v1tab1 [.view1 childsite  0]
set v1tab2 [.view1 childsite 1]
set v1tab3 [.view1 childsite 2]
set v1tab4 [.view1 childsite 3]
set v1tab5 [.view1 childsite 4]
set v1tab6 [.view1 childsite 5]
set v1tab7 [.view1 childsite 6]

# Step 3a. Define the main menu selections.
.menubar configure -menubuttons {
    menubutton file    -text "File"
    menubutton edit    -text "Edit"    -state disabled
    menubutton view    -text "View"
    menubutton options -text "Options" -state disabled
    menubutton tools   -text "Tools"   -state disabled
    menubutton help    -text "Help"
}
# Step 3b.  Define the submenus.
```

```
.menubar add command .file.open \
    -label "Open Device File" \
    -command {# OpenNodeFile}
.menubar add command .file.edit -label "Exit" \
    -command {exit}
.menubar add radiobutton .view.curr_view \
    -variable view -label "Status View"  -value .view1 \
    -command {
        pack forget $curr_view
        pack .view1 -anchor nw -fill both \
          -expand yes \
          -side left
        set curr_view .view1
}
.menubar add command .help.manual -label "On-Line Help" \
    -command {
        set help [hyperhelp .#auto \
          -topics {intro ch1 ch2 ch3 } \
          -helpdir ./help]
        $help showtopic intro
        $help activate
}

.menubar add command .help.about -label "About Ch8-Demo" \
    -command {
        if { [winfo exists .md ] != 1} {
            image create photo logo -file "nms.gif"
            messagedialog .md -title "About Ch8-Demo" \
                -image logo -imagepos w \
                -text "Ch8-Demo \n Version 1.0"
            .md hide Apply
            .md hide Cancel
            .md hide Help
            .md activate
        }
}

set view .view1
set curr_view $view
.view1 select 0
```

```
    # Step 4a: Create scrolled listbox for group display and
selection.
    set labelfont \
        {-*-Courier-Medium-R-Normal--*-120-*-*-*-*-*-*}
    scrolledlistbox .top.groups -textbackground beige\
        -height 1.5i -width 1.5i -vscrollmode static \
        -hscrollmode static -selectmode single \
        -labeltext "Groups" -labelfont $labelfont
    pack .top.groups -side left -fill x

    # Step 4b: Create scrolled textbox for node display and
    # selection.
    set header [format "%4s %12s %8s %13s %11s %8s" \
        "Node" "             Uphours"  " Vendor" \
        "         sysName" " " "sysDescr"]
    scrolledtext .top.nodes  -textbackground beige \
        -labeltext $header -labelpos nw \
        -height 1.5i -labelfont $labelfont -wrap none
    pack .top.nodes -side left -fill x -expand yes

    # Step 5:  Create a label to display status messages.
    label .status.label  -text "Status/Message Area." \
        -bg grey     \
        -relief sunken -height 1
    pack .status.label -fill x -anchor ne -expand yes

    # Step 6a: Create a scrolled canvas to display StatusMap.
    scrolledcanvas $v1tab1.statusmap -confine false \
        -textbackground beige
    $v1tab1.statusmap configure -scrollregion "0 0 800  800"
    pack  $v1tab1.statusmap  -side top  -fill both -expand yes


}
```

Rewritten Test Driver Program Using Rewritten CreateMainWindow

```
#!/bin/sh
# When on Unix, invoke itman \.
exec itman "$0" "$@"


source ch8-demo.itk
```

```
proc gInit { } {

    global nInfo nn sampledata

    set sampledata [list \
        {1 1.3.6.1.4.1.9.1.12 158.121.122.1 Rtr-001 Cisco \
        123.3 "Susan Maxwell (617) 232-2373" \
        "Bldg-001 Boston MA" \
        "Cisco Internetworking Operating System" -1} \
        {0 1.3.6.1.4.1.9.1.9 158.121.122.2 Rtr-002 Cisco \
        1243.3 "Susan Maxwell (617) 232-2373" \
        "Bldg-001 Boston MA" \
        "Cisco Internetworking Operating System" -1} \
        {1 1.3.6.1.4.1.114.1.3.3.1.7 158.121.122.3 \
        Sw-001 3Com 1.6 "Susan Maxwell (617) 232-2373" \
        "Bldg-001 Boston MA" "Lanplex Rev 4.3" -1} \
        {1 1.3.6.1.4.1.114.1.3.3.1.7 158.121.122.4 \
        Sw-002 3Com 2.4 "Susan Maxwell (617) 232-2373" \
        "Bldg-001 Boston MA" "Lanplex Rev 4.3" -1}]

    set n 0
    foreach el $sampledata {
        set nInfo($n,state)       [lindex $el 0]
        set nInfo($n,sysOID)      [lindex $el 1]
        set nInfo($n,addr)        [lindex $el 2]
        set nInfo($n,sysName)     [lindex $el 3]
        set nInfo($n,vendor)      [lindex $el 4]
        set nInfo($n,uphrs)       [lindex $el 5]
        set nInfo($n,sysContact)  [lindex $el 6]
        set nInfo($n,sysLocation) [lindex $el 7]
        set nInfo($n,sysDescr)    [lindex $el 8]
        set nInfo($n,id)          [lindex $el 9]
        incr n +1
    }
    set nn [expr $n -1]
}

proc DisplayNodeList { } {

    global nn gi nInfo groups

    set gi [.top.groups curselection]
```

```
    if { [info exists groups($gi,nodelist)] != 1} { return }
    if { [llength $groups($gi,nodelist)] <= 0} {return}

    .top.nodes configure -state normal
    .top.nodes delete 0.0 end

    foreach n $groups($gi,nodelist) {
        if { $nInfo($n,state) == 1} {
            set line [format "%-15s %9.1f %-15s %-20s %-40s\n" \
            $nInfo($n,addr) $nInfo($n,uphrs) \
            $nInfo($n,vendor) $nInfo($n,sysName) \
            $nInfo($n,sysDescr)]
        } else {
            set line [format "%-15s %9s %-15s %-20s %-40s\n" \
            $nInfo($n,addr) " " $nInfo($n,vendor) \
            $nInfo($n,sysName) $nInfo($n,sysDescr)]
        }
        set tag $nInfo($n,addr)
        .top.nodes  insert end $line $tag
    }
    .top.nodes configure -state disabled
}


proc AddDevice { nindex  } {

    global x y xpos ypos nInfo nn gi width v1tab1

    #This proc adds a node to the $v1tab1.statusmap canvas.

    set view [expr $width -100]
    if {$xpos < $view} { incr xpos 50
    } else { set xpos 50; incr ypos 50}

    #Store initial positions.
    set id [ $v1tab1.statusmap create bitmap \
        $xpos  $ypos  -bitmap @node.xbm -foreground black]
    $v1tab1.statusmap bind current <Enter> {
        set tag [$v1tab1.statusmap find withtag current]
        for {set n 0} {$n <=$nn} {incr n +1} {
            if {$nInfo($n,id) == $tag} {
                .status.label config -text $nInfo($n,addr)
```

```
                    break
              }
          }
      }

      $v1tab1.statusmap bind current <Leave> {
          .status.label config -text ""
      }

      $v1tab1.statusmap bind  current  <Button-1> {
          global x y
          set x %x
          set y %y
       }

      $v1tab1.statusmap bind  current  <B1-Motion> {
          global x y; set newx %x;  set newy %y
          set distx [expr $newx - $x]
          set disty [expr $newy - $y]
          $v1tab1.statusmap move current $distx $disty
          #Store values for next time
              set x $newx
              set y $newy
      }

      $v1tab1.statusmap bind $id <Double-Button-1> {
          $v1tab1.statusmap itemconfigure all -background {}
          set tag [$v1tab1.statusmap find withtag current]
          for {set n 0} {$n <=$nn} {incr n +1} {
              if {$nInfo($n,id) == $tag} {
                  DisplayFrontPanel $n
                  break
              }
          }
      }

      return $id

}

proc DisplayFrontPanel {nindex} {
```

```
global   nInfo view width height curr_view
global   v2tab1 v2tab2 v2tab3 v2tab4 v2tab5

# This routine displays a frontpanel bitmap of a device.
# It also adds hot spots on the bitmap.

# Unpack other views.
pack forget .view1

# Create the .view2 tabnotebook if it does not exist.
if { [winfo exists .view2] != 1} {
    tabnotebook .view2
    # Add pages to view2 tabnotebook.
    .view2 add -label "FrontPanel"          \
        -command {
            .view2 select 0
            .view2 view 0
        }
    .view2 add -label "MIBII Info" \
        -command { MIBIIOps} \
        -state disabled
    .view2 add -label "Host MIB Info"    \
        -command { HostOps} -state disabled
    .view2 add -label "Bridge MIB Info"  \
        -command { BridgeOps} -state disabled
    .view2 add -label "OSPF MIB Info"     \
        -command { OspfOps } -state disabled
    .view2 add -label "RMON MIB Info"     \
        -command { RmonOps } -state disabled
    # Get the childsite frames of these pages.
    set v2tab1 [.view2 childsite  0]
    set v2tab2 [.view2 childsite 1]
    set v2tab3 [.view2 childsite 2]
    set v2tab4 [.view2 childsite 3]
    set v2tab5 [.view2 childsite 4]
    set v2tab6 [.view2 childsite 5]
}

#Create the scrolledcanvas $v2tab1.deviceview if it
#doesn't exist.
if { [winfo exists $v2tab1.deviceview] != 1} {
    scrolledcanvas $v2tab1.deviceview \
```

```
            -confine false -textbackground beige
        $v2tab1.deviceview configure \
            -scrollregion "0 0 800 800"
}


pack .view2 -anchor nw -fill both -expand yes -side left
pack $v2tab1.deviceview -anchor nw -fill both \
    -expand yes -side left
$v2tab1.deviceview delete all
.view2 select 0
set view .view2
set curr_view .view2


if { [string compare 1.3.6.1.4.1.114.1.3.3.1.7 \
    $nInfo($nindex,sysOID)] == 0} {
    # Device is a supported 3Com Lanplex.
    image create photo chassis -file "3comchas.gif"
    image create photo greenport -file "greenport.gif"
    set image chassis
    set heading \
        "Front Panel View of node $nInfo($nindex,addr)"
    if { [winfo exists $v2tab1.deviceview.label] != 1} {
        label $v2tab1.deviceview.label -text $heading \
            -width 60 -bg grey -fg black
        pack $v2tab1.deviceview.label  -side top -fill x
    } else {
        $v2tab1.deviceview.label configure -text $heading
    }
    $v2tab1.deviceview create image 400 100  \
        -image $image -tag chassis
    $v2tab1.deviceview create image 520 100 \
        -image greenport -tag port1
    $v2tab1.deviceview bind port1 <Button-1> {
        .status.label config -text "Port 1 selected"
    }
    $v2tab1.deviceview create image 550 100 \
        -image greenport -tag port2
    $v2tab1.deviceview bind port2 <Button-1> {
        .status.label conf -text "Port 2 selected"
    }
    $v2tab1.deviceview bind  chassis <Button-1> {
```

```
                    .status.label conf -text "Chassis Slected"
            }
        }

}


proc UpdateStatus { n } {

    global nn nInfo v1tab1

    if { $nInfo($n,state) == 1} {
        .top.nodes tag configure $nInfo($n,addr) \
            -foreground darkgreen
        $v1tab1.statusmap itemconfigure $nInfo($n,id) \
            -foreground darkgreen
    } elseif  { $nInfo($n,state) == 0} {
        .top.nodes tag configure $nInfo($n,addr) \
            -foreground red
        $v1tab1.statusmap itemconfigure $nInfo($n,id) \
            -foreground red
    }

}
```

Now, let's put everything together:

```
proc MainApp {
  uplevel #0 {
    # Initialize.
    set xpos 0
    set ypos 0
    set x 0
    set y 0
    set width  800
    set height 550

    CreateMainWindow

    # Add three groups to the group listbox.
    .top.groups insert end "Universal Group"
    .top.groups insert end "Cisco"
    .top.groups insert end "3Com"
```

```
    # Populate nInfo with some sample data.
    gInit

    # Create a list of nodes for each group.
    set groups(0,nodelist) [list 0 1 2 3]
    set groups(1,nodelist) [list 0 1]
    set groups(2,nodelist) [list 2 3]

    # Select index 0 "Universal Group".
    .top.groups selection set 0
    DisplayNodeList

    # Add nodes to the StatusMap.
    for {set n 0} {$n <= $nn} {incr n +1} {
        set nInfo($n,id) [AddDevice $n]
    }

    # Set up things so when the user selects an entry in
    # .top.groups, its corresponding nodes are displayed in
    # .top.nodes.
    .top.groups configure -selectioncommand {
        set gi [.top.groups curselection]
        $v1tab1.statusmap itemconfigure all -background {}
        DisplayNodeList
        if { $gi > 0 } {
            foreach nindex $groups($gi,nodelist) {
                $v1tab1.statusmap \
                    itemconfigure $nInfo($nindex,id) \
                    -background grey
            }
        }
    }

    # Update status color for each node.
    for { set n 0} {$n <= $nn} {incr n +1} {
        UpdateStatus $n
    }

    vwait forever
  }
}
```

Obtaining Additional [Incr Widgets]

The Tcl community is constantly sharing code. There are some very useful Mega-Widgets available within this community that may be of interest to you. One that is especially useful for network management purposes is a `tree` Mega-Widget that is discussed in the book *Tcl/Tk Tools*. A good place to look for additional Itcl Mega-Widgets is the site http://www.tcltk.com.

IN SUMMARY

The first thing we did in this chapter was build a simple `table` widget, which will be used in several of our sample applications. While performing this exercise, we showed how to add scrollbars to a complex, composite widget. In the next section, we revisited canvases, building code to draw an IP path. This example, among other things, showed how to associate mouse events to tag values. Finally, we explored the Itcl Mega-Widgets and rewrote the `CreateMainWindow` code from Chapter 7 to use them.

9 *Socket Programming*

Tcl's `socket` command is used to set up TCP (Transmission Control Protocol) connections. This chapter shows several ways to use sockets within your applications. This chapter covers:

- Overview of socket communications
- Example: simple client-server connection
- Example: adding a Web interface

OVERVIEW OF SOCKET COMMUNICATIONS

The term "socket" is a carryover from the early days, when BSD UNIX first supported the TCP/IP protocol. When two processes want to communicate with each other via TCP, the server side will first request a socket (i.e., channel) to a local port number. Once this server socket is opened, it waits for incoming client connections to the server's host:port address.

A TCP connection is established between the two end-point sockets. It's the combination of host and port numbers that uniquely identify the connection end-points. The TCP protocol provides reliable, bi-directional communications between the two end-points.

The processes at each end-point of the connection simply read and write to what they know to be a channel ID. This communication is very similar to file I/O. When one end wants to terminate the connection, it simply performs a close on its channel ID.

When using socket communications, one must be aware that certain port numbers are reserved for specific network services. For example, FTP has the well-known port assignments of 20 and 21. Unless you intentionally want to connect to a specific network service, you should set up socket connections with port numbers greater than 1024. On UNIX systems, you can usually look at the `/etc/services` file to see if a specific port number is defined by another application.

socket

Tcl's `socket` command supports TCP network protocol connections. This command opens a network socket and returns a channel identifier.

The command to create a client socket has the following syntax:

```
socket ?options? host port
```

Only a few options are supported by the socket command. They are:

`-async`
This is used to request an asynchronous mode of operation. When used, the `socket` request will return immediately, even though the connection has not been established.

`-myaddr address`
This is used mainly when a system has multiple IP addresses and it wants the socket to know it as the address defined by `-myaddr`

`-myport port`
This is used mainly when a client wants the server to be informed that the client connection is from the port defined by `-myport`.

The command to create a server socket is:

```
socket -server command ?-myaddr address? port
```

When an opened server socket receives a new client connection on the specified port, it will spawn a new channel ID and invoke the procedure defined by `-server` command with three arguments. These arguments are:

- The new channel ID that your server application will use for communicating with the client
- The client's host address
- The client's port number

If your computer has multiple IP addresses, the `-myaddr` option allows you to identify a particular address. For example, below we request a server socket using `-myaddr` 158.101.121.58, and we then specify to execute the procedure www whenever a client connection is received on port 2000.

```
socket -server www -myaddr 158.101.121.58 2000
⇒ sock5
```

If at any time we want to close this server socket, we can do so by simply issuing the command:

```
close sock5
```

Clients that wish to communicate with your application will then make connection requests to your server socket. In this case, 158.101.121.58:2000. They can do this simply by issuing the command:

```
socket 158.101.121.58 2000
```

If there is no opened socket on port 2000 on the server, the above client request will return the following error message: couldn't open socket: connection refused. If, on the other hand, the server has opened a socket on port 2000 and the client request is successful, a channel ID will be returned.

The fileevent Command

Remember when we discussed the fileevent command in Chapter 4? Well, the procedure specified by the -server command to handle new client connections to your server socket will typically contain the fileevent command, as in the example below:

```
proc www {channel chost cport} {
        puts "www ... $channel $chost $cport"
        fileevent $channel readable [list Receiver $channel]
}
```

The fileevent command as used above allows your application to do other things when there is no channel data to process. In the example code above, the procedure Receiver is called whenever the channel has data to process; otherwise, the event loop remains open, processing other events.

fconfigure

The fconfigure command is used to set and query options on a channel. The syntax of the fconfigure command is:

```
fconfigure channelId
fconfigure channelId name
fconfigure channelId name value ?name value ...?
```

Here, channelId identifies the channel for which to set or query an option. If no name or value arguments are supplied, the command returns a list containing alternative option names and values for the channel. If name is supplied with no value, the command returns the current value of the given option. If one or more pairs of name and value are supplied, the command sets each of the name options to the corresponding value; in this case, the return value is an empty string.

Channel options that can be changed with the `fconfigure` command are:

`-blocking boolean`

This boolean indicates whether I/O operations on the channel can cause a process to block indefinitely. Channels are normally in blocking mode.

`-buffering newValue`

If `newValue` is `full`, the I/O system will buffer output until its internal buffer is full or until the flush command is invoked. If `newValue` is `line`, the I/O system will automatically flush output for the channel whenever a newline character is output. If `newValue` is `none`, the I/O system will flush automatically after every output operation. The default is for `-buffering` to be set to `full`, except for channels that connect to terminal-like devices; for these channels, the initial setting is `line`.

`-buffersize newSize`

`newSize` is an integer value used to set the size of buffers, in bytes, for this channel to store input or output. The default value is 4096.

`-eofchar char`
`-eofchar {inChar outChar}`

Defines the end-of-file characters for a channel. The default value for `-eofchar` is an empty string in all cases.

`-translation mode`
`-translation {inMode outMode}`

On input, automatically translates the external end-of-line representation into newline characters. Upon output, translates newlines to the external end-of-line representation. The default translation mode, `auto`, handles all the common cases automatically. The `-translation` option provides explicit control over the end-of-line translations.

Channel I/O

Once a channel connection is established, you use the same I/O commands (i.e., `read`, `puts`, `gets`, `flush`) on socket channels as you do on file channels.

Limitations of TCL's Socket Communications

As already discussed, Tcl socket communications are limited to TCP session connections only. In addition, prior to Tcl 8.0, it was also difficult to transfer binary data using Tcl sockets. The Tcl 8.0 `binary` (builds a binary string) and `fcopy` (copies from one channel to another) commands make handling binary data easier than earlier Tcl releases.

If you require additional TCP/IP communications capabilities beyond just simple TCP sockets, look at the publicly available Distributed Programming extension to Tcl/Tk (Tcl-DP). Brian Smith and Lawrence Rowe have an excellent chapter on Tcl-DP in the book *Tcl/Tk Tools* by Mark Harrison. Tcl-DP support includes TCP, UDP IP-multicast protocols and RPC communication capabilities.

Example: Simple Client-Server Communications

Here we illustrate how a client application can connect to a remote server to obtain information from the server application. In this simple example, our client requests a snapshot copy of the array nInfo.

The following occurs on the server machine:

- The procedure gInit populates the array nInfo with sample data.
- The socket command is used to create a server socket listening on port 2000.
- The procedure server is called whenever a new client connection comes in on port 2000. This first outputs a notice to the console that a new channel connection has just been received from a specified client host and port. In practice, you may want to have a similar notice go to an application-specific log file. Second, it configures the new channel with -buffering set to none. This causes the channel to be automatically flushed after each and every write operation. Third, we define via fileevent that whenever this channel is readable, call the procedure Receiver with the channel ID.
- The procedure Receiver retrieves a string from the channel. If it encounters an end-of-file, it closes the channel; otherwise, it checks whether the string is valid. At the moment, the only string we'll accept is get nInfo. If this is received, the command array get nInfo will be evaluated and the result written back to the channel.

Here is our main server code:

```
# Create some sample data so nInfo is populated.
  gInit

# Open socket 2000 to receive HTML requests.
  set foo [catch {socket -server server  2000} msg]
  if {$foo != 0} {
        puts "Error opening server port 2000 ... $msg"
  }
vwait forever
```

and its associated procedures:

```
proc gInit { } {

    global nInfo nn

    # This procedure simply creates some sample data for
    # nInfo.

    set sampledata [list \
        {1 1.3.6.1.4.1.9.1.12 158.121.122.1 Rtr-001 Cisco \
        123.3 "Susan Maxwell (617) 232-2373" \
        "Bldg-001 Boston MA" \
        "Cisco Internetworking Operating System" -1} \
        {0 1.3.6.1.4.1.9.1.9 158.121.122.2 Rtr-002 Cisco \
        " " "Susan Maxwell (617) 232-2373" \
        "Bldg-001 Boston MA" \
        "Cisco Internetworking Operating System" -1} \
        {1 1.3.6.1.4.1.114.1.3.3.1.7 158.121.122.3 \
        Sw-001 3Com 1.6 "Susan Maxwell (617) 232-2373" \
        "Bldg-001 Boston MA" "Lanplex Rev 4.3" -1} \
        {1 1.3.6.1.4.1.114.1.3.3.1.7 158.121.122.4 \
        Sw-002 3Com 2.4 "Susan Maxwell (617) 232-2373" \
        "Bldg-001 Boston MA" "Lanplex Rev 4.3" -1}]

    set n 0
    foreach el $sampledata {
        set nInfo($n,state)       [lindex $el 0]
        set nInfo($n,sysOID)      [lindex $el 1]
        set nInfo($n,addr)        [lindex $el 2]
        set nInfo($n,sysName)     [lindex $el 3]
        set nInfo($n,vendor)      [lindex $el 4]
        set nInfo($n,uphrs)       [lindex $el 5]
        set nInfo($n,sysContact)  [lindex $el 6]
        set nInfo($n,sysLocation) [lindex $el 7]
        set nInfo($n,sysDescr)    [lindex $el 8]
        set nInfo($n,id)          [lindex $el 9]
        incr n +1
    }
    set nn [expr $n -1]
}
```

```
proc server { channel chost cport} {
        puts "connection from $chost:$cport"
        fconfigure $channel -buffering none
        fileevent $channel readable [list Receiver $channel]
}

proc Receiver { channel} {

    global nInfo errorCode errorInfo

    if { [eof $channel] || [catch {gets $channel cmd}]} {
        close $channel
        return
    }

    set err [catch {
            #   check for valid command
            if { [string compare $cmd "get nInfo"] == 0 } {
            set xdata [array get nInfo]
            puts $channel $xdata
            close $channel
            }
    }]

    if { $err != 0} {
        puts "Error in Receiver"
        puts "... errorCode=$errorCode, errorInfo=$errorInfo"
    }


}
```

The following occurs on the client machine:

When the client application wants to get an updated copy of the array nInfo, it calls the procedure get_nInfo. This sets up a client connection to port 2000 on the server host. It then writes the command string get nInfo to its channel and issues a flush command to send this out immediately. Next, it issues a gets command on the channel to get and store the response data into a variable called rcvdata. Lastly, we use the command array set nInfo $rcvdata to set the array nInfo on the client end.

```
proc get_nInfo { } {
```

```
    global nInfo

    set err [catch {
                set chan [socket 158.101.121.58 2000]
                puts $chan "get nInfo"
                flush $chan
                gets $chan rcvdata
                array set nInfo $rcvdata
                close $chan
        }]

    return $err

}
```

We will test this by simply displaying the contents of nInfo on the client machine after calling get_nInfo. Note that for this to work, the server code must first be executed on the server side.

```
get_nInfo
⇒ 0
array get nInfo
⇒ 3,state 1 2,uphrs 1.6 1,sysContact {Susan Maxwell (617)
232-2373} 3,uphrs 2.4 2,addr 158.121.122.3 2,sysOID
1.3.6.1.4.1.114.1.3.3.1.7 0,id -1 3,sysContact {Susan Maxwell
(617) 232-2373} 0,vendor Cisco 2,id -1 2,vendor 3Com 1,sysDe-
scr {Cisco Internetworking Operating System} 0,sysContact
{Susan Maxwell (617) 232-2373} 3,sysDescr {Lanplex Rev 4.3}
1,sysOID 1.3.6.1.4.1.9.1.9 1,addr 158.121.122.2 2,sysContact
{Susan Maxwell (617) 232-2373} 1,id -1 3,sysOID
1.3.6.1.4.1.114.1.3.3.1.7 3,addr 158.121.122.4 1,vendor Cisco
0,sysDescr {Cisco Internetworking Operating System} 0,sysLoca-
tion {Bldg-001 Boston MA} 0,sysName Rtr-001 3,id -1 0,state 1
1,sysName Rtr-002 1,sysLocation {Bldg-001 Boston MA} 3,vendor
3Com 1,state 0 0,uphrs 123.3 2,sysName Sw-001 2,sysLocation
{Bldg-001 Boston MA} 2,sysDescr {Lanplex Rev 4.3} 0,addr
158.121.122.1 0,sysOID 1.3.6.1.4.1.9.1.12 1,uphrs { } 2,state
1 3,sysName Sw-002 3,sysLocation {Bldg-001 Boston MA}
```

ADDING A WEB INTERFACE

There are several ways to add a Web interface to your Tcl applications, including:

- Using the publicly available Tcl-Plugin from the Sunscript site http://www.sunscript.sun.com.

  As discussed in Chapter 15, this requires installing the Tcl-Plugin on each of your client browsers. Then, client users would connect to your Web server or server-based application to retrieve specific Tclets.

- Using the publicly available Tcl Web Server from the Sunscript site www.sunscript.com.

  This allows you to embed a complete Web server inside your application. It currently uses Scotty to provide several useful functions like Discover and MIB browsing. This makes it an excellent starting point for developing a sophisticated network management Web server solution.

- Using Tcl or PERL-based CGI scripts to retrieve information from flat files or databases.

  You could have your Tcl applications write data to flat files or databases and use Tcl or PERL-based CGI scripts to share this information via the Web.

- Simply parsing and sending HTML data via a server socket within your application.

  This simple approach is used in our sample application `StatusMgr` that is described in Chapter 12. Here, all we do is have our application open a server socket on port number 2000 and parse/output application-specific HTML data. Once a Web browser connects to our server port, our application outputs the HTML Home Page that is illustrated in Figure 9.1.

From the Home Page illustrated in Figure 9.1, the user selects a Group and a Request and then presses the "submit" button. Our application then parses the HTML request and sends back an HTML reply, as shown in Figure 9.2.

The server code for this example is pretty much directly from our `StatusMgr` application. One difference is we have shortened the code here by only implementing a response for the `Device Status` request. It is not necessary to show the response to all the requests since they all follow the same concept shown for `Device Status`.

In our Web interface example code, our application code does the following:

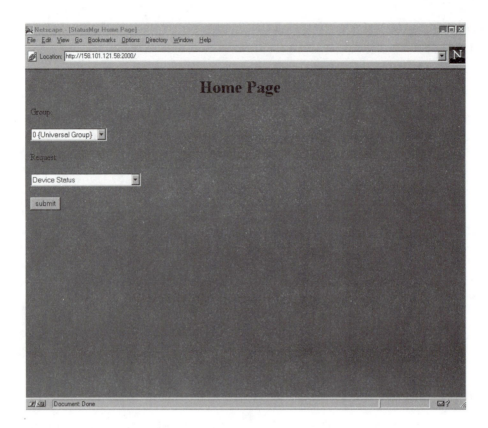

Figure 9.1   Home Page of simple Web interface example.

- Creates sample data.

  Our application calls the procedure `gInit` to populate the array `nInfo` with sample data. It also creates some sample groups, namely "`Universal Group`", `Cisco`, and `3COM`. It associates specific nodes with each group. Our `StatusMgr` application has no need to create sample data because it will be populating `nInfo` with real data. This step is specific for this example.

- Determines its IP address.

  The procedure `www_home` needs to know its IP address to use as follows:

```
puts $channel "<FORM ACTION=http://$myaddr:2000 METHOD=GET>"
```

- Issues a socket command requesting a server connection on port `2000`.

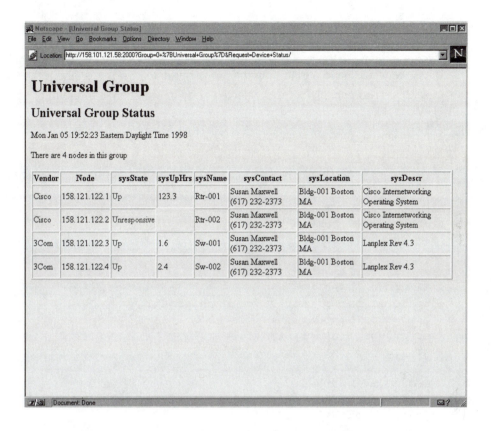

Figure 9.2   Device status page of simple Web interface example.

Besides opening a server socket, this causes the procedure www to be invoked for each new client connection to port 2000. Note that if the system running your server application has multiple IP addresses, you may need to use the -myaddr option here when you open your server socket.

When a client connection arrives on port 2000, invokes the procedure www.

The channel is configured for -buffering equal to none (this eliminates the need to flush after every puts). It issues a fileevent so that the procedure www_receiver is called whenever the specified channel has data to read.

When www_receiver is called, reads a line from the channel and processes the request string.

- www_home creates an HTML form from which users select both desired group and request.

This allows users to quickly specify what information they want back. Note that here we cheated and displayed the value of an internal variable, `gindex`, with the group name in the group selection box. This saved a little work since without it, we would have had to map the group name to `gindex` on the response.

- `www_d_status` simply outputs selected node information in the form of an HTML table.

Here is our main code for this example:

```
# Populate nInfo with some sample data.
   gInit

   # Create group names.
     set groups(0,name) "Universal Group"
     set groups(1,name) "Cisco"
     set groups(2,name) "3Com"
     set gindex 2

   # Create a list of nodes for each group.
     set groups(0,nodelist) [list 0 1 2 3]
     set groups(1,nodelist) [list 0 1]
     set groups(2,nodelist) [list 2 3]

# Determine my address.
   set foo [host2addr [info hostname]]
   set myaddr [octet2inst $foo]

# Open socket 2000 to receive HTML requests.
   set foo [catch {socket -server www 2000} msg]
   if {$foo != 0} {
          puts "Error opening server port 2000 ... $msg"
   }

# Keep event loop open until user manually exists this
# program.
   vwait forever
```

and here are the associated procedures for it:

```
proc www {channel chost cport} {
```

```
    # This procedure occurs when a client connects to
    # our server port 2000. When the new channel has
    # data, it passes it to www_receiver to parse.

    fconfigure $channel -buffering none
    fileevent $channel readable [list www_receiver $channel]
}
```

The procedure www makes the application non-blocking. It uses `fileevent` to call www_receiver when there is new client data to port 2000.

```
proc www_receiver {channel} {

    #Check for end of file or abnormal termination.

    if { [eof $channel] || [catch {gets $channel line}]} {
        close $channel
        return
    }

    if {[catch {set request [lindex $line 1]}]} {
        close channel
        return
    }

    set match " "
    set grpflg " "
    set gi -1
    set grpname " "
    set reqflg " "
    set reqval " "

    set foo \
            [regexp {([^=]+)=([^+]+)+([^&]+)&([^=]+)=(.*)} \
            $request match grpflg gi grpname reqflg reqval]

    if { $foo != 1} {
        catch {www_home $channel}
        return
    }
```

```
if {[string match "Device+Status*" $reqval]} {
    catch {www_d_status $channel $gi}
    return
}

if {[string match "Device+Availability*" $reqval]} {
    #www_d_avail $channel $gi
    catch {www_uconstr $channel}
    return
}

if {[string match "WAN+Interface+Status*" $reqval]} {
    #www_wan_ifstatus $channel $gi
     catch {www_uconstr $channel}
     return
}

if {[string match "LAN+Interface+Status*" $reqval]} {
    #www_lan_ifstatus $channel $gi
    catch {www_uconstr $channel}
    return
}

if {[string match "Historical+Availability+Summary*" \
    $reqval]} {
    #www_g_avail_his $channel $gi
    catch {www_uconstr $channel}
    return $err
}

catch {www_home $channel}
return
```

```
}
```

The procedure www_receiver reads from the specified channel and sets request to the first line of input data.

When a client browser first connects to our server port 2000, this first line of data will be something like:

```
GET / HTTP/1.0.
```

Our regular expression seeks to retrieve a group identifier and page request from a line that fits the following format:

```
/?Group=0+%7BUniversal+Group%7D&Request=Device+Status/ HTTP/1.0
```

The first time a browser connects to our socket, our regular expression will fail to find a line that has the format of a `StatusMgr` page request. Thus, `www_receiver` will call `www_home` to output the Home Page shown in Figure 9.1 back to the client.

From the Home Page, the user chooses a Group and a Request, and presses the "submit" button. Now the line to `www_receiver` will be of one of the following two formats, depending on the requesting browser:

```
/?Group=0+%7BUniversal+Group%7D&Request=Device+Status/ HTTP/1.0
```

or

```
/?Group=0+%7BUniversal+Group%7D&Request=Device+Status HTTP/1.0
```

Our regular expression obtains values for `grpflg`, `gi`, `grpname`, `reqflg` and `reqval`. For example, the values below correspond to valid `StatusMgr` page request:

- line = GET /?Group=0+%7BUniversal+Group%7D&Request=De-
  vice+Status/ HTTP/1.0
- request =
  /?Group=0+%7BUniversal+Group%7D&Request=Device+Status/
- match =
  /?Group=0+%7BUniversal+Group%7D&Request=Device+Status/
- grpflg = /?Group
- gi = 0
- grpname = +%7BUniversal+Group%7D
- reqflg = Request
- reqval = Device+Status/

In this case, `www_receiver` would call `www_d_status` with `$channel` and `$gi` as arguments.

```
proc www_home {channel} {

global groups gindex myaddr

puts $channel "<HTML>"
puts $channel "<head>"
puts $channel "<title>StatusMgr Home Page</title>"
puts $channel "</head>"
puts $channel {<body bgcolor="sky blue">}
puts $channel {<h1 align="center">Home Page</h1>}
puts $channel "<FORM ACTION=http://$myaddr:2000 METHOD=GET>"
```

```
      puts $channel "Group:<P>"
      puts $channel {<SELECT NAME="Group" >}
      for {set g 0} {$g <= $gindex} {incr g +1} {
        set line [list <OPTION>$g $groups($g,name)]
        puts $channel $line
      }
      puts $channel {</SELECT> <P>}
      puts $channel "Request:<P>"
      puts $channel {<SELECT NAME="Request" >}
      puts $channel {<OPTION>Device Status}
      puts $channel {<OPTION>Device Availability}
      puts $channel {<OPTION>WAN Interface Status}
      puts $channel {<OPTION>LAN Interface Status}
      puts $channel {<OPTION>Historical Availability Summary}
      puts $channel {</SELECT> <P>}
      puts $channel {<INPUT TYPE="submit" VALUE="submit">}
      puts $channel {</FORM>}
      puts $channel "</body>"
      puts $channel "</HTML>"
      close $channel


}
```

The procedure www_home creates the Home Page that is displayed in Figure 9.1. From this form, users select a Group and a Request.

```
proc www_d_status { channel gi} {

    global nn nInfo groups

    # This procedure simply outputs an HTML table showing nodal
    # status for a specified group reference by the group index
    # gi.


    # Set up header info.
     set timestamp [clock format [clock seconds]]
     puts $channel  {<HTML>}
     puts $channel \
     "<HEAD><TITLE>$groups($gi,name) Status</TITLE> </HEAD> "
     puts $channel  {<BODY bgcolor="beige">}
     puts $channel  "<H1>$groups($gi,name)</H1>"
```

```
    puts $channel  "<H2>$groups($gi,name) Status</H2>"
    puts $channel  "<p>$timestamp</p>"
    set numnodes [llength $groups($gi,nodelist)]
    puts $channel  "<p>There are $numnodes nodes in this \
     group</p>"
    puts $channel  {<TABLE BORDER> }
    puts $channel  {<TR>  <TH>Vendor</TH>  <TH>Node</TH> \
        <TH>sysState</TH> <TH>sysUpHrs</TH> <TH>sysName</TH> \
        <TH>sysContact</TH> <TH>sysLocation</TH> \
        <TH>sysDescr</TH> </TR>}
    # Output row entries.
    foreach n $groups($gi,nodelist) {
        if { $nInfo($n,state) == 1  } {
            set color green
            set state "<FONT COLOR=$color>Up</FONT>"
        } elseif  {$nInfo($n,state) == 0} {
            set color red
            set state "<FONT COLOR=$color>Unresponsive</FONT>"
        } else {
            set color black
            set state "<FONT COLOR=$color>Unknown</FONT>"
        }
        set hours $nInfo($n,uphrs)
        set vendor $nInfo($n,vendor)
        puts $channel  "<TR>  <TD>$vendor</TD> \
            <TD>$nInfo($n,addr)</TD> \
            <TD>$state</TD> <TD>$hours</TD> \
            <TD>$nInfo($n,sysName)</TD> \
            <TD>$nInfo($n,sysContact)</TD> \
            <TD>$nInfo($n,sysLocation)</TD> \
            <TD>$nInfo($n,sysDescr)</TD>   </TR>"
    }
  }
  puts $channel "</TABLE> </BODY> </HTML>"
  close $channel


}
```

The procedure www_d_status displays a device status for every device in the specified group. Color is used to highlight node states. Red is used to highlight nodes that are not responsive to poll requests. Magenta is used to highlight nodes with one of more down interfaces. Orange is used to highlight nodes with threshold problems.

```
proc www_uconstr {channel} {

    global myaddr

    puts $channel {<HTML>}
    puts $channel {<head>}
    puts $channel {<title>Under Construction Page</title>}
    puts $channel {<body bgcolor="beige">}
    puts $channel {<h1 align="center">Under Construction \
        Page</h1>}
    puts $channel {<P>Sorry, this page is under \
        construction. </P>}
    puts $channel "</body>"
    puts $channel "</HTML>"
    close $channel
}
```

The procedure www_uconstr is used in this example to display that a page request is under construction. For this example, all requests, except the request for Device Status, are under construction.

The procedure gInit is the same precedure from the previous example. Again, it is used to populate nInfo with sample data.

IN SUMMARY

This chapter showed how to build simple client-server code in Tcl using sockets. It then expanded on this example by showing you how to make your applications Web-accessible.

10

A Response Time Monitoring Tool

This tool provides network delay measurements from a workstation to a list of devices. By using this tool to measure network delay to a list of subnets, a network manager can gain insight to how the network is performing at different strategic points. This tool can be used to help troubleshoot network performance problems. It can also be used to obtain a snapshot of delay through your network. Specifically, the tool provides the following information for each address being tested:

- Current delay measurements
- Average delay measurements
- Peak delay measurements
- Percentage of tests that completed; this helps indicate the reachability of a device

CONCEPTS DEMONSTRATED

The implementation of the Network Delay Tool demonstrates the following concepts:

- Using the simple table widget from Chapter 8
- Generating ICMP echo requests with TickleMan
- Using the `after` command to implement a one-second timer
- Using the `time` command to measure the elapsed execution time of a Tcl scipt

Device	Current Delay	Average Delay	Peak Delay	% Completed
www.cisco.com	217 msecs	367	888	100.0
www.3Com.com	230 msecs	369	858	100.0
www.baynetworks.com	220 msecs	505	1555	100.0
www.cabletron.com	183 msecs	192	237	100.0
www.ascend.com	247 msecs	255	300	100.0

Figure 10.1 Network delay tool

NETWORK DELAY CODE

The Network Delay Tool has six procedures:

- NetworkDelay provides the main code section for this tool. The user calls NetworkDelay with an address list, and the procedure kicks off the test.

- InitGlobals initializes all the globals and nInfo array, which are used for maintaining device delay information. InitGlobals also creates the ICMP session used for generating ICMP echo requests.

- BuildApplicationScreen builds the simple table widget and fills in the IP addresses within the table.

- Timer implements a one-second timer.

- PerformDelayTests calls DelayTest for each address in the list. This procedure is initially called by NetworkDelay, and is also called every poll period by Timer.

- DelayTest measures network delay to an IP address. After the delay is measured, the overall average and peak values are maintained within nInfo. DelayTest also writes the delay and percentage of tests completed values into the simple table widget.

```
source book-ch8.itcl

proc NetworkDelay {addrList} {
  global lAddr

#    Main code section:
#
# Initialize globals
```

```
    set lAddr $addrList
    InitGlobals

    BuildApplicationScreen

    after 1000 Timer
    PerformDelayTests
}
```

NetworkDelay is composed of only five commands: save the address list, initialize all globals, build the application screen, start the timer after one second and start performing the delay tests. Even though the procedure exits fairly quickly, the Timer procedure will keep things running. Note that since we will use the simple table widget built in Chapter 8, we source book-ch8.itcl.

```
##############################################################
# InitGlobals procedure
#
#       This procedure initializes all global variables.
#
proc InitGlobals {} {
   uplevel #0 {

            set gPollTries 3
            set gPollTime 60

            set nRows 0
            set nCount 0
            set nState waiting

            foreach el $lAddr {

                    incr nRows 1
                    set nInfo($nRows,sum) 0
                    set nInfo($nRows,count) 0
                    set nInfo($nRows,polltries) 0
                    set nInfo($nRows,max) 0
            }

            set gSnmpId [snmpsession sess1 -icmp -timeout 200]
    }
}
```

gPollTries specifies the number of ICMP echo requests to send out for each test. gPollTime specifies in seconds how often to perform the tests. We've set up three tests per cycle, and we perform the tests every sixty seconds. The array nInfo is used to keep track of the following information per device: the total sum of all the results (used for calculating averages), the total number of successful tests, the total number of test attempts and the peak test result.

The timeout value used in setting up the ICMP session will cause a timeout failure after two seconds.

```
##########################################################
# BuildApplicationScreen procedure
#
#       Build main table, main screen.
#


proc BuildApplicationScreen { } {

    global nRows lAddr
    set f [MakeTable a $nRows 10 "        Device        " \
          "Current Delay" "Average Delay" \
          " Peak Delay " "% Completed"]
    pack $f

    set i 1
    foreach el $lAddr {

          SetTableValue a $i 1 $el
          incr i 1
    }


}
```

BuildApplicationScreen is fairly straightforward. It builds a simple table widget with n rows (n being the number of addresses being tested), ten of which can be displayable, and five columns. After building the table, the IP addresses for each device being tested are written to the first column of each corresponding row.

```
##########################################################
# Timer procedure
#
#       Implement a one-second timer.
#
#
```

```
proc Timer { } {
  global nCount nState gPollTime

  if {$nState != "active"} {
    incr nCount;
    if {$nCount >= $gPollTime} {
        set nCount 0
        PerformDelayTests
    }
  }

  after 1000 Timer
}
```

Timer is used to implement a one-second timer. nState is used to indicate whether Per-formDelayTests is still active. If PerformDelayTests is still active, Timer will return after setting up to be entered in a second. The effect of this is that the countdown to performing the next test starts after the completion of the previous test.

```
##############################################################
# PerformDelayTests procedure
#
#     Call DelayTest for each address in list. Maintain peak,
#     average values, and percent packets received.
#
proc PerformDelayTests { } {
  global lAddr nState

  set nState active
  set i 1
  foreach el $lAddr {

        DelayTest $el $i
        incr i 1
  }
  set nState waiting
}
```

PerformDelayTests cycles through each address being tested, calling DelayTest. Before starting the tests, nState is set to active; upon completion of all tests nState is reset to waiting.

```
###############################################################
# Delay Test procedure
#
#       Perform ping test on address.
#
#       Return number of successful tests.
#
proc DelayTest {addr row} {
  global gSnmpId gPollTries nInfo

    set sum 0
    set count 0

    for {set i 0} {$i < $gPollTries} {incr i 1} {

         set cmd [list $gSnmpId ping $addr 64 { } wait]
         set x [time {set y [eval $cmd]}]

         #
         # First determine if a timeout occurred.
         #

         set n [string first timeout $y]
         if {$n != -1} {
              continue
         }

         set n [lindex $x 0]
         set n [expr $n/1000]

         incr count 1
         set sum [expr $sum + $n]
    }

    incr nInfo($row,polltries) $gPollTries
    incr nInfo($row,count) $count

    set x [expr double($nInfo($row,polltries))]
    set y [expr double($nInfo($row,count))]

    set p [expr ($y/$x)*100.0]
    SetTableValue a $row 5 $p
```

```
if {$count != 0} {

        set avg [expr $sum/$count]
        set s [format "%d msecs" $avg]
        SetTableValue a $row 2 $s

        if {$nInfo($row,max) < $avg} {
                set nInfo($row,max) $avg
                SetTableValue a $row 4 $avg
        }

        set x [expr $sum/1000.0]
        set nInfo($row,sum) [expr $nInfo($row,sum) + $x]

        #
        # Calculate average. Note that values have been
        # converted to seconds; convert back to msecs
        # before displaying value.
        #

        set x $nInfo($row,sum)
        set y [expr double($nInfo($row,count))]

        set avg [expr int(($x/$y)*1000)]
        SetTableValue a $row 3 $avg
    }

    return $count
}
```

DelayTest will send n ICMP echo requests to a device (n being specified by the global gPollTries). The data portion of each echo request will be set to 64 bytes. The time command is used to measure the number of microseconds it takes for the nonblocking ICMP echo request command to execute. The command could complete execution due to one of two reasons: a response to the echo response could be received or a timeout could occur. By searching the result string for the string timeout, we can determine which result occurred.

The results of all the successful tests for this cycle are averaged together and the result written to the "Current Delay" column. The sum of all the test results is maintained so the overall average value can be written to the "Average Delay" column. If a new peak value is detected, it is written to the "Peak Delay" column. The total number of all tests attempted and completed are maintained so the percentage of completed tests can be written to the "% Completed" column.

EXTENDING THE NETWORK DELAY TOOL

We will now show how the Network Delay Tool can be extended to perform the following:

- Indicate the time the peak value was detected
- Change the color of the text within a row of the simple table widget to red if a threshold value is exceeded
- Use a device's TCP connection table to determine the IP addresses to test

To add the first item, we need to modify the `MakeTable` command within `BuildApplicationScreen` to:

```
set f [MakeTable a $nRows 10 "        Device        " \
       "Current Delay" "Average Delay" \
       " Peak Delay " " Peak Time " "% Completed"]
```

and change the code testing for a new peak value within `DelayTest` to:

```
if {$nInfo($row,max) < $avg} {
  set nInfo($row,max) $avg
  SetTableValue a $row 4 $avg
  set s [clock format [clock seconds] -format "%I:%M %p"]
  SetTableValue a $row 5 $s
}
```

After making these changes (and changing the "% Completed" column number to 6), running `NetworkDelay` will give us the results shown in Figure 10.2.

To change a row's text color to indicate a threshold has been exceeded, we need to:

- Pass a threshold value to the procedure `NetworkDelay`
- Write a procedure, `ChangeRowColor`, which can configure the foreground color for each cell within a row
- Test for a threshold exceeded condition in `DelayTest`

Device	Current Delay	Average Delay	Peak Delay	Peak Time	% Completed
www.cisco.com	220 msecs	241	353	12:24 PM	100.0
www.3Com.com	1575 msecs	469	1575	12:29 PM	100.0
www.baynetworks.com	233 msecs	256	380	12:24 PM	100.0
www.cabletron.com	186 msecs	190	240	12:24 PM	100.0
www.ascend.com	254 msecs	264	303	12:24 PM	100.0

Figure 10.2   Network Delay Tool showing peak time.

- Add a "Clear Status" button to reset all red text to black
- Add a command procedure, ClearRowStatus, to be executed when the "Clear Status" button is pressed
- Maintain a list of all rows in the "red" state

Two new procedures, ChangeRowColor and ClearRowStatus, are provided below:

```
proc ChangeRowColor {row color} {
  global gRowsStatusChanged

  for {set i 0} {$i < 6} {incr i} {
      .{a}_Table_frame.r$row.c$i configure -fg $color
  }

  if {$color = "red"} {
      lappend gRowsStatusChanged $row
  }
}


proc ClearRowStatus { } {
  global gRowsStatusChanged

  foreach el $gRowsStatusChanged {
      ChangeRowColor $el black
  }
  set gRowsStatusChanged ""
}
```

Note that to write ChangeRowColor, we needed to know the cell naming convention used within MakeTable. Also, we needed to add each row that is being set to red to the global gRowStatusChanged list.

The new code for BuildApplicationScreen is:

```
proc BuildApplicationScreen { } {

  global nRows lAddr

  set mf [frame .mainFrame]

  set f [MakeTable a $nRows 10 "       Device        " \
      "Current Delay" "Average Delay" " Peak Delay " \
      " Peak Time " "% Completed"]
  pack $f -in $mf -side top
```

```
set cb [button .clearB -text \
    "Clear Status" -command ClearRowStatus]
pack $cb -in $mf -side top
pack $mf

set i 1
foreach el $lAddr {

    SetTableValue a $i 1 $el
    incr i 1
}


}
```

Here we build a main frame and pack within it the frame returned by `MakeTable` and the "Clear Status" button.

Finally, we need to modify `DelayTest` slightly to compare the calculated delay value to the threshold value. The modified code for `DelayTest` is:

```
proc DelayTest {addr row} {
  global gSnmpId gPollTries nInfo gThreshold

  set sum 0
  set count 0

  for {set i 0} {$i < $gPollTries} {incr i 1} {

      set cmd [list $gSnmpId ping $addr 64 { } wait]
      set x [time {set y [eval $cmd]}]

      #
      # First, determine if a timeout occurred.
      #

      set n [string first timeout $y]
      if {$n != -1} {
          continue
      }

      set n [lindex $x 0]
      set n [expr $n/1000]
```

```
        incr count 1
        set sum [expr $sum + $n]
}

incr nInfo($row,polltries) $gPollTries
incr nInfo($row,count) $count

set x [expr double($nInfo($row,polltries))]
set y [expr double($nInfo($row,count))]
set p [expr ($y/$x)*100.0]
SetTableValue a $row 6 $p

if {$count != 0} {

        set avg [expr $sum/$count]
        set s [format "%d msecs" $avg]
        SetTableValue a $row 2 $s

        if {$avg >= $gThreshold} {
                ChangeRowColor $row red
        }

        if {$nInfo($row,max) < $avg} {
                set nInfo($row,max) $avg
                SetTableValue a $row 4 $avg
                set s [clock format [clock seconds] \
                        -format "%I:%M %p"]
                SetTableValue a $row 5 $s
        }

        set x [expr $sum/1000.0]
        set nInfo($row,sum) [expr $nInfo($row,sum) + $x]

        # Calculate average. Note, values have been converted
        # to seconds, convert back to msecs before displaying
        # value

        set x $nInfo($row,sum)
        set y [expr double($nInfo($row,count))]

        set avg [expr int(($x/$y)*1000)]
        SetTableValue a $row 3 $avg
```

Device	Current Delay	Average Delay	Peak Delay	Peak Time	% Completed
www.cisco.com	200 msecs	350	848	04:30 PM	100.0
www.3Com.com	220 msecs	229	290	04:27 PM	100.0
www.baynetworks.com	220 msecs	572	1976	04:27 PM	100.0
www.cabletron.com	200 msecs	340	834	04:28 PM	100.0
www.ascend.com	884 msecs	634	884	04:31 PM	100.0

Clear Status

Figure 10.3   Network Delay Tool after extensions.

```
    }

    return $count
}
```

Wrapping up this section, we will build two procedures, `BuildTcpConnList` and `BuildTcpCB`, which will build a list of IP addresses from a device's TCP connection table. Once the list is built, `NetworkDelay` will be called, and this list will be passed to it.

If there is a server device on your local segment, and you wish to monitor the network delay for all remote addresses currently connected to that server, these routines could be used to automate this for you. Note that if the server is on a local segment, the network delay you measure from your workstation to each of the remote addresses should be the same as the network delay from the server to the remote addresses. This, of course, would not make a lot of sense if you were accessing the server remotely.

```
proc BuildTcpConnList {addr cstr} {
    global gAddrList gDone

    set gAddrList ""
    set gDone 0

    set sid [snmpsession -snmp -tableRows 1]

    set authinfo [list snmpv1 $cstr]
    set vb {tcpConnRemAddress}
    set cb [list BuildTcpCB]

    $sid table $addr $authinfo $vb {0} {} $cb

    vwait gDone
```

```
    NetworkDelay 600 $gAddrList
}

proc BuildTcpCB {result} {
  global gAddrList gDone

    set vblist [GetVarBindList $result]
    set vb [GetVarBind $vblist 1]
    set val [GetValue $vb]

    if {[string length $val] > 0} {
        if {[lsearch $gAddrList $val] == -1} {
            lappend gAddrList $val
        }
    }

    set errorStatus [GetErrorStatus $result]

    if {$errorStatus == "endOfTable" } {
        set gDone 1
    }
}
```

BuildTcpConnList kicks off a table command to collect the tcpConnRemAd-dress column. When the collection is complete, the callback routine sets the variable gDone, which causes BuildTcpConnList to start NetworkDelay, passing it the list of addresses collected. Note that BuildTcpCB checks to make sure an address already hasn't been added to the list before adding it. This is necessary since tcpConnTable could have several entries with the same remote address if the remote address has several active TCP connections to the device.

IN SUMMARY

In this chapter, we showed how to build a useful tool in a relatively small amount of code using some of our previously built procedures. We further showed that trivial functional changes could, in effect, be made trivially. We also showed that more significant functional changes could also be made easily.

11

A Network Discovery Tool

This chapter provides a complete code review of the sample network discovery tool that we described back in Chapter 2. This application is used to discover SNMP-accessible nodes in one or more Class B or C networks. It can also be used to discover individual Class B subnets as long as a subnet mask of 255.255.255.0 is used.

The tool has no GUI and produces both text and HTML files as output. We point out places in the code where we open or close an SNMP session, or issue an SNMP command with a comment line that begins with # SNMP COMMAND. This tool uses convenience routines developed in Chapter 5 for parsing result strings from SNMP operations.

This application goes through a list of Class B or Class C networks as specified by the user in the file `networks.txt`. It does an SNMP poll for each IP address in the range of addresses supported by each network entry. `Discover` throttles sending SNMP requests so that it doesn't flood the line. When the throttle rate is reached (as defined by variable `gThrottleLevel`), `Discover` performs a `vwait`, waiting for an SNMP response to be received. The information per poll is saved in the array `nDisInfo`. For each iteration, newly discovered nodes are written to the output files.

Input files required by this application are:

- `networks.txt`
A user-defined list of networks to discover with associated community name information.

- `vendors.txt`
An application file that contains a list of private enterprise OIDs by vendor. It is a modified copy of the enterprise number file available via ftp://ftp.isi.edu/in-notes/iana/assignments/enterprise-numbers. Long vendor names have been shortened and names have been modified to have no spaces. This file will be available on our Web site.

To understand this application, you need a clear understanding of the contents of the user-created file `networks.txt`. Here is an example of the contents of a valid `networks.txt` file:

```
158 101 *   public admin
207 52 18   public support
```

For this example, `discover.itcl` will use the community strings "public" and "admin" to first poll the address range 158.101.1.1 through 158.101.1.254. Then it will do the same for 158.101.2.1 through 158.101.2.254, and so on through the entire address range of the 158.101 network. Finally it will poll the address range 207.52.18.1 through 207.52.18.254 using the community strings "public" and "support". Note that any number of community strings can be listed on a line. If none are listed, "public" will be used as a default.

Output files created by this application are:

- `discover.txt`

A text file with a line of information per discovered node. The character | is used to delimit fields of information within each line. This delimited text file is easily loaded into spreadsheet or database systems, but remember to ignore the first line of header information.

- `discover.html`

An HTML file with a singe table of information; there is a row for each discovered node.

- `discover.lst`

A text file with a list of discovered nodes and the community name with which each node was discovered.

When you retrieve this application from our Web site, you will be retrieving a zip file that includes three files: `discover.itcl`, `vendors.txt` and `networks.txt`. Note that you will need to modify `networks.txt` to identify the networks you want to discover and the community names to use to discover them.

CONCEPTS DEMONSTRATED

This application demonstrates the following concepts:

- SNMP Get and GetNext polling using the TickleMan API
- Tcl file I/O to create both text and HTML files

GENERAL OVERVIEW OF CODE

The main portion of `discover.itcl` does the following:

- Calls the procedure `InitGlobals` for initialization.
- Sets up an SNMP session, `sessid1`.

- Calls the procedure `OpenVendorFile` with the filename `vendors.txt` to get knowledge of vendors' private enterprise OID numbers, which are later used to identify vendor names from `sysObjectID`.
- Calls the procedure `OpenNetFile` with the filename `networks.txt` to get the user-specified networks to discover and what community names to use during the discovery process.
- Open for writing three output files: `discover.txt`, `discover.html` and `discover.lst`.
- Write header information to files `discover.txt` and `discover.html`.
- For each network entry, read from `networks.txt` and call the procedure `DiscoverSubnet` for each address range for which to discover. Then, call the procedure `Update_nInfo` to write newly discovered nodes to output files.
- Close the output files and SNMP session. Notify the user that the application has completed successfully. Wait for the user to close the application console.

This application, `discover.itcl`, is composed of the following procedures:

- `InitGlobals`

    Defines the varbind list used in discover polls and also defines an array, `ietf`, which specifies the OIDs to use when checking for MIB support.

- `OpenVendorFile`

    Opens and reads `vendors.txt`. Stores a mapping of private enterprise OID numbers to vendor names in the array `vendorName`.

- `OpenNetFile`

    Opens `networks.txt` and reads which networks to discover.

- `DiscoverSubnet`

    Generates SNMP polls through an entire address range between x.x.x.1 and x.x.x.254. For each node that returns an SNMP response, it then checks for MIB support. All node information is stored in the array `nDisInfo`.

- `DisCallBk`

    The callback procedure that processes the Get Response for discover polls. If the error response is `noError`, learned information about the node is saved in the array `nDisInfo`.

- `MibCallBk`

    MIB support is determined by doing a GetNext on the starting OID for a MIB branch. This callback routine processes the resulting Get Response packet. If the response is an OID that is within the OID range for the MIB, the node is identified as supporting that MIB.

- Update_nInfo

Goes through the array nDisInfo looking for new nodes that have not been identified yet to the output files. If a node is new, it writes information about the node to both the output files and to the console so the user can see the progress of the application while it is running.

DETAIL CODE

Here is the main logic code contained in discover.itc:

```
###################################################################
#                          Main Logic
###################################################################

# Initialize globals.

  InitGlobals

# SNMP COMMAND - Create snmp session.

  set sessid1 [snmpsession sess1 -snmp -timeout 200 -retries 0]


# Get vendor name and enterprise numbers.

  OpenVendorFile vendors.txt

# Get list of Class B and Class C networks the user wants to
# discover.

  OpenNetFile networks.txt

# Create and open output files.

  set text_fileid [open discover.txt "w"]
  set html_fileid [open discover.html "w"]
  set lst_fileid  [open discover.lst "w"]

# Write headers for discover.txt.

  puts $text_fileid $timestamp
```

```
    puts $text_fileid " Vendor|      Adress|          \
        ObjectID|         sysName| \
        MIB-Support|         sysLocation|              \
        sysContact|              sysDescr"

# Write headers for discover.html.

    puts $html_fileid "<HTML> <HEAD> \
        <TITLE>$timestamp</TITLE> </HEAD>"
    puts $html_fileid {<BODY bgcolor="Beige">}
    puts $html_fileid "<H1>$timestamp</H1>"
    puts $html_fileid "<TABLE BORDER>"
    set colnames [list Vendor NodeAddr ObjectId sysName \
                MIB-Support sysLocation sysContact sysDescr]
    foreach el $colnames {
        puts $html_fileid "<TH>$el</TH>"
    }
    puts $html_fileid "<TR>"

# Poll through address ranges of each specified network.

  for {set i 1} {$i <= $nnets} {incr i +1} {
    set B1 $netInfo($i,B1)
    set B2 $netInfo($i,B2)
    set B3 $netInfo($i,B3)

    set cstrlist $netInfo($i,cstrlist)

    if {$B3 != "*"} {
        puts "Starting discover on subnet $B1.$B2.$B3 $cstrlist"
        DiscoverSubnet $B1 $B2 $B3 $cstrlist
        Update_nInfo $text_fileid $html_fileid $lst_fileid
        puts  "Finished discover on subnet $B1.$B2.$B3"
    } else {
          for {set n 1 } {$n <= 254 } {incr n 1} {
              puts "Starting discover on subnet $B1.$B2.$n \
                  $cstrlist"
              DiscoverSubnet $B1 $B2 $n $cstrlist
              Update_nInfo $text_fileid $html_fileid $lst_fileid
              puts  "Finished discover on subnet $B1.$B2.$n"
          }
    }
```

```
}

# Close output files and snmp sessions.

puts $html_fileid "</TABLE> </BODY> </HTML>"
flush $text_fileid
flush $html_fileid
flush $lst_fileid
close $text_fileid
close $html_fileid
close $lst_fileid

puts "Discover has completed successfully.  Output files are:"
puts "        discover.html"
puts "        discover.txt"
puts "        discover.lst"
puts "   "
puts "Discover has completed successfully. Closed this console \
      now."

# SNMP COMMAND -- Close the SNMP Session

$sessid1 destroy

# Use vwait so that the application doesn't close its console on
# completion. We want the user to see validation that the
# application successfully completed.

set forever ON
vwait forever
```

Here are the associated procedures contained in discover.itcl:

```
###############################################################
#                       proc InitGlobals
###############################################################

proc InitGlobals { } {

  uplevel #0 {

      # Define SysBindList.
```

```
        set SysBindList [list sysObjectID sysName sysDescr \
                         sysLocation sysContact sysUpTime \
                         ipAdEntAddr.127.0.0.9 ]

    # Define oids for checking MIB support.

        set ietf(rmon)        1.3.6.1.2.1.16
        set ietf(rmon2)       1.3.6.1.2.1.16.11
        set ietf(hostmib)     1.3.6.1.2.1.25
        set ietf(appmib)      1.3.6.1.2.1.27
        set ietf(rdbmsmib)    1.3.6.1.2.1.39
        set ietf(repeatermib) 1.3.6.1.2.1.22
        set ietf(bridgemib)   1.3.6.1.2.1.17
        set ietf(ospfmib)     1.3.6.1.2.1.14
        set ietf(atmmib)      1.3.6.1.2.1.37
        set ietf(ifxmib)      1.3.6.1.2.1.31.1
        set ietf(frmib)       1.3.6.1.2.1.10.37
        set ietf(fddimib)     1.3.6.1.2.1.10.15.71
        set ietf(dot3)        1.3.6.1.2.1.10.7
        set ietf(dot5)        1.3.6.1.2.1.10.9
        set ietf(ds1)         1.3.6.1.2.1.10.18
        set ietf(ds3)         1.3.6.1.2.1.10.30
        set ietf(smds)        1.3.6.1.2.1.10.31
        set ietf(rip2)        1.3.6.1.2.1.23
        set ietf(rmontok)     1.3.6.1.2.1.16.10
        set ietf(ipforw)      1.3.6.1.2.1.4.24
        set ietf(entitymib)   1.3.6.1.2.1.47

        set gPacketCount 0
        set gThrottleLevel 50

    # Define timestamp and date information to date the reports.

        set timestamp [clock format [clock seconds]]
        set date [lrange $timestamp 1 2]

    # Initialize the count of nodes discovered.

        set nnodes 0
    }
}
```

The procedure `InitGlobals` defines the contents of our `SysBindList` to later poll for nodal information. We also define an array, `ietf`, which contains the MIB OID numbers to use in discovering MIB support. By defining these MIB OID numbers in an array, we only have to define one global in the procedures that use these OID numbers, and more importantly, we can easily cycle through these MIB OID numbers by using an `array names` command within a `foreach` loop. `InitGlobals` also defines `gPacketCount`, which is used for controlling the number of outstanding SNMP packets that can be put on the line, and `gThrottleLevel`, which defines the level at which to start throttling SNMP packets to be sent.

```
#############################################################
#                     proc OpenVendorFile
#############################################################

proc OpenVendorFile { vendor_file }  {

    global vendorName

    # This procedure reads a file that identifies vendor
    # enterprise oids. This file is an edited version of
    # the internet available snmp-vendors-contacts.txt
    # file whose contents look like the following:
    #
    #  1 Proteon
    #  2 IBM
    #  3 CMU
    #  .  .
    #  .  .

    set fileid [ open $vendor_file "r"]

    while { [gets $fileid line] >= 0 } {

        #check validity of data

        set num [lindex $line 0]
        set name [lindex $line 1]

        if {$num < 1 || $num > 20000} { continue }

        set vendorName($num) $name
    }
    close $fileid
}
```

The procedure `OpenVendorFile` creates and populates the array `vendorName`, which will be used later to map OID numbers to vendor names.

```
###############################################################
#                       proc OpenNetFile
###############################################################

proc OpenNetFile { net_file }  {

    global netInfo nnets InFile InFileId

    # The contents of this input file are as follows:
    #  <Byte1> <Byte2> <Byte3> <read-community1> <read-community2>
    #    For example, data entries would look like the following:
    #    158 101 121 public support
    #    158 102 *   public support

    set fileid [ open $net_file "r"]
    set nnets 0

    while { [gets $fileid line] >= 0 } {
        # Check validity of data, for example, skip blank lines.
        set len [llength $line]
        if {$len < 2} {
            continue
        }
        set B1 [lindex $line 0]
        set B2 [lindex $line 1]
        set B3 [lindex $line 2]
        if { ($B1 < 1) || ($B1 > 254) } {
            continue
        }

        if { ($B2 < 1) || ($B2 > 254) } {
            continue
        }

        if { ($B3 < 1 || $B3 > 254) && ($B3 != "*") }  {
            continue
        }

        # ok, B1 B2 B3 values are valid, now get community string
        # list.

        if {$len >= 3} {
            set cstrlist [lrange $line 3 end]
        } else {
```

```
                set cstrlist {public}
        }


        # OK, now add new entry to global array netInfo.

        incr nnets +1
        set netInfo($nnets,B1)  $B1
        set netInfo($nnets,B2)  $B2
        set netInfo($nnets,B3)  $B3
        set netInfo($nnets,cstrlist) $cstrlist
    }
    close $fileid
}
```

The procedure OpenNetFile reads the file networks.txt for valid network entries. For each valid network entry, it stores information to array netInfo.

```
###############################################################
#                    proc DiscoverSubnet
###############################################################

proc DiscoverSubnet { B1 B2 B3 cstrlist} {

    global  nDisInfo netInfo SysBindList sessid1 ietf
    global  gPacketCount gThrottleLevel


    # Initialize-Cleanup from previous subnet discover.

        # nDisInfo is an array which we use to store nodal
        # information for each node in the given subnet. This
        # array is reused per subnet, so we need to initialize
        # it per subnet.

        if { [info exists nDisInfo] } {
            unset nDisInfo
        }

    # Here we initialize a fresh nDisInfo array

        for {set n 1 } {$n <= 254} {incr n 1} {
            set addr  "$B1.$B2.$B3.$n"
```

```
        set nDisInfo($n,addr)            $addr
        set nDisInfo($n,rcomm)           "n/a"
        set nDisInfo($n,sysDescr.0)      "n/a"
        set nDisInfo($n,sysName.0)       "n/a"
        set nDisInfo($n,sysObjectID.0)   "n/a"
        set nDisInfo($n,sysContact.0)    "n/a"
        set nDisInfo($n,sysUpTime.0)     -1
        set nDisInfo($n,state)           "unknown"
        set nDisInfo($n,sysLocation.0)   "n/a"
        set nDisInfo($n,nodeaddr)        $addr
        set nDisInfo($n,mibsupport)      ""
  }

# Now we can poll the entire subnet address space
# with each community string in list.

foreach cstr $cstrlist {

      set authinfo1 [list snmpv1 $cstr]
      for {set n 1 } {$n <= 254} {incr n 1} {

          if {$nDisInfo($n,state) == "Reachable"} {continue}

          while {$gPacketCount > $gThrottleLevel} {
             vwait gPacketCount
          }

          set addr $nDisInfo($n,addr)
          set callbk_str [list DisCallBk $n $cstr]
          set cmd [list $sessid1 next $addr $authinfo1 \
             $SysBindList {} $callbk_str]

          # SNMP COMMAND -- Polling for MIB-II info.

          set foo [catch {eval $cmd} reqid]

          if { $foo == 0} {
             incr gPacketCount
          } else {
            puts stderr "SysPoll error polling node $addr"
          }
          update
```

```
    }

    puts "Network $B1.$B2.$B3 $cstr \
        Syspolling complete ..."

    # Pause for outstanding polls to complete.

    while {$gPacketCount > 0} {
        vwait gPacketCount
    }

}

# Now, let's check for MIB support one MIB at a time.

for {set n 1 } {$n <= 254} {incr n 1} {

  if {$nDisInfo($n,state) != "Reachable"} {continue}

    set addr $nDisInfo($n,addr)
    set authinfo [list snmpv1 $nDisInfo($n,rcomm)]
    set nDisInfo($n,mibsupport) "mib-2"

    puts "Checking node $addr mib support"

    # Check node for IETF MIB support.

    set callbk_str [list MibCallBk $n]

    foreach el [array names ietf] {

        while {$gPacketCount > $gThrottleLevel} {
            vwait gPacketCount
        }

        set cmd [list $sessid1 next $addr $authinfo \
            $ietf($el) {} $callbk_str]

        # SNMP COMMAND -- Polling for IETF MIB support.

        set foo [catch {eval $cmd} reqid]
        if { $foo == 0} {
```

```
                        incr gPacketCount
                } else {
                    puts stderr "Error polling node $addr \
                        for $el MIB Support"
                }
                update
            }
        }


        # Pause for outstanding polls to complete.

        while {$gPacketCount > 0} {
            vwait gPacketCount
        }
}
```

The procedure DiscoverSubnet polls all addresses in the address range B1.B2.B3.1 through B1.B2.B3.254 for specified MIB-II information using the community strings from the list until a node responds to one of the community strings. The callback routine used for these polls is DisCallBk. We will poll any of the nodes that responded to a discover poll for various IETF MIB support.

The array nDisInfo is used to temporarily hold nodal information for 254 addresses at a time. We store the nodal information for each iteration of DiscoverSubnet in nDisInfo. The contents are used later by Update_nInfo to write new nodal information to the output files. All of the entries in nDisInfo should be self-explanatory, except for possibly nDisInfo (\$n,nodeaddr).

We use the value of nDisInfo(\$n,nodeaddr) to uniquely identify nodes. We need to uniquely identify nodes because we don't want to report the same node twice in our output files. When we poll nodes, one of the things we poll for is the next entry after 127.0.0.9 in the IP address table. This should give us the first valid IP address in the node's IP address table, after its loopback addresses. We treat this address as the node's unique IP address by storing it in nDis Info(\$n,nodeaddr). Before the procedure Update_nInfo outputs nodal information for a node, it sets unique_addr from nDisInfo(\$n,nodeaddr). Then it checks if the element nInfo(\$unique_addr) exists. If not, the node is determined to be new. Update_nInfo will then write information about the node to the output files and create a new element, nInfo(\$unique_addr).

While gPacketCount is incremented in this routine after generating an SNMP request, it is decremented in the callback routines after either a response or a timeout is received. The code fragments:

```
    while {$gPacketCount > $gThrottleLevel} {
                vwait gPacketCount
        }
```

and

```
        while {$gPacketCount > 0} {
          vwait gPacketCount
        }
```

will cause the script to wait until either the callback routines `DisCallBk` or `MibCallBk` are entered or `gPacketCount` is decremented.

```
################################################################
#                       proc DisCallBk
################################################################

proc DisCallBk { nodeid comm result } {

    global nDisInfo SysBindList vendorName sessid1
    global MibVBList1 MibVBList2
    global errorCode errorInfo gPacketCount


    incr gPacketCount -1

    set err [catch {

        set addr $nDisInfo($nodeid,addr)
        set infcode  [GetErrorStatus $result]

        update
        if {$infcode != "noError"} {
            set nDisInfo($nodeid,state) "Unresponsive"
        }

        if {$infcode == "noError"} {
            ProcessNodeReachable $nodeid $result $comm
        }

    }]

    if { $err != 0} {
        puts "Error in DisCallBk nodeid=$nodeid comm=$comm"
        puts "        errorCode=$errorCode  errorInfo=$errorInfo"
    }
    update
}
```

```
proc ProcessNodeReachable {nodeid result comm} {
        global nDisInfo

        # We have gotten a valid response with data.
        # Mark the node as reachable via $comm.

        set nDisInfo($nodeid,state) Reachable
        set nDisInfo($nodeid,rcomm) $comm

        # OK, let's parse the vb list of the response.

        set vblist [GetVarBindList $result]

        foreach vb $vblist {

                set oid      [GetOID $vb]
                set type     [GetType $vb]

                if { [string compare unknown $type] == 0} {
                    continue
                }

                set val [GetValue $vb]
                if {[string compare OctetString $type] == 0} {
                    set val [octet2text $val]
                }

                # Watch out for non-displayable octet strings.

                if { [string length $val] == 0} {
                    set val [GetValue $vb]
                }

                # We need to uniquely identify nodes.  The way it is
                # done here is to use the first valid IP address
                # supported by the node in its IP address table.
                # Thus, if the oid is ipAddEntAddr, use its
                # value to uniquely identify the node; else,
                # save the oid and value in nDisInfo array as we
                # normally do.
```

```
                    if {[string first ipAdEntAddr $oid] > -1} {
                        set nDisInfo($nodeid,nodeaddr) $val
                    } else {
                        set nDisInfo($nodeid,$oid) $val
                    }
                }
            }
        }
```

The procedure `DisCallBk` parses the result of the SNMP response. It decrements `gPack-etCount`. If the SNMP response is `noError`, `ProcessNodeReachable` is called. The logic for `ProcessNodeReachable` was pulled into a separate routine to make the code more readable. It parses the response and saves the information to the array `nDisInfo`.

```
##############################################################
#                     proc MibCallBk
##############################################################
proc MibCallBk { nodeid result } {

    global nDisInfo errorCode errorInfo
    global ietf gPacketCount

    incr gPacketCount -1

    set err [catch {
    update

    set addr $nDisInfo($nodeid,addr)

    # Now, check if the response is good.

    set infcode  [GetErrorStatus $result]
    if { $infcode == "noError"} {

            # OK, the response is good and the node is reachable...
            # let's parse its response ...

            set vblist [GetVarBindList $result]
            foreach vb $vblist {

                set oidname     [GetOID $vb]
                set type        [GetType $vb]
```

```
        if { [string compare unknown $type] == 0} {
            continue
        }

        set val [GetValue $vb]
        if {[string compare OctetString $type] == 0} {
            set val [octet2text $val]
        }

        # Watch out for non-displayable octet strings.

        if { [string length $val] == 0} {
            set val [GetValue $vb]
        }

        # Here we make sure the oid value is in oid number
        # format and not in oid name format.

        if [catch {set oid [oid2dot $oidname]} err] {
            puts "MibCallBk: can not translate $oidname"
            return
        }

        foreach el [array names ietf] {

            if {[string first $ietf($el) $oid] == 0 && \
                [string first $el \
                $nDisInfo($nodeid,mibsupport)] < 0} {

                # We have discovered ietf mib support.

                append nDisInfo($nodeid,mibsupport) ", $el "
                break
            }
        }
    }
}

}]

if { $err != 0} {
    puts "Error is MibCallBk nodeid=$nodeid "
```

```
        puts "       errorCode=$errorCode   errorInfo=$errorInfo"
    }
    update
}
```

The procedure `MibCallBk` parses the SNMP response and checks the OIDs in the response. It first makes sure the OID is specified as an OID number and not as a OID name. To do this, it uses the TickleMan procedure `oid2dot`. If the beginning of the OID number matches the same OID number string as one of our defined IETF MIBs, we append to `nDisInfo($nodeid,mibsupport)` a string like "rmon2", if it's not already there.

```
###############################################################
#                       proc Update_nInfo
###############################################################

proc Update_nInfo { text_fileid html_fileid lst_fileid } {

    global nInfo nnodes nDisInfo date timestamp vendorName

    # Here we process any new nodes we have found in the subnet
    # just discovered. We want to make sure we don't record nodes
    # that were already found under a different IP address. If
    # nInfo($unique_addr) exists, skip the node, since it was
    # processed before.

    for { set n 1} {$n <= 254} {incr n +1} {
        if {[string compare \
           $nDisInfo($n,state) "Reachable"] != 0 } {
               continue
        }

        set addr $nDisInfo($n,addr)
        set unique_addr $nDisInfo($n,nodeaddr)
        if {[info exists nInfo($unique_addr)] == 1 } {
           continue
        }

        # OK, this is a new node not already discovered.

        incr nnodes +1

        #
        # Create an entry in array nInfo to indicate that a unique
```

```
# address was found.
#

set nInfo($unique_addr) 1

# Save vendor enterprise number.

set num -1

if [catch \
   {set oid [oid2dot $nDisInfo($n,sysObjectID.0)]} err] {
       puts "Update_ninfo: can not translate \
            $nDisInfo($n,sysObjectID.0)"
       continue
}


#
# oid for enterprises is 1.3.6.1.4.1.
# we need to get the vendor number n from the
# oid 1.3.6.1.4.1.n.
#
set len [string length $oid]
set newstr [string range $oid 12 $len]
regexp {([^.]*).([^.]*).} $newstr match num
if { [info exists vendorName($num)] == 1} {
    set vendorname $vendorName($num)
} else {
    set vendorname "n/a"
}

# Output to console so whoever is watching can see
# new nodes as they are discovered.

puts "nnodes = $nnodes"
puts [format "%15s %15s" $vendorname $addr]
puts [format "              %20s %20s" \
         $nDisInfo($n,sysObjectID.0) \
         $nDisInfo($n,sysName.0)]
puts [format "              %10s %20s %20s " \
         $nDisInfo($n,mibsupport) \
         $nDisInfo($n,sysLocation.0) \
         $nDisInfo($n,sysContact.0)]
```

```
puts [format "                %30s" \
        $nDisInfo($n,sysDescr.0)]

# Output info (w/o community names) to text file so we can
# import this info into spreadsheets and database systems
# as an ascii file with fields delimited by |.

puts $text_fileid [format \
        "%15s| %15s| %20s| %20s| %10s| %20s| %20s| %30s" \
        $vendorname $addr $nDisInfo($n,sysObjectID.0) \
        $nDisInfo($n,sysName.0) \
        $nDisInfo($n,mibsupport) \
        $nDisInfo($n,sysLocation.0) \
        $nDisInfo($n,sysContact.0) \
        $nDisInfo($n,sysDescr.0)]

# Output info (w/o community names) to HTML file.

puts $html_fileid [format "<TD>%15s</TD>" $vendorname]
puts $html_fileid \
        [format "<TD ALIGN=RIGHT>%15s</TD>" $addr]
puts $html_fileid [format "<TD>%20s</TD>" \
        $nDisInfo($n,sysObjectID.0)]
puts $html_fileid [format "<TD>%20s</TD>" \
        $nDisInfo($n,sysName.0)]
puts $html_fileid [format "<TD>%10s</TD>" \
        $nDisInfo($n,mibsupport)]
puts $html_fileid [format "<TD>%20s</TD>" \
        $nDisInfo($n,sysLocation.0)]
puts $html_fileid [format "<TD>%20s</TD>" \
        $nDisInfo($n,sysContact.0)]
puts $html_fileid [format "<TD>%30s</TD>" \
        $nDisInfo($n,sysDescr.0)]
puts $html_fileid "<TR>"

# Output node and community info to a file that can be
# used later when we need node and community name info
# to set up node monitoring via snmp.

puts $lst_fileid [format "%15s %30s" $addr \
        $nDisInfo($n,rcomm)]
```

```
      # Flush file i/o so if the program is interrupted, we at
      # least have partial data saved to the output files.

      flush $text_fileid
      flush $html_fileid
      flush $lst_fileid
   }
   flush $text_fileid
   flush $html_fileid
   flush $lst_fileid
}
```

The procedure `Update_nInfo` checks the array `nDisInfo` for nodes that have been discovered. It determines a discovered node's unique address (`unique_addr`) from its corresponding value of `nDisInfo($n,nodeaddr)`. If `nInfo($unique_addr)` does not exist, the node is a newly discovered node and information about the node is written to various output files.

IN SUMMARY

We built, in a fairly small amount of code, a useful application for discovering SNMP devices on a subnet and which MIBs (from a subset of IETF MIBs) are supported on the devices. We further demonstrated how to build an HTML output file to show the results of the discover process. This tool could be extended to show both SNMP-supported devices and devices that respond to an ICMP ping. The tool could further be extended to use the enterprise number of a device to obtain private MIB information, such as the software revision numbers and boards installed on a device.

12

A Status Monitoring Tool

This chapter reviews the sample application, StatusMgr, that we first introduced back in Chapter 2. Figure 12.1 shows the native GUI to this tool.

This application displays information such as device network availability, device reset counts, interface uptimes, interface utilization and interface discards. It also shows on request which devices in your defined groups are routing the most IP traffic, which are generating the most IP traffic, and which are receiving the most IP traffic.

StatusMgr displays nodal states via status colors. It uses the color dark green to indicate network devices that are both reachable and healthy, as far as StatusMgr knows. It uses the color magenta to indicate devices that are reachable, but have one or more interfaces that have administration status set to UP, and operational status set to DOWN. The color orange is used to indicate symptoms based on built-in threshold rules. Finally, the color red is used to indicate nodes that are not reachable via SNMP polling, based on the address and community name values we are using.

StatusMgr can also be accessed remotely via a Web browser. Figure 12.2 shows its Home Page, which is accessible by pointing your browser to URL http://<hostname>:2000.

Although this application is larger in scale than what we feel Tcl is best suited for, Status-Mgr demonstrates that a pure Tcl application is capable of performing a large amount of polling and analysis, even from a mid-level (166Mhz with 32M Memory) PC running WIN95. (Note that performance would be a great deal better if the same PC were running NT Workstation 4.0.)

GENERAL OVERVIEW OF CODE

The code for this application is too large to present in its entirety here, but we will provide a general overview of the code, identifying what data is collected and used. You have seen much of

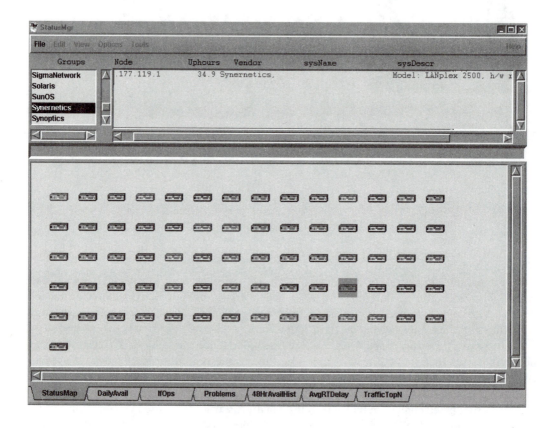

Figure 12.1 StatusMgr application.

the code for this application in previous chapters. The complete application code is freely available from our Web site.

Startup

On startup, StatusMgr does the following:

- Calls the procedure OpenVendorFile, which reads vendor names and enterprise OIDs from the file vendors.txt. You saw this procedure back in Chapter 11.

- Creates two SNMP sessions, one for system polling and one for interface polling. We could have simply used one SNMP session for both system and in-

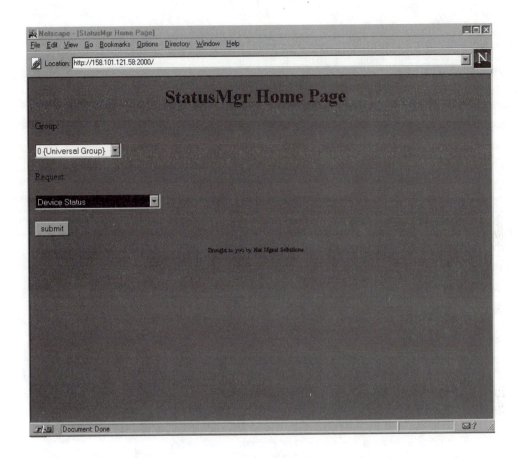

Figure 12.2   StatusMgr Web interface Home Page.

terface polling. It was mainly a personal decision to use two sessions. This makes it easier to reassign different default timeout and retry counts for system polls versus interface polls.

- Calls the procedure `CreateMainWindow` to create the main application window. You saw back in Chapter 8 how `CreateMainWindow` was used to create our main application GUI.

- Opens a server socket connection so users can access this application remotely via their Web browsers' `StatusMgr` Web interface. You saw back in Chapter 9 how we opened a server socket on port 2000 and used the procedures `www`, `www_receiver`, and `www_home` to process and identify data requests from remote Web clients.

After startup, it's up to the user to manually open a file of nodes to monitor. StatusMgr expects its node file to have the extension .cfg. As explained in Chapter 2, this file needs to be manually created by the user. It provides group names, devices in each group and the read and write community names per device. Note that the write community name is optional and is not used by StatusMgr. The following illustrates a sample node file:

```
<group> "Building A"
158.101.121.200 public
58.101.121.58 public
<group> "Building B"
158.101.122.10  public
158.101.122.12  public
```

The user must open a device file via the FILE --> Open Device File menu selection. This informs StatusMgr of what nodes to monitor. This menu selection will call the procedure OpenNodeFile, which reads the selected node file.

Global Variables

Data used by StatusMgr is mainly stored in the following global arrays: nInfo, gValueList, groups and nodes

- The array nInfo is used to store nodal information. It is indexed by <nodeid>, where <nodeid> is an integer number from 0 to nn. Here, nn+1 is the total number of nodes we are monitoring.
- The array gValueList is used to store counter and sysUpTime values. This array is used by the procedures AddValueToList and Rate to calculate things like octets per second or packets per second.
- The array groups is used to store group information. It is indexed by <gid>, where <gid> is an integer number from 0 to gindex. Here, gindex+1 is the total number of node groups. Note that the Universal Group is a system-defined group and has the index value of zero. The array groups maintains both group names and hourly summary statistics for the last 48 hours of operation.
- The array nodes is used to retrieve the nodeid for a specified node address. This array is indexed by node address. Thus, the value of nodes(<node address>) is the node's nodeid.

OpenNodeFile

The procedure OpenNodeFile first performs some initialization by calling the procedure gInit. This sets variables like nn to their initial values.

OpenNodeFile then uses the built-in `tk_getOpenFile` command to create a dialog box for the user to select a `.cfg` file to open. This dialog box is shown in Figure 12.3.

The file selection dialog window shows the user what `*.cfg` files exist in the selected directory path and prompts the user to select one.

After reading the node file, the procedure OpenNodeFile selects the Universal Group and calls DisplayNodeList. This procedure, shown earlier in Chapter 8, updates the textbox in the upper right-hand area of the main application window. This shows the user all nodes that are being monitored. Then OpenNodeFile initiates SNMP polling by calling the procedures SysPoll and IfPoller.

SysPoll primarily performs system status monitoring, while IfPoller mainly collects interface data for traffic monitoring. SysPoll restarts itself every three minutes after its own completion. IfPoller restarts itself every 30 seconds after its own completion.

SysPoll

The first thing SysPoll does on startup is check the time, as demonstrated in Chapter 4. If the hour has incremented since the last invocation of SysPoll, it calls the procedure NewHour. What this does is collect each node's previous hour operational statistics and summarizes this data

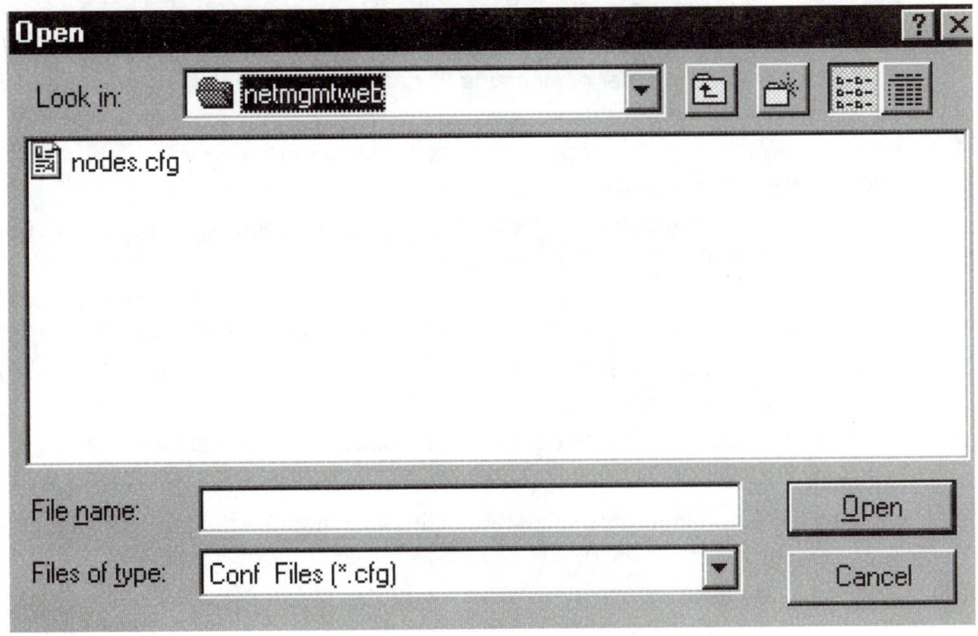

Figure 12.3 Open File dialog box

per group. NewHour then updates the groups array so users can get a summary of group operations for previous hours on-demand.

For each group, NewHour updates the array groups, recording how many nodes in each group had 100 percent availability, partial availability, zero availability and unknown availability for the previous hour. Also included in this is the number of node resets that occurred in the group during the previous hour.

After calling NewHour on hourly changes, SysPoll then polls each node for the following MIB-II information:

- sysUpTime (system uptime in hundredths of a second)
- sysObjectID (vendor's enterprise OID, which is used later to identify vendor name)
- sysName (an administratively-assigned text value identifying node name)
- sysDescr (a text description which normally includes product name and software version)
- sysLocation (an administratively-assigned text string identifying node's location)
- sysContact (an administratively-assigned text string identifying node's support person)
- ipInDiscards (counter of good incoming IP datagrams discarded by the node; useful for identifying periods of congestion)
- ipInDelivers (counter of incoming IP datagrams received by node; useful for identifying top IP receivers)
- ipOutRequests (counter of good IP datagrams generated by node; useful for identifying top IP senders)
- ipOutDiscards (counter of good outgoing IP datagrams discarded by node; useful for identifying periods of congestion)
- ipOutNoRoutes (counter of good IP datagrams discarded because no route could be found in routing tables; useful for identifying routing problems)
- ipRoutingDiscards (counter of routing table discards of valid routes; useful for identifying lack of buffers for large routing tables)
- ipForwDatagrams (counter of forwarded datagrams; useful for identifying top IP packet forwarders)

The returned information identifies the reachability state of nodes and provides information that is stored to the arrays nInfo and gValueList.

IfPoller

IfPoller polls each known interface for each node that is reachable for the following MIB-II information:

- ifIndex (integer index for an entry into ifTable)
- ifType (integer that identifies the type of interface as assigned by the Internet Assigned Numbers Authority)
- ifSpeed (estimated interface speed in bits per second)
- ifAdminStatus (enumerated integer, where up (1), down (2), testing(3))
- ifOperStatus (enumerated integer, where up (1), down (2), testing (3))
- ifLastChange (the value of sysUpTime when the interface entered its current operational state; useful for identifying interface resets and for identifying time in current state)
- ifInOctets (counter of incoming octets for this interface, including framing octets)
- ifOutOctets (counter of outgoing octets for this interface, including framing octets)
- ifInUcastPkts (counter of incoming unicast packets for this interface)
- ifOutUcastPkts (counter of outgoing unicast packets for this interface)
- ifInNUcastPkts (counter of incoming non-unicast, i.e., broadcast and multicast, packets for this interface)
- ifOutNUcastPkts (counter of outgoing non-unicast, i.e., broadcast and multicast, packets for this interface)
- ifInDiscards (counter of good inbound packets discarded; useful for identifying congestion periods)
- ifOutDiscards (counter of good outbound packets discarded; useful for identifying congestion periods)
- ifInErrors (counter of inbound packets received that were discarded due to errors; useful for identifying an interface with some sort of hardware or software problem)
- ifOutErrors (counter of outbound packets received that were discarded due to errors; useful for identifying an interface with some sort of hardware or software problem)

The returned information identifies the UP/DOWN state of interfaces and obtains interface information that is stored to the arrays nInfo and gValueList.

UpdateEvents

`StatusMgr` has a number of MIB threshold rules defined in the procedure `Update-teEvents`. The threshold rules defined in `UpdateEvents` were presented in Chapter 2.

Display Procedures

Much of `StatusMgr`'s code contains display procedures. These procedures take data mainly out of the arrays `groups` and `nInfo`. You saw this earlier in Chapter 9 when we showed `www_d_status`.

The full list of `StatusMgr`'s display procedures that output HTML data back to remote Web browsers include:

- `www_d_status`

  When the Device Status request is selected from `StatusMgr`'s Home Page, this procedure writes back to the remote browser an HTML table showing current node state, problem and system description information for each node of a specified group. This data combines data from the node text box and problem tab of the main application window into one HTML report.

- `www_d_avail`

  When the Device Availability request is selected from `StatusMgr`'s Home Page, this procedure writes back to a remote browser an HTML table showing daily and current hour availability and reset information for each node of a specified group. This data is the same as that shown for the `DailyAvail` tab of the native application window.

- `www_wan_ifstatus`

  When the WAN Interface Status request is selected from `StatusMgr`'s Home Page, this procedure writes back to a remote browser an HTML table showing interface status and information for all WAN interfaces for a specified group. This data is the same as that shown for the `IfOps` tab, but here we output information for WAN interfaces only.

- `www_lan_ifstatus`

  When the LAN Interface Status request is selected from `StatusMgr`'s Home Page, this procedure writes back to a remote browser an HTML table showing interface status and information for all LAN interfaces for a specified group. This data is the same as that shown for the `IfOps` tab, but here we output information for LAN interfaces only.

- www_g_avail_his

    When the Historical Availability Summary request is selected from StatusMgr's Home Page, this procedure writes back to a remote browser an HTML table displaying previous hours' availability and reset information for a specified group, as illustrated in Figures 12.4 and 12.5. This data is the same as that shown for the 48HrAvailHist tab of the native application window.

The full list of display procedures that write to StatusMgr's main application window include:

- DisplayStatus

    When users select a node from the StatusMap and click Mouse Button-3, this creates a top-level window showing detail status, reference and problem data for the selected node.

- DisplayAvail

    When the DailyAvail tab is selected from the notebook, this shows current day and current hour availability and reset information for each node in the selected group.

- DisplayIfOps

    When the IfOps tab is selected from the notebook, this shows detailed ifTable information for each interface of each node in the selected group.

- DisplayProblems

    When the Problems tab is selected from the notebook, this shows all current problems for all nodes and interfaces in the selected group.

- DisplayHistory

    When the 48HrAvailHist tab is selected from the notebook, this shows the selected group's nodal availability and reset summary for each of the last 48 hours that StatusMgr has been running.

- DisplayDelay

    When the AvgRTDelay tab is selected from the notebook, this shows the average round-trip poll response time (based on the last three polls) for each node in the selected group.

- DisplayTrafficLdrs

    When the TrafficTopN tab is selected from the notebook, this shows the Top 10 nodes in each category: IP Forwarders, IP Senders and IP Receivers for the selected group.

Figure 12.4 shows output from the procedure www_g_avail_his. Here, we connected to StatusMgr via its Web Interface and requested a 48-Hour Availability Summary for the Univer-

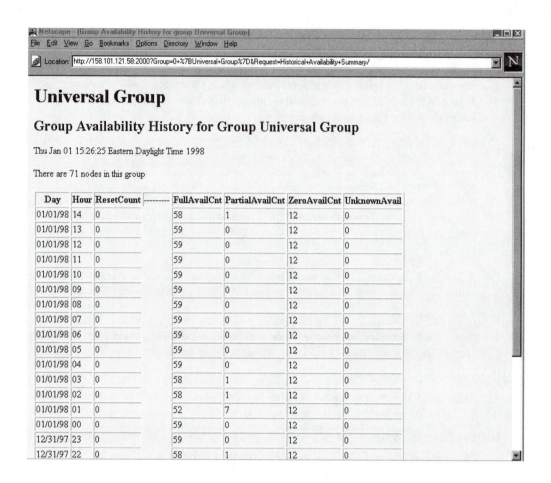

Figure 12.4 Historical availability summary page (for Universal Group) via StatusMgr's Web interface.

sal Group. We can see that over the past several hours, network device availability for all monitored nodes has been stable, except for some partial network unreachability that occurred at around 2:00 on New Year's morning. We can see right away that none of the problems were caused by node failures since the reset counts are all zero.

From here, we could make a daily availability request to see which nodes were affected at this time but our main concern is to simply check to make sure reachability to critical servers was NOT affected. We quickly obtained knowledge of this by going back to our Home Page and selecting Historical Availability Summary on our Novell Group. The results of this are shown in Figure 12.5. This shows us that critical server reachability was stable all evening.

This example has real-world relevance. Network operations during evening backup periods

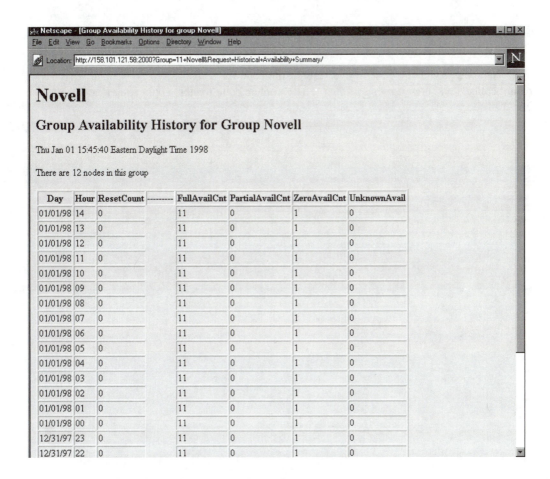

Figure 12.5 Historical availability summary page (for Novell Group)via StatusMgr Web interface.

is often of major interest. Many network managers are spending a great deal of effort to deploy high-speed LAN switches in their networks to keep up with nightly and weekend backup load. We have frequently seen cases where network devices and interfaces are most prone to reset under the high traffic loads of network backups. Resets can occur very quickly and often many monitoring tools don't report them. Thus, network backups take longer than they need to because operation staffs are unaware of evening nodal and interface resets.

The historical availability summary of group operations over the last 48 hours also allows us to easily monitor the reset counts for new releases of network device software. Sometimes, newly released software can be unstable. With `StatusMgr`, we can easily check whether any particular software release is less stable than previous software versions.

IN SUMMARY

Here we provided a general overview of the code for `StatusMgr`, described what SNMP data it collects and how it uses this data. The complete code for this application is available from our Web site.

13

An IP Path Tracing Tool

This tool will use SNMP to trace an IP path from a source to a destination address. It will graphically represent the path in a Tk canvas, showing each hop along the path, the connection type between hops (Ethernet, Token Ring, FDDI ring or serial connection) and the line speed for each connection (see Figure 13.1). The IP forward packet rate for each device along the path will be periodically collected, along with the octet rates for each interface along the path. Information about each hop in the path, such as IP address, interface type, interface line speed, interface bit rates and IP forwarding packet rates, will be provided in a table and will be periodically updated. By using this tool to diagnose IP routing problems, a network manager can gain insight as to what devices and interfaces make up an IP path, how busy the devices are along the path and how busy the interfaces are along the path. Bottlenecks will quickly become obvious. While this tool has immediate usefulness, it can also be used as a base to build very powerful tracing and diagnostic tools.

CONCEPTS DEMONSTRATED

The implementation of this tool brings together concepts from throughout this book. Specifically, this chapter will demonstrate the following:

- The `AddValueToList` and `Rate` procedures from Chapter 3
- The polling loop from Chapter 6
- The simple table widget from Chapter 8
- Drawing an IP path in a canvas from Chapter 8

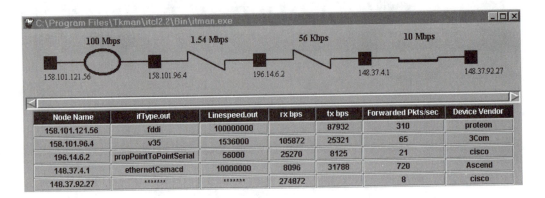

Figure 13.1   IP Path Tracing Tool display (path displayed does not represent a real path).

IP PATH TRACING CODE

The code for this tool will be broken into three sections: routines to trace an IP path and build the necessary data structures, routines to build the user interface and routines to use the polling loop and calculate the statistics obtained from it. We will also provide several routines to extend the canvas example from Chapter 8. The `OpenVendorFile` routine from Chapter 11 will be used, but not presented here.

PART 1—TRACING AN IP PATH

We will trace an IP path by starting at the source address. We will search the device's routing table for a route to the destination address, a route to the subnet of the destination address, a route to the network of the destination address or the default route (0.0.0.0). This will give us the next hop along the path. It will also give us the interface we must exit to get to the next hop. We will then read the local addresses and ifIndex values of the next hop to get the local address and interface number that match the next hop address. This will give us the interface number to get into the next hop. We will repeat this process until we get to the destination address, or until we get a direct route to the destination. (For example, a router could be connected to an Ethernet subnet of a destination address. This would most likely show up in the routing table as a direct route to the Ethernet subnet.)

If, while tracing the path, we come across a device that either doesn't support SNMP or for which we don't have the correct community string information, we will break out of the tracing loop and use the partial path that we built.

This tool is a good example of the 80/20 rule (or maybe the 90/10 rule). It will trace most paths, but there are cases where it will not provide complete information. This tool will not always be correct when there are multiple routes for a destination entry in the routing table. This is because we used the IP routing table from RFC 1213 (MIB II) instead of the newer IP forwarding table defined in RFC 1354, which allows multiple entries for the same destination based on routing protocol and policy. We used the older IP routing table because the newer IP forwarding table is not yet widely deployed. Also, if you have a device which automatically uses load balancing to split the traffic up between several links to a remote device, and this information is not accessible through a private MIB, there is really no way to show this in a path trace, or to show that the traffic is going through several interfaces. This points out a general problem that we have seen through years of building network management products for vendors. It is sometimes very hard or impossible to come up with a solution that solves all of the problems, and there is a tendency for engineers to get stuck because of that. Instead of coming up with something that will be useful 80–90 percent of the time and building on that, they get stuck in a quagmire trying to build something that will handle all possible cases. Moving on ...

This section has been broken into 11 procedures:

- `IpRouteTool` acts as the main driver code.
- `RT_GetNextHop` returns the next hop along the IP path. This routine is called within a path tracing loop by `IpRouteTool`.
- `Rt_IsNextHop` determines whether an entry in an IP routing table is the next hop that should be used. It is called by `RT_GetNextHop`.
- `Rt_IsValidNextHop` checks an IP address and `ipRouteType` value to determine if both the address is a valid IP address and `ipRouteType` represents a valid route.
- `Rt_NetMask` is a convenience routine to logically AND a network mask and an IP address.
- `RT_GetNextInst` determines the next instance to use in our intelligent `ipRouteTable` search.
- `RT_AddToPath` adds a device to the path, and initiates system, local address and interface information to be collected. It is called by `IpRouteTool`.
- `RT_GetSystemInfo` collects system information for a device. It is called by `RT_AddToPath`.
- `RT_GetLocalAddresses` collects local address and ifIndex values. It is called by `RT_AddToPath`.
- `RT_GetLocalAddressesCB` is a callback routine for a table walk issued by `RT_GetLocalAddresses`.
- `RT_CollectInterfaceInfo` collects `ifType`, `ifSpeed` and `ifMtu` values for interfaces along the path. It is called by both `RT_AddToPath` and `RT_GetNextHop`.

```
source book-ch3.itcl
source book-ch6.itcl
source book-ch8.itcl
source book-ch8-canvas-ex.itcl


proc IpRouteTool {src dest} {

    global gPathArr gPathTraceState destAddr nodeIndex cv
    global gPollRate

    OpenVendorFile "vendors.txt"
    RT_BuildUI

    for each el [array name gPathArr] {
        unset gPathArr($el)
    }

    set s [snmpsession -snmp]

    set gPathTraceState working
    set nodeIndex 0
    set srcAddr  [ConvertNameToIpAddr $src]
    set destAddr [ConvertNameToIpAddr $dest]

    if [catch {RT_AddToPath $s $srcAddr} err] {
        set gPathTraceState "error: $err"
    }

    DrawIpHop $cv $nodeIndex $srcAddr 0 0 0

    while {$gPathTraceState == "working"} {
#
#   If route destination has been found, break out of loop.
#
        if {$gPathArr($nodeIndex,ipaddr) == $destAddr} {
            set gPathTraceState pathTraced
            break
        }

        if [catch {
```

```
            set node \
            [RT_GetNextHop $s $nodeIndex $destAddr]} err] {
                set gPathTraceState "error: $err"
                puts "error getting next hop: $err"
                continue
        }


        #
        # If a direct route (3) found to the destination
        # add destination as last hop in path.
        #

        if {$gPathArr($nodeIndex,routeType) == 3} {
                set node $destAddr
        }

        if [catch {RT_AddToPath $s $node} err] {
                set gPathTraceState "error: $err"
        }

        set i [expr $nodeIndex - 1]
        DrawIpHop $cv $nodeIndex $node $i \
            [RT_MapIfTypeToConnType $gPathArr($i,out,type)] \
            $gPathArr($i,out,speed)
    }

    RT_RebuildUITable
    RT_SetupPolling
#
#   Now stay in a simple loop, which after every
#   poll period, produces statistics with the collected
#   data.
#
    set n [expr $gPollRate * 1000]
    while {1} {
            after $n {set x 1}
            vwait x
            RT_UpdateStats
    }
}
```

`IpRouteTool` is the main routine for this application. It is supplied with a source and destination address as parameters. The call to `RT_BuildUI` builds the user interface, which consists of a canvas to graphically represent the discovered IP path and a simple table widget to provide information about the path. In our canvas example in Chapter 8, we provided a routine, `DrawIpPath`, to draw a complete path. Here we will be providing a routine, `DrawIpHop`, which will draw a hop along the path. This way we can draw each hop as it is discovered. The `while` loop in the routine either traces a path to the destination address, or traces a partial path until a failure occurs.

The code fragment:

```
if {$gPathArr($nodeIndex,routeType) == 3} {
    set node $destAddr
}
```

sets the next hop along the path to the destination address if the next hop has a direct connection to the destination address.

Once we break out of the path trace loop, we call `RT_RebuildUITable` to add path information into the simple table widget. We then call `RT_SetupPolling`, which builds a polling list to collect both IP route information for each device along the path and interface information for each interface along the path. We then go into an endless loop, waking up after every polling period, to process the collected path statistics.

```
proc RT_GetNextHop {s i inst} {
       global gPathArr

       set addr $gPathArr($i,ipaddr)
       set authinfo [list snmpv1 $gPathArr($i,cstr)]

       while {$inst != 0} {

              set vblist [list ipRouteDest.$inst]
              set result [$s get $addr $authinfo $vblist {} wait]
              set errorStatus [GetErrorStatus $result]
#
#    If entry in routing table exists, check if actually next hop.
#

              if {$errorStatus == "noSuchName"} {
                     set inst [RT_GetNextInst $inst]
                     continue
              }

              if {$errorStatus == "noError"} {
```

```
if [catch {
    set x [RT_IsNextHop $s $i $inst]} err] {
        error "$err: Unable to trace Next Hop: \
                RT_GetNextHop"
}


#
# If RT_IsNextHop finds a valid entry,
# it will return a list containing the
# corresponding ipRouteIfIndex, ipRouteType,
# ipRouteProto and ipRouteNextHop.
#

if {[llength $x] > 1} {

    set ifindex [lindex $x 0]

    #
    #   Check for a routing loop.
    #   We detect a loop if the outgoing
    #   ifIndex equals the incoming ifIndex.
    #

    if {[info exists gPathArr($i,inIfIndex)]} {
        if {$gPathArr($i,inInIndex) == \
                ifindex} {
            error "Routing loop detected: \
                RT_GetNextHop"
        }
    }

    set gPathArr($i,outIfIndex) $ifindex
    set gPathArr($i,routeType) [lindex $x 1]
    set gPathArr($i,routeProto) [lindex $x 2]
    RT_CollectInterfaceInfo $s $i $ifindex out

    return [lindex $x 3]
}

set inst [RT_GetNextInst $inst]
continue
```

```
        }

        error "$errorStatus: $addr using instance = $inst: \
                RT_GetNextHop"
    }
    error "Unable to trace Next Hop: RT_GetNextHop"
}
```

RT_GetNextHop intelligently searches a device's routing table for the next hop value given a destination address. Routing tables can be huge. If we just blindly walked a routing table to find the next hop value, not only would we add a lot of unnecessary SNMP traffic to the network, but we would also add significantly to the amount of time it takes for our tracing algorithm to complete. Instead, we limit our search to at most 31 table accesses. We start with the destination address as an instance. If an entry exists in the IP routing table, great. Otherwise, we clear the least significant bit within the instance that is set to 1. We will continue to do this until we find the next hop value within the table. Given a destination address of 158.101.121.9, we would first try that address as an instance in our table search, then 158.101.121.8, then 158.101.121.0 and on down to 0.0.0.0 until we find a valid entry.

```
proc RT_IsNextHop {s i inst} {
#
#   Check if row in routing table is the next hop in the route.
#
        global gPathArr destAddr

        set addr $gPathArr($i,ipaddr)
        set authinfo [list snmpv1 $gPathArr($i,cstr)]
        set vblist [list ipRouteNextHop.$inst \
                ipRouteIfIndex.$inst ipRouteProto.$inst \
                ipRouteMask.$inst ipRouteType.$inst]

        set result [$s get $addr $authinfo $vblist {} wait]
        set errorStatus [GetErrorStatus $result]
        if {$errorStatus == "noSuchName"} {return}
        if {$errorStatus != "noError"} {
            error "$errorStatus"
        }
#
#   At this point, data has been collected.
#
        set vblist [GetVarBindList $result]
```

```
      set nextHop [GetValue [GetVarBind $vblist 1]]
      set ifIndex [GetValue [GetVarBind $vblist 2]]
      set routeProto [GetValue [GetVarBind $vblist 3]]
      set mask [GetValue [GetVarBind $vblist 4]]
      set routeType [GetValue [GetVarBind $vblist 5]]
#
#   Compare mask and route-dest to mask and inst.
#
      set v1 [RT_NetMask $mask $destAddr]
      set v2 [RT_NetMask $mask $inst]

      if {$v1 != $v2} {return "notValid"}
#
#   Check if ipRouteType = direct (3).
#
      if {$routeType == 3} {
          return [list $ifIndex $routeType $routeProto $nextHop]
      }

      if {[RT_IsValidNextHop $nextHop $routeType] == 1} {
            return [list $ifIndex $routeType $routeProto $nextHop]
      }

      return "notValid"
}
```

Rt_IsNextHop is passed a session ID, a node index and an instance to use for the IpRouteTable. It queries the device pointed to by the node index for the ipRouteNextHop, ipRouteIfIndex, ipRouteProto, ipRouteMask and ipRouteType values. If an unexpected SNMP error is detected, the routine raises an error which gets caught by RT_GetNextHop. An entry is considered valid if the final destination address ANDed with the network mask equals the instance value ANDed with the network mask and the next hop value is a valid IP address.

```
proc RT_IsValidNextHop {addr type} {
#
#   Return 1 if type is valid and address not one of the
#   following:
#
#       0.x.x.x
#       127.x.x.x
#       1.0.0.0
#
```

```
#    else return 0.
#


#
#    ipRouteType 2 = invalid
#

        if {$type == 2} {
             return 0
        }

        if {$addr == "1.0.0.0"} {
             return 0
        }

        set x [split $addr .]
        if {[lindex $x 0] == 0} {
             return 0
        }

        if {[lindex $x 0] == 127} {
             return 0
        }

        return 1
}


proc RT_NetMask {mask addr} {
#
# AND address with mask.
#

        set a [split $addr .]
        set m [split $mask .]
        set result [list [MaskField $a $m 0] \
                          [MaskField $a $m 1] \
                          [MaskField $a $m 2] \
                          [MaskField $a $m 3]]
        return [join $result .]
}
```

The `MaskField` routine is provided in Chapter 6. This routine simply splits up an IP address and a network mask into four-element lists, logically ANDs each address component against the corresponding network mask components and recreates an address in dotted notation.

```
proc RT_GetNextInst {inst} {

#
#  If instance already equals 0.0.0.0, return 0 to indicate
#  failure
#
    if {$inst == "0.0.0.0"} {
        return 0
    }
#
#  else and off least significant bit.
#
    set x [split $inst .]
    set i 3
#
#  Find first address part that's not zero,
#  moving from right to left.
#
    while {[lindex $x $i] == 0} {
        incr i -1
    }

    set val [lindex $x $i]
    set j 1
    while {[expr $val & $j] == 0} {
        set j [expr $j << 1]
    }

    set val [expr (~$j) & $val]
    return [join [lreplace $x $i $i $val] .]
}
```

`RT_GetNextInst` takes the current instance and clears the least significant bit that is set to 1. It does this by splitting an IP address in dotted notation into a four-element list. Then, starting from the right (list position 3), it finds the first nonzero element. The code:

```
set j 1
while {[expr $val & $j] == 0} {
    set j [expr $j << 1]
}
```

tests whether the first bit in the nonzero element is 1. If not, it keeps shifting the test value right until a 1 is found.

```
proc RT_AddToPath {s addr} {
      global gPathArr destAddr nodeIndex

      incr nodeIndex
      set gPathArr($nodeIndex,ipaddr) $addr
      set gPathArr($nodeIndex,cstr) \
          [lindex [GetPollingInfo $addr] 0]
#
#   Initialize sysObjectID, ifType and ifSpeed. These values
#   should be filled in later.
#
      set gPathArr($nodeIndex,sysobjectid) "n/a"
      set gPathArr($nodeIndex,out,type) 0
      set gPathArr($nodeIndex,out,speed) "n/a"

      RT_GetSystemInfo $s $nodeIndex
      RT_GetLocalAddresses $s $nodeIndex
      if {$nodeIndex != 1} {
#
#   Collect interface information for the incoming interface
#   along the path.
#
              set i [lsearch $gPathArr($nodeIndex,localaddrs) $addr]
              if {$i != -1} {
                  set n [lindex $gPathArr($nodeIndex,ifindexes) $i]
                  set gPathArr($nodeIndex,inIfIndex) $n
                  RT_CollectInterfaceInfo $s $nodeIndex $n in
              }
      }
#
#   check if route destination is one of the device's local
#   addresses. If it is, replace ip address with destination
#   address.
#
      set i [lsearch $gPathArr($nodeIndex,localaddrs) $destAddr]
      if {$i != -1} {
              set $gPathArr($nodeIndex,ipaddr) $destAddr
      }
}
```

RT_AddToPath bumps the node count and adds a discovered device to gPathArr. It calls RT_GetSystemInfo to collect system information about the device, and RT_GetLocalAddresses to collect the local addresses and interfaces for the device. If the device is not the first hop in the path (the source address), it also calls RT_CollectInterfaceInfo to collect information about the incoming interface. The incoming interface number is determined by finding the position of the device address within the collected local addresses, and then matching the ifIndex value that was collected at that position. Finally, the routine checks if the destination address matches one of the device's local addresses, and if it does, it replaces the device address with that destination address.

```
proc RT_GetSystemInfo {s i} {
    global gPathArr

    set addr $gPathArr($i,ipaddr)

    set authinfo [list snmpv1 $gPathArr($i,cstr)]
    set vblist [list sysDescr sysObjectID]

    set result [$s next $addr $authinfo $vblist {} wait]

    set errorStatus [GetErrorStatus $result]
    if {$errorStatus != "noError"} {
        error "$errorStatus: RT_GetSystemInfo"
    }

    set vblist [GetVarBindList $result]
    set gPathArr($i,sysdescr) \
            [GetValue [GetVarBind $vblist 1]]
    set gPathArr($i,sysobjectid) \
            [GetValue [GetVarBind $vblist 2]]
}
```

RT_GetSystemInfo performs a synchronous (blocking) SNMP Get request to collect a device's sysDescr and sysObjectID values. The sysObjectID is used to determine the vendor of the device. If an SNMP error occurs, the routine raises an error, which passes through RT_AddToPath and is caught by IpRouteTool.

```
proc RT_GetLocalAddresses {s i} {
    global gPathArr

    set gPathArr($i,wait) 0

    set addr $gPathArr($i,ipaddr)
```

```
    set authinfo [list snmpv1 $gPathArr($i,cstr)]
    set vblist [list ipAdEntIfIndex]
    set ops {-tableRows 1}
    set cb [list RT_GetLocalAddressesCB $i]

    $s table $addr $authinfo $vblist {0} $ops $cb

    vwait gPathArr($i,wait)
}
```

RT_GetLocalAddresses sets up for a table walk to collect all ipAdEntIfIndex entries. The routine blocks using vwait until all entries have been collected. From ipAdEntI-
fIndex, we get both the local addresses of a device and their corresponding ifIndex values.

```
proc RT_GetLocalAddressesCB {i result} {
    global gPathArr

    set errorStatus [GetErrorStatus $result]
    if {$errorStatus == "timeout"} {
        set gPathArr($i,wait) 1
    }

    set vblist [GetVarBindList $result]

    if {[llength $vblist] == 0} {
        set gPathArr($i,wait) 1
    }

    set oid [GetOID [GetVarBind $vblist 1]]

    lappend gPathArr($i,localaddrs) \
        [GetInstance $oid ipAdEntIfIndex]

    lappend gPathArr($i,ifindexes) \
        [GetValue [GetVarBind $vblist 1]]

    if {$errorStatus == "endOfTable"} {
        set gPathArr($i,wait) 1
    }
}
```

RT_GetLocalAddressesCB is the associated callback routine for the table walk issued
within RT_GetLocalAddresses. It pulls the local address value from the instance portion of a

returned OID, and builds a list of both local addresses and ifIndex values. When either a timeout is detected or the end of the table is reached, RT_GetLocalAddresses is signaled by setting gPathArr($i,wait).

```
proc RT_CollectInterfaceInfo {s i n str} {
     global gPathArr
#
#  Collect interface information for interface along path.
#  n = ifIndex for interface to collect, str identifies
#  whether the interface is "incoming" or "outgoing".
#
     set addr $gPathArr($i,ipaddr)
     set authinfo [list snmpv1 $gPathArr($i,cstr)]
     set vblist [list ifType.$n ifSpeed.$n ifMtu.$n]

     set result [$s get $addr $authinfo $vblist {} wait]

     set errorStatus [GetErrorStatus $result]
     if {$errorStatus != "noError"} {
          return
     }

     set vblist [GetVarBindList $result]

     set gPathArr($i,$str,type) \
          [GetValue [GetVarBind $vblist 1]]

     set gPathArr($i,$str,speed) \
          [GetValue [GetVarBind $vblist 2]]

     set gPathArr($i,$str,mtu) \
          [GetValue [GetVarBind $vblist 3]]
}
```

RT_CollectInterfaceInfo collects ifType, ifSpeed and ifMtu values for interfaces along a path.

PART 2—BUILDING THE USER INTERFACE

This section has been broken into five procedures:

- `RT_BuildUI`, which builds the user interface.
- `RT_RebuildUITable`, which is called after the path is traced, and rebuilds the simple table widget, populating it with discovered information.
- `RT_MapIfTypeToConnType` is a convenience routine which maps an ifType value to eth, ring or serial. This is used for drawing the path within the canvas.
- `RT_MapIfTypeToString` is a convenience routine which maps an ifType number to its corresponding enumerated string.
- `RT_MapEntToVendorName` is a convenience routine which maps an enterprise number to a vendor name.

```
proc RT_BuildUI { } {
        global gNodeSize gConnSize gxOffset gyOffset gAfterId cv
        global rtab

        set gNodeSize 20
        set gConnSize 150
        set gxOffset   30
        set gyOffset   40
        set gAfterId ""

        set mf [frame .mf_RouteTool]
        set rtab [MakeTable routeTool 0 0 \
        "      Node Name    " "      ifType.out      " " " \
        "Linespeed.out " "  rx bps  " " tx bps  " " " \
        "Forwarded Pkts/sec" " Device Vendor "]

        pack $mf
        pack $rtab -in $mf

        set cf [BuildCanvas .rtCanvas 0]
        pack $cf -in $mf -side top -before $rtab

        set cv .rtCanvas.c
}
```

RT_BuildUI builds both a canvas in which to draw a path and a simple table widget with zero rows so that the header is visible. Once a path is traced, the simple table widget is rebuilt with a row count equal to the number of devices in the path.

```
proc RT_RebuildUITable {} {

        global nodeIndex rtab cv gPathArr
```

```
destroy $rtab
set rtab [MakeTable routeTool $nodeIndex 15 \
   "      Node Name    " "      ifType.out      " " \
Linespeed.out " "  rx bps  " "  tx bps  " " \
Forwarded Pkts/sec" " Device Vendor "]

pack $rtab -in .mf_RouteTool -after $cv

for {set i 1} {$i <= $nodeIndex} {incr i} {
       SetTableValue routeTool $i 1 $gPathArr($i,ipaddr)
       if {$i != $nodeIndex} {
              SetTableValue routeTool $i 2 \
                     [RT_MapIfTypeToString \
                            $gPathArr($i,out,type)]
              SetTableValue routeTool $i 3 \
                            $gPathArr($i,out,speed)
       } else {
              SetTableValue routeTool $i 2 "*******"
              SetTableValue routeTool $i 3 "*******"
       }
       SetTableValue routeTool $i 7 \
              [RT_MapEntToVendorName \
                     $gPathArr($i,sysobjectid)]
   }
}
```

RT_RebuildUITable rebuilds the simple table widget, specifying a row count equal to the number of devices within the path. It fills in the Node Name, ifType.out, Linespeed.out and Device Vendor columns. The rx bps, tx bps and Forwarded Pkts/Sec columns will be filled in as data is periodically collected from the devices.

```
proc RT_MapIfTypeToConnType {i} {
#
#   Map ifType to eth, ring or serial.
#
       global ifTypeMap

       if {![info exists ifTypeMap($i)]} {return "unknown"}

       return [lindex $ifTypeMap($i) 0]
}
```

```
proc RT_MapIfTypeToString {i} {
#
#  Map ifType to eth, ring or serial.
#
      global ifTypeMap

      if {![info exists ifTypeMap($i)]} {return "unknown"}

      return [lindex $ifTypeMap($i) 1]
}
```

Array ifTypeMap is provided later in this chapter. It is indexed by an ifType value and has as a value a two-element list composed of the connection type (eth, ring or serial) and the enumerated string value for the ifType value. The above two convenience routines simply map an ifType value to either a connection type or an enumerated string.

```
proc RT_MapEntToVendorName {oid} {

      global vendorName

      if {$oid == "n/a"} {
            return "n/a"
      }

      set oid [split [oid2dot $oid] .]
      set n [lindex $oid 6]
      if { [info exists vendorName($n)] == 1} {
        return $vendorName($n)
      } else {
        return "n/a"
      }
}
```

The array vendorName is populated by the procedure OpenVendorFile, which was presented in Chapter 11.

PART 3—INTEGRATING WITH THE POLLING LOOP

This section has been broken into six procedures:

- `RT_SetupPolling`, which is called after a path has been traced. This routine builds a poll list and then calls the `PollingLoop` procedure detailed in Chapter 6.
- `RT_PollingCallback` acts as the callback routine for the polling loop.
- `RT_UpdateStats` is called every polling period by `IpRouteTool`. It calls `RT_CalcForwardPktRate`, `RT_CalcRxRate`, and `RT_CalcTxRate` for each device within the path.
- `RT_CalcForwardPktRate` calculates the IP forwarded packet rate for a device.
- `RT_CalcRxRate` calculates an interface's receive bit rate.
- `RT_CalcTxRate` calculates an interface's transmit bit rate.

```
proc RT_SetupPolling {} {

    global gMibs gPollRate maxPollSeconds minPollSeconds
    global gHiThreshold gLowThreshold gDeviceThreshold
    global nodeIndex gPathArr

    set gPollRate 30
    set maxPollSeconds [expr $gPollRate * 10]
    set minPollSeconds [expr $gPollRate - 5]
    set gHiThreshold 15
    set gLowThreshold 10
    set gDeviceThreshold 5
    set gMibs [list \
                [list ipForwDatagrams] \
                [list ifOperStatus ifInOctets ifOutOctets]]
#
#   Build polling list.
#
    set pollList ""
    for {set i 1} {$i <= $nodeIndex} {incr i} {

        set addr $gPathArr($i,ipaddr)
        set inst ""
        if {[info exists gPathArr($i,inIfIndex)]} {
            set inst [concat $inst $gPathArr($i,inIfIndex)]
        }

        if {[info exists gPathArr($i,outIfIndex)]} {
```

```
                    set inst [concat $inst $gPathArr($i,outIfIndex)]
            }

            set x [list $addr {0} $inst]
            lappend pollList $x
    }


    PollingLoop $pollList RT_PollingCallback
}
```

`RT_SetupPolling` builds a poll list with an entry for each device within the path. Each entry is a list containing the device's IP address, an instance 0 (used to collect IP route information) and a list of the `ifIndex` numbers for the interfaces of the device that make up a path. The first device (source address) in the path simply has an outgoing interface along the path; the last device simply has an incoming interface. All other devices in the path have both incoming and outgoing interfaces.

For now, the only IP routing information we will periodically collect for a device is its `ipForwDatagrams` counter. For each interface, we will collect `ifOperStatus`, `ifInOctets` and `ifOutOctets`.

```
proc RT_PollingCallback {timeticks name nid inst vblist} {

        set i [string length $inst]
        foreach vb $vblist {
                set val [GetValue $vb]
                set oid [GetOID $vb]
                set j [string length $oid]
                set mibVar [string range $oid 0 [expr $j - $i - 2]]
                AddValueToList $mibVar "$nid,$inst" $val $timeticks
#
#   If ifOperStatus not "up", flush all collected values.
#   For interface only, don't bother logging any more data.
#
                if {$mibVar == "ifOperStatus"} {
                        if {$val != 1} {
                                FlushAllValues "$nid,$inst"
                                AddValueToList $mibVar "$nid,$inst" \
                                        $val $timeticks
                                return
                        }
                }
        }
}
```

RT_PollingCallback is the callback routine that we registered with the polling loop. It goes through a varbind list, pulling the MIB OID Name from the OID, and adds the value to be used for rate calculations using the AddValueToList routine shown in Chapter 3. If an ifOperStatus for an interface is not up, all values for that interface are flushed using the FlushAll-Values routine shown in Chapter 6.

```
proc RT_UpdateStats {} {
        global nodeIndex

        for {set i 1} {$i <= $nodeIndex} {incr i} {
                RT_CalcForwardPktRate $i
                RT_CalcRxRate $i
                RT_CalcTxRate $i
        }
}


proc RT_CalcForwardPktRate {i} {
        global gPathArr

        set addr $gPathArr($i,ipaddr)
        set nid [GetNodeId $addr]
        if {$nid == -1} {
                return
        }

        CheckReady $nid
        set pktRate [Rate ipForwDatagrams "$nid,0"]

        if {$pktRate == -1} {
                return
        }
        SetTableValue routeTool $i 6 [expr round($pktRate)]
}
```

RT_CalcForwardPktRate calculates the IP forwarded packet rate and writes the value into the simple table widget. The routines, CheckReady and GetNodeId, which map an address into a node ID, are shown in Chapter 6.

```
proc RT_CalcRxRate {i} {
        global gPathArr
#
# Get ifIndex number of incoming port.
#
```

```
    if {![info exists gPathArr($i,inIfIndex)]} {
        return
    }
    set inst $gPathArr($i,inIfIndex)
    set addr $gPathArr($i,ipaddr)
    set nid [GetNodeId $addr]
    if {$nid == -1} {
        return
    }
    CheckReady $nid
    if {[CheckOperStatus $nid $inst] == -1} {
        return
    }
    set inRate [Rate ifInOctets "$nid,$inst"]
    if {$inRate == -1} {
        return
    }

    SetTableValue routeTool $i 4 [expr round($inRate) * 8]
}
```

RT_CalcRxRate checks that a device has an incoming interface (the first device in the path won't), and then calculates the receive byte rate for that interface. It converts the value to a bit rate and writes it to the simple table widget.

```
proc RT_CalcTxRate {i} {
    global gPathArr
#
# Get ifIndex number of outgoing port.
#
    if {![info exists gPathArr($i,outIfIndex)]} {
        return
    }

    set inst $gPathArr($i,outIfIndex)
    set addr $gPathArr($i,ipaddr)
    set nid [GetNodeId $addr]
    if {$nid == -1} {
        return
    }

    CheckReady $nid
    if {[CheckOperStatus $nid $inst] == -1} {
```

```
            return
    }

    set outRate [Rate ifOutOctets "$nid,$inst"]
    if {$outRate == -1} {
            return
    }
    SetTableValue routeTool $i 5 [expr round($outRate) * 8]
}
```

RT_CalcTxRate checks that a device has an outgoing interface (the last device in the path won't), and then calculates the transmit byte rate for that interface. It converts the value to a bit rate and writes it to the simple table widget.

MISCELLANEOUS ROUTINES

In the following section, we provide a command to set up the ifTypeMap array and some routines to extend the canvas example from Chapter 8, particularly to draw a hop at a time instead of a complete path.

```
array set ifTypeMap \
  [ list \
  1 {eth other} \
  2 {eth regular1822} \
  3 {serial hdh1822} \
  4 {serial ddnX25} \
  5 {serial rfc877x25} \
  6 {eth ethernetCsmacd} \
  7 {eth iso88023Csmacd} \
  8 {eth iso88024TokenBus} \
  9 {ring iso88025TokenRing} \
 10 {ring iso88026Man} \
 11 {eth starLan} \
 12 {eth proteon10Mbit} \
 13 {eth proteon80Mbit} \
 14 {eth hyperchannel} \
 15 {ring fddi} \
 16 {serial lapb} \
 17 {serial sdlc} \
 18 {serial ds1} \
```

```
19 {serial e1} \
20 {serial basicISDN} \
21 {serial primaryISDN} \
22 {serial propPointToPointSerial} \
23 {serial ppp} \
24 {serial softwareLoopback} \
25 {eth eon} \
26 {eth ethernet3Mbit} \
27 {eth nsip} \
28 {serial slip} \
29 {serial ultra} \
30 {serial ds3} \
31 {serial sip} \
32 {serial frameRelay} \
33 {serial rs232} \
34 {serial para} \
35 {serial arcnet} \
36 {serial arcnetPlus} \
37 {serial atm} \
38 {serial miox25} \
39 {serial sonet} \
40 {serial x25ple} \
41 {serial iso8802llc} \
42 {serial localTalk}\
43 {serial smdsDxi} \
44 {serial frameRelayService} \
45 {serial v35} \
46 {serial hssi} \
47 {serial hippi} \
48 {serial modem} \
49 {serial aal5} \
50 {serial sonetPath} \
51 {serial sonetVT} \
52 {serial smdsIcip} \
53 {serial propVirtual} \
54 {serial propMultiplexor} \
]

proc DrawIpHop {c ndnum name cnum ctype cspeed} {
    AdjustIPPathScrollRegion $c $ndnum $cnum
    if {$ndnum > 0} {
        DrawNode $c [expr $ndnum - 1] $name
```

```
        }

    if {$cnum > 0} {
            switch $ctype {
                eth {DrawEthConn $c [expr $cnum - 1] $cspeed}
                ring {DrawRingConn $c [expr $cnum -1] $cspeed}
                serial {DrawSerialConn $c [expr $cnum - 1] $cspeed}
            }
        }
}
```

DrawIpHop is passed a canvas ID, a node index value, a node name, a connection index value, a connection type and a connection line speed as parameters.

```
proc AdjustIPPathScrollRegion {c i j} {
#
#   If either i or j is greater than gNodeCount,
#   set gNodeCount to the greater of the two and adjust
#   scrolled region size.
#
        global gNodeCount

        if {$i > $j} {
                set n $i
        } else {
                set n $j
        }

        if {$n <= $gNodeCount} {return}

        set gNodeCount $n
        set size [GetIPPathCanvasSize $n]
        if {$size < 800} {return}

        $c configure -scrollregion [list 0 0 $size 100]
}
```

AdjustIPPathScrollRegion is necessary in case the scroll region of the canvas needs to grow due to another node being drawn into it.

```
proc GetIPPathCanvasSize {n} {

        global  gNodeSize gConnSize gxOffset
```

```
    return [expr (($n-1) * ($gConnSize + $gNodeSize)) \
                + ($gxOffset * 2) + $gNodeSize]
}
```

GetIPPathCanvasSize returns the canvas size required to accommodate an n-node path.

IDEAS ON EXTENDING THE IP PATH TRACING TOOL

The IP Path Tracing Tool presented in this chapter, while immediately useful, is really a base that can be used to build more powerful IP path tracing/diagnostic tools. The following could be done to significantly extend this tool:

- Trace both forward and reverse paths. Create a second canvas to show the reverse path (the path from the destination to the source).
- Collect error information. Try to determine if devices along the path are seeing a high number of IP errors, or if the interfaces along the path are being congested or are also seeing high errors. If a potential problem is detected, change the color of the node or connection within the graph to indicate this. If the user clicks on a node or connection, pop up a dialog box to indicate the problems that have been detected.
- Based on sysObjectID information, collect device-specific information to perform a more detailed diagnostic.

IN SUMMARY

In this chapter we showed how to build a useful tool using routines and concepts developed earlier in the book. We further showed how to integrate the polling loop built in Chapter 6.

14

RMONv2 Configuration

This chapter provides tools for both configuring RMONv2 and building an inventory of your current RMONv2 probe configurations. By using RMONv2, you can derive the following information about your network traffic:

- Protocol breakdown by segment
- MAC address-to-network address translation
- Protocol breakdown by network address
- Protocol breakdown for traffic between different network addresses
- A TopN report for protocol traffic between different network addresses
- Protocol breakdown by application layer
- Application traffic breakdown for conversations of a particular protocol between two network addresses
- A TopN report for application traffic between different network addresses

CONCEPTS DEMONSTRATED

This chapter will demonstrate how to configure the RMONv2 protocolDirTable and several other RMONv2 control tables. We will also demonstrate how to access data from some of the related RMONv2 data tables. The RMONv2 control tables which we provide configuration tools for include:

- Protocol Distribution Control Table
- Address Map Control Table
- Host Control Table
- Matrix Control Table

The tools in this chapter will utilize the `GetPollingInfo` routine developed in Chapter 6, as well as several of the convenience routines for accessing SNMP result information shown in Chapter 5.

RMONv2 CONFIGURATION SCRIPTS

RMONv2 is made up of a protocol directory table (protocolDirTable) and a number of control and data tables. The protocolDirTable defines each protocol that the RMONv2 device can monitor. It also defines for each protocol whether the address map group, host groups or matrix groups are supported. If the address map group is supported, address mapping for that protocol can be performed. If host groups are supported, traffic for that protocol arranged by network address and application layer, can be collected. If matrix groups are supported, traffic matrix and TopN reports can be collected for that protocol.

The protocolDirTable is indexed by a protocol identifier and parameter (protocolDirID and protocolDirParameters). The protocolDirID contains a unique octet string for a specified protocol. The protocolDirParameters contains information about a probe's capability with respect to a particular protocol. It is not the scope or intent of this book to explain how to build these objects. However, in Appendix A we provide a complete listing of the file `rmon2ProtList.tcl`, which defines protocol names, identifiers and parameters for a large number of protocols.

A partial listing of `rmon2ProtDir.tcl` is provided below:

```
set rmon2protList [list \
    [list ether2 4.0.0.0.1 1.0] \
    [list llc 4.0.0.0.2 1.0] \
    [list snap 4.0.0.0.3 1.0] \
    [list wgAssigned 4.0.0.0.5 1.0] \
    [list wildcard-ether2 4.1.0.0.1 1.0] \
    [list ether2.idp 8.0.0.0.1.0.0.6.0 2.0.0] \
    [list ether2.ip 8.0.0.0.1.0.0.8.0 2.0.1] \
    [list ether2.arp 8.0.0.0.1.0.0.8.6 2.0.0] \
    [list ether2.vip 8.0.0.0.1.0.0.11.173 2.0.0] \
    [list ether2.vloop 8.0.0.0.1.0.0.11.174 2.0.0] \
    [list ether2.vecho 8.0.0.0.1.0.0.11.175 2.0.0] \
    [list ether2.vloop 8.0.0.0.1.0.0.128.196 2.0.0] \
    [list ether2.vecho 8.0.0.0.1.0.0.128.197 2.0.0] \
    [list ether2.ipx 8.0.0.0.1.0.0.129.55 2.0.0] \
```

Before executing any of our RMONv2 scripts, we will cycle through `rmon2protList` and build an array of protocol identifiers and parameters indexed by protocol name.

```
proc buildRmon2ProtArray {} {
        global gProtDirArray rmon2protList

        foreach el $rmon2protList {

                set descr [lindex $el 0]
                set prot [lindex $el 1]
                set param [lindex $el 2]

                set gProtDirArray($descr,prot) $prot
                set gProtDirArray($descr,param) $param

        }
}
```

For example:

```
source rmon2ProtDir.tcl
buildRmon2ProtArray

puts $gProtDirArray(ether2.arp,prot)
⇒ 8.0.0.0.1.0.0.8.6

puts $gProtDirArray(ether2.arp,param)
⇒ 2.0.0
```

Before trying to write to a device's protocolDirTable, we will first read all the entries from the table and store them in an array, gArrCProt. There are several reasons for doing this. First, it will allow us to build an inventory of what protocols are configured for a device. Second, it will allow us to access the `protocolDirLocalIndex` value assigned for a protocol. This is a unique identifier assigned when an entry is added to the protocolDirTable, and will allow us to correlate protocol information within the RMONv2 data tables. Finally, it will allow us to determine whether we need to add a new entry or modify an existing one.

```
proc collectRmon2ProtocolDir {addr} {
        global gSid gDoneFlag

        set gDoneFlag 0

        set pInfo [GetPollingInfo $addr]
        set comm [lindex $pInfo 0]
```

```
        set authinfo [list snmpv1 $comm]
        set vb [list protocolDirLocalIndex \
                protocolDirAddressMapConfig \
                protocolDirHostConfig \
                protocolDirMatrixConfig]

        set cb [list cbRoutine $addr]
        set op [list -tableRows 1]

        $gSid table $addr $authinfo $vb {0} $op $cb
        vwait gDoneFlag
}
```

The above routine will walk the protocolDirTable. By setting −tableRows to 1, cbRoutine will be called for each collected row. The values for protocolDirID and protocolDirParameters will be determined by the returned OID values. Note that we were able to reference RMONv2 MIB OID Names directly because we had compiled RMONv2 MIB (RFC 2021) using the utility tools supplied with TickleMan. If we hadn't, we would have had to define variables and set them to the OID Numbers. If we were using Scotty, we would have had to add the command "mib load rfc2021.mib" to buildRmon2ProtArray.

```
proc cbRoutine {addr result} {
#
#   Callback routine for collecting protocol directory table.
#
#   For each collected protocol, separate the protocol from the
#   parameter. Save in a global array, using the protocol as an
#   index, a list containing the parameter, address map
#   configuration, host configuration and matrix configuration.

        global gArrCProt gDoneFlag

        set n [expr \
            [string length "protocolDirLocalIndex"] + 1]
        set errorStatus [GetErrorStatus $result]
        set vblist [GetVarBindList $result]

        set vb [GetVarBind $vblist 1]

        set oid [GetOID $vb]    ;# oid string for
                                ;# protocolDirLocalIndex
        set val [GetValue $vb]  ;# Value for protocolDirLocalIndex
```

```
        set p [string range $oid $n end]

        if {[string length $p] == 0} {
            set gDoneFlag 1
            return
        }

        set temp [split $p .]

        set i [lindex $temp 0]
        set prot [lrange $temp 0 $i]
        set prot [join $prot .]
        set param [lrange $temp [expr $i + 1] end]
        set param [join $param .]

        set vb [GetVarBind $vblist 2]    ;# Get the AddressMapConfig
        set amc [GetValue $vb]           ;# value.


        set vb [GetVarBind $vblist 3]    ;# Get the HostConfig value.
        set hc [GetValue $vb]

        set vb [GetVarBind $vblist 4]    ;# Get the MatrixConfig
        set mc [GetValue $vb]            ;# value.
#
#  gArrCProt will be indexed by ip address and protocol
#  identifier. An array element of gArrCProt will be assigned
#  a list containing:
#    protocol local index, configured protocol parameter settings,
#    address map config, host config and matrix config.
#
        set gArrCProt($addr,$prot) [list $val $param $amc $hc $mc]

        if {$errorStatus == "endOfTable"} {
            set gDoneFlag 1
        }
}
```

if oid is set to protocolDirLocalIndex.8.1.0.0.1.0.0.0.240.2.0.0, then:

```
        set p [string range $oid $n end]
```

will set p to 8.1.0.0.1.0.0.0.240.2.0.0.

```
set temp [split $p .]
```

will set temp to "8 1 0 0 1 0 0 0 240 2 0 0". The first element in the list, 8, is the length of the protocol identifier (which gets assigned to the variable ;), so the commands:

```
set prot [lrange $temp 0 $i]
set prot [join $prot .]
```

will set prot to "8.1.0.0.1.0.0.0.240". The commands:

```
set param [lrange $temp [expr $i + 1] end]
set param [join $param .]
```

will set param to "2.0.0". Finally, when "endOfTable" is reached, gDoneFlag will be set, notifying collectRmon2ProtocolDir that collection has been completed. After the protocol directory table has been collected, you could call the following routine, inventoryColProt, to produce an inventory file.

```
proc inventoryColProt {addr fname} {
        global gArrCProt gProtDirArray

        set f [open $fname w]
        set x [array name gArrCProt $addr,*]
        set pList [array get gProtDirArray *,prot]

        foreach el $x {

                set el [lindex [split $el ,] 1]
                set i [lsearch $pList $el]
                if {$i == -1} {
                        puts $f "Unrecognized: $el $gArrCProt($addr,$el)"
                } else {
                        set name [lindex $pList [expr $i - 1]]
                        puts $f "$name, $gArrCProt($addr,$el)"
                }
        }
        close $f
}
```

To understand the above code, remember that gArrCProt is indexed by IP address and protocol identifier. The command:

```
set x [array name gArrCProt $addr,*]
```

will produce a list of all the protocol identifiers discovered for an address (each element of the list will be address,protocol). The first index for `gProtDirArray` is protocol name; the second is either "`prot`" or "`param`". The command:

```
set pList [array get gProtDirArray *,prot]
```

will build a list of all the protocol names and identifiers that we know about (or at least those that were added to `rmon2ProtList`). For each protocol identifier collected from the device, we search to see if it is one we recognize. If it is, we write the protocol name and configuration values to the inventory file; otherwise, we write that the protocol identifier is one we don't recognize. The partial results of running `inventoryColProt`:

```
wildcard-ether2.ip.tcp.smtp,prot, 2490395 4.0.1.0.0 1 3 3
wildcard-ether2.ip.tcp.www-http,prot, 2228245 4.0.1.0.0 1 3 2
Unrecognized: 8.1.0.0.1.0.0.134.221 1703944 2.0.0 1 1 1
wildcard-ether2.ipx.ncp,prot, 1900560 3.0.0.0 1 2 2
wildcard-ether2.ipx.nov-sap,prot, 1966097 3.0.0.0 1 2 2
wildcard-ether2.ip,prot, 327681 2.0.1 3 3 2
wildcard-ether2.ip.tcp,prot, 1179659 3.0.1.0 1 3 2
wildcard-ether2.ip.udp,prot, 1245196 3.0.1.0 1 2 2
wildcard-ether2.ip.ospf,prot, 1835022 3.0.1.0 1 2 2
wildcard-ether2.vip,prot, 655366 2.0.0 2 2 2
wildcard-ether2.ip.tcp.x11,prot, 2162708 4.0.1.0.0 1 3 2
Unrecognized: 8.1.0.0.1.0.0.128.155 524292 2.0.0 2 2 2
wildcard-ether2.ipx,prot, 458755 2.0.0 2 3 2
wildcard-ether2.ip.udp.snmp,prot, 2293783 4.0.0.0.0 1 3 3
wildcard-ether2.ip.tcp.ftp-data,prot, 2097171 4.0.1.0.0 1 3 2
wildcard-ether2.ip.tcp.ftp,prot, 2555932 4.0.1.0.0 1 3 2
wildcard-ether2.ip.udp.router,prot, 2424857 4.0.0.0.0 1 2 2
```

Each line includes either the protocol name or the identifier (for protocols that we haven't added to `rmon2ProtList`), the `protocolDirLocalIndex` value, the configured `param` value and the address map, host and matrix configuration values. For the configuration values, 1 indicates not supported, 2 that support is turned off, and 3 that support is turned on.

The configuration of `protocolDirTable` has been broken into seven routines:

- `configureProtocolDir` is passed an address and a list of protocols and configuration information. For each element in this list, either `addProtocol` is called to add a new protocol or `changeProtocolConfig` is called to change the configuration of an already loaded protocol.
- `addProtocol` adds a new protocol to `protocolDirTable`.
- `changeProtocolConfig` modifies the address map, host or matrix configuration, if necessary.

- checkErrorStatus is a convenience routine to check the error status for the results of an SNMP Get operation. It raises an error if an SNMP error was detected.

- getLocalIndex collects the protocolDirLocalIndex value for a newly added protocol.

- getProtocolDirConfig collects the address map, host and matrix configuration values for a specified protocol. This is necessary since the values returned within a set varbind are not necessarily the values that were configured. For example, if you add a new protocol and set the address map configuration to supportOff (2), and address mapping is not supported for that protocol, the actual value set in the MIB is notSupported (1).

- removeProtocol removes a protocol from the protocolDirTable.

```
proc configureProtocolDir {addr pList} {
  global gArrCProt gProtDirArray

  set pInfo [GetPollingInfo $addr]
  set comm [lindex $pInfo 1]

  foreach el $pList {

      set descr [lindex $el 0]
      set prot $gProtDirArray($descr,prot)

      if {[info exists gArrCProt($addr,$prot)] == 0} {
         if [catch {
            addProtocol $addr $comm $el} err] {
               error "$err: configureProtolDir"
         }
      } else {
         if [catch {
            changeProtocolConfig $prot $addr $comm $el} err] {
               error "$err: configureProtocolDir"
         }
      }
   }
}
```

The code:

```
set prot $gProtDirArray($descr,prot)
if {[info exists gArrCProt($addr,$prot)] == 0} {
```

maps a protocol name to a protocol identifier. Then, by using the `info` command, it determines whether the protocol exists within protocolDirTable for the specified address. Note that the procedure raises an error if one of the underlying procedures raises an error. `configureProtocolDir` should be called within a `catch` command.

```
proc addProtocol {addr comm el} {
        global gArrCProt gProtDirArray gSid

        set authinfo [list snmpv1 $comm]
        set descr [lindex $el 0]
        set amc [lindex $el 1]
        set hc [lindex $el 2]
        set mc [lindex $el 3]
#
#   Create an instance equal to
#   protocolDirID.protocolDirParameters.
#
        set inst \
  "$gProtDirArray($descr,prot).$gProtDirArray($descr,param)"
#
#   Set protocolDirStatus to "createAndWait" (5).
#
        set vb [list protocolDirStatus.$inst 5]
        set vblist [list $vb]
        set result [$gSid set $addr $authinfo $vblist {} wait]
        checkErrorStatus $result addProtocol

        set ocDescr [text2octet $descr]
        set ocOwner [text2octet "rmon2Config"]
#
#   Set remaining fields for new row, then set
#   protocolDirStatus to "active" (1).
#
        set vb1 [list protocolDirDescr.$inst $ocDescr]
        set vb2 [list protocolDirAddressMapConfig.$inst $amc]
        set vb3 [list protocolDirHostConfig.$inst $hc]
        set vb4 [list protocolDirMatrixConfig.$inst $mc]
        set vb5 [list protocolDirOwner.$inst $ocOwner]
        set vb6 [list protocolDirStatus.$inst 1]

        set vblist [list $vb1 $vb2 $vb3 $vb4 $vb5 $vb6]
```

```
    set result [$gSid set $addr $authinfo $vblist {} wait]
    checkErrorStatus $result addProtocol

    if [catch {
        set localIndex [getLocalIndex $addr $comm $inst]} err] {
        error "$err: addProtocol"
    }

    if [catch {
        set cf [getProtocolDirConfig $addr $comm $inst]} err] {
        error "$err: addProtocol"
    }

    set gArrCProt($addr,$gProtDirArray($descr,prot)) \
        [list $localIndex \
            $gProtDirArray($descr,param) \
            [lindex $cf 0] \
            [lindex $cf 1] \
            [lindex $cf 2]]
}
```

A new row is added to protocolDirTable by first creating a unique instance using the protocol identifier and parameter, and then setting protocolDirStatus to "createAndWait" (5). If this is successful, the next step is to set the description, configuration and owner values, and then to set protocolDirStatus to "active" (1). Again, if this is successful we want to next retrieve the local index value created for the entry (protocolDirLocalIndex), as well as the configuration values the RMONv2 device actually used.

Note that checkErrorStatus will raise an error if an SNMP error was detected. The format of the error string will be <SNMP Error>: <procedure name>. Both getLocalIndex and getProtocolDirConfig, which are called by addProtocol, will also raise errors using the same format. addProtocol will catch the error, though, append ": addProtocol" to the error string, and also raise an error. By using this mechanism, we can build a chain of where an error occurred. For example, if a timeout occurred within getLocalIndex, we would end up raising the error "timeout: getLocalIndex: addProtocol".

```
proc changeProtocolConfig {prot addr comm el} {
    global gArrCProt gProtDirArray gSid

    set descr [lindex $el 0]
    set new_amc [lindex $el 1]
    set new_hc [lindex $el 2]
    set new_mc [lindex $el 3]
```

```
        set authinfo [list snmpv1 $comm]

        set x $gArrCProt($addr,$prot)
        set localIndex [lindex $x 0]
        set param [lindex $x 1]
        set amc [lindex $x 2]
        set hc [lindex $x 3]
        set mc [lindex $x 4]

        set inst "$prot.$param"
        set vblist ""
#
#   If any of the values are notSupported (1), don't allow
#   values to be changed.
#
        if {$amc == 1} {
            set new_amc 1
        }

        if {$amc != $new_amc} {
            lappend vblist \
                [list protocolDirAddressMapConfig.$inst $new_amc]
        }

        if {$hc == 1} {
            set new_hc 1
        }

        if {$hc != $new_hc} {
            lappend vblist \
            [list protocolDirHostConfig.$inst $new_hc]
        }

        if {$mc == 1} {
            set new_mc 1
        }

        if {$mc != $new_mc} {
            lappend vblist \
                [list protocolDirMatrixConfig.$inst $new_mc]
        }
```

```
        if {[llength $vblist] == 0} {
            puts "No configuration necessary for $prot"
            return
        }

        set result [$gSid set $addr $authinfo $vblist {} wait]
        checkErrorStatus $result changeProtocolConfig

        if [catch {
            set cf [getProtocolDirConfig $addr $comm $inst]} err] {
            error "$err: changeProtocolConfig"
        }

        set gArrCProt($addr,$prot) [list $localIndex \
                $gProtDirArray($descr,param) \
                [lindex $cf 0] \
                [lindex $cf 1] \
                [lindex $cf 2]]
}
```

changeProtocolConfig will determine if the requested values for protocol-DirAddressMapConfig, protocolDirHostConfig and protocolDirMatrixConfig are different than those being maintained within gArrCProt. If they are, a varbind list will be built and an SNMP Set request sent. Note that after performing the Set operation, we still have to reread these MIB variables to obtain the values used by the RMONv2 device.

```
proc checkErrorStatus {result procname} {
        set errorStatus [GetErrorStatus $result]
        if {$errorStatus != "noError"} {
                error "$errorStatus: $procname"
        }
}
```

checkErrorStatus is a convenience routine that checks a result string for an SNMP error. It raises an error if one occurred.

```
proc getLocalIndex {addr comm inst} {
        global gSid

        set authinfo [list snmpv1 $comm]
        set vblist [list protocolDirLocalIndex.$inst]

        set result [$gSid get $addr $authinfo $vblist {} wait]
        checkErrorStatus $result getLocalIndex
```

```
        set x [GetVarBindList $result]
        set x [GetVarBind $x 1]
        return [GetValue $x]
}
```

getLocalIndex retrieves protocolDirLocalIndex for a specified instance.

```
proc getProtocolDirConfig {addr comm inst} {
        global gSid
#
#   Read configuration variables.
#
        set authinfo [list snmpv1 $comm]
        set vblist [list protocolDirAddressMapConfig.$inst \
                        protocolDirHostConfig.$inst \
                        protocolDirMatrixConfig.$inst]
        set result [$gSid get $addr $authinfo $vblist {} wait]
        checkErrorStatus $result getProtocolDirConfig

        set vblist [GetVarBindList $result]

        set vb [GetVarBind $vblist 1]
        set amc [GetValue $vb]

        set vb [GetVarBind $vblist 2]
        set hc [GetValue $vb]

        set vb [GetVarBind $vblist 3]
        set mc [GetValue $vb]

        return [list $amc $hc $mc]
}
```

getProtocolDirConfig retrieves the protocolDirAddressMapConfig, pro-tocolDirHostConfig and protocolDirMatrixConfig for a specified instance.

```
proc removeProtocol {addr descr} {
        global gArrCProt gProtDirArray gSid
        set pInfo [GetPollingInfo $addr]
        set wrcomm [lindex $pInfo 1]
        set authinfo [list snmpv1 $wrcomm]

        set prot $gProtDirArray($descr,prot)
```

```
set x $gArrCProt($addr,$prot)

set param [lindex $x 1]
set inst "$prot.$param"

set vblist [list [list protocolDirStatus.$inst 6]]

set result [$gSid set $addr $authinfo $vblist {} wait]
checkErrorStatus $result removeProtocol

unset gArrCProt($addr,$prot)
}
```

A protocol is removed from the protocolDirTable by setting `protocolDirStatus` to "`destroy`" (6). We will wrap up this section by providing a convenience routine to map a protocol description to a local index for a specified IP address.

```
proc ConvertDescrToLocalIndex {addr descr} {
     global gArrCProt gProtDirArray

     if {![info exists gProtDirArray($descr,prot)]} {
          error "$descr not recognized: \
               ConvertDescrToLocalIndex"
     }

     set prot $gProtDirArray($descr,prot)
     if {![info exists gArrCProt($addr,$prot)]} {
          error "$descr not configured in $addr:\
                    ConvertDescrToLocalIndex"
     }
     return [lindex $gArrCProt($addr,$prot) 0]
}
```

This routine will be used later in this chapter when we show how to access several RMONv2 data tables.

RMONv2 CONTROL TABLES

Next, we will be building scripts to configure the Protocol Distribution Control Table, Address Map Control Table, Host Control Table and Matrix Control Table. All of these control tables are configured in a consistent way and as such, we will be building several generic routines to control these tables. These routines are:

- collectRmon2ControlInfo correlates a mapping of interface-to-index for a control table. For all of the RMONv2 control tables that we will be describing, after you configure which protocols to monitor through the protocolDirTable, you configure which interfaces to monitor through these RMONv2 control tables. collectRmon2ControlInfo is passed a data source MIB variable for one of the control tables, and issues a table command to collect all entries for that variable.
- cbRmon2Control is the callback routine for collectRmon2ControlInfo.
- setRmon2Control adds a row to a control table.
- removeRmon2Control removes a row from a control table.
- getInstance is a convenience routine for retrieving instance information from an OID.
- getUniqueIndex is a convenience routine for obtaining a unique control index.

These routines will use a global array, gRmon2CtlArr, to map a device's ifIndex number to a control table's index. The index for the array is <ip address, table string, ifIndex>.

```
proc collectRmon2ControlInfo {addr t m} {
#
#       Collect datasource variable for an RMONv2 control table.
#
        global gSid gDoneArr

        set gDoneArr($addr,$t) 0
        set pInfo [GetPollingInfo $addr]
        set comm [lindex $pInfo 1]
        set authinfo [list snmpv1 $comm]

        set vb [list $m]

        set op [list -tableRows 1]
        set cb [list cbRmon2Control $addr $t $m]

        $gSid table $addr $authinfo $vb {0} $op $cb
        vwait gDoneArr($addr,$t)
}
```

```
proc cbRmon2Control {addr t m result} {
      global gDoneArr gRmon2CtlArr

      set errorStatus [GetErrorStatus $result]

      set vblist [GetVarBindList $result]
      set vb [GetVarBind $vblist 1]
      set oid [GetOID $vb]

      set controlIndex [GetInstance $oid $m]

      if {[string length $controlIndex] > 0} {

             set val [GetValue $vb]
             set i [expr [string length "ifIndex"]+1]
             set ifIndex [string range $val $i end]

             set gRmon2CtlArr($addr,$t,$ifIndex) $controlIndex
      }

      if {$errorStatus == "endOfTable"} {
             set gDoneArr($addr,$t) 1
      }
}

proc GetInstance {oid m} {
      set n [expr [string length $m] + 1]
      return [string range $oid $n end]
}
```

We obtain the control index by pulling the instance portion off the OID. The value for a data source variable is in the format ifIndex.n, where n is the ifIndex number. The commands:

```
      set i [expr [string length "ifIndex"]+1]
      set ifIndex [string range $val $i end]
```

will therefore extract the ifIndex number from the value. When collection is complete, the gDoneArr element associated with the address and control table being collected will be set, signaling collectRmon2ControlInfo. By using an array element, we can simultaneously collect RMONv2 control table information for multiple addresses and control tables.

```
proc getUniqueIndex {addr t} {
      global gRmon2CtlArr
```

```
        set x [array get gRmon2CtlArr "$addr,$t,*"]
        set i 1
        foreach {index val} $x {
             if {$val > $i} {
                  set i $val
             }
        }
        return [expr $i + 1]
}


proc setRmon2Control {addr i t miblist} {
        global gSid gIfIndex gLocalIndex gDone gRmon2CtlArr

#
#       Check to see if ifindex is already configured.
#
        if {[info exists gRmon2CtlArr($addr,$t,$i)]} {

             puts "already configured."
             return
        }

        set pInfo [GetPollingInfo $addr]
        set comm [lindex $pInfo 1]
        set authinfo [list snmpv1 $comm]

        set mStatus [lindex $miblist 0]
        set mDataSource [lindex $miblist 1]
        set mOwner [lindex $miblist 2]

        set inst [getUniqueIndex $addr $t]

        set vblist [list [list $mStatus.$inst 5]]
        set result [$gSid set $addr $authinfo $vblist {} wait]

        checkErrorStatus $result setRmon2Control

        set ds "[oid2dot ifIndex].$i"

        set vb1 [list $mDataSource.$inst $ds]
        set vb2 [list $mOwner.$inst [text2octet "monitor"]]
```

```
    set vb3 [list $mStatus.$inst 1]

    set vblist [list $vb1 $vb2 $vb3]

    set n [llength $miblist]
    set j 3
    while {$j < $n} {
          set vb [lindex $miblist $j]

          set oid "[lindex $vb 0].$inst"
          set val [lindex $vb 1]

          lappend vblist [list $oid $val]
          incr j
    }

    set result [$gSid set $addr $authinfo $vblist {} wait]

    checkErrorStatus $result setRmon2Control

    set gRmon2CtlArr($addr,$t,$i) $inst

}
```

setRmon2Control is passed four arguments: an IP address to configure, an ifIndex value for an interface for which to turn on monitoring, a table string identifying the RMONv2 control table and a list of MIB variables. In the MIB variable list, the first element corresponds to the control table's status variable, the second element to the control table's data source variable and the third element to the control table's owner variable. If there are more than three elements in the list, the remaining elements will be MIB variable, value pairs of the remaining MIB variables that need to be set for a control table. This routine will call getUniqueIndex, which will generate a unique index by finding the largest index being used for the control table and bumping the value by one. It will then create a new row by setting the associated status variable to "createAndWait" (5), issuing another Set command and setting the data source, owner, any other necessary MIB variables and status to "active" (1). If successful, it will update gRmon2CtlArr.

```
proc removeRmon2Control {addr i t m} {
    global gSid gRmon2CtlArr

    if {![info exists gRmon2CtlArr($addr,$t,$i)]} {

          return
    }
```

```
    set inst $gRmon2CtlArr($addr,$t,$i)
    set pInfo [GetPollingInfo $addr]
    set comm [lindex $pInfo 1]
    set authinfo [list snmpv1 $comm]

    set vb [list [list $m.$inst 6]]

    set result [$gSid set $addr $authinfo $vb {} wait]

    checkErrorStatus $result setDistControl
    unset gRmon2CtlArr($addr,$t,$i)
}
```

This routine removes an entry from a control table by setting the associated status variable to "destroy" (6). If it is successful, it removes the corresponding entry from gRmon2CtlArr (if an SNMP error occurred, checkErrorStatus will raise an error, causing the routine to exit before the unset command can be executed).

PROTOCOL DISTRIBUTION GROUP

This group enumerates the octets and packets received for a particular protocol (again, for the protocols configured within the protocolDirTable). Each row in the protocolDistControlTable identifies an interface for the RMONv2 device for which monitoring is enabled. The rows in the protocolDistStatusTable are instanced by a control index and protocol index.

We will now provide collect, set and remove routines for controlling protocolDistControlTable. Note that the collect routine must be run before either the set or remove routines.

```
proc collectDistControl {addr} {

    collectRmon2ControlInfo $addr DistControl \
        protocolDistControlDataSource
}


proc setDistControl {addr i} {

    set miblist [list protocolDistControlStatus \
                      protocolDistControlDataSource \
                      protocolDistControlOwner]
```

```
        if [catch {
            setRmon2Control $addr $i DistControl $miblist} err] {
            error "$err: setDistControl"
        }
}

proc removeDistControl {addr i} {

    set m protocolDistControlStatus
    if [catch {
        removeRmon2Control $addr $i DistControl $m} err] {
        error "$err: removeDistControl"
    }
}
```

These routines use the RMONv2 control table routines developed in the previous section. We will now provide a routine which demonstrates how to access data from the `protocolD-istStatsTable`. `getDistStatsData` is passed an address, interface number and protocol name. It collects the packet and octet count for that interface and protocol.

```
proc getDistStatsData {addr ifIndex descr} {
    global gRmon2CtlArr gSid

    if {![info exists gRmon2CtlArr($addr,DistControl,$ifIndex)]} {
        error "$ifIndex not configured: getDistStats"
    }

    set index $gRmon2CtlArr($addr,DistControl,$ifIndex)
    if [catch {
        set protIndex \
            [ConvertDescrToLocalIndex $addr $descr]} err] {
        error "$err: getDistStatsData"
    }

    set pInfo [GetPollingInfo $addr]
    set comm [lindex $pInfo 1]
    set authinfo [list snmpv1 $comm]
    set vblist [list protocolDistStatsPkts.$index.$protIndex \
                    protocolDistStatsOctets.$index.$protIndex]

    set result [$gSid get $addr $authinfo $vblist {} wait]

    checkErrorStatus $result getDistStatsData
```

```
    set vblist [GetVarBindList $result]

    set vb [GetVarBind $vblist 1]
    set pkts [GetValue $vb]

    set vb [GetVarBind $vblist 2]
    set octets [GetValue $vb]

    return [list $pkts $octets]
}
```

The command:

```
    set index $gRmon2CtlArr($addr,DistControl,$ifIndex)
```

maps an `ifIndex` value to the corresponding `protocolDistControlIndex` value. The command:

```
    set protIndex [ConvertDescrToLocalIndex $addr $descr]
```

maps a protocol name to the corresponding `protocolDirLocalIndex` value.

```
    getDistStatsData $addr 1 wildcard-ether2.ip
    ⇒ 19108825 3726203865

    getDistStatsData $addr 1 wildcard-ether2.ip.ospf
    ⇒ noSuchName: getDistStatsData
```

ADDRESS MAP GROUP

The address map group matches each network address to a specific MAC address, and identifies on which port of the RMONv2 device the address was discovered. Each row in the addressMapControlTable identifies an interface for the RMONv2 device for which monitoring is enabled. The rows in the addressMapTable are instanced by a time filter, protocol index, network address and an interface on which the network address was seen. For address mapping to occur for a protocol, the address map configuration for that protocol must be configured to "supportedOn" within the protocolDirTable.

Below are the collect, set and remove routines for configuring the `addressMapCon-trolTable`:

```
proc collectAddressMapControl {addr} {

    collectRmon2ControlInfo $addr AddressMap \
        addressMapControlDataSource
}

proc setAddressMapControl {addr i} {

    set miblist [list addressMapControlStatus \
                    addressMapControlDataSource \
                    addressMapControlOwner]
    if [catch {
        setRmon2Control $addr $i AddressMap $miblist} err] {
        error "$err: setAddressMapControl"
    }
}

proc removeAddressMapControl {addr i} {

    set m addressMapControlStatus
    if [catch {
        removeRmon2Control $addr $i AddressMap $m} err] {
        error "$err: removeAddressMapControl"
    }
}
```

Below is a somewhat kludgey example of how to access the `addressMapTable`. This routine is passed an address of an RMONv2 device, a network address to look up and an interface number. It returns the associated MAC address. The RMONv2 probe we used for testing only seemed to work properly if we passed it a fully instanced OID number; otherwise, an SNMP Get-Next command would always return the first entry in the table. Also, if we tried to perform an SNMP Get command with a fully instanced OID number, the probe would improperly return the first entry in the table. Because of this, we had to subtract 1 from the network address within the instance and use an SNMP GetNext command. This example is provided only as a demonstration of how to access the `addressMapTable`!

```
proc getMacAddress {addr ifIndex ipaddr} {
  global gSid

  if [catch {
```

```
    set i \
      [ConvertDescrToLocalIndex $addr wildcard-ether2.ip]} err] {
      error "$err: getMacAddress"
  }

  set pInfo [GetPollingInfo $addr]
  set comm [lindex $pInfo 1]
  set authinfo [list snmpv1 $comm]
#
#  Kludge to subtract 1 from the nextwork address. This is being
#  done to work around a broken probe implementation!
#
  set x [split $ipaddr .]
  set x [lreplace $x 3 3 [expr [lindex $x 3] - 1]]
  set x [join $x .]

  set oid [oid2dot ifIndex]
#
#  Form fully-instanced oid.
#
  set inst [join [list 0 $i 4 $x 11 $oid $ifIndex] .]

  set result [$gSid next $addr $authinfo \
      [list addressMapPhysicalAddress.$inst] {} wait]

  checkErrorStatus $result getMacAddress
  set vb [GetVarBind [GetVarBindList $result] 1]
  set oid [GetOID $vb]
  set inst [GetInstance $oid addressMapPhysicalAddress]

#
#  get network address from oid instance
#
  set x [split $inst .]
  set x [lrange $x 3 6]
  set x [join $x .]

  if {[string compare $x $ipaddr] != 0} {
      error "not found."
  }
```

```
    set val [GetValue $vb]
    return $val
}
```

RMONv2 HOST GROUPS

The RMONv2 host groups deal with the collection of statistics by host. These groups allow protocol traffic to be decoded based on its network-layer address, and on the application-level protocol discovered at each known network-layer address. Each row in the `hlHostControlTable` identifies an interface for the RMONv2 device for which monitoring is enabled. The `nlHost-Table` is indexed by control index, time filter, protocol index and network address. The `al-HostTable` is indexed by control index, time filter, network-layer protocol index, network address and application-layer protocol index. Entries will be created in these data tables for all protocols whose value of `protocolDirHostConfig` is "supportedOn" within the protocol directory table.

Below are the collect, set and remove routines for configuring the `hlHostControlTable`:

```
proc collectHostControl {addr} {

        collectRmon2ControlInfo $addr HostControl \
            hlHostControlDataSource
}

proc setHostControl {addr i} {
        set NL_MAX 4000
        set AL_MAX 4000

        set miblist \
          [list hlHostControlStatus \
                hlHostControlDataSource \
                hlHostControlOwner \
                [list hlHostControlNlMaxDesiredEntries $NL_MAX] \
                [list hlHostControlAlMaxDesiredEntries $AL_MAX]]
        if [catch {
                setRmon2Control $addr $i HostControl $miblist} err] {
                error "$err: setHostControl"
        }
}
```

```
proc removeHostControl {addr i} {

    set m hlHostControlStatus
    if [catch {
            removeRmon2Control $addr $i HostControl $m} err] {
        error "$err: removeHostControl"
    }
}
```

The following routine demonstrates accessing the nlHostTable. Given an interface, network protocol and network address, the routine getNetworkProtocolStats will read the corresponding entry from the nlHostTable. The routine will retrieve the current value of sysUpTime from the RMONv2 device and subtract mins from it (first converting mins to hundredths of a second) to use as a time filter.

```
proc getNetworkProtocolStats {addr ifIndex descr netaddr mins} {
    global gSid gRmon2CtlArr

    if {![info exists gRmon2CtlArr($addr,HostControl,$ifIndex)]} {
        error "$ifIndex not configured: getNetworkProtocolStats"
    }

    set index $gRmon2CtlArr($addr,HostControl,$ifIndex)
    if [catch {
        set protIndex \
            [ConvertDescrToLocalIndex $addr $descr]} err] {
        error "$err: getDistStatsData"
    }

    set pInfo [GetPollingInfo $addr]
    set comm [lindex $pInfo 1]
    set authinfo [list snmpv1 $comm]
#
#   Get current value for sysUpTime.
#
    set result [$gSid get $addr $authinfo {sysUpTime.0} {} wait]
    checkErrorStatus $result getNetworkProtocolStats

    set vb [GetVarBind [GetVarBindList $result] 1]
    set n [GetValue $vb]
```

```
#
#   Use time filter of current sysUpTime - $mins minutes.
#
    set n [expr $n - ($mins*60*100)]

    set inst [join [list $index $n $protIndex 4 $netaddr] .]

    set vblist [list nlHostInPkts.$inst \
                     nlHostOutPkts.$inst \
                     nlHostInOctets.$inst \
                     nlHostOutOctets.$inst \
                     nlHostOutMacNonUnicastPkts.$inst]

    set result [$gSid get $addr $authinfo $vblist {} wait]
    checkErrorStatus $result getNetworkProtocolStats

    set vblist [GetVarBindList $result]

    set vb [GetVarBind $vblist 1]
    set inpkts [GetValue $vb]

    set vb [GetVarBind $vblist 2]
    set outpkts [GetValue $vb]

    set vb [GetVarBind $vblist 3]
    set inoctets [GetValue $vb]

    set vb [GetVarBind $vblist 4]
    set outoctets [GetValue $vb]

    set vb [GetVarBind $vblist 5]
    set outNUcast [GetValue $vb]

    return \
        [list $inpkts $outpkts $inoctets $outoctets $outNUcast]
}

getNetworkProtocolStats $addr 1 wildcard-ether2.ip $netaddr 5
⇒ 1249 0 141748 0 0
```

From this example, 1,249 packets and 141,748 octets were received from network address $netaddr with a time filter of five minutes ago.

RMONv2 MATRIX GROUPS

Three control tables are associated with the RMONv2 matrix groups: `hlMatrixControlTable`, `nlMatrixTopNControlTable` and `alMatrixTopNControlTopNControlTable`. We are going to provide a solution only for configuring the `hlMatrixControlTable`.

Configuring entries within the `hlMatrixControlTable` will allow statistics to be collected based on conversations between pairs of hosts. Statistics will be collected on both network-layer conversations and application-layer conversations for protocols whose value of `protocolDirMatrixConfig` is "supportedOn" within the protocol directory table. The collected statistics will be written to the `nlMatrixSDTable`, the `nlMatrixDSTable`, the `alMatrixSDTable` and the `alMatrixDSTable`.

```
proc collectMatrixControl {addr} {

        collectRmon2ControlInfo $addr MatrixControl \
                hlMatrixControlDataSource
}


proc setMatrixControl {addr i} {
        set NL_MAX 4000
        set AL_MAX 4000

        set miblist \
            [list hlMatrixControlStatus \
                    hlMatrixControlDataSource \
                    hlMatrixControlOwner \
                    [list hlMatrixControlNlMaxDesiredEntries $NL_MAX] \
                    [list hlMatrixControlAlMaxDesiredEntries $AL_MAX]]
        if [catch {
                setRmon2Control $addr $i MatrixControl $miblist} err] {
                error "$err: setMatrixControl"
        }
}


proc removeMatrixControl {addr i} {

        set m hlMatrixControlStatus
        if [catch {
                removeRmon2Control $addr $i MatrixControl $m} err] {
                error "$err: removeMatrixControl"
        }
}
```

USING THE RMONv2 CONFIGURATION TOOLS

1) Inventory an RMONv2 device's protocol directory table:

```
source rmon2ProtDir.tcl
buildRmon2ProtArray
collectRmon2ProtocolDir $addr
inventoryColProt $addr inventory.txt
```

2) Configure a device's protocol directory table. In this example, we are configuring ospf, snmp and udp protocols, all with configuration settings of "supported-Off" (2).

```
source rmon2ProtDir.tcl
buildRmon2ProtArray
collectRmon2ProtocolDir $addr
set plist [list \
      [list wildcard-ether2.ip.ospf 2 2 2] \
      [list wildcard-ether2.ip.udp.snmp 2 2 2] \
      [list wildcard-ether2.ip.udp 2 2 2]]
configureProtocolDir $addr $pList
```

3) Remove a protocol from a device's protocol directory table. In this example, remove ospf.

```
source rmon2ProtDir.tcl
buildRmon2ProtArray
collectRmon2ProtocolDir $addr
removeProtocol $addr wildcard-ether2.ip.ospf
```

4) Add protocol distribution monitoring for an interface:

```
collectDistControl $addr
setDistControl $addr $ifIndex
```

5) Add network-to-physical address mapping for an interface:

```
collectAddressMapControl $addr
setAddressMapControl $addr $ifIndex
```

6) Add host monitoring for an interface:

```
collectHostControl $addr
setHostControl $addr $ifIndex
```

7) Add RMONv2 matrix monitoring for an interface:

```
collectMatrixControl $addr
setMatrixControl $addr $ifIndex
```

IN SUMMARY

This chapter provided solutions for configuring most RMONv2 control tables, and also provided examples for accessing several related RMONv2 data tables. These short configuration scripts could be used to build an RMONv2 configuration inventory application, as well as an application to consistently configure multiple RMONv2 devices (probes or switches with RMONv2 support).

15 *More Information*

This chapter briefly examines how the Tcl Plug-in could be used with network management applications. In addition, it identifies books and Internet sites with more information on SNMP and Tcl, where to find information on Tcl extension packages, and the availability of Tcl /Java-related products from Sunscript.

TCL PLUG-IN

The SunScript Group freely provides several useful Tcl/Tk add-on and development tools. One is the Tcl Plug-in for Netscape Navigator, Netscape Communicator and Microsoft Internet Explorer. The Tcl Plug-in lets you embed Tcl /Tk scripts (called Tcl applets, or Tclets) in Web pages and run local Tcl/Tk scripts from your browser. It is available from SunScript at: http://sunscript.sun.com/plugin/, and from the Neosoft mirror site at: http://www.neosoft.com/sunsoft/.

Version 1.0 of the Tcl Plug-in for both UNIX and PC systems was first released back in 1996 and was based on Tcl 7.7. Version 2.0b5 of the Tcl Plug-in was made available in December 1997. It is based on Tcl 8.0. The Tclet examples in this chapter use `policy home`, which is supported with Version 2.0b5 of the Tcl Plug-in. Beware, earlier releases of the Tcl Plug-in do not support the `policy` command.

Security Policies

The Tcl Plug-in supports configurable security policies. A security policy defines what a Tclet can do. For example, the default security policy prevents Tcl applets from running other programs, creating sockets, accessing the file system and creating toplevel windows (including menus).

The following is a list of Tcl and Tk commands that are not available under the default security policy:

- `bell`—ring terminal bell
- `cd`—change directory
- `clipboard`—access CLIPBOARD selection
- `exec`—run programs
- `exit`—terminate a process
- `glob`—match filenames in a directory
- `grab`—grab the cursor
- `menu`—display a menu
- `load`—dynamically load shared libraries that implement new Tcl commands in C
- `open`—open a file (Actually, a restricted version of this command is available that lets you open files in the Tcl script library for reading only.)
- `pwd`—query current directory
- `send`—send Tcl commands to other Tk applications
- `socket`—open a network socket
- `source`—load script files
- `tk`—set/query Tk application name
- `tkwait`—block on events (You can use `vwait` to wait for variables to change.)
- `toplevel`—create toplevel windows
- `wm`—control the Window Manager

The Tcl Plug-in allows users to circumvent these default security restrictions according to their comfort level. For example, Tclets that specify `policy` home have the following additional functionality:

- Create socket connections to the origin host from where the Tclet was downloaded. To open a client `socket` to the origin host, specify the `socket` command with an empty string in place of the host address.
- Read and write persistent data to a directory shared by other Tclets that share a common origin URL.
- Use commands like `socket`, `fconfigure`, `open`, `file`, `close`, `puts`, `tell`, `seek` and `glob`.

- **Access functions from the browser package like** ::browser::getURL,
  ::browser::displayURL, ::browser::getForm, browser::display-
  Form **and** ::browser::status.

The default features allowed by policy home can also be changed by the user by simply modifying the home.cfg file in the TclPlug/2.0/Config directory.

See http://sunscript.sun.com/plugin. for a detailed description of security policies under Version 2.0 of the Tcl Plug-in. There you will find 2.0 documentation and example demos of Tclets using different security policies.

The <EMBED> Tag

The <EMBED> tag is used to embed Tclets inside Web pages. This HTML mechanism is commonly used with plug-ins. In general, it allows any type of file to be embedded directly into a Web page, and via defined file extensions, to invoke specified plug-ins as supported by your browser. Most Web browsers will display a message like Plugin Not Loaded when you download a page with a plug-in file and do not have the corresponding plug-in installed.

The <EMBED> tag, as defined under HTML, supports the src, align, width and height attributes. The src attribute indicates the URL of the embedded document. In addition, the HTML <EMBED> tag enables users to specify any number of user-defined parameters to pass to the plug-in.

Within your Tclet, all attribute names and values from the <EMBED> tag are available in the array embed_args. When using the Tcl Plug-in, it is best to specify all attributes in lowercase in your <EMBED> tag statement. This makes name resolution easier later when you use the embed_args array.

Here is an example using the array embed_args in your Tclet. Below we have an HTML page named tclet1.html that embeds the Tclet tclet1.tcl within its page:

```
<html>
<title>Tclet Example: tclet1.tcl</title>
<head>
<body>
<embed src=tclet1.tcl width=400 height=200 string="Hello
World">
</body>
</head>
</html>
```

The Tclet tclet1.tcl has the following contents:

```
foreach { name value} [array get embed_args] {
    frame    .$name
```

```
    label   .$name.label -text $name -width 30
    entry   .$name.entry -textvariable $name -width 30
    pack    .$name.label .$name.entry -side left
    pack    .$name -anchor w -fill x -expand true
    .$name.entry insert 0 $value
}
```

Figure 15.1 shows the result of downloading `tclet1.html`. Here we display the name and value of each attribute available from the array `embed_args`. If we loaded the file `tclet1.tcl` directly into our browser, the only attributes in the array `embed_args` would be `embed_mode=full` and `palette=foreground`.

Note that `embed_mode` will have the value `embed` for embedded Tclets, `full` for full-page Tclets and `hidden` for Tclets with no windows.

You must use the extension `.tcl` to identify Tclets with the `html` `<EMBED>` tag statement, otherwise, the browser won't know to use the Tcl Plug-in on the contents of your Tclets.

For example, the following `embed` statement is wrong:

```
<embed scr=tclet1.itcl width=600 height=600>
```

Here, the browser wouldn't know to invoke the Tcl Plug-in on `.itcl` files.

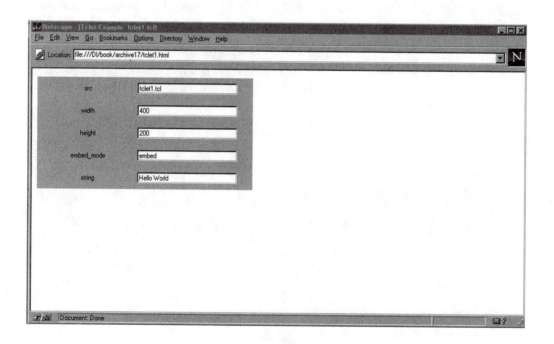

Figure 15.1   Results of downloading tclet1.html.

Instead of specifying `src=<file.tcl>` within the `<EMBED>` tag, you can also place your Tcl scripts in the `<EMBED>` tag using the `type` and `script` arguments as illustrated below:

```
<embed type="application/x-tcl"
script='
  button .b -text "Hello World"
  pack .b
'
```

Practical Uses of the Tcl Plug-in for Network Management

There are several ways in which the Tcl Plug-in can be used for network management purposes, including:

- Providing a graphical client front-end to server-based management applications

  Download a Tclet from a server or server-based application socket. Then, have the Tclet set up a socket connection back to the origin host to retrieve application data used by the Tclet. We will demonstrate this concept in Example #1.

- Displaying graphs of network management report data from server-based files or databases

  More and more network reporting applications today make their data accessible to remote users via the Web. These server-based applications typically create HTML pages with embedded GIF files that show operation data in the form of graphs, bar charts, pie charts, etc. An impressive example of this is the Internet Network Connectivity Monitoring Graphs that is part of Scotty's contributed software and available from http://netmon.itb.ac.id.

Instead of having server-based applications create GIF files for graphing and charting management data, server-based applications could create Tclet files that, when downloaded, display operations data in graphical form. This can be faster than downloading large GIF files. We demonstrate this concept in Example #2.

Example #1: Using the Tcl Plug-in as a Client Front-end to a Server-based Management Application

Here we demonstrate how to create a client-server application using the Tcl Plug-in. Note that this is only a demonstration of a concept, not a robust implementation.

Here we have written a sample server application called `ex1-server.itcl`, and a Tclet called `ex1-client.tcl`. The server application is a simulation of our sample `StatusMgr` application, while the client Tclet is a simulation of `StatusMgr`'s GUI without any SNMP data collection.

The server application, `ex1-server.itcl`, creates artificial data for the arrays `groups` and `nInfo` using `gInit` from earlier chapters. We start this server application on our Web server 158.101.121.58. It opens a server socket on port 2001 and waits for client connections. It parses incoming socket data, looking for application-level commands like `get nInfo` and `get groups`. Upon receipt of these application-level commands, the server application sends back the contents of these arrays to the requesting client. `ex1-server.itcl` is basically the same as the server code from Chapter 9, except the procedure `Receiver` has been expanded as follows:

```
proc Receiver { channel} {

    # This procedure handles client requests.

    global nInfo errorCode errorInfo gi groups

    if { [eof $channel] || [catch {gets $channel cmd}]} {
        close $channel
         return
    }


    set err [catch {
            #  Check for valid command.
            switch $cmd {
                "get nInfo" {set xdata [array get nInfo]
                            puts $channel $xdata
                            close $channel
                            }
                "get groups" {set xdata [array get groups]
                            puts $channel $xdata
                            close $channel
                            }
            }
        }]

    if { $err != 0} {
        puts "Error in Receiver"
        puts "... errorCode=$errorCode, errorInfo=$errorInfo"
    }
```

```
}
```

On the client system, we launch our browser and point it to the following URL:

```
http://158.101.121.58/ex1-client.html.
```

The contents of ex1-client.html are as follows:

```
<html>
<title>Tclet Example#1: ex1-client.tcl</title>
<head>
<body>
<embed src=ex1-client.tcl width=800 height=600">
</body>
</head>
</html>
```

Figure 15.2 shows what the user sees in his/her browser. This GUI behaves as follows: When the user selects different groups from the group listbox, nodes belonging to the selected group are displayed in the node textbox at the upper right-hand cornerof the GUI. As nodes change state, the GUI reflects these state changes both in the node textbox and on the bottom canvas.

ex1-client.tcl

The code for ex1-client.tcl is largely the same code from our test driver in Chapter 7 for CreateMainWindow, except for the following:

- Here we removed menus from CreateMainWindow. Menus are not used with the Tcl Plug-in due to security reasons.
- policy home is specified so our Tclet can set up a socket connection to get node information from its server application.
- The node image used in the .bottom.statusmap canvas is now created from bitmap data that is available with the Tclet. Previously, the procedure AddDevice pulled this data from a file. Here we changed AddDevice to create the node image from bitmap data.
- UpdateStatus is called periodically to track changing node states. This change was added so that you can see nodes changing states on the GUI.

Main logic of ex1-client.tcl:

```
policy home
```

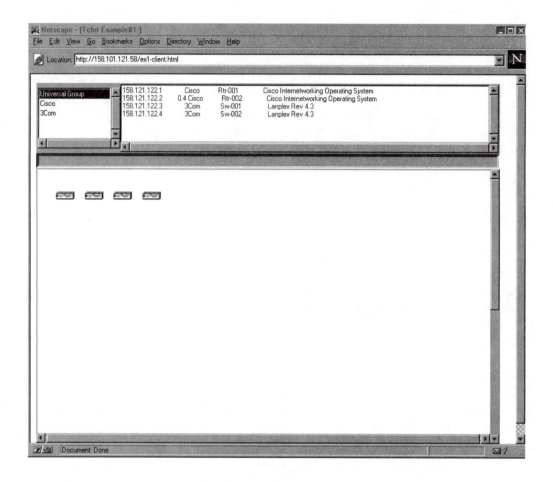

Figure 15.2   Demonstration of StatusMgr's Main GUI Running as a Client Tclet

```
# Initialize.
  set nn -1
  set xpos 0
  set ypos 0
  set x 0
  set y 0
  set width  800
  set height 550

# Create main window.
```

```
    CreateMainWindow

  # Create bitmap_node for stored data.
    set bitmap_node "
    #define node_width 32.
    #define node_height 32.
    static char node_bits[] = {
        0x00, 0x00, 0x00, 0x00, 0x00, 0x00, 0x00, 0x00, 0x00, 0x00,
0x00, 0x00,
        0x00, 0x00, 0x00, 0x00, 0x00, 0x00, 0x00, 0x00, 0x00, 0x00,
0x00, 0x00,
        0x00, 0x00, 0x00, 0x00, 0x00, 0x00, 0x00, 0x00, 0x00, 0x00,
0x00, 0x00,
        0x00, 0x00, 0x00, 0x00, 0xf8, 0xff, 0xff, 0xff, 0x54, 0x55,
0x55, 0xd5,
        0xaa, 0xaa, 0xaa, 0xea, 0xff, 0xff, 0xff, 0xff, 0x01, 0xe0,
0x81, 0xe2,
        0x0f, 0x00, 0x00, 0xe0, 0xaf, 0xeb, 0xff, 0xeb, 0x0f, 0x00,
0x00, 0xe0,
        0xaf, 0x0b, 0xff, 0xe9, 0x01, 0x00, 0x00, 0xe0, 0x01, 0x00,
0x00, 0xe0,
        0xff, 0xff, 0xff, 0x7f, 0xfe, 0xff, 0xff, 0x3f, 0x00, 0x00,
0x00, 0x00,
        0x00, 0x00, 0x00, 0x00, 0x00, 0x00, 0x00, 0x00, 0x00, 0x00,
0x00, 0x00,
        0x00, 0x00, 0x00, 0x00, 0x00, 0x00, 0x00, 0x00, 0x00, 0x00,
0x00, 0x00,
        0x00, 0x00, 0x00, 0x00, 0x00, 0x00, 0x00, 0x00};;"

  # Get array groups from the server application.
    set err [catch {
        set chan [socket "" 2001]
        puts $chan "get groups"
        flush $chan
        gets $chan rcvdata
        close $chan
    }]

    if {$err == 0} {
        array set groups $rcvdata
        .status.label config -text ""
    } else {
```

```
            .status.label config -text "Failure Connecting To Server"
        }

    # Add elements to the group listbox.
        for {set g 0} {$g <= $gi} {incr g +1} {
            .top.groups.listbox insert end $groups($g,name)
        }

    # Get array nInfo.
        get_nInfo
        set nn [expr [llength [array names nInfo *addr]] -1]


    # Select index 0 "Universal Group".
        .top.groups.listbox selection set 0
        DisplayNodeList

    # Add nodes to the StatusMap.
        for {set n 0} {$n <= $nn} {incr n +1} {
            set nInfo($n,id) [AddDevice $n]
        }

    # Set up things so when the user selects an entry in
    # .top.groups.list, its corresponding nodes are displayed
    # in .top.nodes.text.
        bind .top.groups.listbox <ButtonRelease-1> {
            DisplayNodeList
        }

    # Update status color for each node.
        UpdateStatus
```

Procedures used in ex1-client.tcl:

```
proc ScrolledListbox { parent args } {

    # This procedure creates the scrolled listbox for displaying
    # group names .... it is exactly as it was in Chapter 7.
    .
    .
    .
}
```

```
proc ScrolledTextbox { parent args } {

    # This procedure creates a scrolled textbox for displaying
    # node information for selected groups .... it is exactly
    # as it was in Chapter 7.
    .
    .
    .

}


proc CreateMainWindow { } {

    # This procedure creates our main application window.
    # Note it is a slightly different CreateMainWindow than that
    # of Chapter 7. For example, menus have been removed.

    global view curr_view

    # Define broad frame layout of main window.
    frame .top -height 75  -borderwidth 2
    pack .top -side top -fill x
    frame .status -height 18 -borderwidth 3  -relief sunken
    pack .status -side top -fill x
    frame .bottom
    pack .bottom -side top -fill both -expand true


    # Create listbox for group display and selection.
    ScrolledListbox .top.groups -height 5 -selectmode single
    pack .top.groups -side left

    # Create scrolled textbox for node display and selection.
    ScrolledTextbox .top.nodes -height 7
    pack .top.nodes  -side left  -fill x -expand yes

    # Create a label within frame .status for display status
    # messages.
    label .status.label  -text "Status/Message Area." \
                 -relief sunken -height 1
    pack .status.label -fill x -anchor ne -expand yes

    # Create a canvas to display StatusMap.
```

```
canvas .bottom.statusmap -confine false  -relief raised \
        -xscrollcommand ".bottom.statusmap.sx set" \
        -yscrollcommand ".bottom.statusmap.sy set"
scrollbar .bottom.statusmap.sx \
        -command ".bottom.statusmap xview" \
        -orient horizontal
scrollbar .bottom.statusmap.sy \
        -command ".bottom.statusmap yview"
.bottom.statusmap configure -scrollregion "0 0 800  800"
pack  .bottom.statusmap.sy -side right  -fill y
pack  .bottom.statusmap.sx  -side bottom -fill x
pack  .bottom.statusmap  -side top  -fill both -expand yes

}



proc DisplayNodeList { } {

    # This procedure updates the list of nodes in the
    # scrolled text box based on the selected group
    # .... it is exactly as it was in Chapter 7.

        .
        .
        .

}



proc AddDevice { nindex  } {

    # This procedure adds a new node to the canvas
    # .bottom.statusmap. Note that it is slightly different from
    # that of Chapter 7. Here the node bitmap is created from
    # bitmap data rather than from a bitmap file.


    global x y xpos ypos nInfo nn gi width bitmap_node

    set view [expr $width -100]
    if {$xpos < $view} { incr xpos 50
    } else { set xpos 50; incr ypos 50}
```

```
# Create bitmap.
image create bitmap node$nindex -data $bitmap_node

# Store initial positions.
set id [.bottom.statusmap create image $xpos  $ypos\
        -image node$nindex ]

.bottom.statusmap bind current <Enter> {
    set tag [.bottom.statusmap find withtag current]
    for {set n 0} {$n <=$nn} {incr n +1} {
        if {$nInfo($n,id) == $tag} {
            .status.label config -text $nInfo($n,addr)
            break
        }
    }
}

.bottom.statusmap bind current <Leave> {
    .status.label config -text ""
}

.bottom.statusmap bind  current  <Button-1> {
    global x y
    set x %x
    set y %y
}

.bottom.statusmap bind  current  <B1-Motion> {
    global x y; set newx %x;  set newy %y
    set distx [expr $newx - $x]
    set disty [expr $newy - $y]
    .bottom.statusmap move current $distx $disty
    #Store values for next time
        set x $newx
        set y $newy
}

return $id


}
```

```tcl
proc UpdateStatus { } {

    # This procedure is slightly different from that of Chapter 7.
    # Here we loop through the index of nodes, and for each node,
    # update the state color of nodes reflected on the GUI.

    global nn nInfo

    for {set n 0} {$n <= $nn} {incr n +1} {
      if { $nInfo($n,state) == 1} {
         .top.nodes.text tag configure $nInfo($n,addr) \
             -foreground darkgreen
         node$n configure -foreground darkgreen
      } elseif  { $nInfo($n,state) == 0} {
         .top.nodes.text tag configure $nInfo($n,addr) \
             -foreground red
         node$n configure -foreground red
      }
    }

}

proc get_nInfo {} {

    # This procedure periodically gets a new snapshot of the array
    # nInfo from our server. This procedure was not needed in
    # Chapter 7.

    global nInfo nn

    set err [catch {
       set chan [socket "" 2001]
       puts $chan "get nInfo"
       flush $chan
       gets $chan rcvdata
       close $chan
    }]

    if { $err == 0} {
        array set nInfo $rcvdata
```

```
        .status.label config -text ""
        UpdateStatus
        after 60000 get_nInfo
} else {
        # Turn all the nodes black on the map.
        for {set n 0} {$n <= $nn} {incr n +1} {
            .top.nodes.text tag configure $nInfo($n,addr)\
                    -foreground black
            node$n configure -foreground black
        }
        .status.label config \
            -text "Failure Connecting To Server"
}
}
```

Again, *this is only a demonstration of concept* and not a complete implementation. In actuality, it is not as easy as demonstrated here to implement reliable client-server applications.

Example #2: Using the Tcl Plug-in to Display Network Management Graphs

Here we mainly want to make you aware of the availability of Tcl plotting Tclets. Listed in Part 4 of the Tcl FAQ are a few Tcl plotting Tclets available in the public domain for helping you graph and chart data points. Most of these worked well for us on earlier versions of the Tcl Plug-in, but we had some trouble getting them to work with Version 2.0b5 of the Tcl Plug-in.

One package that we found to work with Version 2.0b5 of the Tcl Plug-in is Serious Series. This flexible Tclet produces points, lines, columns, multiple axes, annotations, etc. A Serious Series chart (or set of charts) is defined by the data section of the Serious Series Tclet. The Tclet itself contains first a brief data section and then a program section. The program section is the set of Serious Series Tcl procedures.

Serious Series can be used to create graphs and charts both in Tclets and in native applications. It is quite feature-rich. For us, it worked equally well with version 1.x and 2 .x of the Tcl Plug-in; just add policy home when using it with Version 2.0b5.

Serious Series was made available to the public back in 1996 by John McCaskey. Unfortunately, his account, http://www-leland.stanford.edu/%7Emccaskey, is no longer active. We will make a copy of Serious Series available on our Web site, along with its associated documentation and demo examples.

The Serious Series Tclet includes first a Tcl data section and then a set of Serious Series Tcl procedures. This is pretty common for this type of Tclet tool. All you need to do is copy the Serious Series Tclet and change the brief data section that defines the attributes for the data you want to graph. Since the Serious Series data section is somewhat difficult to explain, we won't try, except to say that you specify values for title, fonts, etc., for your graph and then you specify array values to actually chart. Your resulting graph will be based on how you define your data values.

The following is a sample data section in a Serious Series Tclet:

```
################   Beginning of DATA SECTION   ################
policy home
set title "Daily Network Peak Hour Giga-Packet/Sec Load"
set canvaswidth   700
set canvasheight 550

set rotate true
set pageheight 612; # in points  8.5in x 72 points
set pagewidth  792; # in points  11 in x 72 points

set charts {
    { {  25  50  675 525}  \
        "Daily Network Peak Hour Giga-Packets/Sec Load "  \
        "Chart3Xaxis"   "Chart3Yaxes"   "Chart3Series"}
 }
set Chart3Xaxis {Day 31
        {1 "Jun 1" 3 "Jun 3" 5 "Jun 5" 7 "Jun 7" 9 "Jun 9" \
        11 "Jun 11" 13 "Jun 13" 15 "Jun 15" 17 "Jun 17" \
        19 "Jun 19" 21 "Jun 21" 23 "Jun 23"
        25 "Jun 25" 27 "Jun 27" 29 "Jun 29"}
}
set Chart3Yaxes {
            {"baseline=20" 20 0 20 20.0 1 grid}
}
set Chart3Series {
            {"baseline=20" columns "" "#E44" ""
            {1 20.6 2 100.6 3 101.4 4 101.3 5 101.5 6 \
            101.9 7 21.8 8 22.4 9 102.5 10 102.3 11 \
            102.4 12 102.6 13 102.6 14 102.4 15 21.9 \
            16 21.3 17 101.1 18 178.3 19 201.1 20\
            101.2 21 101.2 22 20.7 23 20.4 24 100.4 25 \
            100.6 26 101.4 27 101.3 28 101.5 29 21.9 30 \
            21.8 }
            }
}
####################   end of DATA SECTION   ####################
```

Figure 15.3 shows the results you see when you download a Serious Series Tclet with the above data section.

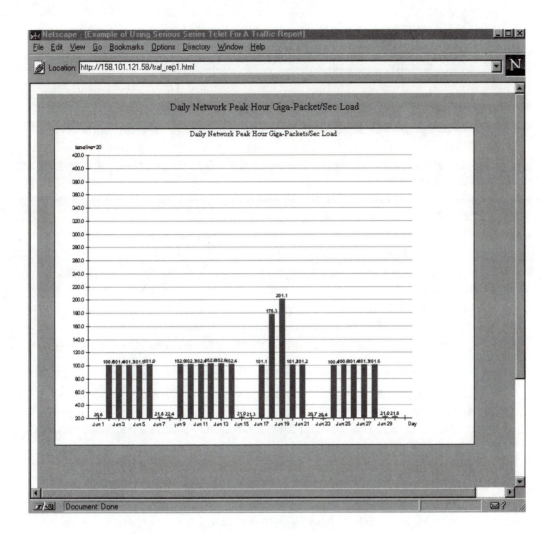

Figure 15.3 A Serious Series Tclet graphing a number of data points.

OTHER BOOKS

There are several good books on SNMP and Tcl, including the following:

- For introductions to SNMPv1 and v2, with some coverage of RMON and RMONv2 MIB definitions:

  - *Managing Internetworks with SNMP* / Mark A. Miller, 2d ed., M&T Books, 1997. ISBN 1-55851-561-5.

- *SNMP, SNMPv2, and RMON : Practical Network Management* / William Stallings, 2d ed., Addison-Wesley, 1996. ISBN 0-201-63479-1.

- *The Simple Book* /Marshall T.Rose, 2d ed., Prentice Hall, 1996. ISBN 0-13-451659-1.

- For guidance on the contents and practical applicability of IETF MIB definitions:

  - *How to Manage Your Network Using SNMP : The Networking Management Practicum* / Marshall Rose and Keith McCloghrie, Prentice Hall, 1995. ISBN 0-13-141517-4.

  - *SNMP : A Guide to Network Management*, Dr. Sidnie Feit, McGraw-Hill, 1995. ISBN 0-07-020359-8.

- For in-depth knowledge of Tcl/Tk, the following books are very useful as both tutorials and reference guides:

  - *Practical Programming in Tcl and Tk*, Brent Welch, 2d ed., Prentice Hall, 1997. ISBN 0-13-616830-2.

  - *Graphical Applications with Tcl & Tk*, Eric Foster-Johnson, 2d ed., M&T Books, 1997. ISBN 1-55851-569-0.

  - *Effective Tcl/Tk Programming: Writing Better Programs in Tcl and Tk*, Mark Harrison and Michael McLennan, Addison-Wesley, 1997. ISBN 0201634740.

  - *Tcl and the Tk Toolkit*, John Ousterhout, Addison-Wesley, 1994. ISBN 0-201-63337-X.

- For useful coverage on several popular Tcl extension packages:

  - *Tcl/Tk Tools*, Mark Harrison, O'Reilly & Associates, 1997. ISBN 1-56592-218-2.

- As introductions to commercial network management systems, the following books are useful. They contain simple explanations of data files used by tools that you can access via Tcl.

  - *Solstice SunNet Manager*, John Graham, McGraw-Hill, 1997. ISBN 0-07-912987-0.

  - *Focus on OpenView*, Nathan Muller, CBM Books, 1995. ISBN 1-878956-48-5.

  - *Multiprotocol Network Management: A Practical Guide to NetView for AIX*, Larry Bennett, McGraw-Hill, 1996. ISBN 0-07-709122-1.

WEB SITES AND NEWSGROUPS

There are several online sites with useful SNMP and Tcl information. Here is a list of some of our favorite sites:

- IETF Home Page

http://www.ietf.org/

- Network Management Resource Database
  http://www.cforc.com/cwk/net-manage.cgi

- Web-based Management Page
  http://www.mindspring.com/~jlindsay/webbased.html

- Network Management Server
  http://netman.cit.buffalo.edu/

- The Simple Web
  http://wwwsnmp.cs.utwente.nl/

- OpenView Forum International WWW Server
  http://www.ovforum.org/

- SNMP Newsgroup
  comp.protocols.snmp

- Tcl with SNMP Extensions
  http://www.net-mgmt-solutions.com/
  http://www.snmp.com/tickleman/
  http://www.snmp.cs.utwente.nl/~schoenw/scotty/
  http://www.gaetner.de/scotty/

- Sun Microsystems Web Pages on Tcl/Tk
  http://sunscript.com/

- Tcl/Tk Information
  http://www.tcltk.com/

- Tcl and Tk World Wide Web Virtual Library
  http://cuiwww.unige.ch/eao/www/TclTk.html

- Tcl Contributed Sources Archive
  http://www.NeoSoft.com/tcl/contributed-software/

- Tcl FAQs, Code & Other Resources
  http://www.cs.uoregon.edu/research/tcl/

Note: There are lots of cool Tclet examples available at http://www.cs.uoregon.edu/research/tcl/code/Tclet/

- **Tcl FAQs**

  http://www.pconline.com/~erc/tclwin.htm

  http://www.teraform.com/%7Elvirden/tcl-faq/

  ftp://ftp.neosoft.com/pub/tcl/sorted/info/faq/

- **Tcl Newsgroups**

  comp.lang.tcl

  comp.lang.tcl.announce

OTHER PACKAGES

Many extension packages available today extend basic Tcl/Tk capabilities. A large list of these extensions is available in Parts 4 and 5 of the Tcl FAQ located at http://www.teraform.com/~lvirden/tcl-faq.

In addition to SNMP and [incr Tcl] support, as mentioned in this book, when building network management applications with Tcl/Tk, you may also want one or more of the following capabilities:

- **Integration with database systems**

  - Commonly used extension packages for this include: oratcl, sybtcl and odbctcl.

- **Sophisticated plotting and graphing of data**

  - BLT is commonly used for this.

- **Integration with non-SNMP devices, such as console programs**

  - Expect is commonly used for this.

- **Sophisticated IP communications support**

  - Tcl-DP is commonly used for this.

The book *Tcl/Tk Tools* by Mark Harrison includes descriptions of several of these extension packages, plus a number of others not mentioned here.

JAVA AND TCL

Tcl is evolving in a synergistic manner with Java. The latest release of the Tcl Plug-in for example, supports a JavaScript policy that provides access to JavaScript routines. In addition, the SunScript group has made the following three products freely available:

- SpecTcl, which is a GUI developer that outputs both Tcl and Java code.
- Jacl (Java Command Language), which is a new Java implementation of Tcl 8.0. With Jacl, you can run Tcl on any system that supports Java. Having a version of Tcl implemented in Java allows Tcl code to run on even more platforms, including the Java Station and many popular Web browsers. Go to http://sunscript.sun.com/java/download.html for an early release copy of Jacl.
- Tcl Blend, which is an early release package for Tcl 8.0 that allows you to load and interact with Java VM. With Tcl Blend, Tcl scripts can invoke Java class methods. Tcl Blend helps to migrate legacy code to Java and also produces hybrid C/Java solutions where C code is used for things that are faster done in C than in Java. Go to http://sunscript.sun.com/java/download.html for an early release copy of Tcl Blend.

Appendix A

The list, given below, rmon2protList, defines a large number of protocols that can be used for the RMONv2 protocol directory table. The list is made up of three components: a protocol name, protocol identifier, and protocol parameter.

```
set rmon2protList [list \
    [list ether2 4.0.0.0.1 1.0] \
    [list llc 4.0.0.0.2 1.0] \
    [list snap 4.0.0.0.3 1.0] \
    [list wgAssigned 4.0.0.0.5 1.0] \
    [list wildcard-ether2 4.1.0.0.1 1.0] \
    [list ether2.idp 8.0.0.0.1.0.0.6.0 2.0.0] \
    [list ether2.ip 8.0.0.0.1.0.0.8.0 2.0.1] \
    [list ether2.arp 8.0.0.0.1.0.0.8.6 2.0.0] \
    [list ether2.vip 8.0.0.0.1.0.0.11.173 2.0.0] \
    [list ether2.vloop 8.0.0.0.1.0.0.11.174 2.0.0] \
    [list ether2.vecho 8.0.0.0.1.0.0.11.175 2.0.0] \
    [list ether2.vloop 8.0.0.0.1.0.0.128.196 2.0.0] \
    [list ether2.vecho 8.0.0.0.1.0.0.128.197 2.0.0] \
    [list ether2.ipx 8.0.0.0.1.0.0.129.55 2.0.0] \
    [list llc.ip 8.0.0.0.2.0.0.0.6 2.0.1] \
    [list llc.vtr 8.0.0.0.2.0.0.0.188 2.0.0] \
    [list llc.ipx 8.0.0.0.2.0.0.0.224 2.0.0] \
    [list snap.idp 8.0.0.0.3.0.0.6.0 2.0.0] \
    [list snap.ip 8.0.0.0.3.0.0.8.0 2.0.1] \
    [list snap.arp 8.0.0.0.3.0.0.8.6 2.0.0] \
    [list snap.vip 8.0.0.0.3.0.0.11.173 2.0.0] \
    [list snap.vloop 8.0.0.0.3.0.0.11.174 2.0.0] \
    [list snap.vecho 8.0.0.0.3.0.0.11.175 2.0.0] \
```

```
[list snap.vloop 8.0.0.0.3.0.0.128.196 2.0.0] \
[list snap.vecho 8.0.0.0.3.0.0.128.197 2.0.0] \
[list snap.ipx 8.0.0.0.3.0.0.129.55 2.0.0] \
[list wgAssigned.ipx 8.0.0.0.5.0.0.0.1 2.0.0] \
[list wildcard-ether2.vtr 8.1.0.0.1.0.0.0.188 2.0.0] \
[list wildcard-ether2.idp 8.1.0.0.1.0.0.6.0 2.0.0] \
[list wildcard-ether2.ip 8.1.0.0.1.0.0.8.0 2.0.1] \
[list wildcard-ether2.arp 8.1.0.0.1.0.0.8.6 2.0.0] \
[list wildcard-ether2.vip 8.1.0.0.1.0.0.11.173 2.0.0] \
[list wildcard-ether2.vloop 8.1.0.0.1.0.0.11.174 2.0.0] \
[list wildcard-ether2.vecho 8.1.0.0.1.0.0.11.175 2.0.0] \
[list wildcard-ether2.vloop 8.1.0.0.1.0.0.128.196 2.0.0] \
[list wildcard-ether2.vecho 8.1.0.0.1.0.0.128.197 2.0.0] \
[list wildcard-ether2.ipx 8.1.0.0.1.0.0.129.55 2.0.0] \
[list ether2.idp.xns-rip 12.0.0.0.1.0.0.6.0.0.0.0.1 3.0.0.0] \
[list ether2.idp.xns-echo 12.0.0.0.1.0.0.6.0.0.0.0.2 3.0.0.0] \
[list ether2.idp.xns-error 12.0.0.0.1.0.0.6.0.0.0.0.3 3.0.0.0] \
[list ether2.idp.xns-pep 12.0.0.0.1.0.0.6.0.0.0.0.4 3.0.0.0] \
[list ether2.idp.xns-spp 12.0.0.0.1.0.0.6.0.0.0.0.5 3.0.0.0] \
[list ether2.ip.icmp 12.0.0.0.1.0.0.8.0.0.0.0.1 3.0.1.0] \
[list ether2.ip.igmp 12.0.0.0.1.0.0.8.0.0.0.0.2 3.0.1.0] \
[list ether2.ip.ggp 12.0.0.0.1.0.0.8.0.0.0.0.3 3.0.1.0] \
[list ether2.ip.tcp 12.0.0.0.1.0.0.8.0.0.0.0.6 3.0.1.0] \
[list ether2.ip.egp 12.0.0.0.1.0.0.8.0.0.0.0.8 3.0.1.0] \
[list ether2.ip.igrp 12.0.0.0.1.0.0.8.0.0.0.0.9 3.0.1.0] \
[list ether2.ip.udp 12.0.0.0.1.0.0.8.0.0.0.0.17 3.0.1.0] \
[list ether2.ip.ospf 12.0.0.0.1.0.0.8.0.0.0.0.89 3.0.1.0] \
[list ether2.vip.vipc 12.0.0.0.1.0.0.11.173.0.0.0.1 3.0.0.0] \
[list ether2.vip.vspp 12.0.0.0.1.0.0.11.173.0.0.0.2 3.0.0.0] \
[list ether2.vip.varp 12.0.0.0.1.0.0.11.173.0.0.0.4 3.0.0.0] \
[list ether2.vip.vrtp 12.0.0.0.1.0.0.11.173.0.0.0.5 3.0.0.0] \
[list ether2.vip.vicp 12.0.0.0.1.0.0.11.173.0.0.0.6 3.0.0.0] \
[list ether2.ipx.nov-rip 12.0.0.0.1.0.0.129.55.0.0.0.1 3.0.0.0] \
[list ether2.ipx.nov-echo 12.0.0.0.1.0.0.129.55.0.0.0.2 3.0.0.0] \
[list ether2.ipx.nov-error 12.0.0.0.1.0.0.129.55.0.0.0.3 3.0.0.0] \
[list ether2.ipx.spx 12.0.0.0.1.0.0.129.55.0.0.0.5 3.0.0.0] \
[list ether2.ipx.ncp 12.0.0.0.1.0.0.129.55.0.0.4.81 3.0.0.0] \
[list ether2.ipx.nov-sap 12.0.0.0.1.0.0.129.55.0.0.4.82 3.0.0.0] \
[list ether2.ipx.nov-netbios 12.0.0.0.1.0.0.129.55.0.0.4.85 3.0.0.0] \
[list ether2.ipx.nov-diag 12.0.0.0.1.0.0.129.55.0.0.4.86 3.0.0.0] \
[list ether2.ipx.nov-sec 12.0.0.0.1.0.0.129.55.0.0.4.87 3.0.0.0] \
[list ether2.ipx.nov-watchdog 12.0.0.0.1.0.0.129.55.0.0.64.4 3.0.0.0] \
```

```
[list ether2.ipx.nov-bcast 12.0.0.0.1.0.0.129.55.0.0.64.5 3.0.0.0] \
[list ether2.ipx.snmp 12.0.0.0.1.0.0.129.55.0.0.144.15 3.0.0.0] \
[list ether2.ipx.snmptrap 12.0.0.0.1.0.0.129.55.0.0.144.16 3.0.0.0] \
[list llc.ip.icmp 12.0.0.0.2.0.0.0.6.0.0.0.1 3.0.1.0] \
[list llc.ip.igmp 12.0.0.0.2.0.0.0.6.0.0.0.2 3.0.1.0] \
[list llc.ip.ggp 12.0.0.0.2.0.0.0.6.0.0.0.3 3.0.1.0] \
[list llc.ip.tcp 12.0.0.0.2.0.0.0.6.0.0.0.6 3.0.1.0] \
[list llc.ip.egp 12.0.0.0.2.0.0.0.6.0.0.0.8 3.0.1.0] \
[list llc.ip.igrp 12.0.0.0.2.0.0.0.6.0.0.0.9 3.0.1.0] \
[list llc.ip.udp 12.0.0.0.2.0.0.0.6.0.0.0.17 3.0.1.0] \
[list llc.ip.ospf 12.0.0.0.2.0.0.0.6.0.0.0.89 3.0.1.0] \
[list llc.vtr.vip 12.0.0.0.2.0.0.0.188.0.0.0.186 3.0.0.0] \
[list llc.vtr.vecho 12.0.0.0.2.0.0.0.188.0.0.0.187 3.0.0.0] \
[list llc.ipx.nov-rip 12.0.0.0.2.0.0.0.224.0.0.0.1 3.0.0.0] \
[list llc.ipx.nov-echo 12.0.0.0.2.0.0.0.224.0.0.0.2 3.0.0.0] \
[list llc.ipx.nov-error 12.0.0.0.2.0.0.0.224.0.0.0.3 3.0.0.0] \
[list llc.ipx.spx 12.0.0.0.2.0.0.0.224.0.0.0.5 3.0.0.0] \
[list llc.ipx.ncp 12.0.0.0.2.0.0.0.224.0.0.4.81 3.0.0.0] \
[list llc.ipx.nov-sap 12.0.0.0.2.0.0.0.224.0.0.4.82 3.0.0.0] \
[list llc.ipx.nov-netbios 12.0.0.0.2.0.0.0.224.0.0.4.85 3.0.0.0] \
[list llc.ipx.nov-diag 12.0.0.0.2.0.0.0.224.0.0.4.86 3.0.0.0] \
[list llc.ipx.nov-sec 12.0.0.0.2.0.0.0.224.0.0.4.87 3.0.0.0] \
[list llc.ipx.nov-watchdog 12.0.0.0.2.0.0.0.224.0.0.64.4 3.0.0.0] \
[list llc.ipx.nov-bcast 12.0.0.0.2.0.0.0.224.0.0.64.5 3.0.0.0] \
[list llc.ipx.snmp 12.0.0.0.2.0.0.0.224.0.0.144.15 3.0.0.0] \
[list llc.ipx.snmptrap 12.0.0.0.2.0.0.0.224.0.0.144.16 3.0.0.0] \
[list snap.idp.xns-rip 12.0.0.0.3.0.0.6.0.0.0.0.1 3.0.0.0] \
[list snap.idp.xns-echo 12.0.0.0.3.0.0.6.0.0.0.0.2 3.0.0.0] \
[list snap.idp.xns-error 12.0.0.0.3.0.0.6.0.0.0.0.3 3.0.0.0] \
[list snap.idp.xns-pep 12.0.0.0.3.0.0.6.0.0.0.0.4 3.0.0.0] \
[list snap.idp.xns-spp 12.0.0.0.3.0.0.6.0.0.0.0.5 3.0.0.0] \
[list snap.ip.icmp 12.0.0.0.3.0.0.8.0.0.0.0.1 3.0.1.0] \
[list snap.ip.igmp 12.0.0.0.3.0.0.8.0.0.0.0.2 3.0.1.0] \
[list snap.ip.ggp 12.0.0.0.3.0.0.8.0.0.0.0.3 3.0.1.0] \
[list snap.ip.tcp 12.0.0.0.3.0.0.8.0.0.0.0.6 3.0.1.0] \
[list snap.ip.egp 12.0.0.0.3.0.0.8.0.0.0.0.8 3.0.1.0] \
[list snap.ip.igrp 12.0.0.0.3.0.0.8.0.0.0.0.9 3.0.1.0] \
[list snap.ip.udp 12.0.0.0.3.0.0.8.0.0.0.0.17 3.0.1.0] \
[list snap.ip.ospf 12.0.0.0.3.0.0.8.0.0.0.0.89 3.0.1.0] \
[list snap.vip.vipc 12.0.0.0.3.0.0.11.173.0.0.0.1 3.0.0.0] \
[list snap.vip.vspp 12.0.0.0.3.0.0.11.173.0.0.0.2 3.0.0.0] \
[list snap.vip.varp 12.0.0.0.3.0.0.11.173.0.0.0.4 3.0.0.0] \
```

```
[list snap.vip.vrtp 12.0.0.0.3.0.0.11.173.0.0.0.5 3.0.0.0] \
[list snap.vip.vicp 12.0.0.0.3.0.0.11.173.0.0.0.6 3.0.0.0] \
[list snap.ipx.nov-rip 12.0.0.0.3.0.0.129.55.0.0.0.1 3.0.0.0] \
[list snap.ipx.nov-echo 12.0.0.0.3.0.0.129.55.0.0.0.2 3.0.0.0] \
[list snap.ipx.nov-error 12.0.0.0.3.0.0.129.55.0.0.0.3 3.0.0.0] \
[list snap.ipx.spx 12.0.0.0.3.0.0.129.55.0.0.0.5 3.0.0.0] \
[list snap.ipx.ncp 12.0.0.0.3.0.0.129.55.0.0.4.81 3.0.0.0] \
[list snap.ipx.nov-sap 12.0.0.0.3.0.0.129.55.0.0.4.82 3.0.0.0] \
[list snap.ipx.nov-netbios 12.0.0.0.3.0.0.129.55.0.0.4.85 3.0.0.0] \
[list snap.ipx.nov-diag 12.0.0.0.3.0.0.129.55.0.0.4.86 3.0.0.0] \
[list snap.ipx.nov-sec 12.0.0.0.3.0.0.129.55.0.0.4.87 3.0.0.0] \
[list snap.ipx.nov-watchdog 12.0.0.0.3.0.0.129.55.0.0.64.4 3.0.0.0] \
[list snap.ipx.nov-bcast 12.0.0.0.3.0.0.129.55.0.0.64.5 3.0.0.0] \
[list snap.ipx.snmp 12.0.0.0.3.0.0.129.55.0.0.144.15 3.0.0.0] \
[list snap.ipx.snmptrap 12.0.0.0.3.0.0.129.55.0.0.144.16 3.0.0.0] \
[list wgAssigned.ipx.nov-rip 12.0.0.0.5.0.0.0.1.0.0.0.1 3.0.0.0] \
[list wgAssigned.ipx.nov-echo 12.0.0.0.5.0.0.0.1.0.0.0.2 3.0.0.0] \
[list wgAssigned.ipx.nov-error 12.0.0.0.5.0.0.0.1.0.0.0.3 3.0.0.0] \
[list wgAssigned.ipx.spx 12.0.0.0.5.0.0.0.1.0.0.0.5 3.0.0.0] \
[list wgAssigned.ipx.ncp 12.0.0.0.5.0.0.0.1.0.0.4.81 3.0.0.0] \
[list wgAssigned.ipx.nov-sap 12.0.0.0.5.0.0.0.1.0.0.4.82 3.0.0.0] \
[list wgAssigned.ipx.nov-netbios 12.0.0.0.5.0.0.0.1.0.0.4.85 3.0.0.0] \
[list wgAssigned.ipx.nov-diag 12.0.0.0.5.0.0.0.1.0.0.4.86 3.0.0.0] \
[list wgAssigned.ipx.nov-sec 12.0.0.0.5.0.0.0.1.0.0.4.87 3.0.0.0] \
[list wgAssigned.ipx.nov-watchdog 12.0.0.0.5.0.0.0.1.0.0.64.4 3.0.0.0] \
[list wgAssigned.ipx.nov-bcast 12.0.0.0.5.0.0.0.1.0.0.64.5 3.0.0.0] \
[list wgAssigned.ipx.snmp 12.0.0.0.5.0.0.0.1.0.0.144.15 3.0.0.0] \
[list wgAssigned.ipx.snmptrap 12.0.0.0.5.0.0.0.1.0.0.144.16 3.0.0.0] \
[list wildcard-ether2.vtr.vip 12.1.0.0.1.0.0.0.188.0.0.0.186 3.0.0.0] \
[list wildcard-ether2.vtr.vecho 12.1.0.0.1.0.0.0.188.0.0.0.187 3.0.0.0] \
[list wildcard-ether2.idp.xns-rip 12.1.0.0.1.0.0.6.0.0.0.0.1 3.0.0.0] \
[list wildcard-ether2.idp.xns-echo 12.1.0.0.1.0.0.6.0.0.0.0.2 3.0.0.0] \
[list wildcard-ether2.idp.xns-error 12.1.0.0.1.0.0.6.0.0.0.0.3 3.0.0.0] \
[list wildcard-ether2.idp.xns-pep 12.1.0.0.1.0.0.6.0.0.0.0.4 3.0.0.0] \
[list wildcard-ether2.idp.xns-spp 12.1.0.0.1.0.0.6.0.0.0.0.5 3.0.0.0] \
[list wildcard-ether2.ip.icmp 12.1.0.0.1.0.0.8.0.0.0.0.1 3.0.1.0] \
[list wildcard-ether2.ip.igmp 12.1.0.0.1.0.0.8.0.0.0.0.2 3.0.1.0] \
[list wildcard-ether2.ip.ggp 12.1.0.0.1.0.0.8.0.0.0.0.3 3.0.1.0] \
[list wildcard-ether2.ip.tcp 12.1.0.0.1.0.0.8.0.0.0.0.6 3.0.1.0] \
[list wildcard-ether2.ip.egp 12.1.0.0.1.0.0.8.0.0.0.0.8 3.0.1.0] \
[list wildcard-ether2.ip.igrp 12.1.0.0.1.0.0.8.0.0.0.0.9 3.0.1.0] \
[list wildcard-ether2.ip.udp 12.1.0.0.1.0.0.8.0.0.0.0.17 3.0.1.0] \
```

```
[list wildcard-ether2.ip.ospf 12.1.0.0.1.0.0.8.0.0.0.0.89 3.0.1.0] \
[list wildcard-ether2.vip.vipc 12.1.0.0.1.0.0.11.173.0.0.0.1 3.0.0.0] \
[list wildcard-ether2.vip.vspp 12.1.0.0.1.0.0.11.173.0.0.0.2 3.0.0.0] \
[list wildcard-ether2.vip.varp 12.1.0.0.1.0.0.11.173.0.0.0.4 3.0.0.0] \
[list wildcard-ether2.vip.vrtp 12.1.0.0.1.0.0.11.173.0.0.0.5 3.0.0.0] \
[list wildcard-ether2.vip.vicp 12.1.0.0.1.0.0.11.173.0.0.0.6 3.0.0.0] \
[list wildcard-ether2.ipx.nov-rip 12.1.0.0.1.0.0.129.55.0.0.0.1 3.0.0.0] \
[list wildcard-ether2.ipx.nov-echo 12.1.0.0.1.0.0.129.55.0.0.0.2 3.0.0.0] \
[list wildcard-ether2.ipx.nov-error 12.1.0.0.1.0.0.129.55.0.0.0.3 3.0.0.0] \
[list wildcard-ether2.ipx.spx 12.1.0.0.1.0.0.129.55.0.0.0.5 3.0.0.0] \
[list wildcard-ether2.ipx.ncp 12.1.0.0.1.0.0.129.55.0.0.4.81 3.0.0.0] \
[list wildcard-ether2.ipx.nov-sap 12.1.0.0.1.0.0.129.55.0.0.4.82 3.0.0.0] \
[list wildcard-ether2.ipx.nov-netbios 12.1.0.0.1.0.0.129.55.0.0.4.85 3.0.0.0] \
[list wildcard-ether2.ipx.nov-diag 12.1.0.0.1.0.0.129.55.0.0.4.86 3.0.0.0] \
[list wildcard-ether2.ipx.nov-sec 12.1.0.0.1.0.0.129.55.0.0.4.87 3.0.0.0] \
[list wildcard-ether2.ipx.nov-watchdog 12.1.0.0.1.0.0.129.55.0.0.64.4 3.0.0.0] \
[list wildcard-ether2.ipx.nov-bcast 12.1.0.0.1.0.0.129.55.0.0.64.5 3.0.0.0] \
[list wildcard-ether2.ipx.snmp 12.1.0.0.1.0.0.129.55.0.0.144.15 3.0.0.0] \
[list wildcard-ether2.ipx.snmptrap 12.1.0.0.1.0.0.129.55.0.0.144.16 3.0.0.0] \
[list ether2.idp.xns-spp.smb 16.0.0.0.1.0.0.6.0.0.0.0.5.255.83.77.66 4.0.0.0] \
[list ether2.ip.tcp.ftp-data 16.0.0.0.1.0.0.8.0.0.0.0.6.0.0.0.20 4.0.1.0.0] \
[list ether2.ip.tcp.ftp 16.0.0.0.1.0.0.8.0.0.0.0.6.0.0.0.21 4.0.1.0.0] \
[list ether2.ip.tcp.telnet 16.0.0.0.1.0.0.8.0.0.0.0.6.0.0.0.23 4.0.1.0.0] \
[list ether2.ip.tcp.smtp 16.0.0.0.1.0.0.8.0.0.0.0.6.0.0.0.25 4.0.1.0.0] \
[list ether2.ip.tcp.domain 16.0.0.0.1.0.0.8.0.0.0.0.6.0.0.0.53 4.0.1.0.0] \
[list ether2.ip.tcp.oracle-sqlnet 16.0.0.0.1.0.0.8.0.0.0.0.6.0.0.0.66 4.0.1.0.0] \
[list ether2.ip.tcp.gopher 16.0.0.0.1.0.0.8.0.0.0.0.6.0.0.0.70 4.0.1.0.0] \
[list ether2.ip.tcp.finger 16.0.0.0.1.0.0.8.0.0.0.0.6.0.0.0.79 4.0.1.0.0] \
[list ether2.ip.tcp.www-http 16.0.0.0.1.0.0.8.0.0.0.0.6.0.0.0.80 4.0.1.0.0] \
[list ether2.ip.tcp.pop3 16.0.0.0.1.0.0.8.0.0.0.0.6.0.0.0.110 4.0.1.0.0] \
[list ether2.ip.tcp.sunrpc 16.0.0.0.1.0.0.8.0.0.0.0.6.0.0.0.111 4.0.1.0.0] \
[list ether2.ip.tcp.nntp 16.0.0.0.1.0.0.8.0.0.0.0.6.0.0.0.119 4.0.1.0.0] \
[list ether2.ip.tcp.netbios-ns 16.0.0.0.1.0.0.8.0.0.0.0.6.0.0.0.137 4.0.1.0.0] \
[list ether2.ip.tcp.netbios-dgm 16.0.0.0.1.0.0.8.0.0.0.0.6.0.0.0.138 4.0.1.0.0] \
[list ether2.ip.tcp.netbios-ssn 16.0.0.0.1.0.0.8.0.0.0.0.6.0.0.0.139 4.0.1.0.0] \
[list ether2.ip.tcp.bgp 16.0.0.0.1.0.0.8.0.0.0.0.6.0.0.0.179 4.0.1.0.0] \
[list ether2.ip.tcp.login 16.0.0.0.1.0.0.8.0.0.0.0.6.0.0.2.1 4.0.1.0.0] \
[list ether2.ip.tcp.vip 16.0.0.0.1.0.0.8.0.0.0.0.6.0.0.2.61 4.0.1.0.0] \
[list ether2.ip.tcp.kerberos 16.0.0.0.1.0.0.8.0.0.0.0.6.0.0.2.237 4.0.1.0.0] \
[list ether2.ip.tcp.oracle-srv 16.0.0.0.1.0.0.8.0.0.0.0.6.0.0.5.245 4.0.1.0.0] \
[list ether2.ip.tcp.oracle-tns 16.0.0.0.1.0.0.8.0.0.0.0.6.0.0.5.246 4.0.1.0.0] \
[list ether2.ip.tcp.oracle-tns-srv 16.0.0.0.1.0.0.8.0.0.0.0.6.0.0.5.247 4.0.1.0.0] \
```

```
[list ether2.ip.tcp.oracle-coauthor 16.0.0.0.1.0.0.8.0.0.0.0.6.0.0.5.249 4.0.1.0.0] \
[list ether2.ip.tcp.oracle-remd 16.0.0.0.1.0.0.8.0.0.0.0.6.0.0.6.35 4.0.1.0.0] \
[list ether2.ip.tcp.oracle-names 16.0.0.0.1.0.0.8.0.0.0.0.6.0.0.6.39 4.0.1.0.0] \
[list ether2.ip.tcp.oracle-em-1 16.0.0.0.1.0.0.8.0.0.0.0.6.0.0.6.212 4.0.1.0.0] \
[list ether2.ip.tcp.oracle-em-2 16.0.0.0.1.0.0.8.0.0.0.0.6.0.0.6.218 4.0.1.0.0] \
[list ether2.ip.tcp.oracle-vp-2 16.0.0.0.1.0.0.8.0.0.0.0.6.0.0.7.16 4.0.1.0.0] \
[list ether2.ip.tcp.oracle-vp-1 16.0.0.0.1.0.0.8.0.0.0.0.6.0.0.7.17 4.0.1.0.0] \
[list ether2.ip.tcp.ngcp 16.0.0.0.1.0.0.8.0.0.0.0.6.0.0.12.128 4.0.1.0.0] \
[list ether2.ip.tcp.x11 16.0.0.0.1.0.0.8.0.0.0.0.6.0.0.23.112 4.0.1.0.0] \
[list ether2.ip.udp.domain 16.0.0.0.1.0.0.8.0.0.0.0.17.0.0.0.53 4.0.1.0.0] \
[list ether2.ip.udp.bootps 16.0.0.0.1.0.0.8.0.0.0.0.17.0.0.0.67 4.0.1.0.0] \
[list ether2.ip.udp.bootpc 16.0.0.0.1.0.0.8.0.0.0.0.17.0.0.0.68 4.0.1.0.0] \
[list ether2.ip.udp.tftp 16.0.0.0.1.0.0.8.0.0.0.0.17.0.0.0.69 4.0.1.0.0] \
[list ether2.ip.udp.sunrpc 16.0.0.0.1.0.0.8.0.0.0.0.17.0.0.0.111 4.0.1.0.0] \
[list ether2.ip.udp.ntp 16.0.0.0.1.0.0.8.0.0.0.0.17.0.0.0.123 4.0.1.0.0] \
[list ether2.ip.udp.netbios-ns 16.0.0.0.1.0.0.8.0.0.0.0.17.0.0.0.137 4.0.1.0.0] \
[list ether2.ip.udp.netbios-dgm 16.0.0.0.1.0.0.8.0.0.0.0.17.0.0.0.138 4.0.1.0.0] \
[list ether2.ip.udp.snmp 16.0.0.0.1.0.0.8.0.0.0.0.17.0.0.0.161 4.0.1.0.0] \
[list ether2.ip.udp.snmptrap 16.0.0.0.1.0.0.8.0.0.0.0.17.0.0.0.162 4.0.1.0.0] \
[list ether2.ip.udp.router 16.0.0.0.1.0.0.8.0.0.0.0.17.0.0.2.8 4.0.1.0.0] \
[list ether2.ip.udp.vip 16.0.0.0.1.0.0.8.0.0.0.0.17.0.0.2.61 4.0.1.0.0] \
[list ether2.vip.vipc.vipc_dgp 16.0.0.0.1.0.0.11.173.0.0.0.1.0.0.0.0 4.0.0.0.0] \
[list ether2.vip.vipc.vipc_rdp 16.0.0.0.1.0.0.11.173.0.0.0.1.0.0.0.1 4.0.0.0.0] \
[list ether2.vip.vspp.vrpc_echo 16.0.0.0.1.0.0.11.173.0.0.0.2.0.0.0.1 4.0.0.0.0] \
[list ether2.vip.vspp.vrte 16.0.0.0.1.0.0.11.173.0.0.0.2.0.0.0.2 4.0.0.0.0] \
[list ether2.vip.vspp.vpcb 16.0.0.0.1.0.0.11.173.0.0.0.2.0.0.0.3 4.0.0.0.0] \
[list ether2.vip.vspp.vmail 16.0.0.0.1.0.0.11.173.0.0.0.2.0.0.0.4 4.0.0.0.0] \
[list ether2.vip.vspp.vftp 16.0.0.0.1.0.0.11.173.0.0.0.2.0.0.0.5 4.0.0.0.0] \
[list ether2.vip.vspp.vfile 16.0.0.0.1.0.0.11.173.0.0.0.2.0.0.0.6 4.0.0.0.0] \
[list ether2.vip.vspp.vsrv 16.0.0.0.1.0.0.11.173.0.0.0.2.0.0.0.7 4.0.0.0.0] \
[list ether2.vip.vspp.vstrtalk 16.0.0.0.1.0.0.11.173.0.0.0.2.0.0.0.15 4.0.0.0.0] \
[list ether2.vip.vspp.vtalk 16.0.0.0.1.0.0.11.173.0.0.0.2.0.0.0.17 4.0.0.0.0] \
[list ether2.vip.vspp.vmgmt 16.0.0.0.1.0.0.11.173.0.0.0.2.0.0.0.18 4.0.0.0.0] \
[list ether2.vip.vspp.vguard 16.0.0.0.1.0.0.11.173.0.0.0.2.0.0.0.19 4.0.0.0.0] \
[list ether2.vip.vspp.smb 16.0.0.0.1.0.0.11.173.0.0.0.2.0.0.2.0 4.0.0.0.0] \
[list ether2.ipx.ncp.nds 16.0.0.0.1.0.0.129.55.0.0.4.81.0.0.0.104 4.0.0.0.0] \
[list ether2.ipx.nov-netbios.smb 16.0.0.0.1.0.0.129.55.0.0.4.85.255.83.77.66 4.0.0.0.0] \
[list llc.ip.tcp.ftp-data 16.0.0.0.2.0.0.0.6.0.0.0.6.0.0.0.20 4.0.1.0.0] \
[list llc.ip.tcp.ftp 16.0.0.0.2.0.0.0.6.0.0.0.6.0.0.0.21 4.0.1.0.0] \
[list llc.ip.tcp.telnet 16.0.0.0.2.0.0.0.6.0.0.0.6.0.0.0.23 4.0.1.0.0] \
[list llc.ip.tcp.smtp 16.0.0.0.2.0.0.0.6.0.0.0.6.0.0.0.25 4.0.1.0.0] \
[list llc.ip.tcp.domain 16.0.0.0.2.0.0.0.6.0.0.0.6.0.0.0.53 4.0.1.0.0] \
```

```
[list llc.ip.tcp.oracle-sqlnet 16.0.0.0.2.0.0.0.6.0.0.0.6.0.0.0.66 4.0.1.0.0] \
[list llc.ip.tcp.gopher 16.0.0.0.2.0.0.0.6.0.0.0.6.0.0.0.70 4.0.1.0.0] \
[list llc.ip.tcp.finger 16.0.0.0.2.0.0.0.6.0.0.0.6.0.0.0.79 4.0.1.0.0] \
[list llc.ip.tcp.www-http 16.0.0.0.2.0.0.0.6.0.0.0.6.0.0.0.80 4.0.1.0.0] \
[list llc.ip.tcp.pop3 16.0.0.0.2.0.0.0.6.0.0.0.6.0.0.0.110 4.0.1.0.0] \
[list llc.ip.tcp.sunrpc 16.0.0.0.2.0.0.0.6.0.0.0.6.0.0.0.111 4.0.1.0.0] \
[list llc.ip.tcp.nntp 16.0.0.0.2.0.0.0.6.0.0.0.6.0.0.0.119 4.0.1.0.0] \
[list llc.ip.tcp.netbios-ns 16.0.0.0.2.0.0.0.6.0.0.0.6.0.0.0.137 4.0.1.0.0] \
[list llc.ip.tcp.netbios-dgm 16.0.0.0.2.0.0.0.6.0.0.0.6.0.0.0.138 4.0.1.0.0] \
[list llc.ip.tcp.netbios-ssn 16.0.0.0.2.0.0.0.6.0.0.0.6.0.0.0.139 4.0.1.0.0] \
[list llc.ip.tcp.bgp 16.0.0.0.2.0.0.0.6.0.0.0.6.0.0.0.179 4.0.1.0.0] \
[list llc.ip.tcp.login 16.0.0.0.2.0.0.0.6.0.0.0.6.0.0.2.1 4.0.1.0.0] \
[list llc.ip.tcp.vip 16.0.0.0.2.0.0.0.6.0.0.0.6.0.0.2.61 4.0.1.0.0] \
[list llc.ip.tcp.kerberos 16.0.0.0.2.0.0.0.6.0.0.0.6.0.0.2.237 4.0.1.0.0] \
[list llc.ip.tcp.oracle-srv 16.0.0.0.2.0.0.0.6.0.0.0.6.0.0.5.245 4.0.1.0.0] \
[list llc.ip.tcp.oracle-tns 16.0.0.0.2.0.0.0.6.0.0.0.6.0.0.5.246 4.0.1.0.0] \
[list llc.ip.tcp.oracle-tns-srv 16.0.0.0.2.0.0.0.6.0.0.0.6.0.0.5.247 4.0.1.0.0] \
[list llc.ip.tcp.oracle-coauthor 16.0.0.0.2.0.0.0.6.0.0.0.6.0.0.5.249 4.0.1.0.0] \
[list llc.ip.tcp.oracle-remd 16.0.0.0.2.0.0.0.6.0.0.0.6.0.0.6.35 4.0.1.0.0] \
[list llc.ip.tcp.oracle-names 16.0.0.0.2.0.0.0.6.0.0.0.6.0.0.6.39 4.0.1.0.0] \
[list llc.ip.tcp.oracle-em-1 16.0.0.0.2.0.0.0.6.0.0.0.6.0.0.6.212 4.0.1.0.0] \
[list llc.ip.tcp.oracle-em-2 16.0.0.0.2.0.0.0.6.0.0.0.6.0.0.6.218 4.0.1.0.0] \
[list llc.ip.tcp.oracle-vp-2 16.0.0.0.2.0.0.0.6.0.0.0.6.0.0.7.16 4.0.1.0.0] \
[list llc.ip.tcp.oracle-vp-1 16.0.0.0.2.0.0.0.6.0.0.0.6.0.0.7.17 4.0.1.0.0] \
[list llc.ip.tcp.ngcp 16.0.0.0.2.0.0.0.6.0.0.0.6.0.0.12.128 4.0.1.0.0] \
[list llc.ip.tcp.x11 16.0.0.0.2.0.0.0.6.0.0.0.6.0.0.23.112 4.0.1.0.0] \
[list llc.ip.udp.domain 16.0.0.0.2.0.0.0.6.0.0.0.17.0.0.0.53 4.0.1.0.0] \
[list llc.ip.udp.bootps 16.0.0.0.2.0.0.0.6.0.0.0.17.0.0.0.67 4.0.1.0.0] \
[list llc.ip.udp.bootpc 16.0.0.0.2.0.0.0.6.0.0.0.17.0.0.0.68 4.0.1.0.0] \
[list llc.ip.udp.tftp 16.0.0.0.2.0.0.0.6.0.0.0.17.0.0.0.69 4.0.1.0.0] \
[list llc.ip.udp.sunrpc 16.0.0.0.2.0.0.0.6.0.0.0.17.0.0.0.111 4.0.1.0.0] \
[list llc.ip.udp.ntp 16.0.0.0.2.0.0.0.6.0.0.0.17.0.0.0.123 4.0.1.0.0] \
[list llc.ip.udp.netbios-ns 16.0.0.0.2.0.0.0.6.0.0.0.17.0.0.0.137 4.0.1.0.0] \
[list llc.ip.udp.netbios-dgm 16.0.0.0.2.0.0.0.6.0.0.0.17.0.0.0.138 4.0.1.0.0] \
[list llc.ip.udp.snmp 16.0.0.0.2.0.0.0.6.0.0.0.17.0.0.0.161 4.0.1.0.0] \
[list llc.ip.udp.snmptrap 16.0.0.0.2.0.0.0.6.0.0.0.17.0.0.0.162 4.0.1.0.0] \
[list llc.ip.udp.router 16.0.0.0.2.0.0.0.6.0.0.0.17.0.0.2.8 4.0.1.0.0] \
[list llc.ip.udp.vip 16.0.0.0.2.0.0.0.6.0.0.0.17.0.0.2.61 4.0.1.0.0] \
[list llc.vtr.vip.vipc 16.0.0.0.2.0.0.0.188.0.0.0.186.0.0.0.1 4.0.0.0.0] \
[list llc.vtr.vip.vspp 16.0.0.0.2.0.0.0.188.0.0.0.186.0.0.0.2 4.0.0.0.0] \
[list llc.vtr.vip.varp 16.0.0.0.2.0.0.0.188.0.0.0.186.0.0.0.4 4.0.0.0.0] \
[list llc.vtr.vip.vrtp 16.0.0.0.2.0.0.0.188.0.0.0.186.0.0.0.5 4.0.0.0.0] \
```

```
[list llc.vtr.vip.vicp 16.0.0.0.2.0.0.0.188.0.0.0.186.0.0.0.6 4.0.0.0.0] \
[list llc.ipx.ncp.nds 16.0.0.0.2.0.0.0.224.0.0.4.81.0.0.0.104 4.0.0.0.0] \
[list llc.ipx.nov-netbios.smb 16.0.0.0.2.0.0.0.224.0.0.4.85.255.83.77.66 4.0.0.0.0] \
[list snap.idp.xns-spp.smb 16.0.0.0.3.0.0.6.0.0.0.0.5.255.83.77.66 4.0.0.0.0] \
[list snap.ip.tcp.ftp-data 16.0.0.0.3.0.0.8.0.0.0.0.6.0.0.0.20 4.0.1.0.0] \
[list snap.ip.tcp.ftp 16.0.0.0.3.0.0.8.0.0.0.0.6.0.0.0.21 4.0.1.0.0] \
[list snap.ip.tcp.telnet 16.0.0.0.3.0.0.8.0.0.0.0.6.0.0.0.23 4.0.1.0.0] \
[list snap.ip.tcp.smtp 16.0.0.0.3.0.0.8.0.0.0.0.6.0.0.0.25 4.0.1.0.0] \
[list snap.ip.tcp.domain 16.0.0.0.3.0.0.8.0.0.0.0.6.0.0.0.53 4.0.1.0.0] \
[list snap.ip.tcp.oracle-sqlnet 16.0.0.0.3.0.0.8.0.0.0.0.6.0.0.0.66 4.0.1.0.0] \
[list snap.ip.tcp.gopher 16.0.0.0.3.0.0.8.0.0.0.0.6.0.0.0.70 4.0.1.0.0] \
[list snap.ip.tcp.finger 16.0.0.0.3.0.0.8.0.0.0.0.6.0.0.0.79 4.0.1.0.0] \
[list snap.ip.tcp.www-http 16.0.0.0.3.0.0.8.0.0.0.0.6.0.0.0.80 4.0.1.0.0] \
[list snap.ip.tcp.pop3 16.0.0.0.3.0.0.8.0.0.0.0.6.0.0.0.110 4.0.1.0.0] \
[list snap.ip.tcp.sunrpc 16.0.0.0.3.0.0.8.0.0.0.0.6.0.0.0.111 4.0.1.0.0] \
[list snap.ip.tcp.nntp 16.0.0.0.3.0.0.8.0.0.0.0.6.0.0.0.119 4.0.1.0.0] \
[list snap.ip.tcp.netbios-ns 16.0.0.0.3.0.0.8.0.0.0.0.6.0.0.0.137 4.0.1.0.0] \
[list snap.ip.tcp.netbios-dgm 16.0.0.0.3.0.0.8.0.0.0.0.6.0.0.0.138 4.0.1.0.0] \
[list snap.ip.tcp.netbios-ssn 16.0.0.0.3.0.0.8.0.0.0.0.6.0.0.0.139 4.0.1.0.0] \
[list snap.ip.tcp.bgp 16.0.0.0.3.0.0.8.0.0.0.0.6.0.0.0.179 4.0.1.0.0] \
[list snap.ip.tcp.login 16.0.0.0.3.0.0.8.0.0.0.0.6.0.0.2.1 4.0.1.0.0] \
[list snap.ip.tcp.vip 16.0.0.0.3.0.0.8.0.0.0.0.6.0.0.2.61 4.0.1.0.0] \
[list snap.ip.tcp.kerberos 16.0.0.0.3.0.0.8.0.0.0.0.6.0.0.2.237 4.0.1.0.0] \
[list snap.ip.tcp.oracle-srv 16.0.0.0.3.0.0.8.0.0.0.0.6.0.0.5.245 4.0.1.0.0] \
[list snap.ip.tcp.oracle-tns 16.0.0.0.3.0.0.8.0.0.0.0.6.0.0.5.246 4.0.1.0.0] \
[list snap.ip.tcp.oracle-tns-srv 16.0.0.0.3.0.0.8.0.0.0.0.6.0.0.5.247 4.0.1.0.0] \
[list snap.ip.tcp.oracle-coauthor 16.0.0.0.3.0.0.8.0.0.0.0.6.0.0.5.249 4.0.1.0.0] \
[list snap.ip.tcp.oracle-remd 16.0.0.0.3.0.0.8.0.0.0.0.6.0.0.6.35 4.0.1.0.0] \
[list snap.ip.tcp.oracle-names 16.0.0.0.3.0.0.8.0.0.0.0.6.0.0.6.39 4.0.1.0.0] \
[list snap.ip.tcp.oracle-em-1 16.0.0.0.3.0.0.8.0.0.0.0.6.0.0.6.212 4.0.1.0.0] \
[list snap.ip.tcp.oracle-em-2 16.0.0.0.3.0.0.8.0.0.0.0.6.0.0.6.218 4.0.1.0.0] \
[list snap.ip.tcp.oracle-vp-2 16.0.0.0.3.0.0.8.0.0.0.0.6.0.0.7.16 4.0.1.0.0] \
[list snap.ip.tcp.oracle-vp-1 16.0.0.0.3.0.0.8.0.0.0.0.6.0.0.7.17 4.0.1.0.0] \
[list snap.ip.tcp.ngcp 16.0.0.0.3.0.0.8.0.0.0.0.6.0.0.12.128 4.0.1.0.0] \
[list snap.ip.tcp.x11 16.0.0.0.3.0.0.8.0.0.0.0.6.0.0.23.112 4.0.1.0.0] \
[list snap.ip.udp.domain 16.0.0.0.3.0.0.8.0.0.0.0.17.0.0.0.53 4.0.1.0.0] \
[list snap.ip.udp.bootps 16.0.0.0.3.0.0.8.0.0.0.0.17.0.0.0.67 4.0.1.0.0] \
[list snap.ip.udp.bootpc 16.0.0.0.3.0.0.8.0.0.0.0.17.0.0.0.68 4.0.1.0.0] \
[list snap.ip.udp.tftp 16.0.0.0.3.0.0.8.0.0.0.0.17.0.0.0.69 4.0.1.0.0] \
[list snap.ip.udp.sunrpc 16.0.0.0.3.0.0.8.0.0.0.0.17.0.0.0.111 4.0.1.0.0] \
[list snap.ip.udp.ntp 16.0.0.0.3.0.0.8.0.0.0.0.17.0.0.0.123 4.0.1.0.0] \
[list snap.ip.udp.netbios-ns 16.0.0.0.3.0.0.8.0.0.0.0.17.0.0.0.137 4.0.1.0.0] \
```

```
[list snap.ip.udp.netbios-dgm 16.0.0.0.3.0.0.8.0.0.0.0.17.0.0.0.138 4.0.1.0.0] \
[list snap.ip.udp.snmp 16.0.0.0.3.0.0.8.0.0.0.0.17.0.0.0.161 4.0.1.0.0] \
[list snap.ip.udp.snmptrap 16.0.0.0.3.0.0.8.0.0.0.0.17.0.0.0.162 4.0.1.0.0] \
[list snap.ip.udp.router 16.0.0.0.3.0.0.8.0.0.0.0.17.0.0.2.8 4.0.1.0.0] \
[list snap.ip.udp.vip 16.0.0.0.3.0.0.8.0.0.0.0.17.0.0.2.61 4.0.1.0.0] \
[list snap.ipx.ncp.nds 16.0.0.0.3.0.0.129.55.0.0.4.81.0.0.0.104 4.0.0.0.0] \
[list snap.ipx.nov-netbios.smb 16.0.0.0.3.0.0.129.55.0.0.4.85.255.83.77.66 4.0.0.0.0] \
[list wgAssigned.ipx.ncp.nds 16.0.0.0.5.0.0.0.1.0.0.4.81.0.0.0.104 4.0.0.0.0] \
[list wgAssigned.ipx.nov-netbios.smb 16.0.0.0.5.0.0.0.1.0.0.4.85.255.83.77.66 4.0.0.0.0] \
[list wildcard-ether2.vtr.vip.vipc 16.1.0.0.1.0.0.0.188.0.0.0.186.0.0.0.1 4.0.0.0.0] \
[list wildcard-ether2.vtr.vip.vspp 16.1.0.0.1.0.0.0.188.0.0.0.186.0.0.0.2 4.0.0.0.0] \
[list wildcard-ether2.vtr.vip.vapp 16.1.0.0.1.0.0.0.188.0.0.0.186.0.0.0.4 4.0.0.0.0] \
[list wildcard-ether2.vtr.vip.vrtp 16.1.0.0.1.0.0.0.188.0.0.0.186.0.0.0.5 4.0.0.0.0] \
[list wildcard-ether2.vtr.vip.vicp 16.1.0.0.1.0.0.0.188.0.0.0.186.0.0.0.6 4.0.0.0.0] \
[list wildcard-ether2.idp.xns-spp.smb 16.1.0.0.1.0.0.6.0.0.0.0.5.255.83.77.66 4.0.0.0.0] \
[list wildcard-ether2.ip.tcp.ftp-data 16.1.0.0.1.0.0.8.0.0.0.0.6.0.0.0.20 4.0.1.0.0] \
[list wildcard-ether2.ip.tcp.ftp 16.1.0.0.1.0.0.8.0.0.0.0.6.0.0.0.21 4.0.1.0.0] \
[list wildcard-ether2.ip.tcp.telnet 16.1.0.0.1.0.0.8.0.0.0.0.6.0.0.0.23 4.0.1.0.0] \
[list wildcard-ether2.ip.tcp.smtp 16.1.0.0.1.0.0.8.0.0.0.0.6.0.0.0.25 4.0.1.0.0] \
[list wildcard-ether2.ip.tcp.domain 16.1.0.0.1.0.0.8.0.0.0.0.6.0.0.0.53 4.0.1.0.0] \
[list wildcard-ether2.ip.tcp.oracle-sqlnet 16.1.0.0.1.0.0.8.0.0.0.0.6.0.0.0.66 4.0.1.0.0] \
[list wildcard-ether2.ip.tcp.gopher 16.1.0.0.1.0.0.8.0.0.0.0.6.0.0.0.70 4.0.1.0.0] \
[list wildcard-ether2.ip.tcp.finger 16.1.0.0.1.0.0.8.0.0.0.0.6.0.0.0.79 4.0.1.0.0] \
[list wildcard-ether2.ip.tcp.www-http 16.1.0.0.1.0.0.8.0.0.0.0.6.0.0.0.80 4.0.1.0.0] \
[list wildcard-ether2.ip.tcp.pop3 16.1.0.0.1.0.0.8.0.0.0.0.6.0.0.0.110 4.0.1.0.0] \
[list wildcard-ether2.ip.tcp.sunrpc 16.1.0.0.1.0.0.8.0.0.0.0.6.0.0.0.111 4.0.1.0.0] \
[list wildcard-ether2.ip.tcp.nntp 16.1.0.0.1.0.0.8.0.0.0.0.6.0.0.0.119 4.0.1.0.0] \
[list wildcard-ether2.ip.tcp.netbios-ns 16.1.0.0.1.0.0.8.0.0.0.0.6.0.0.0.137 4.0.1.0.0] \
[list wildcard-ether2.ip.tcp.netbios-dgm 16.1.0.0.1.0.0.8.0.0.0.0.6.0.0.0.138 4.0.1.0.0] \
[list wildcard-ether2.ip.tcp.netbios-ssn 16.1.0.0.1.0.0.8.0.0.0.0.6.0.0.0.139 4.0.1.0.0] \
[list wildcard-ether2.ip.tcp.bgp 16.1.0.0.1.0.0.8.0.0.0.0.6.0.0.0.179 4.0.1.0.0] \
[list wildcard-ether2.ip.tcp.login 16.1.0.0.1.0.0.8.0.0.0.0.6.0.0.2.1 4.0.1.0.0] \
[list wildcard-ether2.ip.tcp.vip 16.1.0.0.1.0.0.8.0.0.0.0.6.0.0.2.61 4.0.1.0.0] \
[list wildcard-ether2.ip.tcp.kerberos 16.1.0.0.1.0.0.8.0.0.0.0.6.0.0.2.237 4.0.1.0.0] \
[list wildcard-ether2.ip.tcp.oracle-srv 16.1.0.0.1.0.0.8.0.0.0.0.6.0.0.5.245 4.0.1.0.0] \
[list wildcard-ether2.ip.tcp.oracle-tns 16.1.0.0.1.0.0.8.0.0.0.0.6.0.0.5.246 4.0.1.0.0] \
[list wildcard-ether2.ip.tcp.oracle-tns-srv 16.1.0.0.1.0.0.8.0.0.0.0.6.0.0.5.247 4.0.1.0.0] \
[list wildcard-ether2.ip.tcp.oracle-coauthor 16.1.0.0.1.0.0.8.0.0.0.0.6.0.0.5.249 4.0.1.0.0] \
[list wildcard-ether2.ip.tcp.oracle-remd 16.1.0.0.1.0.0.8.0.0.0.0.6.0.0.6.35 4.0.1.0.0] \
[list wildcard-ether2.ip.tcp.oracle-names 16.1.0.0.1.0.0.8.0.0.0.0.6.0.0.6.39 4.0.1.0.0] \
[list wildcard-ether2.ip.tcp.oracle-em-1 16.1.0.0.1.0.0.8.0.0.0.0.6.0.0.6.212 4.0.1.0.0] \
[list wildcard-ether2.ip.tcp.oracle-em-2 16.1.0.0.1.0.0.8.0.0.0.0.6.0.0.6.218 4.0.1.0.0] \
```

```
[list wildcard-ether2.ip.tcp.oracle-vp-2 16.1.0.0.1.0.0.8.0.0.0.0.6.0.0.7.16 4.0.1.0.0] \
[list wildcard-ether2.ip.tcp.oracle-vp-1 16.1.0.0.1.0.0.8.0.0.0.0.6.0.0.7.17 4.0.1.0.0] \
[list wildcard-ether2.ip.tcp.ngcp 16.1.0.0.1.0.0.8.0.0.0.0.6.0.0.12.128 4.0.1.0.0] \
[list wildcard-ether2.ip.tcp.x11 16.1.0.0.1.0.0.8.0.0.0.0.6.0.0.23.112 4.0.1.0.0] \
[list wildcard-ether2.ip.udp.domain 16.1.0.0.1.0.0.8.0.0.0.0.17.0.0.0.53 4.0.1.0.0] \
[list wildcard-ether2.ip.udp.bootps 16.1.0.0.1.0.0.8.0.0.0.0.17.0.0.0.67 4.0.1.0.0] \
[list wildcard-ether2.ip.udp.bootpc 16.1.0.0.1.0.0.8.0.0.0.0.17.0.0.0.68 4.0.1.0.0] \
[list wildcard-ether2.ip.udp.tftp 16.1.0.0.1.0.0.8.0.0.0.0.17.0.0.0.69 4.0.1.0.0] \
[list wildcard-ether2.ip.udp.sunrpc 16.1.0.0.1.0.0.8.0.0.0.0.17.0.0.0.111 4.0.1.0.0] \
[list wildcard-ether2.ip.udp.ntp 16.1.0.0.1.0.0.8.0.0.0.0.17.0.0.0.123 4.0.1.0.0] \
[list wildcard-ether2.ip.udp.netbios-ns 16.1.0.0.1.0.0.8.0.0.0.0.17.0.0.0.137 4.0.1.0.0] \
[list wildcard-ether2.ip.udp.netbios-dgm 16.1.0.0.1.0.0.8.0.0.0.0.17.0.0.0.138 4.0.1.0.0] \
[list wildcard-ether2.ip.udp.snmp 16.1.0.0.1.0.0.8.0.0.0.0.17.0.0.0.161 4.0.1.0.0] \
[list wildcard-ether2.ip.udp.snmptrap 16.1.0.0.1.0.0.8.0.0.0.0.17.0.0.0.162 4.0.1.0.0] \
[list wildcard-ether2.ip.udp.router 16.1.0.0.1.0.0.8.0.0.0.0.17.0.0.2.8 4.0.1.0.0] \
[list wildcard-ether2.ip.udp.vip 16.1.0.0.1.0.0.8.0.0.0.0.17.0.0.2.61 4.0.1.0.0] \
]
```

Index

X